Developing Semantic Web Services

About the Authors

H. Peter Alesso is a technology innovator with twenty years research experience at Lawrence Livermore National Laboratory (LLNL). As Engineering Group Leader at LLNL, he led a team of computer scientists, physicists, and engineers in a wide range of successful software development research projects. Peter has extensive experience with innovative applications across a wide range of supercomputers, workstations, PCs, and wireless devices. He earned an M.S. and an advanced Engineering Degree from M.I.T. and has published several software titles, as well as, numerous scientific journal and conference articles. H. Peter Alesso is the author of, *e-Video: Producing Internet Video as Broadband Technologies Converge*, Addison-Wesley, July 2000, and co-author of *The Intelligent Wireless Web*, Addison Wesley, 2001.

Craig Smith, PhD., a Fellow of the American Association for the Advancement of Science, is an engineer with 30 years experience in research and development of advanced technologies. He currently serves as the Lawrence Livermore Chair Professor at the Naval Postgraduate School in Monterey, CA. He served for three years as Deputy Associate Director of the Energy and Environment Directorate at Lawrence Livermore National Laboratory. He was responsible for a wide range of multimillion-dollar projects and he was a collaborator on several international research initiatives. His areas of interest include sensors, robotics and automated systems; information technology applications; and future energy systems. He has published numerous scientific journal and conference articles on advanced engineering topics. Dr. Smith received his PhD. in Nuclear Science and Engineering from the University of California, Los Angeles (UCLA) in 1975. He is co-author of *The Intelligent Wireless Web*, Addison Wesley, 2001.

Developing
Semantic
Web Services

H. Peter Alesso

Craig F. Smith

CRC Press
Taylor & Francis Group
Boca Raton   London   New York

CRC Press is an imprint of the
Taylor & Francis Group, an **informa** business

AN A K PETERS BOOK

CRC Press
Taylor & Francis Group
6000 Broken Sound Parkway NW, Suite 300
Boca Raton, FL 33487-2742

First issued in hardback 2019

ISBN-13: 978-1-56881-212-0 (pbk)
ISBN-13: 978-1-138-43616-9 (hbk)

Visit the Taylor & Francis Web site at
http://www.taylorandfrancis.com

and the CRC Press Web site at
http://www.crcpress.com

Library of Congress Cataloging-in-Publication Data

Alesso, H. P.
    Developing Semantic Web services / H. Peter Alesso, Craig F. Smith.
        p. cm.
    Includes bibliographical references and index.
        ISBN 1-56881-212-4 (alk. paper)
        1. Semantic Web. 2. Web services. I. Smith, C. F. (Craig Forsythe), 1950- II. Title.

TK5105.88815.A55 2004
025.04--dc22

2004044619

To Chris

To Kathy

Contents

Preface

The inventor of the World Wide Web, Tim Berners-Lee, is also the originator of the next generation Web architecture, the Semantic Web. Currently, his World Wide Web Consortium (W3C) team works to develop, extend, and standardize the Web's markup languages and tools. The objective of the Semantic Web Architecture is to provide a knowledge representation of linked data in order to allow machine processing on a global scale. The W3C has developed a new generation of open standard markup languages which are now poised to unleash the power, flexibility, and above all—logic—of the next generation Web, as well as open the door to the next generation of Web Services.

Currently, Web Services using the .NET and J2EE frameworks are struggling to expand against the limitations of existing Web architecture and conflicting proprietary standards. With software vendors battling for any advantage, Semantic Web Services offer a great reward to the first developer to successfully exploit its latent potential and deliver semantic search, e-mail and collaborative word processing.

Why do we need such a system? Today, the data available within HTML are difficult to manipulate on a large scale. Just think of information about plane schedules, baseball statistics, and product purchasing information. While presently available at numerous sites, its HTML form is problematic. The Semantic Web offers an easier way to publish data that can be accessed and re-purposed as needed.

There are many ways in which the two areas of Web Services and the Semantic Web could interact to lead to the further development of Semantic Web Services. Berners-Lee has suggested that both of these technologies would benefit from integration that would combine the Semantic Web's meaningful content with Web Services' business logic. Areas such as UDDI and WSDL are ideally suited to be implemented using Semantic Web technology. In addition, SOAP could use RDF payloads, remote RDF query and updates, and interact with Semantic Web business rules engines, thereby laying the foundation for Semantic Web Services.

This book presents the complete Language Pyramid of Web markup languages, including: Resource Description Framework (RDF), Web Ontology Language (OWL) and OWL-Services (OWL-S) along with examples and software demos. In addition, it describes the semantic software development tools including: design and analysis methodologies, parsers, validators, editors, development environments, and inference engines. The source code for the "Semantic Web Author," an Integrated Development Environment for semantic markup languages is discussed and available for download at http://www.web-iq.com.

The technology issues of the Next Generation Web create many problematic questions that must be solved before the full power and capability of the Semantic Web Services are available.

The Markup Language Pyramid

Semantic Web Service technological issues that we will specifically address in subsequent chapters include:

1. Why is XML so critical to the future of Web architecture?
2. How will Web Services using .NET and J2EE evolve toward automated discovery and delivery of Web Services?
3. How will Meta-languages, Ontologies, and Inference Engines produce powerful Web search capabilities?
4. Can Semantic Web Services be implemented immediately without waiting for the full development of the Semantic Web?
5. Why would Semantic Web Services lead to open Web standards and a distributed Web?

Our presentations in subsequent chapters are intended to provide persuasive arguments and possible solutions to these questions.

Acknowledgements

We would especially like to acknowledge the online discussion forums, papers, research, and suggestions of the DAML Services Coalition (also known as the OWL-S Coalition) as a whole: Anupriya Ankolenkar, Mark Burstein, Grit Decker, Jerry Hobbs, Ora Lassila, David Martin, Drew McDermott, Sheila McIlraith, Srini Narayanan, Massimo Paolucci, Bijan Parsia, Terry Payne, Marta Sabou, Monika Solanki, Tran Cao Son, Naveen Srinvasan, Katia Sycara, and Honglei Zeng. They were generous and open with all their endeavors.

We would like to thank students: Howard M. Brown, Elangiovan Ginanasekaran, Huong G. Ho, Sui Huang, Eileen M. Jao, Vineet Khosla, Sandeep K. Mirchandani, Al Sary, Xinghai Shao, and Wenyun Shi for their comments and suggestions during early drafts of this work. Their insights helped guide a complex effort.

We would like to thank Rahul Singh of the DriveRDF.org for developing an excellent dll tool called drive which we used as part of out Semantic Web Author software tool.

In addition, we would like to thank software developers: Geoff Chappell, President, Intellidimension, Inc. (www.intellidimension.com) RDF GatewayOne and Chris Sukornyk, President and CEO, Semaview, Java Browser applet for FOAF. They provided software tools for evaluation.

The Organization of this Book

This book is organized into four parts. Just as the Semantic Web is developing from the layered pyramid of markup languages, we have structured the chapters in this book to follow the layering of each additional markup language—one upon the other—in appropriate order.

In the first part of the book, we provide a review and primer for the existing elements of the Web and Web Services within the context of evaluating the Web's current limitations and weaknesses. This assessment provides insight into future requirements for the new Web architecture. Then, in the second part, we present the markup languages, RDF, OWL, and OWL-S. Together, they form the foundation for Semantic Web Services. In the third part of this book, we present the examples, codes, and software tools used to implement the Semantic Web Services. And finally in the fourth part—the Appendices—we present supplemental detailed syntax and source code.

In Part I, we introduce the markup languages that form the foundation of Web: SGML, HTML, and XML, and evaluate their current limitations and requirements. This assessment identifies the needs and requirements for new Web architecture. In Chapter 1, we recall the historic development of the Web and how markup languages are used. In Chapters 2, 3, and 4 we cover the basics of markup languages sequentially from SGML and HTML to XML, respectively. In Chapter 5, we present Web Services as they are currently configured.

In Part II, we introduce the developing markup languages of the Semantic Web. We start in Chapter 6 by laying out the Semantic Roadmap for future development. In Chapters 7 we introduce Resource Description Framework - RDF. In Chapter 8, we present the Web Ontology Language—OWL. In Chapter 9, we explain logic languages, inference and reasoning engines. In Chapter 10, we introduce OWL for Services.

In Part III, we present the examples, codes and tools used to implement the Semantic Web Services. In Chapter 11 we present the Congo.owl example. In Chapter 12, we introduce design and analysis methodologies for Semantic Web Services; including Petri nets and reliability analysis. In Chapter 13, we present editor, language validation and Integrated Development Environments for semantic tools. In Chapter 15, we address the main money maker: semantic search. We conclude in Chapter 16 with a discussion of challenges and opportunities

Finally in Part IV, we provide appendices that include a glossary, a list of acronyms, detailed RDF, and OWL syntax.

Who this Book is For

The primary audience for this book is Web service architects and academic researchers who have a background in HTML and XML and are preparing to deliver Web Services automatically across the Web using the next generation markup languages. This book is also for Web developers with a background in either .NET or J2EE, who are seeking an assessment as well as some insight into the next generation architecture and languages.

Associated Resources

The Semantic Web Organization has developer software resources at http://www.SemanticWeb.org and the World Wide Consortium can be found at http://www.w3.org/Consortium/Activities. In addition, the DAML Services Coalition is available at http://www.daml.org/services/. MIT's AI Laboratory hosts the OXYGEN Project and is available at http://oxygen.lcs.mit.edu/. An associated Web site for this book is available at http://www.web-iq.com to provide reference material, errata, and discussion forums.

In addition, the following element appears throughout the book for edification:

 This icon indicates that the accompanying enclosed text provides expanded details about the topic.

List of Acronyms

A

AI—Artificial Intelligence

ATM—Asynchronous Transfer Mode

C

CERN—European Particle Physics Laboratory

D

DAI—Distributed Artificial Intelligence

DAML—DARPA Agent Markup Language

DARPA—Defense Advanced Research Projects Agency

DC—Dublin Core

DMA—Digraph Matrix Analysis

DNS –Domain Name Service

DOOD –Dylan Object Oriented Database

DOM—Document Object Model

DOCTYPE—Document type declaration

DTD—Document Type Definition

DWDM—Dense Wave Division Multiplexing

E

EJB—Enterprise Java Beans

G

GML—General Markup Language

H

HTML—HyperText Markup Language

HTTP—HyperText Transmission Protocol

I

IEEE—Institute of Electrical and Electronic Engineers

IETF—International Engineering Task Force

IN—Intelligent Networks

IP—Internet Protocol

IPv6—IP version 6

ISP –Internet Service Provider

IT—Information Technology

ITU—International Telecommunications Union

J

JSGF—Java Speech Grammar Format

L

LAN—Local Area Network

M

MIPS—Million Instructions Per Second

N

NIC—Network Interface Card

NLP—Natural Language Processing

N3—Notation 3

O

OIL—Ontology Inference Language

OWL—Web Ontology Language

OWL-S—Web Ontology Language for Services

P

PVM—Parallel Virtual Machine

Q

QoS—Quality of Service

R

RDF—Resource Description Language

RDFS—Resource Description Language Schema

S

SAX—Simple API for XML

SGML—Standard Generalized Markup Language

SHOE—Simple HTML Ontology Extension

SMIL—Synchronized Multimedia Integration Language

SNMP—Simple Network Management Protocol

SOAP—Simple Object Access Protocol

SQL—Structured Query Language

SSML—Speech Synthesis Markup Language

SWAP—Shared Wireless Access Protocol

T

Tb/s—Terabit per second, (1 trillion bits per second)

TM—Topical Maps

TTML –Tagged Text Markup Language

TTS—Text to speech

U

UDDI—Universal Description, Discovery and Integration

UDP—User Datagram Protocol

UML—Unified Modeling Language

URI—Universal Resource Identifier

URIREF—URI reference

V

VoiceXML—Voice XML

W

W3C—World Wide Web Consortium

WAN—Wide area network

WML—Wireless Markup Language

WPAN—Wireless Personal Area Network

WSDL—Web Services Descriptive Language

X

XLink—eXtensible Link Language

XML—eXtensible Markup Language

XSDL—XML Schema Description Language

XSL—eXtensible Style Language

XSL-FO—eXtensible Style Language Format Objects

XSLT—eXtensible Stylesheet Language Transform

Part One

The World Wide Web

Chapter One

The World Wide Web

Overview

It takes no great stretch of the imagination to predict that the World Wide Web will remain an important contributor to our information and communication infrastructure for some time to come. We can conclude this because of the historic development of personal computing and its relationship to networks, which while changing drastically over the last few decades, has nevertheless given birth to the Information Age.

While the capabilities and scope of today's Web is impressive, its continuing evolution into a resource with intelligent features presents many challenges. Currently, the problem with performing intelligent tasks, such as Web Services is that they must rely on proprietary server languages to perform business logic.

The solution of the World Wide Web Consortium (W3C) is to illustrate the path for developing a Web architecture built upon additional layers of open standard markup languages that can be used to deliver business logic through Semantic Web Services. To appreciate this solution, it's important to understand how the development and growth of the World Wide Web with its associated technical compromises has led to its current capabilities and limitations.

In this introductory chapter, we will review the process of developing the Web. We will examine centralized, decentralized, and distributed networks and their vital relationship to open and proprietary Web standards. Also, we will discuss the competition between open stan-

3

dard markup languages and proprietary server-based frameworks, as the basis for expanding Web architecture. In addition, we will discuss the critical role of eXtensible Markup Language (XML) in designing and implementing new Web markup languages. This has a direct bearing on today's Web Services and how they are exploited. This will lead us to evaluate future Web architectures such as the Semantic Web.

Also, we will identify several key questions which will be addressed within this book and which will prove instrumental in providing a roadmap for developing the Semantic Web. Finally, we will offer the observation that Semantic Web Services may be implemented immediately without waiting for full adoption of the Semantic Web.

Background

The history of the Web extends back more than 40 years. Looking back, we can find early signs of relevant network architecture in the 1960s. In 1962, the RAND Corporation began research sponsored by the U.S. Air Force to determine how to develop robust, distributed communication networks for military command and control that could survive and function in the event of a nuclear attack. The concept envisioned a military research network that could survive a nuclear strike, by being sufficiently decentralized so that if any locations were destroyed, the military could still have control of nuclear arms for a counter-attack.

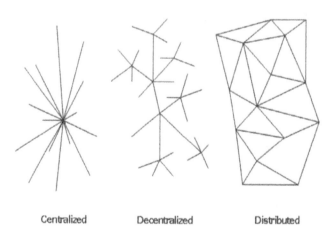

Centralized   Decentralized   Distributed

Figure 1-1. Centralized, decentralized and distributed networks.

Figure 1-1 shows three different network topologies described by the RAND Corporation in August 1964: centralized, decentralized, and distributed. The distributed network structure offered the best survivability.

This initial study led to the development of the ARPANET which, in addition to its robustness against attack, was intended to promote the sharing of super-computers among scientific and military researchers in the United States. In 1969, the ARPANET was created when four nodes in the western U.S. (the University of California at Los Angeles, SRI of Stanford, California, the University of California at Santa Barbara, and the University of Utah) were connected in a system that was to become the precursor to the Internet.

From the very beginning, the ARPANET was a success. Over those first few years, the network developed and expanded as new sites (nodes) were added, and as new capabilities and features were introduced (see Figure 1-2).

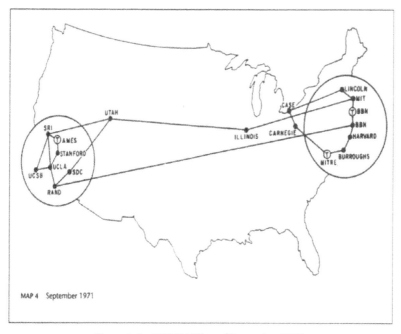

MAP 4   September 1971

Figure 1-2. ARPANET as of September 1971.

In the 1970s, software and protocols were introduced to facilitate email and file transfers. Although the ARPANET was originally designed to allow scientists to share data and access remote computers, email quickly became the most popular application. The ARPANET became a high-speed digital post office as people used it to collaborate on research projects. It was a distributed system of "many-to-many" connections, in a robust, fault-tolerant manner. The system as a whole was distributed, but, because of its limited size, was searchable for a limited amount of information.

At this early stage, the rapidly growing enthusiasm for ARPANET was based upon its reliability, accessibility, and ease of use.

Automation of Document Processing

While the ARPANET emphasized the hardware of the network infrastructure, equally urgent were the efforts being made to develop powerful supporting software. In 1969, Charles Goldfarb, Edward Mosher, and Raymond Lorie of IBM developed the Generalized Markup Language (GML) as a system to build powerful portable interchangeable legal documents. The structure of each type of document was strictly defined in a file called a Document Type Definition (DTD). Within five years, they developed a parser for validating a document. And by 1986, they produced the Standard Generalized Markup Language (SGML) (see Chapter 2).

The purpose of SGML was to provide a powerful all-purpose tool for defining other markup languages that could be streamlined and optimized for more specific tasks. As a result, it wasn't long before SGML gave birth to some of the Internet's primary communication tools (see Figure 1-3) including: HTML (HyperText Markup Language), XHTML (eXtensible HyperText Markup Language), and XML (eXtensible Markup Language).

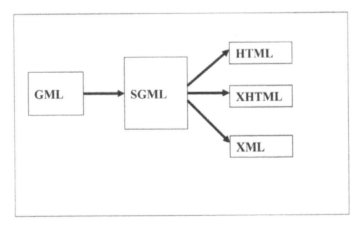

Figure 1-3. The markup language family development.

While XML is already widely used across the Web today, it is still a relatively new technology. XML is a meta-language which means it is a language used to create other languages. XML can provide a basic structure and set of rules for developing any markup language. Using XML, it is possible to create a unique markup language to model just about any kind of information, including Web content. For example, it can even be used to develop a reformulated version of HTML, as was done in the development of XHTML.

XML is basically SGML 'light.' Whereas HTML is merely one SGML document type, XML is a simplified version of the parent language itself. XML 1.0, released in February 1998, was less than a tenth of the size of the SGML specification; however, it had many of the important features of SGML including extensibility, structure, and validity.

The Ever-Expanding ARPANET

While markup languages were being developed, the ARPANET continued to grow; by 1971, it had connected 23 hosts at universities and government research centers around the United States. In 1972, the InterNetworking Working Group (INWG) became the first of several standards-setting entities to govern the growing network. Vinton Cerf, the first chairman of the INWG, later became known as a "Father of the Internet." The following year, the ARPANET went global when it was connected to University College in London, England and the Royal Radar Establishment in Norway.

In 1979, Tom Truscott and Jim Ellis, two graduate students at Duke University, and Steve Bellovin at the University of North Carolina established the first USENET newsgroups. Users from all over the world joined these discussion groups to talk about the net, politics, religion, and many other topics.

ARPANET continued to grow in size and popularity and in 1981 it reached 213 hosts with a new host added every 20 days. By 1987, the number of hosts exceeded 10,000.

The Birth of the Internet

In 1978, Bob Kahn and Vint Cerf and other team members created TCP/IP, the common language of all Internet computers since the 1980s. For the first time the loose collection of networks which made up the ARPANET could be seen as an "internet." TCP and IP were protocols that connected separate networks into a network of networks (the "Internet"). These protocols specified the framework for a few basic services that everyone would need (file transfer, electronic mail, and remote logon) across a very large number of client and server systems. Several computers linked on a local network can use TCP/IP (along with other protocols) within the local network just as they can use the protocols to provide services throughout the Internet. The IP (Internet Protocol) component provides routing from the local network to the enterprise network, then to regional networks, and finally to the global Internet.

TCP/IP

TCP/IP is composed of two layers:

• Internet Protocol (IP)—responsible for moving packets of data from node to node. The IP forwards each packet based on a four-byte destination address (the IP number).

• Transmission Control Protocol (TCP)—responsible for verifying the correct delivery of data from client to server. Since data can be lost in the intermediate network, TCP adds support to detect errors or lost data and to trigger retransmission until the data is correctly received.

The mid-1980s marked a boom in the personal computer and super-minicomputer industries. The combination of inexpensive desktop machines and powerful, network-ready servers allowed many companies to join the Internet for the first time. Corporations began to use the Internet to communicate with each other and with their customers.

By 1988, the Internet had become an important communications tool; however, it also created new concerns about privacy and security in the digital world. In a widely publicized incident, Lawrence Berkeley Laboratory system administrator Clifford Stoll, caught a group of Cyberspies, and wrote bestseller about it. "The Cuckoo's Egg" is a first-person account of tracking a computer hacker through a complicated labyrinth of computer systems. The story ends with the arrest of a ring of spies supported by the KGB.

In 1990, the ARPANET was decommissioned, leaving only the vast network-of-networks called the Internet with over 300,000 hosts. This explosive growth continues to the present day (see Figure 1-4). However, because of this growth, the ability to search items across the Internet had become extremely difficult.

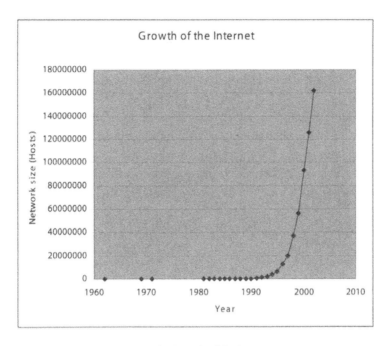

Figure 1-4. Growth of the Internet.

Transition to the World Wide Web

By 1991, three major events and forces converged and accelerated the development of information technology. These three events were the introduction of the World Wide Web, the widespread availability of the network browser, and the unleashing of commercialization.

 In 1991, Tim Berners-Lee, worked at the European Particle Physics Laboratory of the European Organization for Nuclear Research, Conseil Européen pour la Recherche Nucléaire (CERN) in Switzerland. He introduced the concept of the World Wide Web in a relatively innocuous newsgroup, "alt.hypertext," a distributed discussion newsgroup devoted to information about hypertext and hypermedia.

The concept provided the ability to combine words, pictures, and sounds (i.e., to provide multimedia content) on Internet pages. This excited many computer programmers who saw the potential for publishing information on the Internet with the ease of using a word processor but with the richness of multimedia forms.

9

Berners-Lee and his collaborators laid the groundwork for the open standards of the Web. Their efforts included inventing and refining the Hypertext Transfer Protocol (HTTP) for linking Web documents, the Hypertext Markup Language (HTML) for formatting Web documents (a product of SGML), and the Universal Resource Locator (URL) system for addressing Web documents.

HTML is the primary language for formatting Web pages (see Chapter 3). With HTML, the author describes what a page should look like, what types of fonts to use, what color text should be, where paragraphs begin, and many other attributes of the document.

Figure 1-5 shows the client-server relationship over the World Wide Web in which client Web browsers are linked to Web server applications through HTTP communications.

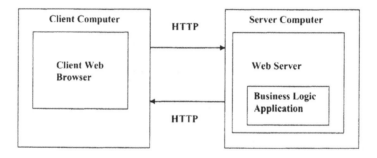

Figure 1-5. Client server relationship.

Hypertext Transfer Protocol (HTTP)

What is Hypertext Transfer Protocol (HTTP)? It's the network protocol used to deliver virtually all files and other data (collectively called resources) on the World Wide Web, whether they're HTML files, image files, query results, or anything else. Usually, HTTP takes place through TCP/IP sockets. Socket is the term for the package of subroutines that provide an access path for data transfer through the network.

Like most network protocols, HTTP uses the client-server model: An HTTP client opens a connection and sends a request message to an HTTP server; the server then returns a response message, usually containing the resource that was requested. After delivering the response, the server closes the connection.

A browser is a software package that creates an HTTP client which sends requests to an HTTP server (Web server) which responds to the client.

The format of an HTTP message is:
<initial line for request or response>
Header1: value1
Header2: value2
Header3: value3

A simple HTTP exchange to retrieve the file at the Universal Resource Locator (URL), first opens a socket to the host www.somehost.com, at port 80 (the default) and then, sends following through the socket:

GET /path/file.html HTTP/1.0
From: someuser@somehost.com
User-Agent: HTTPTool/1.0
[blank line here]

The server responds with the following HTTP and HTML "hello world":
HTTP/1.0 200 OK
Date: Fri, 31 Dec 1999 23:59:59 GMT
Content-Type: text/html
Content-Length: 1354
<html>
  <body>
    Hello World
  </body>
</html>

In 1992, the first audio and video broadcasts took place over a portion of the Internet. These broadcasts, known as the "MBONE" (Multicast Backbone) were introduced at a time when the Internet's size had grown to more than 1,000,000 hosts.

In 1993, Marc Andreesen and a group of student programmers at NCSA (the National Center for Supercomputing Applications located on the campus of University of Illinois at Urbana-Champaign) developed a graphical browser for the World Wide Web called Mosaic. Mosaic, the first graphics-based Web browser, was made freely available. After that, traffic on the Internet expanded at an explosive annual growth rate in excess of 340,000%.

Studies of Internet traffic began to show signs that all Web sites on the Internet are not "equidistant." That is, some sites were acting as hubs and garnishing a dominant share of the through traffic. We can identify two important types of Web sites: hubs and authorities. Some Web sites provide the most prominent sources of primary content, and are called the authorities on the topic; other sites, assemble high-quality guides and resource lists that act as focused hubs, directing users to recommended authorities. Clearly, hubs and authorities lead to an alteration of the distributed nature of the Web (see Appendix C: Graphical Structure of the Web).

In 1994, the World Wide Web Consortium (W3C) was founded under the leadership of Tim Berners-Lee. W3C is comprised of individuals and companies involved with the Internet and the Web. The purpose of W3C is to develop open standards so that the Web evolves in a coherent, single direction.

World Wide Web Consortium (W3C)

The World Wide Web Consortium (W3C) develops interoperable technologies (specifications, guidelines, software, and tools) to lead the Web to its full potential. W3C is a forum for information, commerce, communication, and collective understanding.

More information on W3C is available at: http://www.w3.org/

In 1996, as the "ARPANET-NSFNET-Internet-Web" celebrated its 25th anniversary, the military strategies that influenced its birth become a historic footnote. Approximately 40 million people in almost 150 countries around the world were now connected to the Web. The number of computer hosts approached 10 million. Nevertheless, the reliability and fault tolerant concepts adapted from military doctrine, have been instrumental in the successful rapid growth of the distributed Internet.

Digital Communications

As we shall see there was more to come. The Web was to conquer more than data information transmission. Voice transmission was next.

The Wide Area Network (WAN) services of the 1990's exercised their capabilities through hardware switches and routers. These services were provided through two competing switching technologies: Circuit-switching and Packet-switching. Switches and routers are the essential components of a network's traffic routing function. Switches forward information from one host to another without knowing anything about the paths between the hosts. Routers understand the Internet layer protocol used between hosts. In contrast, circuit-switched networks use dedicated circuits for a particular connection between users during a particular time frame; the circuit remains dedicated for the duration of the message, just as a telephone circuit connects two phones for the duration of a call.

Packet-Switching

In contrast to circuit-switched connections, IP packet-switching does not use a dedicated circuit between two endpoints. Rather, packet-switched connections allow multiple users simultaneous access to multiple locations across a network. Packages of data (packets) are sent from source to destination using the quickest route available. While circuit-switched connections operate the same as a phone call, packet-switched connections are much like sending a series of letters through the mail. Because each packet contains a source and destination address, packets that make up a single transaction can be sent out of order and along different routes. Although packets can be of any size, typical packet sizes range from 100 to 1500 bytes.

Transmitting information in packets can result in vastly increased efficiency and reduced costs to users. All packet-switched services require a connection from the customer site to the access point of the packet-switched network or a connection via the Internet.

Whether to choose circuit-switching or packet-switching depends upon the type of traffic on the networks and the costs involved. Traffic such as video, is sensitive to delays and needs the guaranteed bandwidth of circuited-switched service. Unfortunately, this can be expensive.

The battle between packet-switching and circuit-switching is the battle between IP versus the traditional telephone Asynchronous Transfer Mode (ATM). IP, which comes from the bottom, solves a relatively local problem, multi-platform minicomputer networking and ATM which comes from the top is a protocol of slow evolution, far-sighted but ponderous, slow, and inflexible. ATM developed so slowly that it gave IP/Ethernet an opportunity to come up with Ethernet switching and fast 100 Mbps Ethernet transmission.

By 1999, IP and Ethernet had become well-established and were too firmly entrenched for the corporate marketplace to bypass them in favor of ATM. However, it appears that ATM and IP/Ethernet will continue to co-exist and struggle in their continuing protocol war for some time to come.

Bridging Web Services

While the W3C develops open Web standards, vendors have been customizing their applications for efficient business logic processing through their customized servers and server applications. For example, Web Services can be built on open standards such as Simple Object Access Protocol (SOAP) and Web Service Description Language (WSDL) (see Chapter 5), but then executed through server pages designed for specialized server frameworks (i.e., Java 2 Platform Enterprise Edition (J2EE) and .NET).

Since 1994, Distributed Objects have been developed by many organizations under different names. NeXT called them Portable Distributed Objects, Microsoft called them Component Object Model (COM), IBM called them System Object Model (SOM), and Apple called them OpenDoc. These companies (with the exception of Microsoft) formed the Object Management Group and created a standard called Common Object Request Broker Architecture (CORBA).

The CORBA concept was an architecture that lets applications plug into an "application bus" and call a service. Based on object-oriented units, it called on specialized software components. For the most part, component software developers have been unable to achieve the desired interoperability. This has been because of the lack of universal acceptance which was unachievable without Microsoft's acquiescence. As a result, interchangeable component capabilities were never fully realized.

To actually succeed in developing worldwide distributed component technology standards, it was necessary to find a minimal common ground. XML and HTTP were able to offer just the

14

right minimal technology for their intended application. And SOAP was developed to define the use of XML and HTTP to access services, objects, and servers in a platform-independent manner. As a result, SOAP offers a bridging technology for Web Services.

In 2001, interoperable objects, supported by IBM and Microsoft, were defined as Web Services and were being coupled with a complimentary technology called Universal Discovery Description and Integration (UDDI). Web Services allow companies to publish components and services in a directory that other Web applications can search and implement through a call to the service.

Web Services: Microsoft and Sun Face Off

Microsoft's current approach to Web Services is to build them into Microsoft's .NET framework. The .NET framework uses XML throughout and introduces XML-based remote procedure calls using Simple Object Access Protocol (SOAP) that offers a cross-platform alternative to Distributed Common Object Model (DCOM) and an easier-to-implement alternative to the Internet Inter-ORB Protocol (IIOP). In addition, it introduced a new language, C# with object-oriented Application Programming Interfaces APIs.

SOAP describes commands and parameters that can be passed between browsers and Web Services as part of the Microsoft .NET strategy. SOAP is an implementation of XML that represents one common set of rules about how data and commands will be represented and extended. SOAP consists of three parts: an envelope (a framework for describing what is in a message and how to process it), a set of encoding rules (for expressing instances of application-defined data types), and a convention for representing remote procedure calls and responses. SOAP messages are fundamentally one-way transmissions from a sender to a receiver using HTTP binding.

Web Services Description Language (WSDL) is a new specification to describe networked XML-based services. It provides a way for service providers to describe the format of requests to their systems regardless of the underlying protocol or encoding. WSDL is a part of the effort of Universal Discovery and Description Identification (UDDI) initiative to provide directories and descriptions of such on-line services for electronic business.

In competition with Microsoft's .NET approach (which supports primary Windows), are architectures based on platform independence, such as Java 2 Platform Enterprise Edition (J2EE). In 1995, Sun unveiled the Java platform as a way to create applications that would run on any computer, regardless of the underlying operating system. Java technology has progressed from a tool to animate Web sites to the end-to-end Java 2 platform that spans applications from small consumer devices to enterprise data center servers. The Java programming language is now an important environment used for developing platform-independent Enterprise Internet Portals (EIPs). Java is cross-platform because of the Java Virtual Machine, a device that serves up distributed software on recognized networks; it works independently of the computer's instruction set and architecture.

Java technology has been broadly utilized in applications including; ATM machines, two-way pagers, mobile phones, personal organizers, game machines, cameras, industrial controllers, point-of-sale terminals, and servers. Java technology and XML can be combined to delivery Web Services using J2EE as a foundation.

Adding the strength of XML technologies to Enterprise systems, such as J2EE and CORBA, provides the environment for building highly scalable secure fault-tolerant systems. XML-based technologies SOAP and WSDL provide the means of building a "Web Services" model where business services can be cataloged via UDDI and invoked over the Web though SOAP requests. These services are currently implemented in terms of CORBA, J2EE, or .NET.

The Continuing Development of the Web

Over the past 40 years, the Web has grown from a Cold War concept for responding to the unthinkable effects of a nuclear war, to its present role as the Global Information Superhighway. Just as the railroads of the 19th century enabled the Machine Age and revolutionized the society of the time, the Web is taking us into the Information Age (see Figure 1-6).

16

1969 – ARPANET	The first major use of computers for communication. Built by universities and technology firms with funding from the U. S. Defense Department's Advanced Research Projects Agency (DARPA).
1973 – Internet	A network of networks exchanging packets of data formatted and addressed using TCP/IP.
1992 – MBone	The Multicast Backbone system that allowed people to view real-time information, such as video. Created by IETF.
1996 – Internet2	A consortium of more than 200 universities that created a network of high speed routers and optical fiber links.
1995 – NSFNET	Establishment of the National Science Foundation Network
1996 – The GRID	A collection of public and private organizations that link scattered supercomputers and data into a "grid" to computationally solve problems.
2000 – ABone	The Active Network Backbone to test efficiency of active networking.
2002 – PlanetLab	Academic and corporate networking to create a smarter network that can improve reliability and detect viruses and worms.

Figure 1-6. Timeline of reinventing the Internet.

By 2000, however, Enterprise Information Portals (EIP), such as, AOL, Yahoo, and MSN began serving as centralized entry points for Web surfers and produced focused data flows over the Web. In addition, the introduction of Web Services led to a dichotomy of .NET and J2EE frameworks within the server infrastructure. As a result, the Web moved strongly toward becoming a decentralized network with highly critical hubs.

Limits of Today's Web

The value in reviewing historical development is to draw conclusions by evaluating capabilities and understanding lessons learned. In Table 1-1, we present a summary of the progression of key Web characteristics past and present.

We have found that the Web has changed from the original distributed, high-reliability, open system without a superimposed logic or meta-data. Today, the basic information is still displayed as a distributed open system, but the development of portals, such as, Yahoo, Google, AOL, and MSN has focused Web entry and led to controlling traffic to partisan sites. In addition, business logic has migrated into two segregated server frameworks, active server pages and java server pages. The results has produced a decentralized Web system with critical proprietary portal-centric nodes and frameworks (see Appendix C for a description of how today's data flow paths created distinct flow patterns such as the "Bow-Tie" pattern of the Web).

The current Web is still based on HTML, which describes how information is to be displayed and laid out on a Web page for humans to read. In effect the Web has developed as a medium for humans without a focus on data that could be processed automatically. HTML is not capable of being directly exploited by information retrieval techniques; hence the Web is restricted to manual keyword searches. If you want to find something on the Web, then you have to do it manually.

In the future, we can expect significant improvements in average bandwidth, the use of open standards that will facilitate advanced markup languages, the application of metadata, and the use of inference search to address the problem of the rapid expansion of the size of the global network.

Original Web Characteristics	Current Web Characteristics	Projected Web Characteristics
Distributed	Decentralized, Portal-centric.	Distributed nature competes with decentralization.
High Reliability	Security vulnerabilities.	Specialized subnets.
Fault Tolerant	Segments of Web are fault intolerant.	Internet hubs are fault vulnerable.
Low Bandwidth.	Expanding bandwidth.	High bandwidth.
Information display for humans.	Information display for human, but business logic moved to specialized framework servers (.NET and J2EE).	Semantic Web Servers compete with proprietary server pages for business logic.
Simple Markup Languages	eXensible Markup Language.	Machine-readable information and semantics.
No metadata	Little metadata.	Significant metadata.
Limited search	Keyword search.	Inference/semantic search.
No network logic	Logic on servers.	Logic on Web.

Table 1-1. Web Evolution Comparison.

Original Web Characteristics	Current Web Characteristics	Projected Web Characteristics
Open Standards	Open Web standards compete with proprietary frameworks servers.	Open Web standards compete with proprietary frameworks servers.
Ease of use	More access.	Multimedia access.

Table 1-1 (continued). Web Evolution Comparison.

Because the World Wide Web has its origin in the idea of hypertext, the Web is centered on textual data enriched by illustrative insertions of audio-visual materials. The status quo paradigm of the Web is centered on the client-server interaction, which is a fundamentally asymmetric relationship between providers inserting content into the Web hypertext (server) and users who essentially read text or provide answers to questions by filling out forms (clients). The hyperlinks of the Web represent structures of meaning that transcend the meaning represented by individual texts, but, at present, these Web structures of meaning, lack longevity, and can only be blindly used, e.g. by search engines, which at best optimize navigation by taking into account the statistical behavior of Web users.

There is at present no way to construct complex networks of meaningful relations between Web contents. In fact, the providers have no influence on the links to the contents provided by them and the users have no impact on the available access structures to the content, except by becoming content providers themselves.

This asymmetric client-server relation largely determines the functionalities of the existing Web-software. Web servers are not the standard tools of users, while the Web browsers used by them are restricted to accessing existing information in a standard form. As a consequence, the present Web offers little possibility for (radically) different views of the same underlying content, depriving users of the creative potential inherent in the dynamics of the ever changing Web hypertext.

The Web of the future will thus continue to be essentially based on the representation of meaning by text. However, contrary to the approach of the existing Web, the emerging paradigm is no longer characterized by client-server asymmetry but by informed peer-to-peer interaction, that is, by a cooperation of equally competent partners who jointly act as providers and servers at the same time. Future users will work on shared knowledge by constructing new meaning while accessing the existing body of knowledge represented in the Web through meaningful links. An important framework for creating such meaningful links can be provided by what is presently discussed as the "semantic web," that is, the automated creation of links between machine-understandable metadata. In a further perspective, however, such semantic linking will not be restricted to the use of specifically prepared metadata sets but will exploit the meaningful structure of the Web itself in order to provide a content-based semantic access to information.

In Table 1-2, we identify some of today's basic Web limitations including search, database support, interoperable applications, intelligent business logic, automation, security, and trust.

Web Characteristics	Web Capabilities	Web Limitations
Network	Decentralized with critical portals.	Junction vulnerabilities, vender control, search sink.
Reliability	Secure subnets.	Specialized subnets.
Fault Tolerance	Segments of Internet are fault intolerant.	Internet hubs are fault vulnerable.
Bandwidth	High bandwidth.	Uniformity of bandwidth.
Search	Limited search.	Inference/semantic search not available.
Logic	Business logic on proprietary servers.	Incompatibility problems.

Table 1-2. Web Capabilities and Limitations.

The problem of semantic search through the Web is perhaps its most critical limitation (see Chapter 15). With the current state of the Web, there are two methods of gaining broader information about documents. The first is to use a directory, or portal site, manually constructed by searching the Web and then categorizing pages and links. The problem with this approach is that directories take a tremendous effort to maintain. Finding new links, updating old ones, and maintaining the database technology, all add to a portal's administrative burden and operating costs.

The second method is the search engine. Good search engines pay special attention to metadata (data about data) in the pages that they spider and add to their index databases. In the simplest case, this metadata might take the form of content in meta-tags. More advanced search engines, like Google, rely on more subtle information. For instance, Google's widely touted algorithm evaluates not only the occurrence of keywords on a page, but also the number of outside links to the page itself, as a measure of its popularity.

20

Searching the World Wide Web can be frustrating. Past studies have indicated that search engines index only about 16% of the total content on the Web and that they are biased toward well known information. Moreover, the content on search engines can be at least several months old, although new indexing techniques are making this less likely.

The result of having better standard metadata could be a Web where users and agents could directly tap the latent information in linked and related pages. This would be a powerful paradigm greatly improving the intelligent use of Web resources.

From our review of the historic development of the Web and identifying its key characteristics and limitation in Tables 1-1 and 1-2, we can reach two fundamental conclusions.

To Develop	We Need
Web Services	Web-based logic structure to enable automated services.
Web Search	Semantic analysis to improve relevance.

Table 1-3. Fundamental Needs for Future Web Development.

In the following section, we discuss meeting the goals of compatible Web standards for search and logic. Then in the subsequent sections on the Semantic Web we present the Semantic Web's solution to performing better search and logic using metadata and open Web logic markup languages.

Competing Web Standards

History suggests that the Web will continue to add new layered markup languages upon its current infrastructure in order to expand its capabilities. However, proprietary forces will continue to compete against open standards. The success of Web infrastructure and software is strongly dependant on its ability to support future growth and demands by layering new capabilities upon its existing flexible and durable architecture.

In Table 1-4, we show that under complete open Web standards, the Web should grow in a basic distributed manner. However, proprietary standards will produce a decentralized network with critical portals. And finally, a monopoly on standards would ultimately produce a centralized network around the owner of the standards. The latter two cases will face greater security, trust and reliability difficulties.

Standards	Resultant Network Type
Open Standards	Distributed
Proprietary Specialized Server Logic	Decentralized
Monopoly Standards	Centralized

Table 1-4. How Standards Produce Network Types.

How will the standards of new Web languages be resolved? We have concluded that future search and Web Services will need metadata and logic constructs available globally. Therefore we must address how global standards for search and logic will evolve.

Global Web standards (open vs proprietary) are truly a key element for the future of the Web. But how can we assure that the Web remains primarily based upon compatible standards despite fierce vender competition for various standards' control?

Traditionally, standards have evolved through one of three methods:

1. A vendor dominates a market and sets a de facto standard (e.g., telephony by AT&T, or PC operating systems by Microsoft). This would lead to a Web monopoly and a centralized network.

2. Vendors and markets collaborate in ways that may not be clearly attributed to any one organization, but over time emerge with a leader (e.g., TCP/IP). This would lead to the Web as a decentralized network.

3. Standards organizations establish standards that are so useful that they are rapidly universally adopted (e.g., HTML by W3C). This would lead to a Web as a distributed network.

In the current situation, vendors support different frameworks on their specialized Web servers. The J2EE framework works to optimize UNIX flavor servers for Web service applications provided by one group of vendors and .NET framework works to optimize Windows servers for Web service applications provided by Microsoft and its supporters. So long as the business logic is controlled by vendor-specific frameworks, interoperability, overall efficiency, inference, and smooth growth will remain problematic. Moving toward an open markup language standard will level the playing field worldwide and allow business logic, inference, and other intelligent applications to be more uniformly utilized.

Ultimately, there will be a competition between proprietary developers working toward focusing data flow through their portals and over their specialized framework servers and open standards which allow business logic to be implemented directly on the Web.

Semantic Web Roadmap

While search engines that index HTML pages find many answers to searches and cover a huge part of the Web, they return many irrelevant answers. There is no notion of "correctness" to such searches. By contrast, logical engines have typically been able to restrict their output to that which is a provably correct answer, but have suffered from the inability to go through the mass of connected data across the Web to construct valid answers. The growth of the Web has resulted in a combinatorial explosion of possibilities that is becoming quite intractable.

If an engine of the future combines a reasoning engine with a search engine, it may actually be able to produce useful results. It will be able to reach out to indexes which contain very complete lists of all occurrences of a given term, and then use logic to weed out all but those which can be of use in solving the given problem.

Tim Berners-Lee, the inventor of the WWW, URIs, HTTP, and HTML is also the originator of the next generation Web: the Semantic Web (see Chapter 6). Currently, his World Wide Web Consortium team works to develop, extend, and standardize the Web, as well as its languages and tools. The objective of the Semantic Web is to provide an efficient way of representing typed and linked data on the World Wide Web, in order to allow machine processing on a global scale. While the Semantic Web technologies are still developing, the future of the endeavor appears bright.

The Semantic Web will bring structure and meaningful content to the Web, creating an environment where software agents can carry out sophisticated tasks for users. The first steps in weaving the Semantic Web with the existing Web are already under way. In the near future, these developments will provide new functionality as machines become better able to "understand" and process the data.

The essential property of the World Wide Web is its universality though the power of hypertext. And while today's Web is produced primarily for human consumption, the next generation Web will to a great extent facilitate machine as well as human consumption. At the end of the process we will have databases, programs, and sensor output that can automatically function with little or no human intervention.

For the Semantic Web to function, computers must have access to structured collections of information and sets of inference rules that they can use to conduct automated reasoning.

Artificial-intelligence researchers have long studied such systems and produced today's knowledge representation. It is currently in a state comparable to that of hypertext before the advent of the Web. Knowledge representation contains the seeds of important applications, but to fully realize its potential, it must be linked into a comprehensive global system.

The objective of the Semantic Web, therefore, is to provide a framework that expresses both data and rules for reasoning from a Web based knowledge representation.

Adding logic to the Web means using rules to make inferences, choose courses of action and answer questions. A combination of mathematical and engineering issues complicates this task. The logic must be powerful enough to describe complex properties of objects, but not so powerful that agents can be tricked by being asked to consider a paradox.

Two important technologies for developing the Semantic Web are already in place: XML and the Resource Description Framework (RDF). XML lets everyone create their own tags. Scripts, or programs, can make use of these tags in sophisticated ways, but the script writer has to know how the page writer uses each tag. In short, XML allows users to add arbitrary structure to their documents, but says nothing about what the structure mean.

The Importance of XML

Why is eXtensible Markup Language (XML) so important? Just as HTML is an open standard that allows information exchange and display over the Internet, XML is an open standard that allows data to be exchanged between applications over the Internet (see Chapter 4). XML is the bridge to exchange data between the two main software development frameworks over the Web: J2EE and .NET.

While we can consider XML as a highly functional subset of SGML, it is not implemented and used as a single markup language. Instead, it too is a meta-language that allows users to design their own markup languages. In effect, XML is a "lever." A "lever" in the sense that Archimedes suggested over two thousand years ago, when he stated that the "right lever" could "move" the earth. Only XML is the "lever" that will shape the future architecture of the Web by designing the future Web languages.

The road map for achieving connected applications and associated logical data is called the Semantic Web. The underlying idea is the ability to resolve the semantics of a particular node by following an arc until a familiar node is found.

The Semantic Web offers an easier way to publish data that can be accessed and re-purposed on demand. The Semantic Web is built on syntaxes which use Uniform Resource Identifier (URI), to represent data, usually in triples-based structures where the triplets are subject, predicate and object. Many triplets of URI data can be held in databases, or interchanged on the Web using Resource Description Framework (RDF) (see Figure 1-7).

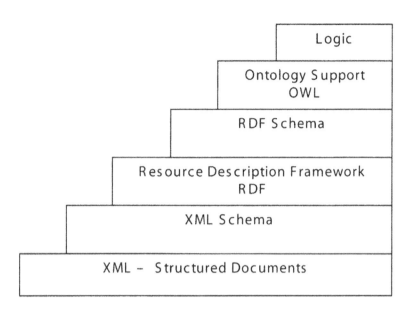

Figure 1-7. Web Language Pyramid.

Resource Description Framework - RDF Metadata

The general model of the Semantic Web is based on Resource Description Framework (RDF) which contains the concept of an assertion and allows assertions about assertions. Meta-assertions make it possible to do rudimentary checks on a document (see Chapter 7). In RDF, a schema allows us to check, for example, that a driver's license has the name of a person.

The schema language typically makes simple assertions about allowable combinations. The constraints expressed in the schema language are easily expanded into a more powerful logical layer (the next layer).

The logic layer provides documents with rules that discriminates one type of document from another, providing checking of documents for self-consistency; and the resolution of a queries. The layer is a predicate logic (using NOT, AND, OR functions).

We may want to make inferences that can only be made by understanding the semantics of the schema language in logical terms. A requirement of RDF is the ability to convert a document from one RDF schema into another.

The RDF model does not say anything about the form of the reasoning engine. RDF at the logical level already has the power to express inference rules; it acts as a query engine of specific algorithms and indices.

25

RDF is a model of statements made about resources and associated URI. Its statements have a uniform structure of three parts: predicate, subject, and object.

For example: The author [predicate] of War and Peace [subject] is Tolstoi [object].

RDF can be used to encode the above natural-language statement, as well as, say, an object-oriented model.

With RDF we can express such statements in a formal way that software agents can read and act on. It lets us express a collection of statements as a graph, as a series of (subject, predicate, object) triples, or even in XML form. The first form is the most convenient for communication between people, the second for efficient processing, and the third for flexible communication with agent software.

If a portal were to create a directory of business sites, it could use RDF document to help RDF-enabled agents and tools better understand the information on that site (see Chapter 13).

Making an Inference

In artificial intelligence, scientists recognize that although computers are beginning to overtake the human brain in terms of sheer processing speed and storage capacity, they still cannot approach the level of human intelligence in terms of general purpose cognitive capability. At least one reason for this is that the brain doesn't stubbornly store and categorize every scrap of every detail that we use as the basis of thought. The brain can make connections between partially-stored information, and assemble this into intelligence.

The Semantic Web won't be possible until software agents have the means to figure out some things by themselves (see Chapter 9). Fortunately, artificial intelligence gives us two tools to help make this possible. First, knowledge representation is a field that defines how we might represent, in computers, some of what is stored between our ears. Second, inference is a way of using formal logic to approximate further knowledge from what is already known. An Inference Engine is a software application that processes the knowledge (see Chapter 6) to derive resulting conclusions.

Building Ontologies

All of this forms a system of representing and synthesizing knowledge that is often referred to as an ontology. The leading ontology system using RDF is Web Ontology Language (called OWL) (see Chapter 8).

OWL allows us to formally express ontologies. W3C RDF provides some classification and rules but OWL goes much further. In fact, one way to look at OWL is as the business rules for the Semantic Web, yet it's much more flexible than most business-rules languages.

Most of OWL's power comes from primitives for expressing classifications. OWL provides a toolbox of class expressions, which bring the power of mathematical logic and set theory to the tricky and important task of mapping ontologies through classifications.

Before the Semantic Web can become a reality however, it faces several challenges including:

- Complexity—Semantics are complex, and it won't be an easy technology to use.

- Abuse—Practices like meta-tag spamming, and even trademark hijacking, show that any system that lets people set their own context is subject to abuse. Semantic Web technologies will need a mostly automated system for establishing trust. This concept is often referred to as the Web of trust.

- Proprietary Technology—Because of the diversity in developers and development tools, Semantic Web technology will have to be politically and technically open for implementation and use. If it requires royalty payments to any party, open source advocates and competing Web technology vendors will boycott it. If it requires a specific plug-in or module, most developers and users won't even bother installing it.

Semantic Web Services

With the new generation of Web markup languages including OWL, there has also developed an ontology of services, called OWL-S, that could facilitate automated functions.

The following are the fundamental automatic OWL-S tasks:

1. Automatic Web-service discovery—involves the automatic location of Web Services. For example, the user may want to find a service that sells airline tickets between two cities.

2. Automatic Web-service invocation—involves the automatic execution of an identified Web-service by a computer program or agent. For example, the user could request the purchase of an airline ticket. Currently, a user must go to the Web site offering that service, fill out a form, and click on a button to execute the service. Execution of a Web service can be thought of as a collection of function calls. The OWL-S markup of Web services provides a declarative, computer-interpretable API for executing these function calls. A software agent interprets the markup and evaluates what information is necessary, what information will be returned, and how to execute it automatically.

3. Automatic Web-service composition and interoperation—involves the automatic selection, composition, and interoperation of Web Services. For example, for travel arrangements. The user must select the Web Services, specify the composition manually, and make sure that any software needed for the interoperation is custom-created. With the OWL-S markup of Web Services, the information necessary to select and compose services will be encoded at the service Web sites. Software can be written to manipulate these representations, together with a specification of the objectives of the task, to achieve the task automatically.

4. Automatic Web-service execution monitoring—individual services and compositions of services often require some time to execute. A user may want to know during this period what the status is. For example, a user may want to make sure that a hotel reservation has already been made.

OWL-S will provide descriptors for the execution of services (see Chapters 10). We provide a detailed OWL-S Semantic Web service called Congo.owl in Chapter 11.

Conclusion

In this chapter, we provided an introduction to the Web and a survey of how it developed using markup applications and distributed networking. We showed that under complete open Web standards, the Web should grow in a basic distributed manner. However, using competing proprietary standards will produce a decentralized network with critical portals. We considered the possibility of a monopoly which would produce a centralized network around the owner of the standards.

We found that XML was a highly functional subset of SGML that will have tremendous influence on the Web's future. In effect, XML is a "lever" that will shape the architecture of the Web by designing the future Web languages.

We discussed how the Web will evolve while packaging knowledge in ways that are increasingly accessible to the emerging technologies for Semantic Web Services.

Finally, the Semantic Web Service technological issues that we will specifically address in subsequent chapters answering the following questions:

1. Why is XML so critical to the future of Web architecture?
2. How will Web Services using .NET and J2EE evolve toward automated discovery and delivery?
3. How will meta-languages, ontologies, and inference engines produce powerful Web search capabilities?

4. Can Semantic Web Services be implemented immediately without waiting for the full development of the Semantic Web?

5. Why would Semantic Web Services lead to open Web standards and a distributed Web?

Chapter Two

Markup Languages

Overview

Programming a computer requires creating a sequence of instructions that the computer will use to perform a corresponding series of tasks. While it is possible to create programs directly in machine language, it is uncommon for programmers to work at this level because of the abstract nature of the instructions. It is better to write programs in a simple text file using a high-level programming language which later can be compiled into executable code.

Of course, there are easier ways to program rather than create fully compiled programs. Instead of compiling source code once and then running programs using the executable code, it is possible to use what are called "scripting languages." Scripting languages are similar to compiled languages, except that instead of transforming the source code into executable code to be run later, the compiler runs the code as it is being compiled. For running very simple programs, it is hard to beat running scripts.

Then, why isn't everything run on scripts? Running the compiler and the program at the same time is a processing burden on the computer, and scripts tend to run slower than executable code.

There is also another level of programming to consider called "stateless programming." Browsers, such as Internet Explorer or Netscape Navigator, view Web pages written in a language called HyperText Markup Language, or HTML. The HTML program can be written to a simple text file and then assigned a certain file type that is recognized by a browser. It is also possible to utilize script programming embedded within HTML. In addition, HTML can include compiler directives that call server pages with proprietary compiled programming. As a result, simple-text HTML is empowered with important capabilities to call complex business logic programming residing on servers both in the frameworks of Microsoft's .NET and Sun's J2EE. These frameworks support Web Services and form a vital part of today's Web.

Currently, the open standards on the Web are layered as markup languages starting with HTML (see Chapter 3) and XML (see Chapter 4). In this chapter, we provide a brief primer for Standard Generalized Markup Language (SGML) in order to establish the heritage of subsequent markups. We introduce the importance of markup languages, in general, for supporting future business logic on the Web. In addition, we summarize other key markup languages including HTML and XML, and indicate their relationship to SGML and the future development of Web Services.

Background

In early 1969, Charles F. Goldfarb joined IBM's Cambridge Scientific Center and began work that focused on how to apply computers to the practice of law. That project required the integration of a text editing application, an information retrieval system, and a page composition program. The legal documents were to be kept in a data repository and would be processed by queries. The selected documents would be revised and tailored using the text editor and returned to the data repository, or rendered for presentation by the composition program.

Such a task might be routine for current word processing systems, but it was well beyond the capabilities of any document processing system in 1969. In fact, in those days, different applications required manual integration and were not only not designed to work together, they frequently were not even able to run on the same operating system. The problem was that, even when the team got programs to communicate with one another, they found that the programs individually required different procedural markup for their document files. Obviously, such incompatibility was a problem of huge proportions, demanding a general solution.

As a result, Charles Goldfarb, together with Edward Mosher and Raymond Lorie, developed the Generalized Markup Language (GML) to enable integrated text editing, formatting, and information retrieval for shared documents.

Markup

Because the software applications of the time were text-based with no graphical capabilities, the text contained within the documents were "marked up" using textual commands. These markups surrounded the text and explained how to handle it for printing. This included notations for boldface, underline, font sizing, placement, and other commands. Editors have been using markup for decades to indicate changes and revisions. Word processors implemented a way in which markup could be encoded in a computer-based system.

GML was based on the generic coding ideas of Rice and Tunnicliffe: namely, the separation of the formatting of a document from its content. Instead of implementing a simple tagging scheme, however, GML introduced the concept of a formally-defined document type with an explicit nested element structure. Major portions of GML were implemented in mainframe publishing systems by IBM and achieved substantial industry acceptance.

After the completion of GML, Goldfarb continued his research on document structures, creating additional concepts, such as short references, link processes, and concurrent document types that were not part of GML, but were later to be developed as part of Standard Generalized Markup Language (SGML).

In 1978, the American National Standards Institute (ANSI) committee on Information Processing established the committee for Computer Languages for the Processing of Text, whose members included Charles Card and Norman Scharpf. Goldfarb was asked to join the committee and eventually to lead a project to develop a text description language standard based on GML. The committee supported the effort of developing Goldfarb's basic language design for SGML into a standard. The first working draft of the SGML standard was published in 1980. Major adopters included the U.S. Internal Revenue Service (IRS) and the U.S. Department of Defense.

In 1984, the SGML project, which had been authorized by the International Organization for Standardization (ISO) as well as ANSI, reorganized. In 1985, a draft proposal for an international standard was published, and the final text, developed by Anders Berglund, then of the European Particle Physics Laboratory (CERN) was issued as ISO 8879 in 1986.

It wasn't long before SGML would give birth to the Internet's primary communication tools including HTML (HyperText Markup Language), XHTML (eXtensible HyperText Markup Language), and XML (eXtensible Markup Language) under the direction of Tim Berners-Lee.

However, the software development approaches leading to using markup languages for the Web bear some discussion. Table 2-1 summarizes the evolution of software development approaches for communications, business logic, and data from 1970 to the present.

	General	Communication Mechanism	Business Logic	Data
1970s	Mainframe centric	Proprietary protocols	Assembly, Cobol	Data passed as binary and stored in files.
1980s	Client/Server	Proprietary protocols by operating system/platform—flavors of Unix	Predominately 4GL—many based upon SQL database products	Data passed as binary and stored in relational databases.
1990s	Enterprise oriented	Component models —CORBA, DCOM, RMI	Object-oriented programming and procedural programming N-tier architecture	Data passed as binary and stored in relational databases.
2000s	Global Business Network	Internet (HTTP) and XML. Open Web Services, SOAP, WDSL	Software agents	XML data transfer.

Table 2-1. Software Development Approaches.

The progression from 1970 proprietary communication network protocols toward open Internet standards in 2003 (HTTP, SOAP) has resulted in global access for information and data. In addition, XML has opened the door to interoperable data exchange on a global basis. The evolution of business from local mainframe Intranets with restricted access into globally connected organizations using business logic running on servers establishes a trend toward building more logic into Web capabilities. The march toward more power and openly available logic on the Web is presented in Figure 2-1.

This figure shows the Markup Language Pyramid starting from XML and XML Schema (see Chapter 4), followed by Resource Description Framework (RDF) and RDF Schema (see Chapter 7). On top of this structure, Ontology and Logic are included in the mix through the Web Ontology Language (OWL) (see Chapter 10).

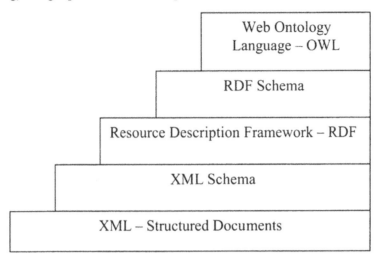

Figure 2-1. The markup language pyramid.

The timeline under which these languages have grown is illustrated in Figure 2-2. The figure shows how new RDF and OWL have grown compared to the Web's main display language HTML and the recent data structuring language XML.

SGML Primer

Every language is based upon a vocabulary. For native languages we call the vocabulary element words. However, in a formal language, they could also be symbols. It is characteristic of languages that some sequences of words (or symbols) are recognized as correct, well-formed sentences. The grammar syntax or structure of the language determines if it is well formed. In fact, we define the set of rules governing a language as its syntax. Beyond sentence structure we must also evaluate the sentence meaning. We define the meaning of a sentence as its semantics. Syntax and semantics are intimately related and form the basis of applying each language.

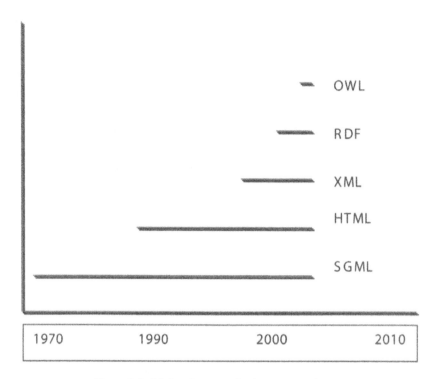

Figure 2-2. Markup language development timeline.

The root of markup languages can be found in the Standard Generalized Markup Language (SGML). SGML will set the starting point for syntax, well-formedness, and validity. Many characteristics of SGML are repeated throughout the development of its progeny languages. So it is worthwhile to review its key features and parental syntax.

In 1986, SGML became an international standard for defining descriptions of the structure and content of different types of electronic documents. SGML is used for describing thousands of different document types in many fields of human activity, from technical documentation to a patient's clinical records.

SGML has withstood the test of time. However, various barriers exist to delivering SGML over the Web. These barriers include a lack of widely supported stylesheets, complex and unstable software due to SGML's broad and powerful options, and obstacles to interchange of SGML data because of varying levels of SGML compliance among software packages. These difficulties have condemned SGML to being a successful niche technology, rather than a mainstream Web tool. However, the SGML language has produced other markup languages that are vital for the development of the Web including HTML and XML.

In general, people who create the component pieces of electronic documents normally think of them in terms of two groups: content and markup. This corresponds with the approach taken by SGML to divide a document into separate content and markup pieces. As a result, an SGML document consists of several parts:

1. The SGML declaration which specifies which characters and delimiters may appear in the application.
2. The document type definition (DTD) which defines the syntax of markup constructs. The DTD may include additional definitions such as numeric and named character entities.
3. A specification that describes the semantics to be ascribed to the markup. This specification also imposes syntax restrictions that cannot be expressed within the DTD.
4. Document instances containing data (content) and markup. Each instance contains a reference to the DTD to be used to interpret it.

In the following sections, we will provide a brief explanation of these SGML features. Many of these features reappear in similar form in later languages in subsequent chapters.

Document Type Declaration

The document type declaration (<!DOCTYPE>) tag tells the parser which DTD governs the current document. Usually the DTD is incorporated by reference to a PUBLIC or SYSTEM name by which the parser or SGML application can find the DTD. The declaration portion of an SGML document will also declare document-specific components:

- Entities used in the document (also addressable as PUBLIC or SYSTEM entities),
- Any notation types not declared in the main DTD.

The SGML declaration indicates the SGML rules of the current document: the character set, characters used as control characters, SGML object capacities, and which SGML features can be used in the document, among other items.

The SGML interpreter, or parser, reads the SGML declaration in order to learn which character set to respect, what codes will act as process control and record ends and starts, what characters should be ignored as SGML data, the capacity needed to store SGML objects encountered by the parser as it parses the document tree structure, and what SGML features will be used in the document type and thus must be interpretable by the parser.

Document Type Definition (DTD)

The DTD contains a formal statement not only of the document elements (the tag set), but of the element hierarchy and other interrelationships, the possible sequences of tags, and the required number of occurrences of the elements. The parser uses the rules laid down in the DTD to enforce conformity to the DTD in SGML documents.

The DTD is either included in a <!DOCTYPE> tag or contained in an external file and referenced from a <!DOCTYPE> tag.

Element declarations are prefaced in the DTDs by the reserved word "ELEMENT." After this reserved word, the next component is the element name.

Element inclusions indicate that, from this point in the hierarchy, the listed element(s) may occur at any point in the document. Such inclusions are often used for elements such as tables and figures that can occur at random in the midst of many content models. Inclusions are noted by preceding the list with the "+" symbol, enclosed in parentheses.

Element exclusions indicate that, from this point in the hierarchy, the listed element(s) may not occur. The exclusions are noted by preceding the list with the "-" symbol, enclosed in parentheses.

The content model defines the required and optional contents of the element, indicated by nested element names or type of character indicators such as "#PCDATA."

<!ELEMENT deflist - - (title?, (term, def)+) >

Sequence indicators in the DTD give rules for sequencing elements and text within the element. Occurrence indicators determine whether and how many of an element must occur in the contents of the declared element.

Sequence Indicator	Symbol Used	Meaning
Sequential elements.	, (comma)	Elements must be in specified order, and are separated by a comma,
Elements that are alternatives.	| (vertical bar)	Elements separated by the vertical bar are considered alternatives and are not listed in any particular order (OR),

Table 2-2. Sequence and Occurrence Indicators.

Sequence Indicator	Symbol Used	Meaning
Elements that are included but in no particular sequence.	& (ampersand)	Elements are included and separated by the ampersand. They are not listed in any particular order (AND),
Optional element, single occurrence if present.	? (question mark)	
Optional element, may occur more than once.	* (asterisk)	
Required element, single occurrence.	unsigned element name	
Required element, must occur at least once, can occur many times.	+ (plus sign)	

Table 2-2 (continued). Sequence and Occurrence Indicators.

In Example 2-1, a DTD is created for a book entitled "Sample Book."

Example 2-1. Creating a DTD for sample book.

Sample Book
   by Anonymous
Chapter 1. Hello
Chapter 2. Goodbye

An example of the Document Type Definition for the above Text file is:

```
<!DOCTYPE Book [
    <!ELEMENT Book (Title, Chapter+)>
    <!ATTLIST Book Author CDATA #REQUIRED>
    <!ELEMENT Title (#PCDATA)>
    <!ELEMENT Chapter (#PCDATA)>
    <!ATTLIST Chapter id ID #REQUIRED>
]>
```

The DTD for Example 2-1 defines precisely those elements needed for one document or for a group of similarly structured documents. The element declarations indicate the "official" name of an element, which will appear inside delimiters as a tag (<chapter> for example) and describe what information each element may contain.

Character data that may contain special characters, cross-references, emphasis tags, and general entities is called "#PCDATA" for parse-able character data; the parser continues to parse PCDATA. CDATA is character data that is not parsed, meaning the parser discontinues parsing until the end of the CDATA element.

Tags

There are two primary object types for tags in a SGML document,: elements, inserted as tags and the entities corresponding to local attributes for special characters, stored text, and external files.

The SGML document begins by defining a character set, generally based on the ASCII standard characters. Then the SGML element names, inside 'tags,' are inserted into text to indicate the beginnings and ends of logical objects. From the user's point of view, markup is mixed with the data using standard characters.

To distinguish between the two types of content, SGML inserts delimiter characters which let the software recognize that certain characters should be read in TAG mode. Characters used as delimiters from ISO 8879, which describes a base set, include open and close angle brackets to set off start tags. Tags are used to demark content. The name of the tag is expressed in alphanumeric characters inside the less than (<) and greater than (>) symbols. For example:

```
start element:   <tagname>
close element: </tagname>
```

The names of the elements and attributes and their order in the hierarchy (among other things) form the markup language used by the document. This language can be defined by the document author or it can be inferred from the document's structure. In Example 2-1, the language contains three elements: Book, Title, and Chapter. The Book element contains a single Title element and one or more Chapter elements. The Book element has an Author attribute and the Chapter element has an ID attribute.

An SGML document type definition declares element types that represent structures or desired behavior. HTML includes element types that represent paragraphs, hypertext links, lists, tables, images, etc.

Each element type declaration generally consists of three parts: a start tag, content, and an end tag. The element's name appears in the start tag (written <element-name>) and the end tag (written </element-name>).

Parsers

SGML can be validated using special parsing software. SGML applications all work with some form of parsing software.

An SGML parser does three jobs, it:

- Validates the structure and syntax of the DTD before parsing the document instance.
- Parses the document structure so that at any point in the document the parser knows the current markup state.
- Checks for markup errors in the document.

In an SGML document, empty elements contain no character data or other elements. Empty tags mark things like cross-references and index entries that will be created by the application system. Empty tags are also often used to insert external files in non-SGML notations, such as graphic files.

For non-empty elements, one or more attributes follow the name of the element inside the tag markers. These attributes are separated by a space from the tag name and from each other attribute name. Each attribute is followed by an "=" sign, and the value of the attribute is enclosed in quotes.

Entities are used to refer to special typographic characters or symbols, external files (an external entity), or replacement ("boilerplate") text (a general entity). In the document instance, external and general entities are called out in the form "&name;" This syntax represents an entity name prefaced by "&" followed by ";" (semicolon).

Entities must be declared in either the DTD or the particular document instance. To be available for all documents in the class, entities should be declared in DTD. Entities, such as graphics used only within a document instance, should be part of the document type declaration at the top of the document.

The Relationship between SGML, HTML, and XML

SGML is a complete document language. In addition, SGML creates powerful all-purpose tools for defining other markup languages including HTML, XHTML, and XML.

XML is a subset of SGML meant to work efficiently with Web data. As a reduced version of SGML, XML is also used to define other markup languages that manipulate data or improve communication protocols for Web Services.

Figure 2-3 shows the markup language hierarchy. XML is a direct descendant of SGML and inherits many of SGML's powers and capabilities. As a child language, it will have an important impact on the future of Web architecture.

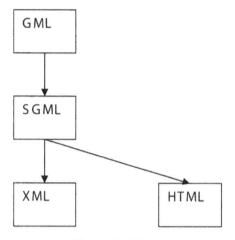

Figure 2-3. Markup language hierarchy.

SGML Capabilities and Limitations

Table 2-3 shows the capabilities and limitations of SGML. SGML is a powerful technology, but it is not Web deployable by itself. Instead, SGML provides the basis for a leaner and Web-appropriate markup language, XML.

Capabilities	Limitations
Powerful Intranet document definitions.	Too complex for Web data and applications.
Enables legacy applications for corporations.	The Web needs a more abstract and a more semantic approach for Web Services.

Table 2-3. SGML Capabilities and Limitations.

Conclusion

In this chapter, we provided a brief primer for Standard Generalized Markup Language (SGML) in order to provide a foundation for other markups. We introduced the role and importance of markup languages, in general. In addition, we summarized other key markup languages including HTML and XML, and indicated their relationship to SGML and the future development of Web Services.

Chapter Three

HyperText Markup Language (HTML)

Overview

Browsers, such as Internet Explorer or Netscape Navigator view Web pages written in HyperText Markup Language (HTML). The HTML program can be written to a simple text file that is recognized by a browser and it can call embedded script programming. In addition, HTML can include compiler directives that call server pages with proprietary compiled programming. As a result, simple-text HTML is empowered with important capabilities to call complex business logic programming residing on servers both in the frameworks of Microsoft's .NET and Sun's J2EE. These frameworks support Web Services and form a vital part of today's Web.

In this chapter, we review the development, features, and limitations of HyperText Markup Language (HTML). We start with this basic markup language and follow the Markup Language Pyramid step-by-step as we move from chapter-to-chapter throughout this book. We will learn how open Web markup standards compete with the proprietary server frameworks.

Background

Vannevar Bush is credited with developing the principles underlying modern hypertext research. Bush earned his B.S. and M.S. from Tufts University in 1913. By 1932, he was Vice President and Dean of the School of Engineering at MIT. In 1938, Bush was elected President of the Carnegie Institution. This position afforded him a highly visible platform to help influence the scientific policy and strategy of the United States. On the eve of World War II, Bush met with President Franklin D. Roosevelt to present his plan for mobilizing military research. He proposed a new organization called the National Defense Research Committee (NDRC). The President approved the plan and Bush was appointed Chairman of the NDRC. Soon, the NDRC was subsumed into the newly created Office of Scientific Research and Development (OSRD) with Bush serving as its Director.

As a result of this extraordinary career, Bush was able to write the article "As We May Think," published in 1945 in the Atlantic Monthly, in which he first proposed his idea for the Memex Machine. This machine was designed to help people sort through the enormous amount of published information available throughout the world. His article described a Memex as a "device in which an individual stores his books, records and communications." The device was automated to provide speed, accuracy, and flexibility. It was intended to be an enlarged, intimate supplement to one's memory.

The Memex Machine was to be an information storage and retrieval device, based on microfilm technology, that would consist of a desk with viewing screens, a keyboard, selection buttons and levers, and microfilm storage device. The machine would augment human memory by allowing the user to make links, or "associative trails," between documents (see Figure 3-1).

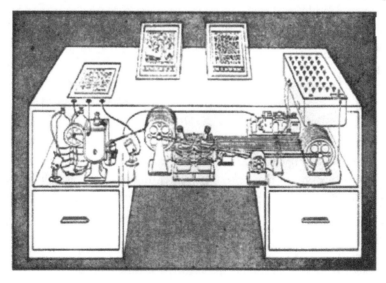

Figure 3-1. Memex Machine in the form of a desk.

While continuing his pursuit of the Memex concept, Bush continued to propose the basics of hypertext. He suggested the notion of blocks of text, joined by links, and he introduced the terms: links, linkages, trails, and web, through his descriptions of a new type of "textuality." Bush's article greatly influenced the creators of "hypertext" and its development for use in modern information systems, including the Internet. It wasn't until 1967 that Ted Nelson first coined the term "hypertext."

The history of the development of HyperText Markup Language (HTML) represents an unusual but interesting tale. From its simple start as a particular on-line application of SGML, past the political maneuverings of the large entrenched browser companies, HTML has weathered the storms of growth and innovation in the ever-expanding Web. As recently as a few years ago, the battle for control of the web markup standard pitted Microsoft against Netscape, both touting W3C compliance.

In 1990, when Tim Berners-Lee laid the foundation for the World Wide Web, he included three primary components:

- HTTP (HyperText Transfer Protocol).
- URLs (Universal Resource Locators).
- HTML (HyperText Markup Language).

These three components represent the essential ingredients leading to the explosive growth of the World Wide Web. Berners-Lee was the primary developer of HTML, assisted by his colleagues at CERN.

The original idea behind HTML was a modest one. When Berners-Lee was putting together his first elementary browsing and authoring system for the Web, he quickly created a highly limited hypertext language that would minimally serve his purposes. Berners-Lee was aware of what SGML had to offer and he realized that he could create a simple DTD based upon SGML that would allow users to create simple hypertext-linked documents. He named this DTD application, HTML. Since it was text-based, any editor or word processor could be employed to create or convert documents for the Web. And it was so easy that it could be mastered in a day. As the Web flourished and use of HTML became widespread, the limitations of the language began to foil continued progress.

As it turned out, the simplicity of HTML was itself a problem. As more content moved to the Web, those creating browsers realized that this simple markup language needed more capability. So the browser developers began implementing new features, and when the Web community liked them, they stayed. For example, although early browsers were simply text-based, there was an immediate desire to display graphic figures and icons on Web pages.

In 1993, a college student named Marc Andreessen added the tag <img> to his Mosaic browser to allow the insertion of graphic images. Other people objected, saying this addition was too limited. They wanted the tags <include> or <embed> to be introduced to allow the addition of any sort of medium to a Web page, with content negotiation. However, that was too big a modification for Mosaic. So Mosaic settled with the <img> tag, and it would be years before the ability to include media in a page by using the tags <embed>, <applet> or <object> would appear.

While Mosaic was busy issuing the <img> tag, Berners-Lee went off to start the nascent World Wide Web Consortium (W3C), and Marc Andreesen began a start-up company called Netscape.

HTML continued to expand, with new and more powerful tags being added, such as, <background>, <frame>, <font>, and <blink>. Microsoft introduced <marquee>, <iframe>, and <bgsound> and started competing for control of the HTML standard. During this time, the W3C debated a new version of HTML, version 3.0, which included an outline for many new features that nobody would ever support, such as <banner> and <fig> (see Table 3-1).

HTML Version	Date	Implementation Key Changes	Comment
HTML 1.0	1992	Initial version.	Limited DTD of SGML, developed by Berners-Lee.
HTML 2.0	November 1995	Added image representation with the <img> tag.	An initiative designed for the Mosaic Browser.
HTML 3.0	Not implemented	Attempt to add additional tags, including <background>, <frame>, <font>, <blink>, <marquee>, <iframe>, <bgsound> and others.	A W3C initiative to incorporate features being independently introduced by Netscape and Microsoft; Version 3.0 was not implemented.
HTML 3.2	January 1997	Version 3.3 toned-down the changes proposed for 3.0 to be consistent with existing standards.	Established a common basis for content providers and browser developers.

Table 3-1. HTML Versions and Key Changes.

HTML Version	Date	Implementation Key Changes	Comment
HTML 4.0	December 1997		The last version of HTML.
XHTML 1.0	2000	Reformulation of HTML 4.0 as an XML application.	

Table 3-1 (continued). HTML Versions and Key Changes.

By 1995, Netscape and Microsoft, the two leading browser developers, were heading toward two completely proprietary versions of HTML. This would have forced people to choose one browser or the other and surf content specifically created for that platform. Content providers would either have to choose between vendors or spend more resources creating multiple versions of their pages. There are still vestiges of this competition lingering on today's Web. The HTML group of W3C started collecting and recording current practice in the shipped versions of browsers, rather than designing a new or future version. Finally the unattainable version of the language, HTML 3.0 was dropped entirely, and work was begun on HTML 3.2, which, ironically, was less sophisticated, but more realistic. It gave content providers and browser developers a common reference. The subsequent HMTL 4.0 was the last formal release of HTML.

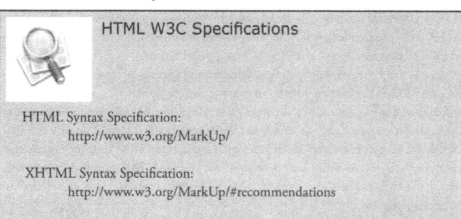

HTML W3C Specifications

HTML Syntax Specification:
   http://www.w3.org/MarkUp/

XHTML Syntax Specification:
   http://www.w3.org/MarkUp/#recommendations

XHTML 1.0, released January 26, 2000 created an entirely new approach to implementing HTML, taking in ideas from XML (see Chapter 4), which is a far more complicated markup language than HTML. XHTML is a family of current and future document types and modules that reproduce and extend HTML, reformulated in XML. XHTML family document types are all XML-based, and are ultimately designed to work in conjunction with XML-based user agents. XHTML has had a series of specifications developed.

The XHTML basic document type includes the minimal set of modules required to be an XHTML host language document type. It includes support for images, forms, basic tables, and objects. It is designed for Web clients that do not support the full set of XHTML features; for example, Web clients such as mobile phones, PDAs, pagers, and set-top boxes. The document type is rich enough for content authoring.

While this new approach was a step in the direction of open standards, vendor competition still drives conflict in this area. The standards war continues to flare up as new versions of various markup languages are introduced but, for the moment at least, the Web has made progress in implementing stable, open, new versions of its base language. This continues the drive toward a Web as a distributed network.

HTML Versions

HTML, a specific DTD of SGML, is the most frequently used document type on the Web. It defines a single, fixed type of document with markup that lets you describe a common class of simple, office-style reports, with headings, paragraphs, lists, illustrations, and access for hyper-text and multimedia.

HTML was defined to allow the transfer, display, and linking of documents over the Internet and was the key enabling technology for the WWW. Prior to the emergence of the Internet, it was unusual to hear the word "page" used to describe elements of data. But HTML Web pages have amazing similarities with paper pages. Both are optimized for visual clarity and are focused on usability without the document structure to support automation.

While the initial version of HTML, Version 1.0, was very limited providing a rudimentary ability to present text on the Web, HTML 2.0 expanded this ability by adding new features. HTML 2.0 was the standard for Web site design until January 1997, and it defined many core HTML features. As more and more people started using HTML, webmasters wanted more tags to enhance the look of their sites. In 1994, HTML 3.2 was released and included all of the browser-specific tags.

HTML 4.0 was recommended by the W3C in December 1997, and was the last iteration of classic HTML. Most of the new functionality introduced with this version is from the ill-fated HTML 3.0 specification, as well as a host of trimmings on old tags, internationalization, and support for HTML's new supporting presentational language, cascading stylesheets. Browser support was provided by Microsoft in their Internet Explorer browsers IE5 and IE6.

XHTML 1.0 is specified in three "flavors." The user specifies which of these variants he is using by inserting a line at the beginning of the document. For example, the HTML for a document may start with a line which says that it is using XHTML 1.0 Strict. Thus, if using a tool to validate the document, the tool will know which variant was used. Each variant has its own DTD which sets out the rules and regulations for using XHTML in a succinct and definitive manner. The "flavors" or options are:

- XHTML 1.0 Strict—This is used together with W3C's Cascading Style Sheet language (CSS) to get font, color, and layout effects, for clean structural markup, free of any markup associated with layout.
- XHTML 1.0 Transitional—This is used to generate Web pages for the general public. The idea is to take advantage of XHTML features, including stylesheets.
- XHTML 1.0 Frameset—This is used to partition the browser window into two or more frames.

Subsequent to the introduction of XHTML 1.0, Versions 1.1 and 2.0 were developed.

XHTML 1.1 is a module-based version of XHTML. While XHTML 1.1 looks very similar to XHTML 1.0 Strict, it is designed to serve as the basis for future extended XHTML family document types, and its modular design makes it easier to add other modules as needed or integrate into other markup languages. XHTML 1.1 plus MathML 2.0 document type is an example of such an XHTML family document type.

XHTML 2.0 is a markup language intended for rich, portable web-based applications. While the ancestry of XHTML 2.0 comes from HTML 4.0, XHTML 1.0, and XHTML 1.1, it is not intended to be backward compatible with these earlier XHTML versions. Application developers familiar with its earlier ancestors will be comfortable working with XHTML 2.0.

HTML Primer

HTML defines display directives for documents on the World Wide Web. Directives are enclosed in brackets.

Directives normally affect the text between the opening and the closing of the directive. A directive is closed using the same designator as the opening directive, but preceded by a slash.

Table 3-2 lists the directives that enable the formatting of most basic documents.

Name	Description
A	anchor, creates a hypertext link to another page
APPLET	Java applet
B	bold text style
BASE	document base URI
BLOCKQUOTE	long quotation
BODY	document body
BR	forced line break
CENTER	shorthand for DIV align=center
COL	table column
EM	emphasis
FONT	local change to font
FORM	interactive form
FRAME	creates a subwindow
H1,H2,H3,H4,H5,H6	heading
HEAD	document head
HR	horizontal rule
HTML	document root element
I	italic text style
IMG	embedded image to be placed
INPUT	form control
LABEL	form field label text
LI	list item
LINK	a media-independent link
MENU	menu list
META	generic meta information
OBJECT	generic embedded object
P	paragraph

Table 3-2. HTML Elements that Format Most Basic Documents.

Name	Description
SCRIPT	script statements
SELECT	option selector
STRONG	strong emphasis
STYLE	style info
TABLE	table
TBODY	table body
TD	table data cell
TEXTAREA	multi-line text field
TH	table header cell
TITLE	document title
TR	table row
U	underlined text style

Table 3-2 (continued). HTML Elements that Format Most Basic Documents.

Tags

HTML uses a wide variety of tags. HTML tags are always enclosed in angle-brackets (< >) and are case-insensitive; that is, it doesn't matter whether you type them in upper or lower case. Tags typically occur in begin-end pairs. These pairs are in the form,

```
<tag>  ...  </tag>
```

where the `<tag>` indicates the beginning of a tag-pair, and the `</tag>` indicates the end. These pairs define containers. Any content between the container tags has the rules of that container applied to it.

The first and last tags in a document should always be the HTML tags. These are the tags that tell a Web browser where the HTML in your document begins and ends. The simplest and most basic of all possible Web documents is the following code for a blank page:

```
<HTML>
</HTML>
```

53

An element is a fundamental component of the structure of a text document. Some examples of elements are heads, tables, paragraphs, and lists. Think of it this way: you use HTML tags to mark the elements of a file for your browser. Elements can contain plain text, other elements, or both.

The HEAD tags contain all of the document's header information.

The TITLE container is placed within the HEAD structure. Between the TITLE tags, the title of the document is detailed. This will appear at the top of the browser's title bar, and will also appear in the history list. Finally, the contents of the TITLE container go into your bookmark file, if you create a bookmark to a page.

The BODY container comes after the HEAD structure. Between the BODY tags, all of the information that gets displayed in the browser window is located. All of the text, the graphics, and links, and so on occur between the BODY tags.

Example 3-1 illustrates these HTML features that create the Web page in Figure 3-2:

Example 3-1. Listing 3-1. HTML Hello World.

```
<HTML>
    <HEAD>
        <TITLE>Document Title</TITLE>
    </HEAD>
    <BODY>
        Hello World ....
    </BODY>
</HTML>
```

The heading structures are most commonly used to set apart document or section titles. For example, the phrase "HTML Syntax Primer" at the beginning of this section is a heading.

There are six levels of headings, from Heading 1 through Heading 6. Heading 1 (H1) is "most important" and Heading 6 (H6) is "least important." By default, browsers will display the six heading levels in the same font, with the point size decreasing as the importance of the heading decreases.

The block of HTML in Listing 3-1 would just string the content into one line of text. However, as you might suspect, paragraphs are quite common in Web pages. The overall structure of a Web page is composed of a number of sections, each of which is composed of one or more paragraphs. Each paragraph is composed of words, and each word of letters.

The beginning of a paragraph is marked by <P>, and the end by </P>.

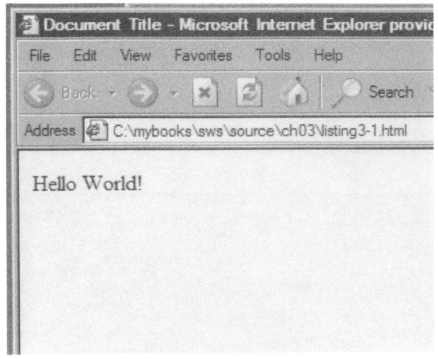

Figure 3-2. HTML Page for Example 3-1.

So what if we want to end a line after a certain word, but don't want to start a new paragraph? Well, what we need is a line break, which is invoked by using the <BR> tag. This forces a line break wherever we place it in the content.

Blockquotes are handy for those long pieces of text which are quoted material and therefore need to be set apart and indented. That is exactly what the blockquote tag does. For example:

<blockquote> This section of text is surrounded by the blockquote tags. A blockquote can exist inside of a paragraph, and always lives on its own line (which is to say, there is an implied line break before and after the blockquote, just as with headings or paragraphs themselves).</blockquote>

Just like most other things in HTML, the blockquote tags form a container.

Various tags are standard, including the meta tags (used for ....), background tags (used for setting document, color, background color/image) as well as the body tag.

The <a> and </a> tags are used to create links from one Web page to another.

Another HTML parameter is HREF. The value assigned to the HREF parameter indicates the URL that will be used for navigation when a person clicks on the text associated with the Link. The associated text is the text between the `<a HREF="..."` > and the `</a>` tags.

Tables

Example 3-2 presents a simple table that illustrates some of the features of the HTML table model.

Example 3-2. Listing 3-2. HTML Simple Table.

```
<HTML>
  <HEAD>
    <TITLE>Document Title</TITLE>
  </HEAD>
  <BODY>
    Hello World ....
          <TABLE border="1"
        summary="This table gives some statistics about
            fruit flies: average height and weight,
            and percentage with red eyes (for both
            males and females).">
<CAPTION><EM>A test table with merged cells</EM></CAPTION>
<TR><TH rowspan="2"><TH colspan="2">Average
    <TH rowspan="2">Red<BR>eyes
<TR><TH>height<TH>weight
<TR><TH>Males<TD>1.9<TD>0.003<TD>40%
<TR><TH>Females<TD>1.7<TD>0.002<TD>43%
        </TABLE>
  </BODY>
</HTML>
```

The Table for Example 3-2 is displayed in Internet Explorer in Figure 3-3 as follows:

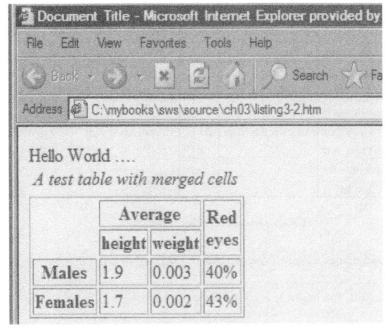

Figure 3-3. HTML table for Example 3-2.

HTML Example

As a practical example, let's take a table of book data and produce the markup needed to display it on a Web page. Tables make it easier to line up choices both vertically and horizontally. When using tables in forms, make sure all the table tags are included between the form tags.

Let's take a look at a database table that contains information about some computer books and create an HTML file that can be used to display the file on a Web page.

Product ID	Title	Author	Date	Publisher	ISBN	Price
1	Developing Semantic Web Services	H. Peter Alesso & Craig Smith	2004	A.K. Peters, Ltd.	1568812124	$39.00
2	The Intelligent Wireless Web	H. Peter Alesso & Craig F. Smith	2001	Addison-Wesley	0201730634	$39.00

Table 3-3. Book Catalog.

Product ID	Title	Author	Date	Publisher	ISBN	Price
3	e-Video: Producing Internet Video	H. Peter Alesso	1999	Addison-Wesley	0201703149	$39.00
4	ASP Fast and Easy Web Development	Michael D. Thomasson	2002	Prima-Tech	0761536183	$29.00
5	JavaServer Pages Fast and Easy Web Development	Aneesha Bakharia	2002	Prima-Tech	0761534288	$29.00

Table 3-3 (continued). Book Catalog.

The HTML coding needed to represent Table 3-3 is given in the following Listing 3-3.

Example 3-3. Listing 3-3. HTML Table.

```
<HTML>
    <HEAD>
 <TITLE>Generate XML from a Database</TITLE>
 <META http-equiv=Content-Type content="text/html;
charset=utf-8">
    <META content="MSHTML 6.00.2800.1170"
name=GENERATOR>
    </HEAD>
    <BODY>
<H2>Generate XML from a Database </H2>
<TABLE border=1>
    <TBODY>
    <TR>
        <TD><B>ProductID</B> </TD>
        <TD><B>Author</B> </TD>
        <TD><B>Title</B> </TD>
```

```
<TD><B>ISBN</B> </TD>
    <TD><B>Publisher</B> </TD>
    <TD><B>Price</B> </TD></TR>
  <TR>
    <TD>1</TD>
    <TD>H. Peter Alesso &amp; Craig F. Smith</TD>
    <TD>Developing Semantic Web Services</TD>
    <TD>1568812124</TD>
    <TD>A. K. Peters, Ltd.</TD>
    <TD>39</TD></TR>
  <TR>
    <TD>2</TD>
    <TD>H. Peter Alesso &amp; Craig F. Smith</TD>
    <TD>The Intelligent Wireless Web</TD>
    <TD>0201730634</TD>
    <TD>Addison-Wesley</TD>
    <TD>39</TD></TR>
  <TR>
    <TD>3</TD>
    <TD>H. Peter Alesso</TD>
    <TD>e-Video: Producing Internet Video</TD>
    <TD>0201703149</TD>
    <TD>Addison-Wesley</TD>
    <TD>39</TD></TR>
  <TR>
    <TD>4</TD>
    <TD>Michael D. Thomasson</TD>
    <TD>ASP Fast and Easy Web Development</TD>
    <TD>0761536183</TD>
    <TD>Prima-Tech</TD>
    <TD>24.99</TD></TR>
  <TR>
    <TD>5</TD>
```

```
<TD>Aneesha Bakharia</TD>
    <TD>JavaServer Pages Fast and Easy Web Devel-
opment</TD>
    <TD>0761534288</TD>
    <TD>Prima-Tech</TD>
    <TD>24.99</TD></TR>
</TBODY>
</TABLE>
  </BODY>
</HTML>
```

The file for Example 3-3 is rendered as Figure 3-4 within Internet Explorer.

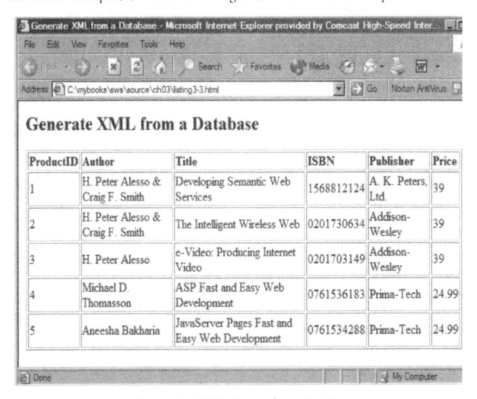

Figure 3-4. HTML display of Example 3-3.

HTML Meta Tags

While HTML does not support semantics directly, it does have crude support for metadata in the form of meta tags. Meta tags are optional HTML tags that are included between the <head> tags. Meta tags provide supplemental information about a Web page in a standardized form that search engines can use. The following sample illustrates how meta tags are implemented:

```
<HEAD>
<TITLE>A Concise Document Title</TITLE>
<META NAME="author" CONTENT="the author's name">
<META NAME="description" CONTENT="a brief description
of the web file">
<META NAME="keywords" CONTENT="keywords relevant to the
document">
<META NAME="date" CONTENT="Month Date, Year">
<META NAME="revised" CONTENT="Month Date, Year">
<LINK REL="link_type" HREF="URL" TYPE="type of docu-
ment">
</HEAD>
```

The "title" tag provides bibliographical information about the document and is also used to index the page based on the keywords in the title. The "author" tag also provides a bibliographic record of the HTML file. Note that if the person who created the content of the file is not the same person who did the HTML markup for the file, both the "author" and the "creator" can be listed in separate tags. The "description" tag is the short summary of a Web page that the search engine will display in search results. It should enable the person looking at it to easily determine the content of the page. The "keywords" tag lets you explicitly list the keywords you want associated with your page which is used by many search engines to index your HTML files. The "date" tag is used to indicate the date on which the document was created, and the "revised" tag indicates the most recent revision date. Finally, the "link" tag gives developers a way to define relationships with other documents. Although the link tag has been part of HTML for many versions, few browsers take advantage of it.

There are many different meta tags, but the most important in search engine rankings are keywords, description and title. The title and description are displayed in search results (see Chapter 15).

The HTML title tag isn't really a meta tag. Whatever text is placed in the title tag will appear in the reverse bar of a browser when they view the Web page. The title tag, however, is crucial for search engines. The text used in the title tag is one of the most important factors in how a search engine may decide to rank the Web page. In addition, all major crawlers will use the text of the title tag as the text they use for the title of the page in Web site listings.

The meta description tag allows the developer to influence the description of his page in the crawlers. The first meta tag is the one that says "name=description". However, some engines, such as Google, ignore the meta description tag and instead automatically generate its own description of the page. Others may support it partially.

The meta keywords tag allows additional text for crawler-based search engines to index along with the body copy. How does this help? Well, for most major crawlers, it doesn't. That's because most crawlers now ignore the tag.

Meta tags have never been a guaranteed way to gain a top ranking on crawler-based search engines. Today, the most valuable feature they offer developers is the ability to control to some degree how their Web pages are described by some search engines (see Chapter 15 on semantic search).

HTML Capabilities and Limitations

By itself, HTML Version 4.0 does not support the structure and semantics needed for complex applications demanded by future Web architecture. At best, HTML meta tags are of low value.

However, HTML is an easy to use and flexible alternative to traditional presentation and hyperstack software for the preparation of instructional material. An advantage of HTML is that it scales well. You can make a single HTML document and put it on one computer where it will be read. You can hand out diskettes with it for people to read on their own computers or you can put it onto a network server, all without changing a single word of the text. The same document serves on a reader, a whole class, or the entire Internet.

HTML Capabilities	HTML Limitations
Displays and prints as appropriate for the implementing device.	Data on HTML pages is not capable of being redirected to different purposes.
Needs only simple tools for generation.	
Supports proprietary server frameworks J2EE and .NET.	
Enables legacy applications to use Web technologies.	Web search requires more abstract and a more semantic support.

Table 3-4. HTML Capabilities and Limitations.

Conclusion

In this chapter, we reviewed the development, features, and limitations of HyperText Markup Language (HTML). We started with this basic markup language and we will continue to follow the Markup Language Pyramid step-by-step as we move from chapter to chapter throughout this book. We saw how open Web markup standards compete with the proprietary server frameworks.

We explored the question, "Can HTML provide support for the development of Web Services and the Semantic Web?" We found that HTML appears sufficiently extensible to provide display of information as required across many different devices and for expanding Web architecture. In addition, we saw the limitations of meta data support in HTML for search engines and the need for improvement in the area of semantics.

Chapter Four

eXtensible Markup Language (XML)

Overview

While eXtensible Markup Language (XML) is already widely used across the Web today, it is still a relatively new technology. XML is a meta-language, which means it is a language used to create other languages. XML can provide a basic structure and set of rules for developing any markup language. Using XML, it is possible to create a unique markup language to model just about any kind of information, including Web content. It can even be used to develop a reformulated version of HTML, for example, as was done in the development of XHTML.

HTML is viewed using a Web browser such as Internet Explorer or Netscape Navigator which are applications specifically designed to interpret HTML and display the results. On the other hand, there is no such thing as a generic "XML viewer." In fact, XML is not a replacement for HTML, but rather a complementary technology. To view XML documents, we must use a specially designed XML language called eXensible StyleSheet Language (XSL). XSL is used in conjunction with HTML code to describe in more detail how XML data is to be displayed in a Web browser.

XML is both a powerful and essential language for today's Web Services. Why is XML so important? Just as HTML is the open standard that allows information to be displayed over the Web, XML is the open standard that allows data to be exchanged between applications and databases over the Web. As such, XML is the interoperable bridge for exchanging data between

J2EE and .NET, the essential frameworks supporting today's Web Services. Yet, despite the recognition of XML's importance today, we must recognize its weaknesses when it comes to semantics and logic. As a result, we must consider, "What is XML, how is it used, and how can it be extended to construct appropriate meta-languages for the architecture of Semantic Web Services?"

In this chapter, we present a primer for XML and some of its more important associated languages including XML Schema and XSL. We conclude with an evaluation of XML's strengths and weaknesses, as well as its utility to help develop the markup languages for future Web architectures.

Background

In Chapter 2, we discussed how IBM scientists developed the Generalized Markup Language (GML) for describing documents and their formatting, and how in 1986 the International Standards Organization (ISO) adopted a version of GML called Standard Generalized Markup Language (SGML). SGML offered a highly sophisticated system for marking up documents so that their appearance would be independent of specific software applications. It was big, powerful, filled with options, and well suited for large organizations that needed exacting document standards.

But during the early development of the Internet, it became apparent that SGML's sophistication made the language unsuitable for quick and easy Web publishing. Clearly the Web needed a simplified markup system, one in which practically anyone could quickly gain proficiency. In Chapter 3, we described how Tim Berners-Lee developed HyperText Markup Language (HTML), which is little more than one specific SGML document type definition (DTD). Because it is so easy to learn and to implement, and because early Web browsers supported it, HTML quickly became the basis of the burgeoning Web.

One of the problems with HTML, however, was that it quickly proved to be too simplistic. It was superb for the early days of the Web—with text-based documents that featured headings, bulleted lists, and hyperlinks to other documents—but as soon as Web authors began demanding multimedia and page-design features, the original version of HTML could not provide the capability. Straightforward in-line graphics couldn't be manipulated and page design suffered because of it.

Why was solving this issue so difficult? Quite simply, HTML wasn't extensible. Although over the years, Microsoft was able to add tags that work only in Internet Explorer and Netscape was able to add tags that work only in Navigator, Web site developers had no way of adding their own tags.

The solution was eXtensible Markup Language (XML). Proposed in late 1996 by the World Wide Web Consortium (W3C), it offered some of SGML's power while avoiding the language's complexity, enabling Web authors to produce fully customized documents with a high degree of design consistency. It offered these things because XML is basically, SGML 'light.' Whereas HTML is merely one SGML document type definition, XML is a simplified version of the parent language itself.

XML 1.0, released in February 1998, was less than a tenth of the size of the SGML specification; however, it had many of the important features of SGML including extensibility, structure, and validity. It was designed to be interoperable with both SGML and HTML. XML emerged as a way to overcome the shortcomings of both. All of the non-essential, unused, cryptic parts of SGML were eliminated by Tim Bray and C.M. Sperberg-McQueen and the XML specification was only 26 pages, as opposed to over 500 pages for SGML.

While we can consider XML as a highly functional subset of SGML, it is not implemented and used as a single markup language. Instead, it too is a meta-language that allows users to design their own markup languages. In effect, XML is a "lever." Only XML is the "lever" that will shape the future architecture of the Web by designing the future Web languages.

XML Primer

Although XML's parent language, SGML, has provided considerable functionality for documentation, XML has simplified the process of defining and using metadata. The very nature of XML is that of a structured document representing the information to be exchanged, as well as the metadata encapsulating its meaning. As a result, XML provides a good representation of extensible, hierarchical, formatted information and its required encoded metadata.

Markup text, in general, needs to be differentiated from the rest of the document text by delimiters. And just as in HTML, the angle brackets (< >) and the names they enclose are delimiters called tags. Tags demarcate and label the parts of the document and add other information that helps define the structure. XML lets you name the tags anything you want, unlike HTML, which limits you to predefined tag names. You can choose element names that make sense in the context of the document. Tag names are case-sensitive, although either case may be used as long as the opening and closing tag names are consistent.

The text between the tags is the content of the document, raw information that may be the body of a message, a title, or a field of data. The markup and the content complement each other, creating an information entity with partitioned labeled data in a handy package. XML is really meant as a way to hold content so that, when combined with other resources, such as a stylesheet, the document becomes a finished product with style and polish.

In its simplest form, an XML document is comprised of one or more named elements organized into a nested hierarchy. An element consists of an opening tag, some data, and a closing tag. For any given element, the name of the opening tag must match that of the closing tag. A closing tag is identical to an opening tag except that the less-than symbol (<) is immediately followed by a forward-slash (/). Keeping this simple view, we can construct the major portions of the XML document to include the following six ingredients:

1. XML Declaration (required).
2. Document Type Definition (or XML Schema).
3. Elements (required).
4. Attributes.
5. Entity.
6. Notations.

We will present the basic syntax for these six key portions of an XML document in the following sections.

XML Declaration

The top of an XML document contains special information called the document prolog. At its simplest, the prolog merely says that this is an XML document and declares the version of XML being used. The XML declaration is an announcement to the XML processor that this document is marked up in XML. The declaration begins with the five-character delimiter "<?xml" followed by some number of property definitions each of which has a property name and value in quotes. The declaration ends with the two-character closing delimiter "?>".

The prolog can hold additional information that nails down such details as the DTD being used, declarations of special pieces of text, the text encoding, and instructions to XML processors.

An example of a well-formed XML declaration is:

```
<?xml version = "1.0" encoding="iso-8859-1" standalone ="yes" ?>
```

Following the XML declaration is a document type declaration that links to a DTD in a separate file. This is followed by a set of declarations. These parts together comprise the prolog.

Document Type Definition (DTD)

The Document Type Definition (DTD) is used for validating the XML document. A DTD is a collection of parameters that describe a document type and includes specific information about the sequence, frequency, and hierarchy of the XML document's elements, attributes, and character data.

By referring to a DTD, we are requesting that the parser compare the document instance to a document model, a process called validity checking. Checking the validity of the document is optional, but it is useful if we need to ensure that the document follows predictable patterns and includes required data.

The DTD has its own declaration (the document type declaration) which starts with the literal string "<!DOCTYPE" followed by the root element, which is the first XML element to appear in the document and the one that contains the rest of the document. To include a DTD within the document, it is necessary to include the URI of the DTD, so the XML processor can find it. After that, there comes the internal subset which is bound on either side by square brackets. The declaration ends with a closing ">".

The internal subset provides a place to put various declarations for use in your document. These declarations might include entity definitions and parts of DTDs. The internal subset is the only place declarations are used within the document itself.

The internal subset is used to augment or redefine the declarations found in the external subset. The external subset is the collection of declarations existing outside the document, like in a DTD. The URI in the document type declaration points to a file containing these external declarations. Internal and external subsets are optional.

We will return to further describe the details of DTD and XML Schema right after we present the rest of the XML documents components (elements, attributes, entities, and notations).

Elements

Elements are the building blocks of a document. We can separate a document into parts so they can be rendered differently or used by a search engine. Elements can be containers, with a mixture of text and other elements. Elements may be arranged in a nested hierarchy, but only one element in the document can be designated as the root document element. The root document element is the first element that appears in the document. In Listing 4-1, <BOOKCATALOG> is the root element and it has a child element described by tag <BOOK>. The child element <BOOK> has six children: ProductID, Author, Title, Publisher, ISBN, and Price.

Listing 4-1. BookCatalog.

```
<BOOKCATALOG>
      <BOOK>
      < ProductID >1</ProductID >
      <Author>H. Peter Alesso</Author>
      <Title>Developing Semantic Web Services
      </Title>
      <Publisher>A.K. Peters, Lmt.</Publisher>
      <ISBN>1568812124</ISBN>
      <Price>$39.00</Price>
      <BOOK>
</BOOKCATALOG>
```

Sometimes it is necessary to convey more information about an element than its name and content can express. The use of attributes allows describing details about the element more clearly. An attribute can be used to give the element a unique label so it can be easily located, or it can describe a property about the element, such as the location of a file at the end of a link. It can be used to describe some aspect of the element's behavior or to create a subtype.

Attributes

An attribute specifies properties of the element that you modify and consists of a name/value pair. Attribute values must be contained in matching single or double quotes. The element may include zero or more attributes.

Attributes are parts or properties of elements, that modify our book example to include the title element as an attribute:

```
<BOOK Title=" Developing Semantic Web Services ">...</BOOK>
```

Namespace

A namespace is a group of element and attribute names. An element exists within a particular namespace and should be validated against that namespace's DTD. By appending a namespace prefix to an element or attribute name, you tell the parser which namespace it comes from. The namespace differentiates element names preventing naming collisions.

Consider, for example, the word 'table' which could be a piece of furniture or a mathematical table. We have two different meanings with the same name, but how can we express that fact without causing a namespace collision? The solution is to have each element or attribute specify which namespace it comes from by including the namespace as a prefix.

For example, we could differentiate 'table' by using two very different and unique prefixes, each associated with a different URI, f:table and m:table. The associated namespaces are xmlns: f="http://www.furniture.com" and xmlns:m="http://www.math.com". This quickly differentiates the various uses of the name 'table.'

Comments

As with any code, it's a good idea to document your work with comments so that other programmers can understand it. A comment begins with the combination of characters "<!--" and ends with the combination of characters "-->".

Entities—Special Symbols

There are a few special symbols in XML that must be entered differently than other text characters. The reason for this is that they are recognized in parts of the XML document such as tags. XML reserves certain characters including less-than (<), greater than (>), and ampersand (&).The XML specification provides the following predefined character entities, so that you can express these characters safely:

Name	Value
&amp	&
&apos	'
&gt	>
&lt	<
&quot	"

Root Element

The root element encloses the rest of the document. The XML declaration must be on the first line followed by the document type declaration and then the closing root element.

Five Fundamental XML Syntax Rules

The key to XML's simplicity and accuracy is maintained through five fundamental rules:

1. Tag names are case-sensitive.
2. Every opening tag must have a corresponding closing tag (except empty tags).
3. A nested tag pair cannot overlap another tag.
4. Attribute values must appear within quotes.
5. Every document must have a root element.

These rules are more restrictive than those of HTML, but are consistent with the rules of XHTML. The XML document is evaluated by a parser which checks that the document follows the above syntax rules and is therefore "well-formed."

XML Family of Languages

XML is a meta-language for describing data; but by itself XML doesn't actually do anything. To implement and use XML effectively, we need to employ a number of additional support languages. XML has a family of associated languages used for parsing, manipulating, and interfacing. We can think of these associate languages as the XML family.

In addition, we can break this family down into several categories: XML validation languages (DTD, XML Schema), XML APIs/location languages (DOM, SAX) XML location languages (XPath, XPointer, and XLink), XML display languages (XSL, XSLT, XSL-FO), and XML Web Services Languages (SOAP, WDSL, UDDI).

Figure 4-1 shows the grouping relationships between XML and associated languages.

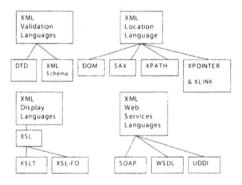

Figure 4-1. XML family of languages.

XML Parsing and Validation Languages

The XML parsing and validation languages are DTD and XML Schema.

Document Type Definitions (DTDs)

XML authors can create any XML structure they desire in order to describe their data. However, an XML author cannot be sure that the structure he created won't be changed by another XML author. There needs to be a way to ensure that the XML structure remains stable. DTD fulfills this role by providing a roadmap for describing and documenting the structure that makes up an XML document. As a result, the DTD determines the validity of an XML document by defining a set of rules for the document.

An XML document is considered "well-formed" if that document is syntactically correct according to the syntax rules of XML. However, that does not mean the document is necessarily valid. In order to be considered valid, an XML document must be validated, or verified, against a particular DTD. The DTD will define the elements required by an XML document, the elements that are optional, the number of times an element should (could) occur, and the order in which elements should be nested. The DTD markup also defines the type of data for an XML element and the attributes that may be associated with those elements. A document, even if well-formed, is not considered valid if it does not follow the rules defined in the associated DTD.

A validating XML parser will check an XML document to ensure that all required elements are present and that no undeclared elements have been added. The hierarchical structure of elements defined in the DTD must be maintained. The values of all attributes are checked to ensure that they meet defined guidelines. No undeclared attributes will be allowed and no required attributes may be omitted. The XML document is defined and validated by the DTD from start to finish.

Although validation is optional, an XML author can reference a DTD from the XML document and use a validating XML parser during processing. An author can thereby ensure the integrity of the data structure.

DOCTYPE

The DTD has its own declaration called the document type declaration which starts with the literal string "<!DOCTYPE" followed by the root element. Then comes the internal subset which is bound on either side by square brackets. The declaration ends with a closing " >".

The following code shows the general syntax of a document type declaration:

```
<!DOCTYPE RootElem SYSTEM ExternalDTDRef [InternalDTDDecl] >
```

Elements Defined in the DTD

All elements in a valid XML document are defined with an element declaration in the DTD. An element declaration defines the name and all allowed contents of an element. Element names must start with a letter or an underscore and may contain any combination of letters, numbers, underscores, dashes, and periods. However, element names must never start with the string "xml." Colons should not be used in element names because they are normally used to reference namespaces.

Each element in the DTD should be defined with the following syntax:

```
<!ELEMENT elementname rule >
```

ELEMENT is the tag name that specifies that this is an element definition, elementname is the name of the element, and rule is the definition to which the element's data content must conform.

In a DTD, the elements are processed from the top down. A validating XML parser will expect the order of the appearance of elements in the XML document to match the order of elements defined in the DTD. Therefore, elements in a DTD should appear in the order you want them to appear in an XML document. If the elements in an XML document do not match the order of the DTD, the XML document will not be considered valid by a validating parser.

Attributes Defined in DTD

Attributes work alongside elements and are important to the construction of DTDs. Attributes are used to specify additional information about an element. Attributes form a name/value pair that describes a particular property of the element. Attributes are declared in a DTD using attribute list declarations, in the form:

```
<!ATTLIST ElementName AttrName AttrType Default>
```

The attribute has the name Attrname and a type, AttrType, as well as a default value, Default. There are four different types of default:

#REQUIRED—the attribute is required.
#IMPLIED—the attribute is optional.
#FIXED value—the attribute has a fixed value.
default—the default value for the attribute.

In addition to the default value, one of ten types of attributes is specified:

CDATA—unparsed character data

Enumeration—a series of string values

NOTATION—a notation declared elsewhere in the DTD

ENTITY—an external binary entity

ENTITIES—multiple external binary entities

ID—a unique identifier

IDREF—a reference to an ID declared elsewhere

IDREFS—multiple references to an ID's declared elsewhere

NMTOKEN—a name consisting of XML token characters

NMTOKENS—multiple names consisting of XML token characters

DTDs are tightly integrated with the documents they describe. In order to use a DTD with a document, we must associate the DTD with the document using the document type declaration. A DTD can be internal, residing within the body of an XML document, or it can be external, referenced by the XML document.

Let's take a quick look at two DTDs—one internal and one external. Listing 4-2 shows an internal DTD.

Listing 4-2. An Internal DTD.

```
<?xml version="1.0"?>
<!DOCTYPE message [
<!ELEMENT message (#PCDATA)>
]>
<message>
        Hello World!
</message>
```

In Listing 4-2, the internal DTD is contained within the document type declaration, which begins with "<!DOCTYPE" and ends with "]>". The document type declaration will appear after the XML declaration and before the root element, and identify that section of the XML document as containing a DTD. Following the document type declaration (DOCTYPE), the root element of the XML document is defined. The DTD tells us that this document will have a single element message that will contain parsed character data (#PCDATA).

NOTE: The document type declaration should not be confused with the Document Type Definition (DTD).

Now, let's take a look at Listing 4-3 and see a DTD as an external file.

Listing 4-3. An External DTD.

```
<?xml version="1.0"?>
<!DOCTYPE message SYSTEM "message.dtd">
<message>
      Hello World!
</message>
```

In Listing 4-3, the DTD is contained in a separate file called "message.dtd." For this example, the contents of message.dtd are assumed to be the same as the contents of the DTD in Listing 4-2. The keyword SYSTEM in the document type declaration lets us know that the DTD is going to be found in a separate file. A URL could have been used to define the location of the DTD.

XML Schema—XSD

DTD was the original approach to validating XML documents; however, XML Schema is a new technology designed to replace DTDs with a more powerful and intuitive approach. The XML Schema process of creating a schema for an XML document is called data modeling because it resolves a class of data into elements and attributes that can be used in an XML document. Once the data model is established, it is possible to create structured XML documents that adhere to the model. Documents that adhere to the schema data model can be identified as valid XML documents. A valid XML document is an XML application that has been approved by a parser application.

XML Schema allows defining markup languages by carefully describing the elements and attributes that can be used to code in XML. An entire XML Schema can not be included inside an XML document as was used with a DTD, but it is possible to reference a schema namespace within the root element of the XML document.

Unlike DTD, schemas created in XML Schema are coded in XML. Since the XML Schema language is an XML markup language, elements and attributes are used according to XML syntax.

XML Schema documents start with the XML declaration, followed by the reference namespace as:

```
<?xml version="1.0">
<xsd:schema xmlns:xsd="http://www.w3.org/2001/XMLSchema">
</xsd:schema>
```

In this code, the xmlns:xsd attribute is used to set the XML Schema namespace which is the standard W3C URI.

The XML Schema language is defined by the elements and attributes and their data types which require four basic components:

1. Element declarations.
2. Attribute declarations.
3. Content models.
4. Data type declaration.

Through these four components, the XML Schema document includes the following specifics: elements, attributes, which elements are child elements, the order of child elements, the number of child elements, whether an element is empty, data types for elements and attributes, and default and fixed values for elements and attributes.

Table 4-1 lists some key XML declaration syntax forms.

Term	Syntax	Means
XML declaration	<?xml version="1.0"?>	Identifies version.
Schema declaration	<xsd:schema xmlns: xsd="namespace">	Identities document as XML schema.
Element declaration	<xsd:element name="name">	Defines element.
Attribute declaration	<xsd:attribute name="name" type="datatype">	Can define datatype, such as xsd:string.

Table 4-1. XML Declaration Syntax.

Element Declarations

XML Schema documents always contain elements, starting with the root element. The subsequent elements may be either simple or complex types. In Table 4-2 we list the various XSD element declarations.

all	documentation	notation
annotation	element	redefine
any	extension	restriction
anyAttribute	field	schema
appInfo	group	selector
attribute	import	sequence
attributeGroup	include	simpleContent
choice	key	simpleType
complexContent	keyref	union
complexType	list	unique

Table 4-2. XSD Element Declarations.

Elements within the XML Schema can be declared using the <element> tag. The element's type can be defined elsewhere within the schema. For instance an element defined as a child of the <schema> element can be referenced anywhere within the schema document. Whereas an element defined when it is declared can only have that definition used once. An element's type can be defined as a <complexType> element, a <simpleType> element, a <complexContent> element, or a <simpleContent> element.

The <simpleType> and <complexType> elements work much the same way. They provide a way to extend or restrict the existing type definition.

The basic construct of an element declaration using <element> within the XML Schema is:

```
<element name="" [type=""] [abstract=""] [block=""]
[default=""] [final=""] [fixed=""] [minOccurs=""]
[maxOccur=""] [nillable=""] [ref=""]
[substitutionGroup=""]/>
```

From this there are many options available.

simpleType Element Declarations

The simpleType element definitions are declared elements that can not contain any other elements and or attributes. The schema element can hold the definition of the target namespace and several default options.

We define the title and author elements from Listing 4-1 as simple types. They don't have attributes or non-text children and can be described directly within a degenerate element. The type (xsd:string) is prefixed by the namespace prefix associated with XML Schema, indicating a predefined XML Schema data type (see Listing 4-4).

Listing 4-4. XML Schema for simpleType Elements.

```
<xsd:element name="Title" type="xsd:string"/>
<xsd:element name="author" type="xsd:string"/>
```

complexType Element Declarations

We can define the XML element named "Book" in Listing 4-1 as a complexType. This element has attributes and non-text children, thus we consider it a complexType.

W3C XML Schema lets us define the cardinality of an element (i.e., the number of its possible occurrences) with some precision. We can specify both minOccurs (the minimum number of occurrences) and maxOccurs (the maximum number of occurrences). Here, maxOccurs is set to unbounded which means that there can be as many occurrences of the character element as the author wishes. Both attributes have a default value of one.

Listing 4-5. XMLSchema Complex Type.

The Book element contains child element "Title"

```
<xsd:element name="Book">
<xsd:complexType>
<xsd:element ref="Title" type="xsd:string"maxOccurs="U
      nbounded"/>
</xsd:complexType>
</xsd:element>
```

The Complex type definitions are for elements that can contain elements and attributes. Complex types are built up from simple type elements. For example, we show the complex type in Listing 4-5.

A <complexType> element may contain one of the following elements:

- all.
- choice.
- complexContent.
- group.
- sequence.
- simpleContent.

One powerful aspect of complex types is the ability to organize elements into sequences and choices. A sequence is a list of child elements that must appear in a particular order, whereas a choice is a list of child elements from which only one may be used. Using Listing 4-1, we can specify the list of all its children in the same way in Listing 4-6 and include the sequence element.

Listing 4-6. XML Schema Complex Type.

```
<xsd:element name="Book">
 <xsd:complexType>
  <xsd:sequence>
   <xsd:element name="ProductID" type="xsd:int"
       minOccurs="0" />
   <xsd:element name="Title" type="xsd:string"
       minOccurs="0" />
   <xsd:element name="Author" type="xsd:string"
       minOccurs="0" />
   <xsd:element name="Date" type="xsd:string"
       minOccurs="0" />
   <xsd:element name="Publisher" type="xsd:string"
       minOccurs="0" />
   <xsd:element name="ISBN" type="xsd:float"
       minOccurs="0" />
   <xsd:element name="Price" type="xsd:decimal"
       minOccurs="0" />
  </xsd:sequence>
 </xsd:complexType>
```

Listing 4-7. XML Schema ComplexType.

```
<xsd:element name="BOOKCATALOG" >
 <xsd:complexType>
  <xsd:element name="Book">
   <xsd:complexType>
   <xsd:element name="Title" type="xsd:string"
      minOccurs="0" />
   </xsd:complexType>
  </xsd:element>
 </xsd:complexType>
```

Finally, after putting it all together, we produce the XML Schema in Listing 4-8 which represents the validating requirement for the original XML file in Listing 4-1. One of the key features of such a design is to define each element and attribute within its context and allow multiple occurrences of a same element name to carry different definitions. In Listing 4-1, there were no attributes, all nodes were identified as elements. As a result, the XML Schema for Listing 4-1 produces Listing 4-8 which includes the complexType element for BOOKCATALOG including complexType Book.

Listing 4-8. Schema.

```
<?xml version="1.0" encoding="utf-8"?>
<xsd:schema xmlns:xs="http://www.w3.org/2001/XMLSchema">
<xsd:element name="BOOKCATALOG" >
 <xsd:complexType>
  <xsd:choice maxOccurs="unbounded" >
   <xsd:element name="Book" >
    <xsd:complexType>
     <xsd:sequence>
      <xsd:element name="ProductID" type="xsd:int"
           minOccurs="0" />
      <xsd:element name="Title" type="xsd:string"
           minOccurs="0" />
```

```
            <xsd:element name="Author" type="xsd:string"
                minOccurs="0" />
            <xsd:element name="Date" type="xsd:string"
                minOccurs="0" />
            <xsd:element name="Publisher" type="xsd:string"
                minOccurs="0" />
            <xsd:element name="ISBN" type="xsd:float"
                minOccurs="0" />
            <xsd:element name="Price" type="xsd:decimal"
                minOccurs="0" />
        </xsd:sequence>
      </xsd:complexType>
      </xsd:element>
    </xsd:choice>
  </xsd:complexType>
 </xsd:element>
</xsd:schema>
```

Content Models

The content model defines what type of content (text, other elements, or a combination) can be contained within an element.

There are four types of content models for XML Schema elements:

- Text—the element can contain only text.
- Empty—the element cannot contain child elements or text.
- Element—the element can contain child elements.
- Mixed—the element can contain child elements and text and use compositor elements to define the structure for child elements.

Attribute Declarations

Attribute declarations include a name and a type. They are always simple type definitions because attribute declarations can't contain elements or other attributes. However, attribute declarations are contained within a complex type definition and they must be declared at the very end of the complex type (see Listing 4-6).

Data Type Declaration

XML Schema not only provides control over XML documents, but also provides control over document data. XML Schema control over data is included through data types. A data type specifies what kind of data to expect. XML Schema supports 44 different data types including;

> String types—xsd:string
> Boolean types—xsd:boolean
> Number types—xsd:interger, xsd:decimal, xsd:float, xsd:double
> Date and time—xsd:time, xsd:date
> Custom type—xsd:simpletype

Each of the 44 data types has a list of constraints that can be used to further define the data described with an element or attribute. For example, the string data type has both minLength and maxLength constraints that can be specified as minimum and maximum lengths for the string. If we need to be sure that the value of a first_name element is a string with at least one character but less than 15 characters, we can specify that as part of the string data type for the element.

Simple data corresponds to basic pieces of information such as numbers, strings, text, dates, times, lists, and so on.

Examples of XML Schema data types that were used in Listing 4-8 are:

```
<xsd:element name="Book" type="xsd:string"/>
<xsd:element name="Title" type="xsd:string"/>
<xsd:element name="ISBN" type="xsd:float"/>
```

Databases allow for similar data type controls to carefully guide the data stored in different database fields. When creating an XML document that requires moving data to a database, a schema is used to create rules for the data in the document that are compatible with the rules of the database.

Notations and Entities

Although notations and entities can be used within XML Schema they are limited to attribute values and can only be used if there is a preceding notation declaration in the schema such as:

```
<xsd:notation name="jpg" public="image/jpg"
system="JPGViewer.exe" />
```

In this example, the notation declaration includes the name of the notation and values for the public and system attributes.

Parsers

A parser is an application that reads the XML document and determines if it meets the XML syntax requirements to be well-formed. XML parsers come in two flavors:

1. Non-validating: the parser does not check a document against any DTD or XML Schema. It only checks that the document is well-formed (that it contains proper markup according to XML syntax rules).
2. Validating: in addition to checking that the XML document is well-formed, the parser verifies that the document conforms to a specific DTD or XML Schema.

Some of the better known validating parsers include:

- Xerces—The Apache XML Project maintains XML parsers in Java, C++, and Perl.
- JavaSoft's XML Parser—Sun's entry into the world of XML parsers.
- Oracle XML Parser—parser through either SAX or DOM.
- XMLBooster—generates XML parsers for COBOL, C, Java, etc.
- SXP—Silfide XML is a parser and a complete XML API in Java.
- MSXML—Microsoft's XML parser in Java is included in IE4.
- DXP—a validating XML parser written in Java.

Recommendations

XML, DTD, XML Schema, XPath and XSL recommendations can be found at the following W3C sites respectively:

http://www.w3.org/XML/
http://www.w3.org/TR/REC-xml.
http://www.w3.org/XML/Schema
http://www.w3.org/TR/xpath
http://www.w3.org/Style/XSL/

XML Interfacing/Location Languages

XML documents form tree structures and can be exploited through various means. Document Object Model (DOM) is a technology for constructing the entire tree model for a given XML document and provides Application Programming Interfaces (API) for developers. An alternative technology that does not require so much memory storage and preprocessing is Simple APIs for XML (SAX) which is based upon event-triggers.

XML linking and location technology is considerably more powerful than HTML. Three languages come together to make linking and locating nodes possible in XML including XPath, XPointer, and XLink. Despite the power of these languages, current browsers only support XPath.

XML Path Language (XPath)

XPath is a standard for creating expressions that can be used to find a specific piece of information within an XML document. XPath gets its name from its use of a path notation for navigating through the hierarchical structure of an XML document. The XPath data model breaks XML documents into a graphical structure-trees, not text. XPath can indicate nodes by position, relative position, type, content, and several other criteria.

To understand how XPath works, first visualize the XML document as a tree of nodes which consist of elements and attributes. An XPath expression can then be considered a kind of roadmap that indicates branches of the tree to follow to the desired data. XPath consists of simple string expressions that have the ability to locate nodes based upon nodes' type, name, or value, or by the relationship of the nodes to other nodes. In addition, the XPath expression is able to find nodes and return any of the following: a node set, a Boolean value, a string value, or a numerical value.

XPath expressions may be composed using a set of operators and special characters. In Table 4-3 we list the various operators and special characters which are most often used in XPath.

Operators and Special Characters	Description
/	Selects the child from the node set on the left side of the character.
//	Specifies that the matching node set should be located at any level within the XML document.
.	Specifies that the current context should be used.
*	wildcard

Table 4-3. Operators and Special Characters.

The XML Path Language provides a declarative notation, termed a pattern, that is used to select the desired set of nodes from an XML document. Each pattern describes a set of matching nodes to select from a hierarchical XML document and each describes a navigation path to the desired set of nodes. The navigation path is similar to a directory file system but describes navigating a hierarchical tree of nodes.

Each "query" of an XML document occurs from a starting node and navigates to a desired node set. A location path is made up of three steps: an axis, a node test, and an optional predicate. This is shown as:

```
axis::node test [predicate]
```

Using this syntax an XPath expression could locate all the <c> nodes by:

```
/a/b/child::*
```

Alternatively, we could abbreviate this as:

```
/a/b/c
```

The axes portion of the location step identifies the hierarchical relationship for the desired nodes. An axis for a location step is given in Table 4-4.

Axis	Specifies
Ancestor	Query should locate the ancestors of the current context node.
Attribute	Attributes of the current context node are desired.
Child	Immediate children of the current context node are desired.
Descendant	In addition to the immediate children of the current context node.
Following	Nodes in the same document as the current context node that appear after the current context node should be selected.

Table 4-4. Axes.

XPath is used by other XML-based technologies including; XSLT, XPointer, XLink, and XML Schema. XSLT uses XPath expressions to match and select particular elements in the input document for copying into the output document. XPointer uses XPath expressions to identify the particular point in an XML document to which an XLink links. XML Schema uses XPath expressions to define uniqueness and co-occurrence constraints.

Before we can use XSL to transform the elements in an XML file, we must pick a particular element to transform. XPath is the mechanism for selecting that piece of the document.

XPath expressions can also represent numbers, strings, or Boolean expressions. This lets XSLT stylesheets carry out simple arithmetic for purposes such as numbering and cross-referencing figures, tables, and equations. String manipulation in XPath lets XSLT perform tasks such as making the title of a chapter upper case.

An XPath expression is evaluated to yield an object, which has one of the following four basic types:

1. node-set (an unordered collection of nodes without duplicates).
2. boolean (true or false).
3. number (a floating-point number).
4. string (a sequence of characters).

Expression evaluation occurs with respect to context. XSLT and XPointer specify how the context is determined for XPath expressions. The context consists of:

- a node (the context node).
- a pair of non-zero positive integers (the context position and the context size).
- a set of variable bindings.
- a function library.
- the set of namespace declarations in scope for the expression.

Both XSLT and XPointer extend XPath by defining additional functions; some of these functions operate on the four basic types; others operate on additional data types defined by XSLT and XPointer.

The namespace declarations consist of a mapping from prefixes to namespace URIs.

XPath expressions often occur in XML attributes. To avoid a quotation mark in an expression being interpreted by the XML processor as terminating the attribute value, the quotation mark can be entered as a character reference entity (" or ').

One important kind of expression is a location path. A location path selects a set of nodes relative to the context node. The result of evaluating an expression that is a location path is the node set containing the nodes selected by the location path. Location paths can recursively contain expressions that are used to filter sets of nodes.

XPath defines common semantics and syntax for addressing XML-expressed information, and bases these primarily on the hierarchical position of components in the tree. This ordering is referred to as document order in XPath, while in other contexts this is termed parse order. Alternatively, we can access an arbitrary location in the tree based on points in the tree having unique identifiers.

An XPath expression can be the value of an attribute in an XML vocabulary as in the following examples:

```
select="Book"
```

The above attribute value expresses all children named "Book" of the current focus element.

```
match="Bookcatalog/Book"
```

The above attribute value expresses a test of an element being in the union of the element types named "Bookcatalog" and "Book."

The XPath syntax looks a lot like addressing subdirectories in a file system or as part of a URI. Multiple steps in a location path are separated by either one or two oblique "/" characters. Filters can be specified to further refine the nature of the components of the information being addressed.

```
select="Bookcatalog/Book[1]"
```

The above illustration selects only the first "Book" child of "Bookcatalog" the focus element.

XML Pointer Language (XPointer)

XPointer is the language used as a fragment identifier for any URI reference that locates a resource. XPointer is an extension of XPath which is used by XLink to locate remote link resources. Its relative addressing allows links to places with no anchors. XPointer/XPath expressions often survive changes in the target document and can point to substrings in character data and to the whole tree. XPointer is used as the basis for a fragment identifier for any URI reference that locates a resource.

XPointer has been split into a framework for specifying location schemes and three schemes: element(), xmlns() and xpointer(). The framework and the first two schemes form the XPointer recommendation, and provide a minimal inventory of mechanisms.

The xpointer() scheme, which is based on the XML Path Language (XPath), is still under development. It supports addressing into the internal structures of XML documents. It allows for traversals of a document tree and its internal parts are based on various properties, such as element types, attribute values, character content, and relative position

XML Linking Language (XLink)

XLink adds hyperlinks in XML documents to link to documents, audio, video, and database data. XLink is also intended to link to a broad class of applications besides browsers.

Similar to HTML Web pages, XML documents can also benefit from linking to each other. XML linking provides support for traditional one-way linking, along with advanced links for two-way links. Links in XML are more powerful than HTML when you consider XLink and XPointer functions.

HTML hyperlinks are based upon the concept of connecting one resource (a source) to another (a target). The source is usually displayed on a Web page via text or an image. HTML link always involve two resources and always go in one direction. XLink offers multi-linking and descriptive capabilities.

XML Linking Language allows elements to be inserted into XML documents in order to create and describe links between resources. It uses XML syntax to create structures that can describe links similar to the simple unidirectional hyperlinks of today's HTML, as well as more sophisticated links.

XLink comes in two kinds of links: extended links and simple links.

Extended links offer full XLink functionality, such as inbound and third-party arcs, as well as links that have arbitrary numbers of participating resources. As a result, their structure can be fairly complex, including elements for pointing to remote resources, elements for containing local resources, elements for specifying arc traversal rules, and elements for specifying human-readable resource and arc titles. XLink defines a way to give an extended link special semantics for finding linkbases; used in this fashion, an extended link helps an XLink application process other links.

Simple links offer shorthand syntax for a common kind of link, an outbound link with exactly two participating resources. Because simple links offer less functionality than extended links, they have no special internal structure. While simple links are conceptually a subset of extended links, they are syntactically different. For example, to convert a simple link into an extended link, several structural changes would be needed.

Simple API for XML (SAX)

Simple API for XML (SAX) is an interface for event-based parsing of XML documents. The SAX technology triggers events in the XML document to aid the XML parser in evaluating if the XML document is well-formed. SAX is a publicly developed standard for the events-based parsing of XML documents. SAX defines a programmatic interface that models the XML information through a sequence of method calls.

SAX facilitates the search of large documents to extract small pieces of information.

An event-based API, SAX, reports parsing events (such as the start and end of elements) directly to the application through callbacks, and does not usually build an internal tree. The application implements handlers to deal with the different events, much like handling events in a graphical user interface.

A SAX parser is required to read an XML document and fire events based on what is encountered in it. Events are fired when they encounter:

- open element tags.
- close element tags.
- #PCDATA and CDATA sections.
- processing instructions, comments, entity declarations.

Document Object Model (DOM)

The XML Document Object Model (DOM) is a W3C specification for programming interfaces for XML documents. DOM provides a standard programming interface to a wide variety of framework applications—.NET and J2EE. With the XML DOM, a programmer can create an XML document, navigate its structure, and add, modify, or delete its elements.

The XML DOM is designed to be used with any programming language and any operating system. Programming languages such as, JavaScript, VBScript, Java, C#, C++, and others can connect to XML through DOM.

DOM is both a programming interface hierarchy and a method for locating and exposing data for manipulation. It identifies each unique object in a document based on its position in the document's hierarchy. DOM consists of a complex system of relationships that a processor application dissects.

A program called an XML parser can be used to load an XML document into the memory. Its information can be retrieved and manipulated by accessing the DOM. The DOM represents a tree view of the XML document. The Microsoft XML parser supports all the necessary functions to traverse the node tree, access the nodes and their attribute values, insert and delete nodes, and convert the node tree back to XML.

Every object in the DOM is called a "node," whether it's an element, attribute, CDATA section, comment, or processing instruction.

SAX and DOM are radically different APIs for accessing XML documents. Table 4-5 provides a comparison.

DOM	SAX
Is tree based on a hierarchy of nodes.	Invokes methods based upon events \<start> and \</end> tags without a tree.
W3C Standard	Public standard
Often provides easier access to manipulate data.	Requires less memory and gives better performance.

Table 4-5. Comparing DOM and SAX.

XML Display Languages

XML display languages include XSL, XSLT and XSL-FO.

eXensible Style Language (XSL)

eXtensible Style Language (XSL) allows XML content to be displayed in a more understandable context than raw XML code. Formatting XML content for display purposes involves determining the layout and positioning of the content along with font and colors used to render the content. XML documents are formatted using special instructions known as styles. A style can be something as simple as a font size or as powerful as a transformation of an XML element to an HTML element. The general mechanism used to apply formatting to XML documents is known as stylesheets.

XSL consists of three parts:

- XPath—a language for defining parts of an XML document.
- XSLT—a language for transforming XML documents.
- XSL Formatting Objects—a vocabulary for formatting XML documents.

XSL is a newer technology than Cascading Stylesheets (CSS) which applies to HTML. Both Internet Explorer and Netscape Navigator support a subset of XSL called XSL Transformations (XSLT). The layout and formatting portion of XSL is known as XSL-Format Objects (XSL-FO), but is not fully supported by the browsers yet.

A stylesheet contains a series of formatting descriptions that determine how elements are displayed on a Web page. The stylesheet determines exactly how to display data in an XML document.

XSL makes it possible to convert data described with one DTD, or schema, into data described by a different DTD, or schema. If your system requires a particular XML vocabulary to work, but data arrives with a different vocabulary, XSL can be used to translate.

XSL can transform XML into HTML, filter and sort XML data, and format XML data. For example, an XML-based data exchange for loan refinancing accepts loan applications, but wants to verify credit history. XML can format the data and XSL will convert the data as needed to the loan office format.

The transformation and formatting capabilities of XSL can function independently of each other. XSL can also add completely new elements into the output file or remove elements. It can rearrange and sort the elements and test and make decisions about which elements to display.

XSL Transformation (XSLT)

XSLT is the transformation component of the XSL stylesheet technology. XSLT consists of an XML-based markup language that is used to create stylesheets for transforming XML documents. XSLT processors read both an XML document and an XSLT stylesheet. The processor produces a new XML document based on the instructions in the XSLT stylesheet.

XSLT uses a powerful pattern-matching mechanism to select portions of the XML document for transformation. When a pattern is matched the tree is transformed. An integral part of XSLT is XPath technology which is used to select nodes for parsing and generating text. XSLT processors can also be made to output essentially arbitrary text, though XSLT is designed primarily for XML-to-XML and XML-to-HTML transformations.

XML Trees

Every well-formed XML document is a tree. A tree is a data structure composed of connected nodes beginning with a top node called the root. The root is connected to its child nodes, each of which is connected to zero or more children of its own, and so forth. Nodes that have no children of their own are called leaves. A diagram of a tree looks much like a genealogical descendant chart that lists the descendants of a single ancestor. Thus, a tree is a hierarchical structure.

In XSLT, elements, attributes, namespaces, processing instructions, and comments are all counted as nodes. Thus, XSLT processor models an XML document as a tree that contains seven kinds of nodes:

- The root.
- Elements.
- Text.
- Attributes.
- Namespaces.
- Processing instructions.
- Comments.

The DTD and document type declaration are specifically not included in this tree. However, a DTD may add default attribute values to some elements, which then become additional attribute nodes in the tree.

It is important to understand how an XSL stylesheet is processed and applied to an XML document. The process starts with an XML processor reading an XML document and processing it in meaningful pieces called nodes. After the document has been processed into a tree, a special processor called an XSL processor begins to apply the rules of an XML stylesheet to the document tree.

The XSL processors start at the root node (root element) and use it as the basis for performing pattern matching. Pattern matching is the process of using patterns to identify nodes in the tree that are to be processed according to XML stylesheets. The patterns are stored within constructs known as templates. The XSL processor analyzes the templates and patterns associated with them to process different parts of the document tree. When a match is made, the portion of the identified tree is processed by the appropriate stylesheet template. At this point, the rules of the template are applied to the content to generate a result tree. The result tree is itself a tree of data, but the data in this case has been transformed by the stylesheet (see Figure 4-2).

Node Type	Value
Root	The value of the root element.
Element	The concatenation of all parsed character data contained in the element, including character data in any of the descendants of the element.
Text	The text of the node; essentially the node itself.

Table 4-6. Node Types.

Node Type	Value
Attribute	The normalized attribute value as specified by Section 3.3.3 of the XML 1.0 recommendation; basically the attribute value after entities are resolved and leading and trailing white space is stripped; does not include the name of the attribute, the equals sign, or the quotation marks.
Namespace	The URI of the namespace.
Processing instruction	The data in the processing instruction; does not include the processing instruction , <? or ?>.
Comment	The text of the comment, <!-- and --> not included.

Table 4-6 (continued). Node Types.

The XSL processor is responsible for performing two tasks:

- Constructing a result tree from the transformation of a source document tree.
- Interpreting the result tree for formatting purposes.

The first task is known as tree transformation and involves transforming a source tree of document content into a result tree (see Figure 4-2). The second task exams the result tree for formatting information and requires the use of XSL-FO; it is not currently supported by most Web browsers.

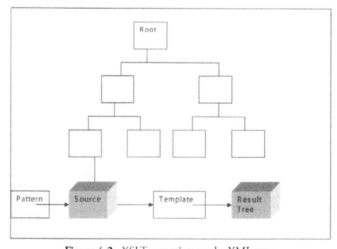

Figure 4-2. XSLT operating on the XML tree.

94

Attaching XSLT Stylesheets

Instead of preprocessing the XML file, we can send the client both the XML file and the XSLT file that describes how to render it. The client is then responsible for applying them. In this case, the XSLT stylesheet must transform the document into an XML application the client understands.

Attaching an XSLT stylesheet to an XML document requires simply inserting an XML-stylesheet processing instruction in the prolog immediately after the XML declaration. This processing instruction should have a type attribute with the value text/xml and an href attribute whose value is a URL pointing to the stylesheet. For example:

```
<?xml version="1.0"?>
<?xml-stylesheet type="text/xml" href="mystylesheet.xsl"?>
```

Pattern-Matching Mechanisms for XSL

The purpose of an XSLT stylesheet is to process the nodes of an XML document and apply a pattern-matching mechanism to determine which nodes are to be transformed. Both the pattern matching and the details of each transformation are defined in the stylesheet. An XSLT stylesheet consists of templates that describe patterns and expressions which are used to match XML content for transformation purposes. The three fundamental constructs in an XSL stylesheet are as follows:

- Templates.
- Patterns.
- Expressions.

Templates

A template is an XSL construct that describes output to be generated based upon certain pattern-matching criteria. Template rules defined by xsl:template elements are a very important part of an XSLT stylesheet. Each xsl:template element has a match attribute that specifies which nodes of the input document the template is matched.

The content of the xsl:template element is the actual template to be instantiated. A template may contain both text that will appear literally in the output document and XSLT instructions that copy data from the input XML document to the result. Because all XSLT instructions are in the http://www.w3.org/1999/XSL/Transform namespace, it's possible to distinguish between the elements that are literal data to be copied to the output and instructions. For example, this template is applied to the root node of the input tree:

```
<xsl:template match="/">
  <html>
    <head>
    </head>
    <body>
    </body>
  </html>
</xsl:template>
```

When the XSLT processor reads the input document, the first node it sees is the root (see Table 4-3). This rule matches that root node and tells the XSLT processor to emit this text:

```
<html>
  <head>
  </head>
  <body>
  </body>
</html>
```

This text is well-formed HTML. Because the XSLT document is itself an XML document, its contents are well-formed XML.

XSL:apply-templates Element

To process the children of the root we use the element xsl:apply-templates. By including xsl:apply-templates in the output template, we tell the formatter to compare each child element of the matched source element against the templates in the stylesheet, and, if a match is found, output the template for the matched node. The template for the matched node may itself contain xsl:apply-templates elements to search for matches for its children. When the formatting engine processes a node, the node is treated as a complete tree.

Select Attribute

The select attribute uses the same kind of patterns as the match attribute of the xsl:template element. If no select attribute is present, all child element, text, comment, and processing instruction nodes are selected.

Patterns and Expressions

Patterns and expressions are used in XSLT templates to perform matches and are used to determine what portion of an XML document is passed through a particular template for transformation. A pattern describes a particular branch of an XML tree. A root pattern is "/" which means that contact is the root element of the document.

Expressions are similar to patterns in that they impact nodes selected for transformation. However, expressions are capable of carrying out processing of their own, such as numerical calculations. For example, expressions include built-in functions, such as Xsl:value-of. The following is a simple example of an expression:

```
<xsl:value-of select="sum(@price)"/>
```

The xsl:value-of element computes the value of a node. The select attribute of the xsl:value-of element specifies exactly which something's value is being computed. This code demonstrates how to use the standard sum() function to calculate the sum of the price attributes within a particular set of elements.

Using XSLT, we can convert XML into display formats; make XML into tool-specific formats, such as typesetting languages; and automatically add numbering, cross-references, tables of contents, and generated text. XSLT can be used to convert documents tagged according to our DTD into documents tagged according to someone else's tag set (see Table 4-8).

Element	Description
xsl:apply-imports	Applies a template rule from an imported stylesheet.
xsl:apply-templates	Applies a template rule to the current element or to the current element's child nodes.
xsl:attribute	Adds an attribute.
xsl:attribute-set	Defines a named set of attributes.
xsl:call-template	Calls a named template.
xsl:choose	Used in conjunction with <xsl:when> and <xsl:otherwise> to express multiple conditional tests.
xsl:comment	Creates a comment node in the result tree.
xsl:copy	Creates a copy of the current node (without child nodes and attributes).

Table 4-8. XSLT.

Element	Description
xsl:copy-of	Creates a copy of the current node (with child nodes and attributes).
xsl:decimal-format	Defines the characters and symbols to be used when converting numbers into strings, with the format-number() function.
xsl:element	Creates an element node in the output document.
xsl:fallback	Specifies an alternate code to run if the XSL processor does not support an XSL element.
xsl:for-each	Loops through each node in a specified node set.
xsl:if	Contains a template that will be applied only if a specified condition is true.
xsl:import	Imports the contents of one stylesheet into another. Note: An imported stylesheet has lower precedence than the importing stylesheet.
xsl:include	Includes the contents of one stylesheet into another. Note: An included stylesheet has the same precedence as the including stylesheet.
xsl:key	Declares a named key that can be used in the stylesheet with the key() function.
xsl:message	Writes a message to the output (used to report errors).
xsl:namespace-alias	Replaces a namespace in the stylesheet to a different namespace in the output.
xsl:number	Determines the integer position of the current node and formats a number.
xsl:otherwise	Specifies a default action for the <xsl:choose> element.
xsl:output	Defines the format of the output document.
xsl:param	Declares a local or global parameter.
xsl:preserve-space	Defines the elements for which white space should be preserved.
xsl:processing-instruction	Writes a processing instruction to the output.
xsl:sort	Sorts the output.

Table 4-8 (continued). XSLT.

Element	Description
xsl:strip-space	Defines the elements for which white space should be removed.
xsl:stylesheet	Defines the root element of a stylesheet.
xsl:template	Rules to apply when a specified node is matched.
xsl:text	Writes literal text to the output.
xsl:tranform	Defines the root element of a stylesheet.
xsl:value-of	Extracts the value of a selected node.
xsl:vaarible	Declares a local or global variable
xsl:when	Specifies an action for the <xsl:choose> element
xsl:with-param	Defines the value of a parameter to be passed

Table 4-8 (continued). XSLT.

XSLT functions are listed in Table 4-9.

Name	Description
current()	Returns the current node.
document()	Used to access the nodes in an external XML document.
element-available()	Tests whether the element specified is supported by the XSLT processor.
format-number()	Converts a number into a string.
function-available()	Tests whether the function specified is supported by the XSLT processor.
generate-id()	Returns a string value that uniquely identifies a specified node.
key()	Returns a node-set using the index specified by an <xsl:key> element.
system-property()	Returns the value of the system properties.
unparsed-entity-uri()	Returns the URI of an unparsed entity.

Table 4-9. XSLT Functions.

eXtensible Styles Language—Formatting Objects (XSL-FO)

eXtensible Styles Language—Formatting Objects (XSL-FO) represents the formatting component of XSL stylesheet technology and is designed to be a functional superset of CSS. XSL-FO provides instructions for the basics of these standards. Without XSL-FO, XML users are obliged to use proprietary formatting and print tools in order to present the information with the appropriate navigation tools for a paginated environment. Typical pagination navigation includes the use of headers and footers, page numbers and page number citations, as well as floating constructs and footnotes, all of which are supported by XSL-FO and go beyond the available presentation mechanisms available in a Web browser. We can, therefore, use XSL-FO to present our information electronically in a page-based format to users.

We often take the printed form of information for granted. When we want to produce a paginated presentation of XML information, we must offer a different set of navigation tools to the consumers of our documents. These navigational aids include headers, footers, page numbers, and page number citations.

This collection of fixed-sized folios may, indeed, have different geometries of page sizes and margin widths used therein, but each page once rendered is fixed in its particular geometry. Layout and typesetting controls give us the power to express our information on pages in a visually pleasing and meaningful convention, conveying information in the presentation itself.

Many aspects of layout are, indeed, applicable on electronic displays and recommendations such as CSS have defined presentation semantics in areas such as font, margin, and color properties. Paginating marked-up information is not something new. The Document Style Semantics and Specification Language (DSSSL) is an international standard originally intended for use with SGML documents, though it also works unchanged with XML documents.

Accepting that HTML and CSS are suitable and sufficient for browser-oriented rendering of information, the W3C set out to define a collection of pagination semantics for print-oriented rendering. These pagination semantics are equally suitable for an electronic display of fixed-size folios of information, such as page-turner browsers and Portable Document Format (PDF) readers.

XSL-FO combines the heritage of CSS and DSSSL in a well-thought-out and robust specification of formatting semantics for paginating information. While well-written for its intended purpose, the document remains out of reach for many people who just want to write stylesheets and print their information.

The key objects of XSL-FO include:

- document element for XSL-FO <root>.
- collection of definitions of page geometries selection pattern <layout-master-set>.
- definition of information for a sequence of pages with common static information <page-sequence>.
- content that is flowed to as many pages as required <flow>.

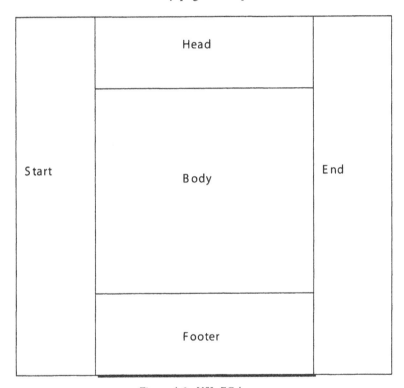

Figure 4-3. XSL-FO layout.

Paginated information includes navigation tools, such as page numbers, page number citations, and headers.

This transforms XML into a final display form by transforming instances of our XML vocabularies into instances of a particular rendering vocabulary.

We can transform information into a combination of HTML and CSS for Web browsers or choose an alternate transformation of XSL-FO for paginated display (be that paginated to a screen, to paper, or perhaps sound).

Example 4-1

Let's develop one example (Example 4-1) that will explore XML, XPath, XSL, and XSD all at once. Let's start with the database given in Table 3-3 called Book Catalog which we introduced in Chapter 3. Then let's create the following files: an XML File, its Schema XSD, and a XSL stylesheet for displaying the data as an HTML page.

First Listing 4-9 shows the XML document.

Example 4-1. Listing 4-9. The XML Document.

The following presents the XML document tags and an associated XML listing using Table 3-3 Book Catalog from Chapter 3:

```
<?xml version="1.0" standalone="yes"?>
<BOOKCATALOG>
  <BOOK>
      <ProductID>1</ProductID>
      <Title>Developing Semantic Web Services</Title>
      <Author>H. Peter Alesso &amp; Craig F. Smith
      </Author>
      <Date>2004</Date>
      <Publisher>A. K. Peters, Ltd.</Publisher>
      <ISBN>1568812124</ISBN>
      <Price>39</Price>
  </BOOK>
  <BOOK>
      <ProductID>2</ProductID>
      <Title>The Intelligent Wireless Web</Title>
      <Author>H. Peter Alesso &amp; Craig F. Smith
      </Author>
      <Date>2001</Date>
      <Publisher>Addison-Wesley</Publisher>
      <ISBN>0201730634</ISBN>
```

```
        <Price>39</Price>
  </BOOK>
  <BOOK>
      <ProductID>3</ProductID>
      <Title>e-Video: Producing Internet Video</Title>
      <Author>H. Peter Alesso</Author>
      <Date>1999</Date>
      <Publisher>Addison-Wesley</Publisher>
      <ISBN>0201703149</ISBN>
      <Price>39</Price>
  </BOOK>
  <BOOK>
      <ProductID>4</ProductID>
      <Title>ASP Fast and Easy Web Development</Title>
      <Author>Michael D. Thomasson</Author>
      <Date>2002</Date>
      <Publisher>Prima-Tech</Publisher>
      <ISBN>0761536183</ISBN>
      <Price>24.99</Price>
  </BOOK>
  <BOOK>
    <ProductID>5</ProductID>
      <Title>JavaServer Pages Fast and Easy
      Web Development</Title>
      <Author>Aneesha Bakharia</Author>
      <Date>2002</Date>
      <Publisher>Prima-Tech</Publisher>
      <ISBN>0761534288</ISBN>
    <Price>24.99</Price>
  </BOOK>
</BOOKCATALOG>
```

Using the XSD information in the previous sections, we construct the following XML Schema (XSD) file for Example 4-1 and the XML document.

Example 4-1 (continued). **Listing 4-10.** The XML Schema XSD file for the XML document in Listing 4-9.

```xml
<?xml version="1.0" standalone="yes"?>
<xsd:schema id="BOOKCATALOG" xmlns="" xmlns:xs="http://
www.w3.org/2001/XMLSchema" xmlns:msdata="urn:schemas-
microsoft-com:xml-msdata">

    <xsd:element name="BOOKCATALOG" msdata:
IsDataSet="true">
      <xs:complexType>
        <xsd:choice maxOccurs="unbounded">
          <xsd:element name="BOOK">
            <xsd:complexType>
              <xsd:sequence>
                <xsd:element name="ProductID" type="xsd:
int" minOccurs="0" />
                <xsd:element name="Title" type="xsd:string"
minOccurs="0" />
                  <xsd:element name="Author" type="xsd:
string" minOccurs="0" />
                <xsd:element name="Date" type="xsd:string"
minOccurs="0" />
                  <xsd:element name="Publisher" type="xsd:
string" minOccurs="0" />
                  <xsd:element name="ISBN" type="xsd:inte-
ger" minOccurs="0" />
                  <xsd:element name="Price" type="xsd:deci-
mal" minOccurs="0" />
              </xsd:sequence>
            </xsd:complexType>
          </xsd:element>
        </xsd:choice>
      </xsd:complexType>
```

```
    </xsd:element>
  </xsd:schema>
```

Now in order to display the XML document in a table on a HTML Web page, we will need to create an XSL stylesheet for Example 4-1. The XSL Stylesheet Listing 4-11 will display Example 4-1 as an HTML table shown in Figure 4-4.

Example 4-1 (continued). **Listing 4-11.** XSL Document.

```
<?xml version="1.0"?>
<xsl:stylesheet version='1.0'  xmlns:xsl='http://www.
w3.org/1999/XSL/Transform'>
<xsl:template match="/">
  <html>
  <body>
    <table border="1">
      <tr>
<td><b>ProductID</b></td>
      <td><b>Author</b></td>
      <td><b>Title</b></td>
      <td><b>ISBN</b></td>
      <td><b>Publisher</b></td>
      <td><b>Price</b></td>
      </tr>
      <xsl:for-each select="BOOKCATALOG/BOOK">
      <tr>
      <td><xsl:value-of select="ProductID" /></td>
      <td><xsl:value-of select="Author" /></td>
      <td><xsl:value-of select="Title" /></td>
      <td><xsl:value-of select="ISBN" /></td>
      <td><xsl:value-of select="Publisher" /></td>
      <td><xsl:value-of select="Price" /></td>
      </tr>
```

```
          </xsl:for-each>
        </table>
      </body>
      </html>
   </xsl:template>
</xsl:stylesheet>
```

The HTML page display from the Example 4-1 XSL file produces Figure 4-4 and the following HTML file listing 4-12.

Figure 4-4. The Web page generated from our Example 4-1 XML and XSL files.

The resultant HTML file after displaying the XML file using the XSL stylesheet is shown in Listing 4-12.

Example 4-1 (continued). **Listing 4-12.** HTML Document.

```
<HTML><HEAD><TITLE>Generate XML from a Database</TI

TLE>
```

```
<META http-equiv=Content-Type content="text/html;
charset=utf-8">
<META content="MSHTML 6.00.2800.1170" name=GENERATOR></
HEAD>
<BODY>
<H2>Generate XML from a Database </H2>
<TABLE border=1>
  <TBODY>
  <TR>
    <TD><B>ProductID</B> </TD>
    <TD><B>Author</B> </TD>
    <TD><B>Title</B> </TD>
    <TD><B>ISBN</B> </TD>
    <TD><B>Publisher</B> </TD>
    <TD><B>Price</B> </TD></TR>
  <TR>
    <TD>1</TD>
    <TD>H. Peter Alesso &amp; Craig F. Smith</TD>
    <TD>Developing Semantic Web Services</TD>
    <TD>1568812124</TD>
    <TD>A. K. Peters, Ltd.</TD>
    <TD>39</TD></TR>
  <TR>
    <TD>2</TD>
    <TD>H. Peter Alesso &amp; Craig F. Smith</TD>
    <TD>The Intelligent Wireless Web</TD>
    <TD>0201730634</TD>
    <TD>Addison-Wesley</TD>
    <TD>39</TD></TR>
  <TR>
    <TD>3</TD>
    <TD>H. Peter Alesso</TD>
    <TD>e-Video: Producing Internet Video</TD>
    <TD>0201703149</TD>
```

107

```
     <TD>Addison-Wesley</TD>
   <TD>39</TD></TR>
<TR>
   <TD>4</TD>
   <TD>Michael D. Thomasson</TD>
   <TD>ASP Fast and Easy Web Development</TD>
   <TD>0761536183</TD>
   <TD>Prima-Tech</TD>
   <TD>24.99</TD></TR>
<TR>
   <TD>5</TD>
   <TD>Aneesha Bakharia</TD>
   <TD>JavaServer Pages Fast and Easy Web Development</TD>
   <TD>0761534288</TD>
   <TD>Prima-Tech</TD>
   <TD>24.99</TD></TR></TBODY></TABLE></BODY></HTML>
```

A Tree View

Elements divide the document into its constituent parts. This diagram, called a tree because of its branching shape, is a useful representation for discussing the relationships between document parts. The top element is called the root element. You'll often hear it called the document element because it encloses all the other elements and thus defines the boundary of the document. The rectangles at the end of the element chains are called leaves, and represent the actual content of the document. Every object in the picture with arrows leading to or from it is a node.

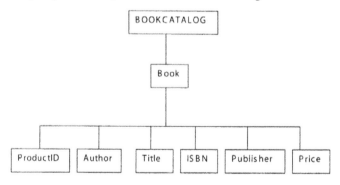

Figure 4-5. Example 4-1 (continued) XML tree.

XMLSPY: An Example of XML Development Tools

XMLSPY is the XML development environment for designing, editing, and debugging enterprise-class applications involving XML, XML Schema, XSL/XSLT, SOAP, WSDL and Web service technologies. It is used for J2EE, .NET, and database developers.

XMLSPY is a comprehensive and easy-to-use product family that facilitates all aspects of XML application development. XMLSPY adds advanced functionality including XSLT debugging, WSDL editing, and XML schema-driven code generation (in C++ and Java).

The stylesheet designer is a new approach to automate the writing of complex XSLT stylesheets using an intuitive drag-and-drop user interface. Stylesheet designer creates advanced electronic forms for use with authentic view. Authentic view is a word processor type editor supporting electronic form-based data input, graphical elements, tables, as well as real-time validation using XML Schema.

XML and Databases

Most Web applications store their data in relational databases. So far we have found that XML can be used not only for document format, but also as a way to store data in a structured manner that may be used in conjunction with Web applications to connect to databases.

If spreadsheets are 'number crunchers,' then databases are 'information crunchers.' Databases excel at managing and manipulating structured information. What is 'structured information'? Consider the phone book which contains items of information (name, address, and phone number) about phone subscribers in a particular area. Each subscriber's information takes the same form. In database vocabulary, the phone book is a table which contains a record for each subscriber. Each subscriber record contains: name (string), address (number/string), and phone number (number). The records are sorted alphabetically by the name field called the key field. Other examples are customer lists, business card files, and parts inventories. Using a database program we can design a database to keep track of many kinds of information.

Relational Model

The Relational Database Model was developed at IBM in the late 1960s by Dr. E. F. Codd while he was looking to solve the problems with the existing database models. The Relational Model became the foundation of modern database technology. At the core of the Relational Model is the concept of tables (also called relations) in which all data is stored. Each table is made up of records (horizontal rows also known as tuples) and fields (vertical columns). How or where the tables of data are stored makes no difference. Each table can be identified by a unique name and that name can be used by the database to find the table.

A database can contain a single table of information, such as the phone book, or many tables of related information.

An order entry system for a business, for example, will consist of many tables:

1. An orders table to track each order.
2. An orders detail table for tracking each item.
3. A customer table so you can see who to bill.
4. An inventory table showing the goods you have.
5. A suppliers table, so you can see to re-order stock.
6. A payments table to track payments for orders.

Each of these tables will be linked to one or more of the other tables, so that we can tie information together to produce reports or answer questions. Multi-file databases like this are called relational databases. Relational databases provide exceptional power and flexibility in storing and retrieving information.

Relational Database Programs (RDBMS)

Database programs create and maintain a computer database often called a database management system, or DBMS. Just as databases range from simple single-table lists to complex multi-table systems, database programs range in complexity. Relational Database Programs (RDBMS) are designed to handle multi-file databases.

Database program tools perform the following:

1. Design the structure of the database.
2. Create data entry forms to get information into the database.
3. Validate the data entered and check for inconsistencies.
4. Sort and manipulate the data in the database.
5. Query the database (that is, ask questions about the data).
6. Produce flexible reports both on screen and on paper, that make it easy to comprehend the information stored in the database.

Analytic Databases

On Line Analytical Processing (OLAP) databases are static, read-only databases which store archived data used for analysis. For example, a company might store sales records and use that database to analyze marketing strategies in relationship to demographics. On the Web, analytic databases are used for inventory catalogs such as Amazon.com. An inventory catalog analytical database usually holds information about products in inventory.

Web pages are generated dynamically by querying the list of available products in the inventory against some search parameters. The dynamically-generated page will display the information about each item (such as title, author, ISBN) which is stored in the database.

Operational Databases

On Line Transaction Processing (OLTP) databases are used to manage more dynamic bits of data. These allow us to modify the data (add, change, or delete). They are used to track real-time information. For example, to track warehouse/stock quantities. As customers order products from an online Web store, an operational database can be used to keep track of how many items have been sold and when the company will need to reorder stock.

Client/Server Databases

There are many types of relational databases and not all of them will be useful for Web applications. In particular, client/server databases rather than the stand-alone packages are best used for the Web. A client/server database works like a database server that is left running 24 hours a day, and 7 days a week. Thus, the server can handle database requests at any hour. Database requests come in from "clients" who access the database through its interface or by connecting to a database socket. Requests are handled as they come in.

Structured Query Language (SQL)

Structured Query Language (SQL) is used to communicate with relational database management systems. SQL statements are used to perform tasks such as updating data on a database or retrieving data from a database. Some common relational database management systems that use SQL are: Oracle, Sybase, Microsoft SQL Server, Access, and Ingres, etc. The standard SQL commands such as "Select," "Insert," "Update," "Delete," "Create," and "Drop" can be used with a database.

Integrating XML with Databases

Now that we have covered relational databases and how they work, we will discuss how to integrate XML into database applications and Web Services.

Is the Web a global database? No, it lacks a Web Schema. However, interconnectivity between corporate, educational, and other databases is possible with XML. And XML Schema allows us to fashion an appropriate relationship to our databases.

XML and database integration is important because XML provides a standard technique to describe data. By leveraging XML, a company can convert its existing corporate data into a format that is consumable by its trading partners. A trading partner can import the XML data into its system using the given format or they convert the data to a different XML format using XSLT.

A large number of XML database solutions exist. They generally come in two varieties: database mapping and native XML support. Native XML support actually stores the XML data in the document in its native format, as a stored file. Database mapping consists of mapping the XML document onto the database fields. The system dynamically converts SQL result sets to XML documents. These tools continue to store the information in relational databases management systems (RDBMS) format. They provide an XML conversion process that is implemented as a server-side Web application. When the data is retrieved it represents an XML document.

The simplest approach to integrating XML and relational databases is just to insert an XML document into a field in a database. We could also retrieve the field, feed it to a parser, apply XSLT transformations to it, and process it using SAX or DOM technology to create a data structure for the XML document.

However, there are trade-offs involved. If you break up the XML document into normalized tables, restoring them to the original data structures can be a lot of work. For example, data stored in an Oracle database on a server in a supplier's system must be imported into a database when a company receives it. In this case, XML would make a good intermediary for the data because it's easy to write programs that import and export data and because by using XML, the data can be used in future applications.

Another example could be a service that syndicates news articles. The news articles would be distributed via XML files so that they could be easily transformed for presentation on the Web.

Connecting to a Database with Java

There are two basic approaches to modeling databases in XML using Java. The least used requires using applets and client side Java Virtual Machine (JVM). However, since applet and JVM are not universally supported this has not been successful.

The second method is to use server-side servlets and Java Database Connectivity (JDBC) API. JDBC is the Java2 standard database access interface with SQL. It provides users with a uniform interface to various relational database systems regardless of different implementations.

Java servlets are server-side components that reside on the Web server or application server and utilize HTTP protocol.

A key advantage of using servlets is promoting the thin-client interface. The servlets handle the request on the server side and respond by generating an HTML page dynamically. Then, the browser only has to support HTML.

The Java Architecture for XML Binding (JAXB) provides a framework for representing XML documents as Java objects. Using JAXB framework, we can guarantee that the documents are well-formed and have the option for schema validation.

JAXB is easier to use and more efficient than processing documents with SAX or DOM API. JAXB is similar to DOM, but the API is simpler. The JAXB binding schema requires the following steps:

1. Review the database schema.
2. Construct the desired XML document.
3. Define a schema for the XML document.
4. Create the JAXB binding schema.
5. Generate the JAXB classes based upon the schema.
6. Develop a Data Access Object (DAO).
7. Develop a servlet for HTTP access.

To establish a connection with the DBMS there are two additional steps to be implemented for Java 2 (see Figure 4-6):

1. Load the driver.
2. Make the connection.

.NET Database Connection

Microsoft's Active-X Data Objects (ADO.NET) is an evolution of the ADO data access model that performs database connectivity for the .NET framework. It was designed specifically for the Web with scalability, statelessness, and XML in mind. ADO.NET uses Connection and Command objects, and introduces the DataSet, DataReader, and DataAdapter. The important distinction between this evolved stage of ADO.NET and previous data architectures is that there exists an object, the DataSet, that is separate and distinct from any data stores.

The DataSet is an always disconnected record set that knows nothing about the source or destination of the data it contains. Inside a DataSet, much like in a database, there are tables, columns, relationships, constraints, and views. A DataAdapter is the object that connects to

113

the database to fill the DataSet. Then, it connects back to the database to update the data there, based on operations performed while the DataSet held the data. In the past, data processing has been primarily connection-based. In an effort to make multi-tiered apps more efficient, data processing is turning to a message-based approach that revolves around chunks of information.

DataAdapter provides a bridge to retrieve and save data between a DataSet and its source data store. It requests with the appropriate SQL commands to the data store. The XML-based DataSet object provides a consistent programming model that works with all models of data storage: flat, relational, and hierarchical.

It does this by having no 'knowledge' of the source of its data, and by representing the data that it holds as collections and data types. No matter what the source of the data within the DataSet is, it is manipulated through the same set of standard APIs exposed through the DataSet and its subordinate objects.

The OLE DB and SQL Server .NET Data Providers (System.Data.OleDb and System. Data.SqlClient) that are part of the .Net Framework provide four basic objects: the Command, Connection, DataReader, and DataAdapter.

For issuing SQL commands against a database we use:

- DataReaders—For reading a forward-only stream of data records from a SQL Server data source.
- DataSets—For storing, remoting and programming against flat data, XML data and relational data.
- DataAdapters—For pushing data into a DataSet, and reconciling data against a database.

When dealing with connections to a database, there are two different options: SQL Server .NET Data Provider (System.Data.SqlClient) and OLE DB .NET Data Provider (System.Data. OleDb). Connections are used to 'talk to' databases, and are represented by provider-specific classes such as SQLConnection. Commands travel over connections and resultsets are returned in the form of streams which can be read by a DataReader object.

ADO.NET: Execute a Command

Commands are issued against databases to take actions against data stores. For example, you could execute a command that inserts or deletes data. Commands include any command that can be issued against a database, and in the case of the OleDbCommand, can be data store specific. Whatever the command may be, the OleDbCommand or SqlCommand can be used to get the command to your back-end data store.

ADO.NET: Get Out Parameters from a Stored Procedure

Some stored procedures return values through parameters. When a parameter in a SQL statement or stored procedure is declared as "out," the value of the parameter is returned back to the caller; the value is stored in a parameter in the parameters collection on the OleDbCommand or SqlCommand objects. If the connection and command name are not set, you can still establish the parameters, but you have to create the collection of parameters and expected types.

ADO.NET: Populate a DataSet from a Database

Getting data from a database is easy, and working with data is easier than before. If you want the results from a database as a forward-only, read-only stream of data, you can execute a command and retrieve the results using the DataReader (see Figure 4-6).

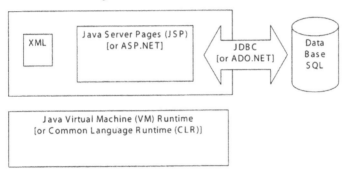

Figure 4-6. XML and databases.

XML Web Services Languages

XML plays a vital role in Web Services. The three enabling Web Services languages are XML languages: Simple Object Access Protocol (SOAP), Web Services Descriptive Language (WSDL), and Universal Description, Discovery and Integration (UDDI). Both J2EE and .NET frameworks support these open XML standards (see Figure 4-7).

- The Simple Object Access Protocol (SOAP) is a means of facilitating platform agnostic exchange of structured XML data packets between applications and components over the Internet. SOAP implementations allow transaction sharing amongst peers in a decentralized, distributed environment via HTTP, SMTP, and other native Internet transport protocols.

115

- A Web Services Descriptive Language (WSDL) description is an XML document that gives all the pertinent information about a Web service including its name, the operations that can be called on it, the parameters for those operations, and the location to send requests. WSDL is written in XML. WSDL is not yet a W3C standard.

- Universal Description, Discovery and Integration (UDDI) is a directory service where businesses can register and search for Web services. UDDI is a platform independent framework for describing services, discovering businesses, and integrating business services by using the Internet. UDDI is a directory of web service interfaces described by WSDL. UDDI communicates via SOAP. UDDI is built into the Microsoft .NET platform.

The Web needs to be augmented with a few other platform services, which maintain the ubiquity and simplicity of the Web, to constitute a more functional platform. The full-function Web services platform can be thought of as XML plus HTTP plus SOAP plus WSDL plus UDDI. We will present each of these languages in greater detail in Chapter 5 along with a discussion and example of Web Services.

Figure 4-7 illustrates a client-server-database three tier relationship. It starts between a client computer that starts a Web browser and connects to the Web. The Web connection uses HTTP to communicate to a server application running on a server computer on the Web. The client may interact with a Web service that passes SOAP messages back and forth between the client and the server as well as to a third tier database.

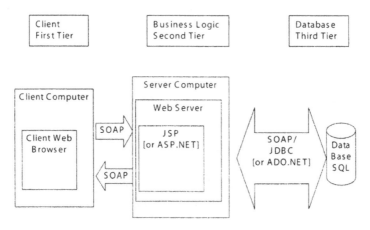

Figure 4-7. XML and the Client-Server relationship.

XML Capabilities and Limitations

Table 4-10 is a general comparison between the markup languages, HTML, SGML, and XML.

SGML	HTML	XML
Powerful for formatting all document types.	Displays and prints as appropriate for the implementing device.	Simple data exchange.
Powerful for generating all markup languages.	Needs more abstract and semantic language for complex tasks.	Needs more abstract and semantic language for complex tasks.
Too complex for the Internet transport over limited network bandwidth.	HTML is meant for human consumption.	Takes advantage of Internet protocols (HTTP) for transportation.
		You can define your own set of tags.
		XML is able to use legacy applications.
		Some XML files require considerable memory and processing capabilities.

Table 4-10. Markup Language General Comparisons.

The Importance of XML

Why is XML so important? Just as HTML is an open standard that allows information exchange and display over the Internet, XML is an open standard that allows data to be exchanged between applications over the Internet. XML is the bridge to exchange data between the two main software development frameworks over the Web: J2EE and .NET.

XML lets everyone create their own tags. Scripts, or programs, can make use of these tags in sophisticated ways, but the script writer has to know how the page writer uses each tag. In short, XML allows users to add arbitrary structure to their documents, but says nothing about what the structure means.

Unfortunately, while XML provides data exchange between applications, it lacks semantics. As a result, programs cannot determine the intended interpretation of XML tags. While XML will continue to play an important role in the development of the Semantic Web, it does not provide a full solution.

Although one might derive some semantics from the structure of the documents, the semantics of each element (XML tag) is not defined. As a result, its interpretation relies on the implicit knowledge applied in application programs. Before we can develop a Web with semantics, resources on the Web will need to be represented in or annotated with structured machine-understandable descriptions of their contents and relationships. This requires vocabularies and formally defined domain ontology.

While we can consider XML a highly functional subset of SGML, it is not implemented and used as a single markup language. Instead, it too is a meta-language that allows users to design their own markup languages. With XML, Web architects can design any and all of the Web Service Languages they will need. And any modifications to XML syntax will have ripple effects on all of its off-spring languages.

Conclusion

In this chapter, we presented a primer for XML and some of its more important associated languages including XML Schema and XSL. We concluded with an evaluation of XML's strengths and weaknesses, as well as a discussion of its utility in developing the markup languages for future Web architectures.

Part Two

The Semantic Web

Chapter Five

Web Services

Overview

The task of creating and deploying Web Services is not all that different than what developers currently do for traditional Web applications. The tendency on all platforms is to automate as much as possible in creating Web Services under interoperable standards. The most advanced vision for the next generation of Web Services is the development of Web Services over Semantic Web Architecture. Support of Semantic Web related technologies includes languages RDF (see Chapter 7) and OWL (see Chapter 8).

To realize the vision of Semantic Web Services, an ontology for Web Services is required to make them machine-understandable and use-apparent (see Chapter 10). Integral to this effort will be the automation of three main functions: service discovery, execution, and composition and interoperation.

In this chapter, we introduce XML-based Web Services and provide a survey comparing Microsoft's .NET and Sun's J2EE frameworks. We discuss the motives and opportunities for evolving today's XML-based Web Services into automated functions leading toward Semantic Web Services.

In addition, we provide a simple Web Service example in the "Hello, World" tradition. We see how to use ASP.NET to create a working Web Service with either a text editor or with Visual Studio, VS.NET, and learn about the basic technologies behind .NET Web Services.

Background

The concept of Web Services is not new. It has been around from the early days of the Internet. Since 1994, distributed objects that could support Web Services were being developed by several organizations under different names. NeXT called them Portable Distributed Objects, Microsoft called them Component Object Model (COM), IBM called them System Object Model (SOM), and Apple called them OpenDoc. These companies (with the exception of Microsoft) formed the Object Management Group and converged upon a standard called Common Object Request Broker Architecture (CORBA).

In 1996, Marc Andreessen, co-founder of Netscape, described how businesses could use Internet Inter-ORB Protocol (IIOP) to request services from one another across a wide variety of platforms. Familiar Web Services include Business to Consumer (B2C) search engines, stock tickers, FedEx tracking, and credit card services. They typically offer interfaces for Web visitors, as well as proprietary Application Programming Interfaces (API) for Business-to-Business (B2B) transactions. Every day more and more services come online, each trying to carve out a business model that provides a new or enhanced service. The goal of all these services is a common, standards-based open interface for application access through the Web.

If Web Services could be fully realized, they could streamline almost any business that needs to communicate with other businesses, like suppliers, banks, and shipping companies. For example, a motorcycle company that offers pre-installed aftermarket options could create an application that lets the salespeople custom design and order a bike for their customers. Using Web Services, the application could verify the credit of the customer, check the availability and order the stock bike, lookup and order custom parts, and arrange and track the shipping of the final product, all without a person picking up the phone.

With Web Services, a business could offer more custom parts from more companies because all the computers are talking a common language, regardless of differing server platforms. By automating the supply chain process, more resources can be devoted to promoting the business and to customer management.

Attempts to achieve full global Web Services through CORBA (Common Object Request Broker Architecture), IIOP (Internet Inter ORB Protocol), Sun's Java RMI (Remote Method Implementation) on the Java platform, and DCOM (Distributed Component Object Model) on the Windows platform did gain some success, albeit mostly intranet/extranet implementations. But working against these protocols has been the complexity of implementation, binary compatibility, and homogenous operating environment requirements.

J2EE platform vs .NET platform

As a result, Web applications have developed into a "two horse" race between the Java 2 Enterprise Edition (J2EE) platform and the Windows .NET Enterprise platform which is likely to continue well into the future. While Sun would like to see everyone programming on the Java platform, and Microsoft would like the same on the Windows platform, there are developers in each camp who won't or can't switch. Most corporations actually support both platforms. In order for Web Services to work across the Web, developers need a set of standards to discover and use without being locked into one environment. Specifically, what is really needed for Web Services to be widely successful are text-based (not binary) Internet protocols, usable on any platform or from any language.

Several components are required to make a Web service work. These include a way to discover a service provider on the Web; a way to discover what services are available on a particular site; a way to describe how to interface with the service; a way to execute the functions provided by the service; a standard messaging format; and last but not least, a way to represent the data in the exchange. The cooperation of many industry players is necessary for the standards to develop for these components and thereby create a successful Web service infrastructure.

HTTP on TCP/IP for Web Services

Before the Web, getting all the major software vendors to agree on a transport protocol for cross-network application services might have been impossible. But the Web rendered that decision academic, by specifying lower-level transports for standardized communication.

The Web uses HTTP running on TCP/IP. TCP/IP was already a mature standard by the time the Web went mainstream in 1994, and by 1997, HTTP had become a universal business standard (see Chapter 1).

HTTP is stable and has excellent reliability and scalability features, such as load balancing and transparent caching. Every resource exposed through HTTP has a URI. That means that every resource can refer to every other resource. There are no boundaries between applications—just a "Web" of linked resources.

Therefore, the existing Web protocol, HTTP, already makes the transfer and addressing of networked data as natural, standardized, and well understood as the storing of data in file systems and databases. It provides a solid foundation for Web Services.

XML-based Web Services

With HTTP and TCP/IP in place, all that was needed for Web Services to proceed was some kind of messaging and data encapsulation standard. But it was XML's invention that really paved the way for Web Services. As a widely heralded, platform-independent standard for data description that could also be used to describe message-passing protocols, XML was a logical choice for the job of standardized application-to-application communication.

HTTP methods can work on any kind of data using an XML vocabulary. This is where incompatibility creeps into the system. Using SQL does not automatically make a program designed for one database schema work with another. Similarly, programs expecting different XML vocabularies will not automatically work together.

However, there are filters for relational databases, and there are tools for mapping between XML vocabularies such as XSLT (see Chapter 4). Another technique for managing XML interoperability issues is the standardization and sharing of schemas through registries, repositories, and standards bodies.

Web Service Standards—SOAP, WSDL, and UDDI

XML officially became a standard in February 1998 and several attempts at an XML protocol for inter-process communication were made. It was the Simple Object Access Protocol (SOAP), developed by Dave Winer, CEO of Userland Software, Microsoft engineers Bob Atkinson and Mohsen Al-Ghosein, and Don Box, co-founder of DevelopMentor Incorporated, that formed the basis for Web Services. Electronic marketplaces were a hot concept in December 1999, when Microsoft held a private meeting with IBM and others to demonstrate SOAP 1.0.

SOAP had a lot of things going for it. It was platform agnostic, flexible, and general-purpose. Its main drawback was vendor distrust of Microsoft. IBM was the first major vendor to adopt SOAP and by 2000, SOAP was gaining wider acceptance. IBM and Microsoft were also each working on a way to programmatically describe how to connect to a Web service. After some discussion, protocol proposals from Microsoft and IBM merged. IBM contributed Network Accessible Service Specification Language (NASSL) and Microsoft offered both Service Description Language (SDL) and SOAP Contract Language. In the fall of 2000, the merged specification, Web Services Description Language (WSDL), was announced.

With SOAP and WSDL, companies could create and describe their Web Services. But someone still needed to provide a way to advertise and locate Web Services. In March 2000, IBM, Microsoft, and Ariba started working on the solution: Universal Description, Discovery, and Integration (UDDI). In September 2000, UDDI 1.0 was announced.

With SOAP, WSDL, and UDDI in place, the de-facto standards of Web Services had arrived. But it wasn't until the end of 2000, that five major IT software infrastructure vendors announced their commitment to Web Services. Oracle, HP, Sun, IBM, and Microsoft, an unlikely alliance, stated their intention to support and deploy the Web Services standards in their products.

.NET Web Services

For Web Services to work, everyone has to agree on a communication methodology, including identifying, accessing, and involving services. SOAP describes commands and parameters that can be passed between browsers and Web Services. Microsoft's current approach to Web Services is to build them into the .NET framework.

The .NET framework uses XML throughout and introduces XML-based remote procedure calls using SOAP that may offer a cross-platform alternative to Distributed Component Object Model (DCOM) and an easier-to-implement alternative to IIOP. In addition, Microsoft introduced a new programming language, C#.NET with a well-developed library of XML-related supported methods (see Chapter 14).

SOAP describes commands and parameters that can be passed between browsers and Web Services as part of .NET. SOAP is an implementation of XML that represents one common set of rules about how data and commands will be represented and extended.

SOAP consists of three parts: an envelope (a framework for describing what is in a message and how to process it), a set of encoding rules (for expressing instances of application-defined data types), and a convention for representing remote procedure calls and responses. SOAP messages are fundamentally one-way transmissions from a sender to a receiver (and vice-a-versa) using HTTP binding.

WDSL also provides a way for service providers to describe the format of requests to their systems regardless of the underlying protocol or encoding. WSDL is a part of the effort of the UDDI initiative to provide directories and descriptions of such on-line services for electronic business.

J2EE Web Services

In competition with Microsoft's .NET approach (which currently supports primary Windows), are architectures based on platform independence, such as Java 2 Platform, Enterprise Edition (J2EE). In 1995, Sun unveiled the Java platform as a way to create applications that would run on any computer, regardless of the underlying operating system. Java technology has progressed from a tool to animate Web sites to the end-to-end Java 2 platform that spans applications from small consumer devices to enterprise data center servers. The Java programming language is now an important environment used for developing platform independent Enterprise Information Portals (EIP). Java is cross-platform because of the Java Virtual Machine (JVM), a device that serves up distributed software on recognized networks; it works independent of the computer's instruction set and architecture. Java technology includes ATM machines, 2-way pagers, mobile phones, personal organizers, game machines, cameras, industrial controllers, point-of-sale terminals, and servers. Java technology and XML can be combined to deliver Web Services using J2EE as a foundation.

Adding the strength of XML technologies to enterprise systems such as J2EE and CORBA, provides the environment for building highly scalable secure fault-tolerant systems. XML-based technologies SOAP and WSDL provide the means of building a "Web Services" model where business services can be catalogued through UDDI and invoked over the Web through SOAP requests. These services could be implemented in terms of CORBA, J2EE, or .NET.

Discovery Web Services

Currently, there are several methods of discovering Web Services—from simple and manual to complex and automated. At the manual end of the spectrum, techniques include e-mail, Web browsing, phone calls, and word-of-mouth. Unfortunately, if a service provider changes any aspect of their service, the change must be manually communicated to all those who are currently using the service.

Next, consider publishing services and service descriptions on various Web sites via formatted files, such as, Microsoft's DISCO and IBM's ADS can be used to create standardized file formats and look-up definitions. DISCO simply provides a file containing XML references to other files that actually describe the service. Sophisticated methods, such as WSDL are more automated because they allow discovery using HTTP GET operations through browsers and Web crawlers.

Still, this only provides a list of services and their associated descriptions. It is still a manual process for a business to review this list and make a decision on which provider and service shall be chosen. The actual use and invocation of the Web service also requires manual intervention and programming techniques.

The next category of discovery is that of Web service brokers. Brokers, SalCentral, Xmethods, and Silicon Hills Group, actively manage services for service providers by providing a means to publish, promote, sell, test, and support their Web Services.

The final approach to Web service discovery is automated and dynamic service registries, such as UDDI. The UDDI registry providers facilitate these registries via Web page interfaces. But, UDDI registries provide Applications Programming Interfaces (APIs) for publishing, finding, and binding services. This makes UDDI registries more dynamic and complex than any other type of Web service discovery method.

The UDDI specifications define a way to publish and discover information about Web Services. UDDI aims to automate the process of publishing your preferred way of doing business finding trading partners and interoperate with them over the Internet.

Simple Object Access Protocol (SOAP)

The task of creating and deploying Web Services is not all that different than what developers currently do for traditional Web applications. On all platforms, the tendency is to automate as much as possible in creating Web Services. Most programmers don't need to know the exact details of encodings and envelopes; instead, they can use a SOAP toolkit, such as Microsoft's Visual Studio.

A Web service consists of three components: a listener to receive the message, a proxy to take the message and translate it into an action, and the application code to implement that action. The listener and proxy components should be completely transparent to the application code. The code shouldn't even recognize that it is being invoked through a Web Service interface.

There is a long list of SOAP implementations available to developers. The three most popular tools are Microsoft's .NET, Apache SOAP for Java, and SOAP::Lite for Perl. No matter which toolkit is used, the fundamental process of creating, deploying, and using SOAP Web Services is basically the same.

The integration of SOAP toolkits varies with the transport layer. While some implement their own HTTP servers, some expect to be installed as part of a particular Web server, so that rather than serving up a Web page, the HTTP daemon hands the SOAP message to the toolkit's proxy component, which does the work of invoking the code behind the Web service.

 HTTP

The Hypertext Transfer Protocol (HTTP) is a generic and stateless protocol for distributed, collaborative, hypermedia information systems. It allows performing operations on resources which are identified by URIs. It has four main methods:

Get – means get the information that is identified by the request URI. Usually it is the action we take when browsing sites and clicking hyperlinks—we ask the web server for the resources that is identified by Request-URLs.

Post – means make a request to the Web server so that the server accepts the resources encapsulated in the request, which will be the new subordinate of the resource identified by the Request-URI in the Request-Line. Usually it is what we do when filling and sending the HTML form to the server to buy something.

Put – means make a request that sends updated information about a resource if the resource identified by the Request-URI exists, otherwise the URI will be regarded as a new resource. The main difference between the POST and PUT requests lies in the different meaning of the Request-URI. In a POST request, the URI is to identify the resource that will handle the enclosed entity. As for the PUT request, the user agent knows what URI is its aim and the Web server cannot redirect the request to other resources. Unfortunately most Web browsers don't implement this functionality, which makes the Web, to some extent, a one-way medium.

Head – is similar to GET except that the server doesn't return a message-body in the response. The benefit of this method is that we can get meta-information about the entity implied by the request without transferring the entity-body itself. We can use this method to check if hypertext links are valid, or if the content was recently modified.

By using HTTP, the Semantic Web can benefit from all these functionalities for free. In addition, almost all HTTP servers and clients support all these features.

Whether the transport is built-in or pluggable, all SOAP toolkits provide the proxy component, which parses and interprets the SOAP message to invoke application code. When the proxy component is handed a SOAP message by a listener, it must do three things:

1. Deserialize from XML into native format for passing off to the code.
2. Invoke the code.
3. Serialize the response back into XML and transport to listener and requester.

A SOAP message is an ordinary XML document containing the following four elements:

1. Envelope element—identifies the XML document as a SOAP message.
2. Header element—that contains header information.
3. Body element—that contains call and response.
4. Fault element—that provides information about errors.

Listing 5-1 illustrates a basic SOAP message structure.

Listing 5-1. Basic SOAP Document.

```
<?xml version="1.0"?>
<soap:Envelope
xmlns:soap="http://www.w3.org/2001/12/soap-envelope"
soap:encodingStyle="http://www.w3.org/2001/12/soap-en-
coding">
    <soap:Header>
    </soap:Header>
        <soap:Body>
            <soap:Fault>
            </soap:Fault>
        </soap:Body>
</soap:Envelope>
```

Despite differences in how various SOAP implementations accomplish these tasks, all SOAP Web-service tools follow this same pattern. Later in this chapter, we will detail an example Web service which will discuss the development process for Microsoft's Visual Studio.

Web Services Description Language (WSDL)

WSDL is a specification that defines how to describe Web Services in a common XML grammar. WSDL describes four critical pieces of data:
- Interface information describing all publicly available functions.
- Data type information for all message requests and message responses.
- Binding information about the transport protocol to be used.
- Address information for locating the specified service.

WSDL represents a contract between the service requestor and the service provider. Using WSDL, a client can locate a Web service and invoke any of its publicly available functions. With WSDL-aware tools, we can also automate the development process and enable applications to integrate new services. WSDL provides a common language for describing services and a platform for automatically integrating those services.

WSDL is divided into six major elements (definitions, types, messages, portTypes, binding, and service) as described in Table 5-1.

Elements	Description
<definitions>	Root WSDL element. It defines the name of the Web service, declares multiple namespaces used throughout the remainder of the document, and contains all the service elements described here.
<types>	What types will be transmitted. The types element describes all the data types used between the client and server. WSDL is not tied exclusively to a specific typing system, but it uses the W3C XML Schema specification as its default choice. If the service uses only XML Schema built-in simple types, such as strings and integers, the types element is not required.
<message>	What messages will be transmitted. The message element describes a one-way message, whether it is a single message request or a single message response. It defines the name of the message and contains zero or more message part elements, which can refer to message parameters or message return values.
<portType>	What operations (functions) will be supported. The portType element combines multiple message elements to form a complete one-way or round-trip operation. For example, a portType can combine one request and one response message into a single request/response operation, most commonly used in SOAP services.
<binding>	How will the messages be transmitted on the wire? What SOAP-specific details are there? The binding element describes the concrete specifics of how the service will be implemented on the wire. WSDL includes built-in extensions for defining SOAP services; therefore SOAP-specific information goes here.
<service>	Where the service is located. The service element defines the address for invoking the specified service. Most commonly, this includes a URL for invoking the SOAP service.

Table 5-1. WSDL Specification Categories.

WSDL Specification Categories

The <portType> element is the most important WSDL element. It defines a Web service, the operations that can be performed, and the messages that are involved. The <portType> element can be compared to a function library (or a module or class) in a traditional programming language.

The <message> element defines the data elements of an operation. Each message can consist of one or more parts. The parts can be compared to the parameters of a function call in a traditional programming language.

The <types> element defines the data type that are used by the Web service. For maximum platform neutrality, WSDL uses XML Schema syntax to define data types.

The <binding> element defines the message format and protocol details for each port.

The main structure of a WSDL document is shown in Listing 5-2.

Listing 5-2. Basic WSDL Document.

```
<definitions>
    <types>
            definition of types........
    </types>
    <message>
        definition of a message....
    </message>
    <portType>
            definition of a port.......
    </portType>
    <binding>
            definition of a binding....
    </binding>
</definitions>
```

A WSDL document can also contain other elements, like extension elements and a service element that make it possible to group together the definitions of several Web services in one single WSDL document. The following is a WSDL example of a simplified fraction document:

131

```
<message name="getTermRequest">
    <part name="term" type="xs:string"/>
</message>
<message name="getTermResponse">
    <part name="value" type="xs:string"/>
</message>

<portType name="glossaryTerms">
  <operation name="getTerm">
      <input message="getTermRequest"/>
      <output message="getTermResponse"/>
  </operation>
</portType>
```

In this example, the portType element defines "glossaryTerms" as the name of a port, and "getTerm" as the name of an operation. The "getTerm" operation has an input message called "getTermRequest" and an output message called "getTermResponse."

The WSDL operation types are defined in Table 5-2.

Operation Type	Definition
One-way	The operation can receive a message but will not return a response
Request-response	The operation can receive a request and will return a response
Solicit-response	The operation can send a request and will wait for a response
Notification	The operation can send a message but will not wait for a response

Table 5-2. WSDL Operation Types.

Listing 5-3 shows a one-way operation type example.

Listing 5-3. WSDL One-Way Operation.

```
<message name="newTermValues">
```

132

```
    <part name="term" type="xs:string"/>
    <part name="value" type="xs:string"/>
</message>

<portType name="glossaryTerms">
   <operation name="setTerm">
      <input name="newTerm" message="newTermValues"/>
   </operation>
</portType >
```

The request-response example is shown in Listing 5-4. In this example the port "glossary-Terms" defines a request-response operation called "getTerm." The "getTerm" operation requires an input message called "getTermRequest" with a parameter called "term," and will return an output message called "getTermResponse" with a parameter called "value."

Listing 5-4. WSDL Request-Response Operation.

```
<message name="getTermRequest">
   <part name="term" type="xs:string"/>
</message>

<message name="getTermResponse">
   <part name="value" type="xs:string"/>
</message>

<portType name="glossaryTerms">
  <operation name="getTerm">
      <input message="getTermRequest"/>
      <output message="getTermResponse"/>
  </operation>
</portType>
```

Binding to SOAP

Listing 5-5 shows an example of a binding to SOAP.

133

Listing 5-5. WSDL Binding to SOAP.

```
<message name="getTermRequest">
   <part name="term" type="xs:string"/>
</message>

<message name="getTermResponse">
   <part name="value" type="xs:string"/>
</message>
<portType name="glossaryTerms">
  <operation name="getTerm">
     <input message="getTermRequest"/>
     <output message="getTermResponse"/>
  </operation>
</portType>

<binding type="glossaryTerms" name="b1">
<soap:binding style="document transport="http://schemas.
xmlsoap.org/soap/http" />
  <operation>
    <soap:operation
     soapAction="http://example.com/getTerm"/>
    <input>
      <soap:body use="literal"/>
    </input>
    <output>
      <soap:body use="literal"/>
    </output>
  </operation>
</binding>
```

The binding element has two attributes: the name attribute and the type attribute. The name attribute defines the name of the binding, and the type attribute points to the port for the binding. In Listing 5-5 this is the "glossaryTerms" port.

The soap:binding element has two attributes: the style attribute and the transport attribute. The style attribute can be "rpc" or "document." The transport attribute defines the SOAP protocol to used: HTTP. The operation element defines each operation that the port exposes. For each operation the corresponding SOAP action has to be defined. Also, the input and output are encoded as "literal."

Universal Description, Discovery and Integration (UDDI)

Prior to the Universal Description, Discovery and Integration UDDI project, no industry-wide approach was available for businesses to reach their customers and partners with information about their products and Web services. Nor was there a uniform method that detailed how to integrate the systems and processes that are already in place at and between business partners. Nothing attempted to cover both the business and development aspects of publishing and locating information associated with a piece of software on a global scale.

A business can register three types of information into a UDDI registry.

White Pages
> Basic contact information and identifiers about a company, including business name, address, contact information, and unique identifiers, e.g., tax IDs. This information allows others to discover the Web Service based upon the business identification.

Yellow pages
> Information that describes a Web service using different categorizations. This information allows others to discover your Web Service based upon its categorization.

Green pages
> Technical information that describes the behaviors and supported functions of a Web service hosted by your business. This information includes pointers to the grouping information of Web services and where the Web services are located.

UDDI has several different uses, based on the perspective of who is using it. From a business analyst's perspective, UDDI is similar to an Internet search engine for business processes. Typical search engines, such as AskJeeves, organize and index URLs for Web sites. However, a business exporting a Web service needs to expose much more than a simple URL. A business analyst can browse one or more UDDI registries to view the different businesses that expose Web Services and the specifications of those services. However, business users probably won't browse a UDDI registry directly, since the information stored within it is not necessarily reader friendly. A series of marketplaces and business search portals could crop up to provide business analysts with a more user-oriented approach to browsing the services and businesses hosted in a UDDI registry.

Software developers use the UDDI Programmer's API to publish services (i.e., put information about them in the registry) and query the registry to discover services matching various criteria. Even though the API provided by UDDI allows random searching for businesses, it's not feasible for a program to select new business partners dynamically. Realistically, it's more likely that business analysts with specific knowledge of the problem at hand will use UDDI portals to discover potentially interesting services and partners, and technologists will write programs to use the services from companies that have already been discovered.

Both business analysts and software developers can publish new business entities and services. Business analysts can use portals attached directly to a particular UDDI server or to a more general search portal that supports UDDI.

The UDDI project also defines a set of XML Schema definitions that describe the data formats used by the various specification APIs. These documents are all available for download at http://www.uddi.org. The UDDI project releases their specifications in unison. The current version of all specification groups is version 2.0. The specifications include:

- UDDI replication—which describes the data replication processes and interfaces to which a registry operator must conform.
- UDDI operators—which outlines the behavior and operational parameters.
- UDDI Programmer's API—which defines a set of functions that all UDDI registries support for inquiring about services hosted.
- UDDI data structures—which covers the specifics of the XML structures contained within the SOAP messages defined by the UDDI Programmer's API.

The UDDI XML API schema is not contained in a specification; rather, it is stored as an XML Schema document that defines the structure and data types of the UDDI data structures.

Creating ASP.NET Web Services

Using the .NET Framework we will present a simple "Hello, World" service using HTTP, SOAP, WSDL, and several other technologies that form the basis for Web Services. Microsoft's Visual Studio provides a simple "Hello, World" service example within Visual C# sample code which requires just a few simple steps to execute.

In the following sections, we'll create a simple Web service in the "Hello, World" tradition. We'll see how to use ASP.NET to create a working Web service (with either a text editor or with VS.NET) and learn about the basic technologies behind .NET Web Services.

Creating "Hello, World" Web Service with Inline Code

While Visual Studio .NET provides a feature-rich integrated development environment for .NET development, it's not required to create .NET Web Services. Applications can also be created using a simple text editor, such as Notepad and the command-line tools that ship with the .NET Framework SDK.

We must place all of our code in one or more text files. Assign each the file extension .asmx and place them in an Internet Information Server (IIS) folder on a server that has the .NET Framework installed. Once you save the code to a folder served by the IIS Web server, it's ready to run. When running IIS locally we must save the file to a location on your local drive (e.g., c:\inetpub\wwwroot\). When using a remote server we might have to use File Transfer Protocol (FTP).

Once a text editor and file location have been selected, it's time to write the code.

Example 5-1 lists the code for a C# version of the "Hello, World" application; this version delivers its familiar message over the Web through an exposed method called HelloWorld(). To identify the class and method as a Web Service to the compiler, this code uses some special notations. It also includes an ASP.NET directive.

To create a C# version of the HelloWorld() Web service, enter the code from Example 5-1 exactly as it appears in Listing 5-2, and save the file to the Web server under the c:\inetpub\wwwroot folder (or whatever folder is the Web root folder for your system) with the name HelloWorld.asmx.

Example 5-1. Listing 5-6. HelloWorld: C# Web Service.

```
<%@ WebService Language="C#"
Class="Example5-1.HelloWorldService" %>
using System.Web.Services;
namespace Example5-1
{
  public class HelloWorldService: WebService
  {
    [WebMethod]
    public string HelloWorld()
    {
```

```
        return "Hello World";
    }
  }
}
```

Example 5-1 begins with a WebService directive (similar to the page directive that begins most .aspx pages) and an ASP.NET statement declaring that the code that follows is a Web service:

```
<%@ WebService Language="C#" Class="Example5-1.HelloWorldSer vice" %>
```

The HelloWorld Web Service requires that we assign values to two WebService directive attributes: language and class. The required language attribute identifies the programming language—the class has been written in C#. The class attribute tells ASP.NET the name of the class to expose as a Web service.

Because a Web service application can comprise multiple classes, we must tell .NET which class to expose, a step analogous to declaring a Main() method to indicate the entry point of a .NET console application or component.

The next line in the example is a statement that tells the compiler to alias the System.Web.Services namespace to the local namespace. For C#, this directive is:

```
using System.Web.Services;
```

This directive allows us to refer to objects in the System.Web.Services namespace without having to fully qualify the request. An example is the next line, which is our class declaration. With the using statement, it looks as follows in C#:

```
using System.Web.Services;
public class HelloWorldService: WebService
```

Without the using statement, it would have to be written fully as:

```
public class HelloWorldService: System.Web.Services.WebService
```

Importing a namespace does not give us access to any of the additional namespaces that appear to be nested in that namespace. In other words, if we were to import the System.Web namespace, we would not be able to refer to the System.Web.Services.WebService class as Services.WebService. While a namespace like System.Web.Services may "appear" to be nested in the System.Web namespace, that is not the case. They are implemented as two different assemblies.

.NET allows us to put the classes of an application into a unique namespace. In C#, this is done with the namespace keyword and the following syntax:

```
namespace name
{
... type declaration ...
}
```

In Example 5-1, the HelloWorldService class is placed in the Example 5-1 namespace with the following statement:

```
namespace Example5-1
{...
}
```

Namespaces provide a means of grouping pieces of code that might be written and maintained by other developers. When the class definitions of your Web service exist within a namespace, we must specify the namespace along with the class name in our WebService directive as in Example 5-1:

```
<%@ WebService Language="C#" Class="Example5-1.HelloWorldService" %>
```

This line tells ASP.NET to look for the class HelloWorldService in the namespace Example 5-1.

Central to Example 5-1 is a class called HelloWorldService. This class is a subclass of System.Web.Services.WebService. By inheriting from the WebService class, a Web service gains direct access to the ASP.NET intrinsic objects, such as application and session.

While inheriting from the WebService class is a common approach for creating a .NET Web Service, it is by no means necessary. We can rewrite the previous examples without this inheritance. However, if you need access to the Application and Session objects without inheriting from WebService, we'll need to use the System.Web.HttpContext object explicitly.

The HelloWorldService class exposes a single method, the public method HelloWorld, which takes no arguments and returns a string containing the text "Hello World." To expose a method as a part of a Web service, we must include the WebMethod attribute, which tells the compiler to treat it as such. Any method marked with the WebMethod attribute must be defined as public. Class methods exposed as Web Services follow the same object-oriented rules as any other class, and therefore methods marked private, protected, or internal are not accessible and will return an error if we attempt to expose them using the WebMethod attribute.

This simple example has created a complete Web service out of an arbitrary method. We could just as easily have substituted a method that retrieves a record from a data store. Additionally, you could have used any of the languages supported by the .NET Framework in place of C#. By inheriting from the System.Web.Services.WebService class, we are able to take advantage of an API that insulates us from the underlying SOAP/XML message exchanges.

A namespace is a container for types such as classes, interfaces, structs, and enums. The source code for objects in a namespace does not have to be stored in the same file, but can instead span multiple files. When the set of source code constituting a namespace is compiled into a library, this library is called a managed DLL, or an assembly. Assemblies are the building blocks of .NET applications and the fundamental unit of deployment. They comprise a collection of types and resources that provide the CLR (Common Language Runtime) with the information it needs to be aware of type implementations. Their contents can be referenced and used by other applications using Visual Studio .NET or a .NET command-line compiler.

To put this Web service to work, just copy it to the Web server as you would any other resource. This ease of deployment is the main benefit of in-line coding. The biggest drawback is that your presentation code and business logic are lumped into the same file. Visual Studio .NET can be used to create and deploy this Web service without stepping outside its Integrated Development Environment (IDE) by using the so-called code-behind approach.

Creating "Hello, World" Web Service with VS.NET (in 10 steps)

Microsoft's Visual Studio .NET (VS.NET) provides features to aid in creating complex Web services. This section takes you through the process of creating the "Hello World" Web service using VS.NET.

To make use of the automation in VS.NET, you must first configure it to communicate with your Web server. You can use either FrontPage Extensions or Universal Naming Convention (UNC) file shares. To keep things simple, we'll assume you have installed Microsoft's Internet Information Server 5.0 (IIS) on your local workstation.

FrontPage Extensions can be installed as a part of IIS.

Step 1: Preparing to use the MS Internet Information Server

Once you've installed FrontPage Server Extensions on your local workstation, you can reach the Administrative Tools and the IIS Manager through the Control Panel for Windows XP. Figure 5-1 shows IIS Manager with the server running the local host.

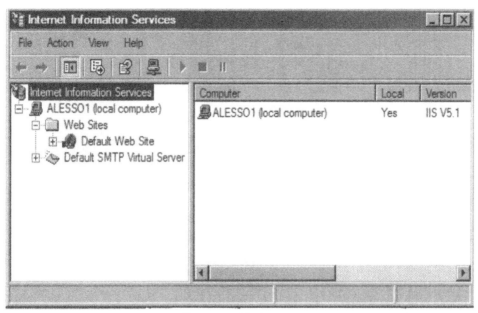

Figure 5-1. IIS Manager.

An ASP.NET Web service consists of a collection of resources (.asmx Web Services, global. asax, configuration information, and compiled components stored in the \bin directory) that run as a IIS virtual application. IIS allows you to divide an instance of a Web server into multiple separate virtual applications. Each of these virtual applications has its own set of application mappings, debugging options, and configuration options. When you create a Web service project using VS.NET, this virtual application configuration is done automatically.

Step 2: Preparing a New Visual Studio Project

To create a new Web Service, start Visual Studio .NET and select the New Project button on the default Start page. You'll see the screen in Figure 5-2. A solution is the outermost container, containing zero or more projects.

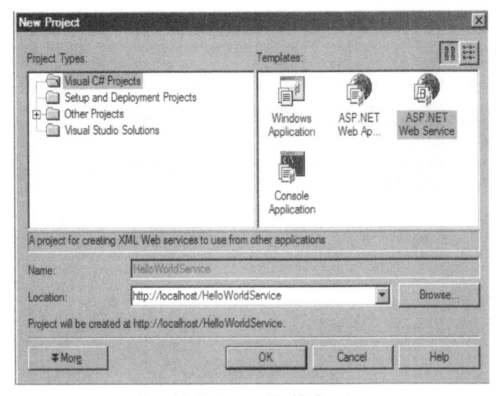

Figure 5-2. Creating a new Visual Studio project.

Here you have the option to create a variety of project types from a list of templates. Under Visual C# Projects, one template option creates an ASP.NET Web service, while our examples use the C# language, the same option is also available for a Visual Basic project or a Managed C++ project. In addition to selecting a project language and template, you must specify a project name and location. The location for the HelloWorldService should be the URL of the IIS Web server you just configured to work with FrontPage Extensions (e.g., http://localhost). For this example, we'll use the project name "HelloWorldService."

Once you click OK, the IDE (Integrated Development Environment) creates a new solution and project and automatically populates the project with several files. The IDE will also create a virtual folder under IIS with the same name as the project name, which, in this case, is HelloWorldService.

The contents of your new project are displayed in the Solution Explorer window, which should appear on the right side of the VS.NET IDE, as shown in Figure 5-3.

Figure 5-3. The Visual Studio .NET Solution Explorer.

When you create a new project without specifying the name of an existing solution, VS.NET creates a new solution whose name is the same as the one you chose for your project. In Figure 5-3, a solution named HelloWorldService has been created; it contains one project, also called HelloWorldService.

Visual Studio .NET also automatically creates several assembly references and files (see Figure 5-3). In this example, VS.NET has included assembly references to the System, System. Data, System.Web, System.Web.Services, and System.XML namespaces.

The five other files that appear in Figure 5-3 are AssemblyInfo.cs, Global.asax, HelloWorldService.vsdisco, Service1.asmx, and Web.config. The only file you really need to create the Web Service is the .asmx file. The four other files provide additional features and functionality that will help you as you build more complex services. Each of these is described as follows.

- AssemblyInfo.cs—An information file that provides the compiler with metadata (name, version, etc.) about the assemblies in the project.
- Global.asax file—Customizable file to handle application-level events (e.g., Application_OnStart).

- HelloWorldService.vsdisco—An XML file used for dynamic discovery of Web Services.
- Web.config—An XML file containing configuration information for the application.

The most important file in our example is the sample service page named Service1.asmx. By double-clicking it, Visual Studio .NET displays a blank design page. If we were dealing with an .aspx ASP.NET Web application, this design page could be used to design the user interface for the page, but since we're developing an .asmx Web service that will be consumed by a machine rather than a person, this design view is not as useful to us.

To see .asmx.cs select Show All Files from the Project menu tab. The Solution Explorer view will change to look like Figure 5-3.

This new view displays all of the files associated with the HelloWorldService project. Notice that the Service1.asmx file now has a tree expander icon to the left of it. Click on the icon, and you'll see another file beneath the Service1.asmx file called Service1.asmx.cs. Elsewhere, you'll also notice a folder called \bin, which is used to store the project's compiled assemblies generated by Visual Studio .NET.

Step 3: Create a new ASP.NET Web Service Project

When you create a new ASP.NET Web Service project, Visual Studio .NET generates boilerplate code as well. The contents of the source file HelloWorldService.asmx.cs should resemble Figure 5-4.

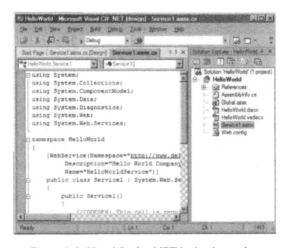

Figure 5-4. Visual Studio .NET boilerplate code.

144

This code (Figure 5-4) begins by importing several namespaces generally required for Web Services and automatically generating namespace and class definitions. In this example, the namespace and class definitions are HelloWorldService and Service1, respectively.

The namespace definition is generated based on the project name. The service name is always autogenerated as Service1. Change this to HelloWorldService. Your service will run just fine if the names don't match up, but keeping the names consistent can help make managing your service easier.

Example 5-1 (continued). **Listing 5-7.** C# Source Code for HelloWorld.

```csharp
using System;
using System.Web;
using System.Web.Services;

namespace Example5-1
{
  public class HelloWorldService : System.Web.Services.
WebService
  {
    public HelloWorldService() {}
    // WEB SERVICE EXAMPLE
    // The HelloWorld() example service returns the
      string Hello World
    // To build, uncomment the following lines, then
      save and build the project
    // To test this Web Service, press F5

    //[WebMethod]
    //public string HelloWorld()
    //{
    //return "Hello World";
    //}
  }
}
```

This code (Listing 5-7) should look familiar since it is nearly identical to the code shown earlier in Example 5-1. All you need to do to make it look like the earlier example is remove the comments in front of the HelloWorld() method and [WebMethod] attribute. Notice, however, that the WebService directive that was present in the in-line code example is missing:

```
<%@ WebService Language="C#" Class="Example5-1.HelloWorldService" %>
```

Recall that this directive is required to tell the compiler which class file to use as the entry point for the Web service. So where is it? When you wrote the inline code Listing 5-1 example, you included both the directive and the source code for the HelloWorld class in the same file. By contrast, when Visual Studio .NET creates Web Service code, it separates the WebService directive and the source code using an approach known to ASP.NET developers as code-behind.

The code-behind approach to programming Web Services involves separating the WebService directive from the supporting C# code. In this model, the .asmx page contains only one line, the WebService directive, while the supporting source code is placed on its own page, which, in the case of C#, has the file extension .asmx.cs, as in the preceding example. This page must be compiled into an assembly and placed in the \bin directory of your Web service before the service can be used. Visual Studio .NET takes care of this process for you automatically.

When you send a request to your Web service for the first time, ASP.NET reads the Web-Service directive to find out the name of the class file containing its supporting logic. ASP.NET knows to look for the compiled class in an assembly in the \bin directory of the project. If there are multiple assemblies in the \bin directory, ASP.NET will look through each of them until it finds the appropriate class.

One of the advantages of storing your code in a compiled form is that source code is not left on your production Web servers. The disadvantage to using the code-behind model is that deployment requires an additional step—compiling the source code. Because Visual Studio .NET uses the code-behind model, simply posting the source pages to the server as in the in-line example will not work. If you do so, you will get an error when you try to access the service. Instead, it's necessary to save your .asmx page to the server and compile your source code, saving it to the project's \bin directory. VS.NET automates this process for you through its build feature. Once your application is complete, select Build Solution from the Build menu and VS.NET will compile your Web service and transfer the .asmx page and associated compiled assembly to the Web server for you.

Step 4: The HelloWorldService

Unlike Active Server Pages, Web Services are not designed to be viewed in a browser. Instead, Web Services are consumed by a client application using protocols such as HTTP GET, HTTP POST, SMTP, or SOAP over HTTP. Some of these protocols, such as SOAP, are more appropriate for server-to-server communication, while others, such as HTTP GET, are more frequently associated with the model of traditional Web-page access.

A Web service that uses HTTP GET as a transport protocol can be accessed in much the same way as a regular Web page. All that is necessary to access such a page is to point a Web browser to the service endpoint. In our example, the endpoint is an .asmx page. But how do you know which protocols HelloWorldService will support, since there is no mention of HTTP or SOAP in the example code? The answer is that, by default, all .NET Web Services try to support HTTP GET, HTTP POST, and SOAP. We say "try," because in many cases the Web service may be too complex for HTTP GET support. Additionally, because Web services are applications that expose functionality to Web-service clients, and as a result have no required graphical user interface, .NET provides a pre-established Web service test page that is displayed when you point your browser to an .asmx page. If you open a browser and type in the URL of the .asmx Web service you just created, you'll see the IE test page shown in Figure 5-5.

Figure 5-5. HelloWorldService test page.

Step 5: HelloWorldService Test Page

The page in Figure 5-5 is generated by the .NET HTTP runtime each time it receives a request for an .asmx page. The page template is itself an ASP.NET .aspx page named DefaultWsdlHelp-Generator.aspx and is stored in the \WINNT\Microsoft.NET\Framework\[version]\Config directory on the server that hosts the Web service.

The test page displays the HelloWorldService service name along with the HelloWorld() method and a link to the service description. The service name and any additional information about this service are retrieved through a process called reflection, which uses the System. Reflection namespace to reveal information about existing types via metadata.

The runtime also automatically creates a service description from the .asmx page, an XML document that conforms to WSDL. If you click the service description link, you'll see the WSDL page. This page can also be viewed in a browser by appending WSDL to the page URL, as in HelloWorldService.cs.asmx?WSDL. The service description for our service is shown in Figure 5-6.

Figure 5-6. HelloWorldService description.

You can see that the WSDL document includes information about the service namespaces, protocols supported, data types used, and Web methods exposed in an XML-based format. This type of information is particularly important for an application looking to use our service.

The WSDL specification is important for the various Web service development platforms. Web-service interoperability and development platforms must all abide by the same version of WSDL as well as the same version of SOAP if they are to work together. The .NET framework currently implements SOAP 1.1.

Getting back to the service test page: if you mouse over the HelloWorld link, you'll see the destination URL:

http://localhost/HelloWorldService.cs.asmx?op=HelloWorld

Step 6: Exercising the HelloWorld Web Method of the Web Service

By clicking this link, you will call the .asmx page, passing a parameter called op (standing for operation) along with the name of the service. This action is the same as calling the HelloWorld Web method of the Web service using HTTP GET. The output page is shown in Figure 5-7.

Figure 5-7. HelloWorldService Invocation Page.

Here you'll see the name of the service and method along with a button to test the service. Through reflection, the logic in the (DefaultWsdlHelpGenerator.aspx test) page is able to determine the signature of our HelloWorld method. Because our Web method takes no arguments, the page need only provide a button for invocation. If our method had a different signature—for example, if it reads a string of text—the .aspx help page would also provide a text box to capture this string and pass it, using HTTP GET, to the Web method when the form was submitted. This text box method works fine for simple data type arguments, but if the Web method were to require an object, this approach would not work.

Beneath the Invoke button, there are also sample service interactions for SOAP, HTTP GET, and HTTP POST.

```
<form action='http://localhost/HelloWorldService/
HelloWorldService.cs.asmx/HelloWorld'  method="GET">

. . .
</form>
```

You can invoke the Web method using the IE test page by opening a Web browser and navigating to the service's URL. You will see a page listing the service's operation, which should be HelloWorld. Click the HelloWorld operation to navigate to the Web method invocation page. This is a page that allows you to test the operation by clicking a button labeled Invoke. Click the button to invoke the service.

Invoking the example service produces the results shown in Figure 5-8.

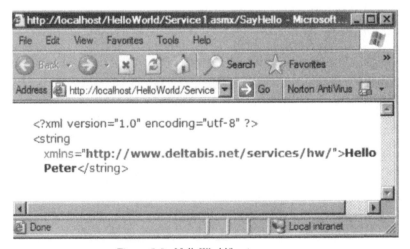

Figure 5-8. HelloWorldService output.

Had you used SOAP to access the service, you would have received a message in the SOAP format; however, since IE isn't designed to either write or read SOAP messages by itself, you're limited to using HTTP GET and HTTP POST.

The response document begins with the following XML declaration:

```
<?xml version="1.0" encoding="utf-8" ?>
```

which identifies the document as an XML document and identifies the encoding of the document to be UTF-8 Unicode. While the encoding type may vary, all XML processors are required to support UTF-8 and UTF-16 Unicode encodings.

The first and only element in the output document is an element called string, which contains the output of our method and has one attribute called xmlns:

xmlns="http://tempuri.org"

This namespace declaration specifies that all unprefixed elements in this document come from the namespace tempuri.org.

One of the features missing from our HelloWorld Web service is information about what it does. To tell a client about the functionality provided by our service, we need a way to document it. .NET provides an attribute for this purpose, WebServiceattribute (a member of the System. Web.Services namespace), which you can use to let clients know where to find information about a Web service. As with other attribute types, the WebServiceAttribute class inherits from System.Attribute. For convenience, the compiler will let you omit the attribute part of the class name in most usage contexts, allowing you to use just WebService instead (not to be confused with the WebService directive in an .asmx page). For simplicity, we'll leave off the attribute part throughout this text as well. The WebService attribute has two properties;

1. Namespace—Sets the XML namespace for the service.
2. Description—Adds a text/HTML description of the service that becomes part of the service description (WSDL) document.

As discussed earlier, XML namespaces are important in the XML world for uniquely identifying the elements and attributes of an XML document. XML namespaces have nothing to do with the .NET's namespaces, which are used to organize classes.

DISCO

So far, we have known where to look for the files and Web Services documents. More commonly, we won't know the exact URL or WDSL document of the Web service we desire.

151

Microsoft created a simple solution for single servers using DISCO documents. DISCO documents allow a client to discover the Web Service offered by a given Web server. You simply create a DISCO file and place it on the virtual root of the Web service. Visual Studio .NET automatically creates a DISCO file for you.

Step 7: Referencing HelloWorld Web Service

Microsoft's VS.NET provides features to aid you in creating complex Web Services. This section takes you through the process of creating the client application for the "Hello, World" service using Visual Studio .NET.

Client Application for "Hello, World" Web Service

To consume the service you created in the last six steps, you need to use the Web Services Description Language command-line tool (WSDL.exe) included in the SDK to create a proxy class that is similar to the class defined in the .asmx file. (It will contain only the WebMethod methods.) Then, you compile your code with this proxy class included.

WSDL.exe accepts a variety of command-line options, however to create a proxy only one option is required: the URI to the WSDL. In this example, we are passing a few extra options that specify the preferred language, namespace, and output location for the proxy. We are also compiling against a previously saved WSDL file instead of the URI to the service itself.

Once the proxy class exists, you can create objects based on it. Each method call made with the object then goes out to the URI of the XML Web service (usually as a SOAP request).

Building Web Service Clients Using the .NET Framework

Clients communicate with Web Services using standard Web protocols, using XML-encoded messages to send and receive messages between themselves. This makes it possible for client applications running on any platform to access Web Services as long as they use standard Web protocols and understand the XML-encoded messages. There are three protocols that Web clients can use to communicate with Web Services namely, HTTP GET, HTTP POST, and SOAP.

The various steps that are involved in creating a Web-service client using C# and the .NET framework are as follows:

1. Generate a proxy for the Web Service.
2. Compile the proxy as a DLL library.
3. Create a Visual C#—Console Application Project.

4. Develop the client.cs class file.

5. Build the project files.

Step 8: Generate a Proxy Class for the Web Service

The .NET SDK simplifies the process of creating Web-service clients by providing the WSDL (wsdl.exe) utility. This utility generates proxy source code for an existing Web service, just as IDL compilers generate DCOM proxies for DCOM components. The only difference between IDL and WSDL is that WSDL is a language that describes the interface of a software component that is XML-based.

The above command creates a proxy for the OIDServer Web Service from the WSDL document obtained from the URL

http://localhost/OIDServer/OIDServer.asmx?WSDL. The proxy uses SOAP as its protocol to talk to the Web Service and is generated as a C# source file which is shown in Listing 5-4.

Step 9: Create a Visual C#—Console Application Project

In Visual Studio, we create a simple Web client form made of two buttons, a text box and two labels (see Figure 5-9). In addition, we reference the Web service "Hello, World" and establish a relationship between the client and the Web service.

Figure 5-9. Hello, World client interface.

Step 10: Develop the Client.cs Class File

Create a new Visual C# ASP.NET Web service project. Create a reference to the OIDServer. dll library.

Listing 5-8 presents the C# code for the Hello World Client Interface that is shown in Figure 5-9.

Listing 5-8. C# Code for Hello World Client Interface.

```csharp
using System;
using System.Drawing;
using System.Collections;
using System.ComponentModel;
using System.Windows.Forms;
using System.Data;
namespace HelloWorldServiceClient
{
    public class Form1 : System.Windows.Forms.Form
    {
        private System.Windows.Forms.Button button1;
        private System.Windows.Forms.Label label1;
        private System.Windows.Forms.PictureBox pictureBox1;
        private System.Windows.Forms.Button button2;
        private System.Windows.Forms.TextBox textBox1;
        private System.Windows.Forms.Label label2;
        private System.ComponentModel.Container components = null;

        public Form1()
        {
            InitializeComponent();
        }
        protected override void Dispose( bool disposing )
        {
            if( disposing )
            {
                if (components != null)
```

```
                {
                        components.Dispose();
                }
        }
        base.Dispose( disposing );
}
[STAThread]
static void Main()
{
        Application.Run(new Form1());
}
private void button1_Click(object sender,
        System.EventArgs e)
{
        HelloWorldServiceClient.localhost.
            HelloWorldService ws = new
            HelloWorldServiceClient.
            localhost.HelloWorldService();
        MessageBox.Show(
            ws.HelloWorld(textBox1.Text + "\r
            \n" + "\r\n" + "Best Wishes,"
            + "\r\n" + "\r\n" + "From Your
            Web Server"));
}
private void button2_Click(object sender,
    System.EventArgs e)
{
        this.Close();
}
}
```

Figure 5-10 shows the Hello, World client after it is started. We enter the name "Peter" and then we click the button "Start Web Service." After the client communicates with the IIS server to connect to and invoke the Web service, Hello, World, a response message box is placed on the screen that says, "Hello Peter..." providing the Web service execution and response.

Figure 5-10. Hello, World service execution and response.

Comparing .NET and J2EE

The .NET platform has an array of technologies under the Microsoft umbrella as an alternative to J2EE and CORBA. Table 5-3 lists the various characteristics, computer codes and features of J2EE and .NET and comments on their differences. Even with the J2EE and .NET differences, Web services still provide the advantage of easy integration. We can illustrate this by considering a B2B scenario. Prior to Web Services, consider Company A that was built with Microsoft technology and wished to connect to Company B built with Java servlets. The integration process would be difficult and further complicated when Company A subsequently wants to connect to Company C built on COBRA/C++. The second connection would require a whole new lengthy integration effort.

With Web Services using SOAP, the process of integrating Companies A, B, and C would be reduced by an order of magnitude. SOAP is an XML technology that describes remote procedure calls (RPC) similar to Java Remote Method Invocation (RMI), but is platform and language independent. Thus a C++ program can execute methods from a Java platform, running on the other side of the world.

As a result, the potential of Web Services presents countless possibilities. For example, consider adding validated standardized AI methods and procedures available from AI servers or AI portals (such as CYC), as Web Services. Remote application programs could call these validated successful AI methods and procedures for their own application's execution.

All vendors of Enterprise Information Portal (EIP) capabilities describe their services as intelligent, but this is currently met with skepticism since the level of training to install, implement, maintain, and operate the varied services is so extensive. What AI applications could be included through Web Services to improve intelligent services? If we remain reluctant to speak of today's most powerful Web applications as intelligent, what will it take to change that?

J2EE	Microsoft.NET	Comments
Java	C# Programming Language	C# and Java both derive from C and C++. C# borrows some of the component concepts from JavaBeans (properties/ attributes, events, etc.), and adds some of its own (like metadata tags). Java runs on any platform with a Java VM. C# only runs in Windows for now.
Java core API	.NET Common Components	High-level .NET components will include support for distributed access using XML and SOAP.
Java Virtual Machine and CORBA IDL and ORB	IL Common Language Runtime	.NET common language runtime allows code in multiple languages to use a shared set of components on Windows. Java's Virtual Machine spec allows Java bytecodes to run on any platform with a compliant JVM.

Table 5-3. Comparison of J2EE and .NET.

J2EE	Microsoft.NET	Comments
Java ServerPages (JSP)	Active Server Pages+ (ASP+)	ASP+ uses Visual Basic, C#, for code snippets, compiled into native code through the common language runtime. SPs use Java code (snippet, or JavaBean references), compiled into Java byte codes.
JJDBC, EJB, JMS, and Java XML Libraries (XML4J, JAXP)	ADO+ and SOAP-based Web Services	ADO+ is built on an XML data interchange on top of HTTP (AKA, SOAP). .NET's Web Services assume SOAP messaging models. EJB, JDBC leave the data interchange protocol at the developer's discretion, and operate on top of HTTP, RMI/JRMP, or IIOP.

Table 5-3 (continued). Comparison of J2EE and .NET.

Web Services Capabilities and Limitations

The original concept of distributed objects was intended to develop a Web architecture that would let applications plug into an "application bus" and call a service. Based on object-oriented units, it would call on specialized software components. To actually succeed in developing component technology standards, it was necessary to find a minimal common ground. XML and HTTP seem to have been able to offer just the right minimal technology.

It took unprecedented vendor cooperation and commitment on the design of the core standards (SOAP, WSDL, and UDDI) to make Web Services happen.

Today, developers can build a SOAP wrapper around their payroll systems and in effect build their own protocol. Web-service developers must decide how to group their logical objects into services. They must create some technique to correlate messages sent to the service with particular objects. For each message they send they must also choose an XML representation for the message.

Today's tools make it seem easy by removing or hiding many options necessary to actually make these new protocols succeed. Visual Studio .NET is a widespread Web Services creation toolkit that makes Web-service construction easy. A developer takes an existing class, clicks a few buttons, and has a Web service.

The problem is that this technique obviates any advantages that Web Services were to provide over DCOM and CORBA. In particular, Web Services were supposed to more cleanly separate a service's interface from its implementation. This aspect of Web Services, termed loose binding, requires a thorough understanding of XML. Loose binding allows implementations to evolve while the public interface is static. In order to make Web Services easy, the tool vendors ripped out this benefit.

Corporations that use Web Services technologies to invent new protocols may get poor economies of scale.

Pitfalls of Web Services

Every technology has its faults. Although Web Services do a great job at solving certain problems, they bring along issues of their own. Some of these pitfalls are inherent to the technological foundations upon which Web Services are based, and others are based on the specifications themselves. It is important to know the issues:

- Availability—The Web has never been 100% available. It follows that Web services, which use the same infrastructure will not be 100% available either. Even if the server is up and running, the required ISP might not be.
- Matching Requirements—Any general service will run into specialized requirements. Some customers might require the one extra little feature that nobody else needs. Web Services, however, are envisioned as a "one size fits many customers" technology.
- Immutable Interfaces—If you invest in creating a Web service for your customers, you have to avoid changing any of the methods that you provide and the parameters that your customers expect. You can create new methods and add them to the service, but if you change existing ones, your customers' programs will break.
- Guaranteed Execution—The whole idea behind having a computer program instead of doing a job by hand is that the program can run unattended. HTTP is not a reliable protocol in that it doesn't guarantee delivery or a response.

Performance Issues

Web Services rely on HTTP—the same communication protocol upon which Web pages are requested and delivered. HTTP was designed to enable one server to handle hundreds of requests quickly by not maintaining a long-term stateful connection between the clients and the server. Instead, HTTP initiates a fresh connection with the server and maintains it only as long as it needs to transfer the data. This tends to make HTTP very transactional in nature.

Although the HTTP communication transaction enables the server side to handle many clients, it also means time is wasted creating and terminating connections. Other technologies—such as DCOM, CORBA, and RMI—don't have this problem because they maintain the connection throughout the application lifecycle.

Lack of Standards

Another set of issues associated with Web Services deals with incomplete standards. If the guiding principle of Web Services is to create an open standardized interchange system for remote program execution, the utilization of any vendor-specific solutions should be avoided. The current Web Services specifications and standards are lacking in the following areas:

- Security and Privacy—Anything sent over the Internet can be viewed by others. At present, the only approved option for sending sensitive information to Web Services is a Secure Socket Layer (SSL) program. SSL over HTTP is sometimes called HTTPS. The disadvantage is that SSL is slower than unencrypted HTTP transactions and is therefore unsuited for large data transfers. In addition, SSL is much more secure than most sales statistics need. Such a transaction shouldn't ordinarily be sent as clear text though. SSL encrypts the entire data stream, not just the sensitive parts.
- Authentication—Authentication answers the question, "Who is contacting me?" At present, the standards ignore this issue and delegate it to the Web Services container. This causes proprietary solutions to be created and breaks down the promise of portability.
- Non-repudiation—Provides solid proof that communication took place. This is also delegated to the Web Services container.
- Transaction—Many activities that would be well suited to Web Services are very complex. They involve dozens of smaller actions that must either be all complete or all rolled back.
- Billing and Contracts—To charge for the use of the service, a way for pricing contracts to be negotiated and maintained needs to be created. The current specifications provide

for service discovery, but do not contain a mechanism for handling pricing for the service or performing automatic billing for the use of the service.

- Provisioning—This is the adding of valid user accounts to a system to allow users to access the service. Currently, there is no agreed upon standard way to do this. The service provider and consumer need a mechanism to exchange provisioning information, and the service provider must know who it trusts as a source of that user information.
- Scalability—Because it is possible to expose existing component systems such as Enterprise Java Beans as Web services, it should be possible to leverage the load-balancing and other scalability mechanisms that already exist. But are there unforeseen stumbling blocks along this path? Does there need to be a new kind of "Web service" application server? Some vendors have come up with mechanisms to provide for load balancing, but no standard for it currently exists.
- Testing—Because of the new structure of Web Services and the decoupling of the clients from the server, testing of Web-service–based solutions can be challenging. Short of adopting a "try it and see if it works" mentality, there really are few ways to test a Web-service system.

The Next Generation of Discovery Services

The successful development of Web Services will greatly depend on the ability to automate as much of the Web Services process as possible under interoperable standards. Matchmaking, or service discovery, is one important aspect of Web Services' e-commerce interactions and advanced matchmaking services require rich and flexible metadata that are not supported by current industry standards, such as UDDI and ebXML.

The most advanced vision for the next generation of Web Services is the development of Web Services over Semantic Web Architecture. The Semantic Web initiative at W3C is generating technologies and tools that could fulfill the requirement for advanced matchmaking services (see Chapter 6). Support of Semantic Web related technologies includes tools, such as RDF and OWL-S.

To realize this vision of Semantic Web Services, a semantic markup of Web Services is required that makes them machine-understandable and use-apparent. This provides support for automated Web-service composition and interoperability. Integral to this effort will be three main functions: service discovery, execution, and composition and interoperation.

Automatic Web-service discovery involves automatically locating Web Services that provide a particular service with appropriate properties. With semantic markup, the Web-service discovery uses computer-interpretable semantic markup at the service Web sites, with a service registry (and/or ontology-based search engine) to automatically locate appropriate services.

Automatic Web-service execution involves a program or agent that automatically executes a discovered Web service. Semantic markup of Web Services should provide a computer-interpretable API for executing services. The markup then tells the agent what input is required, what information is returned, and how to execute the service automatically.

Automatic Web-service composition and interoperation is the automatic selection, composition, and interoperation of appropriate Web services to perform a task (see Chapter 10). The information necessary to select, compose, and respond to services is encoded at the service Web site. With a specification of the task's objectives Software can manipulate this markup to achieve the task automatically.

Of these three tasks, none is entirely realizable with today's Web, primarily because of a lack of a suitable markup language. Academic research on Web-service discovery is growing out of agent matchmaking research. Recent industrial efforts have focused primarily on improving Web-service discovery and aspects of service execution through initiatives, such as the Universal Description, Discovery, and Integration (UDDI) standard service registry and ebXML, an initiative of the United Nations and OASIS (Organization for the Advancement of Structured Information Standards) to standardize a framework for trading partner interchange.

Conclusion

In this chapter, we provided an introduction to XML-based Web Services and a survey compared .NET and J2EE. We discussed the basis of evolving today's XML-based Web Services into automated functions leading toward the Semantic Web. In addition, we detailed a simple "Hello, World" Web service example for .NET

Part Two

The Semantic Web

Chapter Six

The Semantic Web

Overview

In this chapter, we provide an introduction to the Semantic Web and discuss its background and potential. By laying out a road map for its likely development, we describe the essential stepping stones including: knowledge representation, inference, ontology, search and search engines. We also discuss several supporting semantic layers of the Markup Language Pyramid: Resource Description Framework (RDF) and Web Ontology Language (OWL).

In addition, we discuss using RDF and OWL for supporting software agents, Semantic Web Services, and semantic searches.

Background

Tim Berners-Lee invented the World Wide Web in 1989 and built the World Wide Web Consortium (W3C) team in 1992 to develop, extend, and standardize the Web. But he didn't stop there. He continued his research at MIT through Project Oxygen[1] and began conceptual development of the Semantic Web. The Semantic Web is intended to be a paradigm shift just as powerful as the original Web.

---

[1] MIT's Project Oxygen is developing technologies to enable pervasive, human-centered computing and information-technology services. Oxygen's user technologies include speech and vision technologies to enable communication with Oxygen as if interacting directly with another person, saving much time and effort. Automaton, individualized knowledge access, and collaboration technologies will be used to perform a wide variety of automated, cutting-edge tasks.

The goal of the Semantic Web is to provide a machine-readable intelligence that would come from hyperlinked vocabularies that Web authors would use to explicitly define their words and concepts. The idea allows software agents to analyze the Web on our behalf, making smart inferences that go beyond the simple linguistic analyses performed by today's search engines.

Why do we need such a system? Today, the data available within HTML Web pages is difficult to use on a large scale because there is no global schema. As a result, there is no system for publishing data in such a way to make it easily processed by machines. For example, just think of the data available on airplane schedules, baseball statistics, and consumer products. This information is presently available at numerous sites, but it is all in HTML format which means that using it has significant limitations.

The Semantic Web will bring structure and defined content to the Web, creating an environment where software agents can carry out sophisticated tasks for users. The first steps in weaving the Semantic Web on top of the existing Web are already underway. In the near future, these developments will provide new functionality as machines become better able to "understand" and process the data.

This presumes, however, that developers will annotate their Web data in advanced markup languages. To this point, the language-development process isn't finished. There is also ongoing debate about the logic and rules that will govern the complex syntax. The W3C is attempting to set new standards while leading a collaborative effort among scientists around the world. Berners-Lee has stated his vision that today's Web Services in conjunction with developing the Semantic Web, should become interoperable.

Skeptics, however, have called the Semantic Web a Utopian vision of academia. Some doubt it will take root within the commercial community. Despite these doubts, research and development projects are burgeoning throughout the world. And even though Semantic Web technologies are still developing, they have already shown tremendous potential in the areas of semantic groupware (see Chapter 13) and semantic search (see Chapter 15). Enough so, that the future of both the Semantic Web and Semantic Web Services (see Chapter 11) appears technically attractive.

The Semantic Web

The current Web is built on HTML, which describes how information is to be displayed and laid out on a Web page for humans to read. In effect, the Web has developed as a medium for humans without a focus on data that could be processed automatically. In addition, HTML is not capable of being directly exploited by information retrieval techniques. As a result, the

Web is restricted to manual keyword searches. For example, if we want to buy a product over the Internet, we must sit at a computer and search for most popular online stores containing appropriate categories of products.

We recognize that while computers are able to adeptly parse Web pages for layout and routine processing, they are unable to process the meaning of their content. XML may have enabled the exchange of data across the Web, but it says nothing about the meaning of that data. The Semantic Web will bring structure to the meaningful content of Web pages, where software agents roaming from page-to-page can readily carry out automated tasks.

We can say that the Semantic Web will become the abstract representation of data on the Web. And that it will be constructed over the Resource Description Framework (RDF) (see Chapter 7) and Web Ontology Language (OWL) (see Chapter 8). These languages are being developed by the W3C, with participations from academic researchers and industrial partners. Data can be defined and linked using RDF and OWL so that there is more effective discovery, automation, integration, and reuse across different applications.

Figure 6-1 illustrates how Semantic Web languages are built upon XML (see Chapter 4) and climbs up the Markup Language Pyramid to RDF (see Chapter 7) and OWL (see Chapter 8).

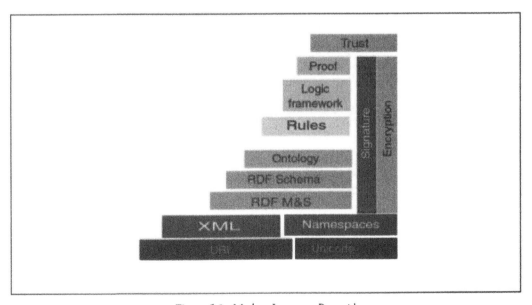

Figure 6-1. Markup Language Pyramid.

These languages are conceptually richer than HTML and allow representation of the meaning and structure of content (interrelationships between concepts). This makes Web content understandable by software agents, opening the way to a whole new generation of technologies for information processing, retrieval, and analysis.

Two important technologies for developing the Semantic Web are already in place: XML and RDF. XML lets everyone create their own tags. Scripts, or programs, can make use of these tags in sophisticated ways, but the script writer has to know how the page writer uses each tag. In short, XML allows users to add arbitrary structure to their documents, but says nothing about what the structure means.

If a developer publishes data in XML on the Web, it doesn't require much more effort to take the extra step and publish the data in RDF. By creating ontologies to describe data, intelligent applications won't have to spend time translating various XML schemas.

In a closed environment, Semantic Web specifications have already been used to accomplish many tasks, such as data interoperability for business-to-business (B2B) transactions. Many companies have expended resources to translate their internal data syntax for their partners. As everyone migrates towards RDF and ontologies, interoperability will become more flexible to new demands.

Another example of applicability is that of digital asset management. Photography archives, digital music, and video are all applications that are looking to rely to a greater degree on metadata. The ability to see relationships between separate media resources as well as the composition of individual media resources is well served by increased metadata descriptions and enhanced vocabularies.

The concept of metadata has been around for years and has been employed in many software applications. The push to adopt a common specification will be widely welcomed.

For the Semantic Web to function, computers must have access to structured collections of information and sets of inference rules that they can use to conduct automated reasoning. AI researchers have studied such systems and produced today's Knowledge Representation (KR). KR is currently in a state comparable to that of hypertext before the advent of the Web. Knowledge Representation contains the seeds of important applications, but to fully realize its potential, it must be linked into a comprehensive global system.

The objective of the Semantic Web, therefore, is to provide a language that expresses both data and rules for reasoning as a Web-based knowledge representation.

Adding logic to the Web means using rules to make inferences and choosing a course of action. A combination of mathematical and engineering issues complicates this task (see Chapter 9). The logic must be powerful enough to describe complex properties of objects, but not so powerful that agents can be tricked by a paradox.

Intelligence Concepts

The concept of Machine Intelligence (MI) is fundamental to the Semantic Web. Machine Intelligence is often referred to in conjunction with the terms Machine Learning, Computational Intelligence, Soft-Computing, and Artificial Intelligence. Although these terms are often used interchangeably, they are different branches of study.

For example, Artificial Intelligence involves symbolic computation while Soft-Computing involves intensive numeric computation.

We can identify the following sub-branches of Machine Intelligence that relate to the Semantic Web:

- Knowledge Acquisition and Representation.
- Agent Systems.
- Ontology.

Although symbolic Artificial Intelligence is currently built and developed into Semantic Web data representation, there is no doubt that software tool vendors and software developers will incorporate the Soft-Computing paradigm as well. The benefit is creating adaptive software applications. This means that Soft-Computing applications may adapt to unforeseen input.

Knowledge Acquisition is the extraction of knowledge from various sources, while Knowledge Representation is the expression of knowledge in computer-tractable form that is used to help software-agents perform. A Knowledge Representation language includes Language Syntax (describes configurations that can constitute sentences) and Semantics (determines the facts and meaning based upon the sentences).

For the Semantic Web to function, computers must have access to structured collections of information. But, traditional knowledge-representation systems typically have been centralized, requiring everyone to share exactly the same definition of common concepts. As a result, central control is stifling, and increasing the size and scope of such a system rapidly becomes unmanageable. In an attempt to avoid problems, traditional knowledge-representation systems narrow their focus and use a limited set of rules for making inferences. These system limitations restrict the questions that can be asked reliably.

XML and the RDF are important technologies for developing the Semantic Web; they provide languages that express both data and rules for reasoning about the data from a knowledge-representation system. The meaning is expressed by RDF, which encodes it in sets of triples, each triple acting as a sentence with a subject, predicate, and object. These triples can be written using XML tags. As a result, an RDF document makes assertions about specific things.

Subject and object are each identified by a Universal Resource Identifier (URI), just as those used in a link on a Web page. The predicate is also identified by URIs, which enables anyone to define a new concept just by defining a URI for it somewhere on the Web. The triples of RDF form webs of information about related things. Because RDF uses URIs to encode this information in a document, the URIs ensure that concepts are not just words in a document, but are tied to a unique definition that everyone can find on the Web.

Search Algorithms

The basic technique of search (or state space search) refers to a broad class of methods that are encountered in many different AI applications; the technique is sometimes considered a universal problem-solving mechanism in AI. To solve a search problem, it is necessary to prescribe a set of possible or allowable states, a set of operators to change from one state to another, an initial state, a set of goal states, and additional information to help distinguish states according to their likeliness to lead to a target or goal state. The problem then becomes one of finding a sequence of operators leading from the initial state to one of the goal states.

Search algorithms can range from brute force methods (which use no prior knowledge of the problem domain, and are sometimes referred to as blind searches) to knowledge-intensive heuristic searches that use knowledge to guide the search toward a more efficient path to the goal state (see Chapters 9 and 15).

Search techniques include:

- **Brute force**
  1. Breadth-first.
  2. Depth-first.
  3. Depth-first iterative-deepening.
  4. Bi-directional.
- **Heuristic**
  1. Hill-climbing.
  2. Best-first.
  3. A*.
  4. Beam.
  5. Iterative-deepening-A*.

Brute force searches entail the systematic and complete search of the state space to identify and evaluate all possible paths from the initial state to the goal states. These searches can be breadth-first or depth-first. In a breadth-first search, each branch at each node in a search tree is evaluated, and the search works its way from the initial state to the final state considering all possibilities at each branch, a level at a time. In the depth-first search, a particular branch is followed all the way to a dead end (or to a successful goal state). Upon reaching the end of a path, the algorithm backs up and tries the next alternative path in a process called backtracking.

The depth-first iterative-deepening algorithm is a variation of the depth-first technique in which the depth-first method is implemented with a gradually increasing limit on the depth. This allows a search to be completed with a reduced memory requirement, and improves the performance where the objective is to find the shortest path to the target state.

The bi-directional search starts from both the initial and target states and performs a breadth-first search in both directions until a common state is found in the middle. The solution is found by combining the path from the initial state with the inverse of the path from the target state.

These brute force methods are useful for relatively simple problems, but as the complexity of the problem rises, the number of states to be considered can become prohibitive. For this reason, heuristic approaches are more appropriate to complex search problems where prior knowledge can be used to direct the search.

Heuristic approaches use knowledge of the domain to guide the choice of which nodes to expand next and thus avoid the need for a blind search of all possible states.

The hill-climbing approach is the simplest heuristic search; this method works by always moving in the direction of the locally steepest ascent toward the goal state. The biggest drawback of this approach is that the local maximum is not always the global maximum and the algorithm can get stuck at a local maximum thus failing to achieve the best results.

To overcome this drawback, the best-first approach maintains an open list of nodes that have been identified but not expanded. If a local maximum is encountered, the algorithm moves to the next best node from the open list for expansion. This approach, however, evaluates the next best node purely on the basis of its evaluation of ascent toward the goal without regard to the distance it lies from the initial state.

The A* technique goes one step further by evaluating the overall path from the initial state to the goal using the path to the present node combined with the ascent rates to the potential successor nodes. This technique tries to find the optimal path to the goal. A variation on this approach is the beam search in which the open list of nodes is limited to retain only the best nodes, and thereby reduce the memory requirement for the search. The iterative-deepening-A* approach is a further variation in which depth-first searches are completed, a branch at a time, until some threshold measure is exceeded for the branch, at which time it is truncated and the search backtracks to the most recently generated node.

A classic example of an AI-search application is computer chess. Over the years, computer chess-playing software has received considerable attention, and such programs are a commercial success for home PCs. In addition, most are aware of the highly visible contest between IBM's Deep Blue Supercomputer and the reigning World Chess Champion, Garry Kasparov in May 1997. Millions of chess and computing fans observed this event in real-time where, in a dramatic sixth game victory, Deep Blue beat Kasparov. This was the first time a computer has won a match with a current world champion under tournament conditions.

Computer chess programs generally make use of standardized opening sequences, and end game databases as a knowledge base to simplify these phases of the game. For the middle game, they examine large trees and perform deep searches with pruning to eliminate branches that are evaluated as clearly inferior and to select the most highly evaluated move.

We will explore semantic search in more detail in Chapter 15.

Thinking

The goal of the Semantic Web is to provide a machine-readable intelligence. But, whether AI programs actually think is a relatively unimportant question, because whether or not "smart" programs "think," they are already becoming useful.

Consider, for example, IBM's Deep Blue. In May 1997, IBM's Deep Blue Supercomputer played a defining match with the reigning World Chess Champion, Garry Kasparov. This was the first time a computer had won a complete match against the world's best human chess player. For almost 50 years, researchers in the field of AI had pursued just this milestone.

Playing chess has long been considered an intellectual activity, requiring skill and intelligence of a specialized form. As a result, chess attracted AI researchers.

The basic mechanism of Deep Blue is that the computer decides on a chess move by assessing all possible moves and responses. It can identify up to a depth of about 14 moves and value-rank the resulting game positions using an algorithm prepared in advance by a team of grand masters.

Did Deep Blue demonstrate intelligence or was it merely an example of computational brute force? Our understanding of how the mind of a brilliant player like Kasparov works is limited. But indubitably, his "thought" process was something very different than Deep Blue's. Arguably, Kasparov's brain works through the operation of each of its billions of neurons carrying out hundreds of tiny operations per second, none of which, in isolation, demonstrates intelligence.

One approach to AI is to implement methods using ideas of computer science and logic algebras. The algebra would establish the rules between functional relationships and sets of data structures. A fundamental set of instructions would allow operations including sequencing, branching and recursion within an accepted hierarchy. The preference of computer science has been to develop hierarchies that resolve recursive looping through logical methods. One of the great computer science controversies of the past five decades has been the role of GOTO-like statements. This has risen again in the context of Hyperlinking. Hyperlinking, like GOTO statements, can lead to unresolved conflict loops (see Chapter 12). Nevertheless, logic structures have always appealed to AI researchers as a natural entry point to demonstrate machine intelligence.

An alternative to logic methods is to use introspection methods, which observe and mimic human brains and behavior. In particular, pattern recognition seems intimately related to a sequence of unique images with a special linkage relationship. While Introspection, or heuristics, is an unreliable way of determining how humans think, when they work, Introspective methods can form effective and useful AI.

The success of Deep Blue and chess programming is important because it employs both logic and introspection AI methods. When the opinion is expressed that human grandmasters do not examine 200,000,000 move sequences per second, we should ask, "How do they know?" The answer is usually that human grandmasters are not aware of searching this number of positions, or that they are aware of searching a smaller number of sequences. But then again, as individuals, we are generally unaware of what actually does go on in our minds.

Much of the mental computation done by a chess player is invisible to both the player and to outside observers. Patterns in the position suggest what lines of play to look at, and the pattern recognition processes in the human mind seem to be invisible to that mind. However, the parts of the move tree that are examined are consciously accessible.

> Suppose most of the chess player's skill actually comes from an ability to compare the current position against images of 10,000 positions already studied. (There is some evidence that this is at least partly true.) We would call selecting the best position (or image) among the 10,000, insightful. Still, if the unconscious human version yields intelligent results, and the explicit algorithmic Deep Blue version yields essentially the same results, then couldn't the computer and its programming be called intelligent too?
>
> For now, the Web consists primarily of huge number of data nodes (containing texts, pictures, movies, sounds). The data nodes are connected through hyperlinks to form 'hyper-networks' can collectively represent complex ideas and concepts above the level of the individual data. However, the Web does not currently perform many sophisticated tasks with this data. The Web merely stores and retrieves information even after considering some of the "intelligent applications" in use today (including intelligent agents, EIP, and Web Services). So far, the Web does not have some of the vital ingredients it needs, such as a global database scheme, a global error-correcting feedback mechanism, a logic layer protocol, or universally accepted knowledge bases with inference engines. As a result, we may say that the Web continues to grow and evolve, but it does not learn.
>
> If the jury is still out on defining the Web as intelligent, (and may be for some time) we can still consider ways to change the Web to give it the capabilities to improve and become more useful (see Chapter 9).

Knowledge Representation and Inference

An important element of AI is the principle that intelligent behavior can be achieved through processing of symbol structures representing increments of knowledge. This has given rise to the development of knowledge-representation languages that permit the representation and manipulation of knowledge to deduce new facts. Thus, knowledge-representation languages must have a well-defined syntax and semantics system, while supporting inference.

First let's define the fundamental terms "data," "information," and "knowledge." An item of data is a fundamental element of an application. Data can be represented by population and labels. Information is an explicit association between data things. Associations are often functional in that they represent a function relating one set of things to another set of things. A rule is an explicit functional association from a set of information things to a resultant information thing. So, in this sense, a rule is knowledge.

Knowledge-based systems contain knowledge as well as information and data. The information and data can be modeled and implemented in a database. Knowledge-engineering methodologies address design and maintenance knowledge, as well as the data and information.

Logic is used as the formalism for programming languages and databases. It can also be used as a formalism to implement knowledge methodology. Any formalism that admits a declarative semantics and can be interpreted both as a programming language and database language is a knowledge language.

Three well-established techniques have been used for knowledge representation and inference: frames and semantic networks, logic based approaches, and rule based systems.

Frames and semantic networks also referred to as slot and filler structures, capture declarative information about related objects and concepts where there is a clear class hierarchy and where the principle of inheritance can be used to infer the characteristics of members of a subclass from those of the higher level class. The two forms of reasoning in this technique are matching (i.e., identification of objects having common properties), and property inheritance in which properties are inferred for a subclass. Because of limitations, frames and semantic networks are generally limited to representation and inference of relatively simple systems.

Logic-based approaches use logical formulas to represent more complex relationships among objects and attributes. Such approaches have well-defined syntax, semantics and proof theory. When knowledge is represented with logic formulas, the formal power of a logical theorem proof can be applied to derive new knowledge. However, the approach is inflexible and requires great precision in stating the logical relationships. In some cases, common-sense inferences and conclusions cannot be derived, and the approach may be inefficient, especially when dealing with issues that result in large combinations of objects or concepts.

Rule-based approaches are more flexible. They allow the representation of knowledge using sets of IF-THEN or other condition action rules. This approach is more procedural and less formal in its logic and as a result, reasoning can be controlled in a forward or backward chaining interpreter.

In each of these approaches, the knowledge-representation component (i.e., problem-specific rules and facts) is separate from the problem-solving and inference procedures.

Resource Description Framework (RDF)

The Semantic Web is built on syntaxes which use the Universal Resource Identifier (URI) to represent data in triples-based structures using Resource Description Framework (RDF) (see Chapter 7). A URI is a Web identifier, such as "http:" or "ftp:." The syntax of URIs is governed by the IETF, publishers of the general URI specification the W3C maintains a list of URI schemes.

In an RDF document, assertions are made about particular things having properties with certain values. This structure turns out to be a natural way to describe the vast majority of the data processed by machines. Subject, predicate, and object are each identified by a URI.

The RDF triplets form webs of information about related things. Because RDF uses URIs to encode this information in a document the URIs ensure that concepts are not just words in a document, but are tied to a unique definition. All the triples result in a directed graph whose nodes and arcs are all labeled with qualified URIs.

The RDF model is very simple and uniform. The only vocabulary is URIs which allow the use of the same URI as a node and as an arc label. This makes self-reference and reification possible, just as in natural languages. This is appreciable in a user-oriented context (like the Web), but is difficult to cope with in knowledge-based systems and inference engines.

Once information is in RDF form, data becomes easier to process. We illustrate an RDF document in Example 6-1. This piece of RDF basically says that a book has the title "e-Video: Producing Internet Video," and was written by "H. Peter Alesso."

Listing 6-1. Sample RDF /XML.

```
<rdf:RDF xmlns:rdf="http://www.w3.org/1999/02/22-rdf-
syntax-ns#"
    xmlns:dc="http://purl.org/dc/elements/1.1/"
    xmlns:foaf="http://xmlns.com/0.1/foaf/" >
    <rdf:Description rdf:about="">
        <dc:creator rdf:parseType="Resource">
            <foaf:name>H. Peter Alesso</foaf:name>
        </dc:creator>
        <dc:title>e-Video: Producing Internet Video</dc:
title>
    </rdf:Description>
</rdf:RDF>
```

The benefit of RDF is that the information maps directly and unambiguously to a decentralized model that differentiates the semantics of the application from any additional syntax. In addition, XML Schema restricts the syntax of XML applications and using it in conjunction with RDF may be useful for creating some datatypes.

The goal of RDF is to define a mechanism for describing resources that makes no assumptions about a particular application domain, nor defines the semantics of any application.

RDF models may be used to address and reuse components (software engineering), to handle problems of schema evolution (database), and to represent knowledge (Artificial Intelligence).

However, modeling metadata in a completely domain independent fashion is difficult to handle. How successful RDF will be in automating activities over the Web is an open question. However, if RDF could provide a standardized framework for most major Web sites and applications, it could bring significant improvements in automating Web-related activities and services (see Chapter 11). If some of the major sites on the Web incorporate semantic modeling through RDF, it could provide more sophisticated searching capabilities over these sites (see Chapter 15).

We will return to a detailed presentation of RDF in Chapter 7.

RDF Schema

The first "layer" of the Semantic Web is the simple data-typing model called a schema. A schema is simply a document that defines another document. It is a master checklist or grammar definition. The RDF Schema was designed to be a simple data-typing model for RDF. Using RDF Schema, we can say that "Desktop" is a type of "Computer," and that "Computer" is a sub class of "Machine". We can also create properties and classes, as well as, creating ranges and domains for properties.

All of the terms for RDF Schema start with namespace http://www.w3.org/2000/01/rdf-schema#.

The three most important RDF concepts are "Resource" (rdfs:Resource), "Class" (rdfs:Class), and "Property" (rdf:Property). These are all "classes," in that terms may belong to these classes. For example, all terms in RDF are types of resource. To declare that something is a "type" of something else, we just use the rdf:type property:

```
rdfs:Resource rdf:type rdfs:Class .
rdfs:Class rdf:type rdfs:Class .
rdf:Property rdf:type rdfs:Class .
rdf:type rdf:type rdf:Property .
```

This means "Resource is a type of Class, Class is a type of Class, Property is a type of Class, and type is a type of Property."

We will return to a detailed presentation of RDF Schema in Chapter 7.

Ontology

A program that wants to compare information across two databases has to know that two terms are being used to mean the same thing. Ideally, the program must have a way to discover common meanings for whatever databases it encounters. A solution to this problem is provided by the Semantic Web in the form of collections of information called ontologies. Artificial-intelligence and Web researchers use the term ontology for a document that defines the relations among terms. A typical ontology for the Web includes a taxonomy with a set of inference rules.

Ontology and Taxonomy

```
We can express an Ontology as:
    Ontology = < taxonomy, inference rules>
And we can express a taxonomy as:
    Taxonomy = < {classes}, {relations}>
```

The taxonomy defines classes of objects and relations among them. For example, an address may be defined as a type of location, and city codes may be defined to apply only to locations, and so on. Classes, subclasses, and relations among entities are important tools. We can express a large number of relations among entities by assigning properties to classes and allowing subclasses to inherit such properties.

Inference rules in ontologies supply further power. An ontology may express the rule "If a city code is associated with a state code, and an address uses that city code, then that address has the associated state code." A program could then readily deduce, for instance, that an MIT address, being in Cambridge, must be in Massachusetts, which is in the U.S., and therefore should be formatted to U.S. standards. The computer doesn't actually "understand" this, but it can manipulate the terms in a meaningful way.

The real power of the Semantic Web will be realized when people create many programs that collect Web content from diverse sources, process the information and exchange the results. The effectiveness of software agents will increase exponentially as more machine-readable Web content and automated services become available. The Semantic Web promotes this synergy—even agents that were not expressly designed to work together can transfer semantic data.

178

The Semantic Web will provide the foundations and the framework to make such technologies more feasible.

Web Ontology Language (OWL)

In 2003, the W3C began final unification of the disparate ontology efforts into a standardizing ontology called the Web Ontology Language (OWL). OWL is a vocabulary extension of RDF. OWL is currently evolving into the semantic markup language for publishing and sharing ontologies on the World Wide Web.

OWL facilitates greater machine readability of Web content than that supported by XML, RDF, and RDFS by providing additional vocabulary along with formal semantics.

OWL comes in several flavors as three increasingly-expressive sublanguages: OWL Lite, OWL DL, and OWL Full. By offering three flavors, OWL hopes to attract a broad following.

We will return to detailed presentation of OWL in Chapter 8.

Inference

A rule may describe a conclusion that one draws from a premise. A rule can be a statement processed by an engine or a machine that can make an inference from a given generic rule. The principle of "inference" derives new knowledge from knowledge that we already know. In a mathematical sense, querying is a form of inference and inference is one of the supporting principles of the Semantic Web.

For two applications to talk together and process XML data, they require that the two parties must first agree on a common syntax for their documents. After reengineering their documents with new syntax, the exchange can happen. However, using the RDF/XML model, two parties may communicate with different syntax using the concept of equivalencies. For example, in RDF/XML we could say "car" and specify that it is equivalent to "automobile."

We can see how the system could scale. Merging databases becomes recording in RDF that "car" in one database is equivalent to "automobile" in a second database.

Indeed, this is already possible with Semantic Web tools, such as a Python program called "Closed World Machine" or CWM.

Unfortunately, great levels of inference can only be provided using "First Order Predicate Logic," FOPL languages, and OWL is not entirely a FOPL language.

First-order Logic (FOL) is defined as a general-purpose representation language that is based on an ontological commitment to the existence of objects and relations. FOL makes it easy to state facts about categories, either by relating objects to the categories or by quantifying.

For FOPL languages, a predicate is a feature of the language which can make a statement about something, or to attribute a property to that thing.

Unlike propositional logics, in which specific propositional operators are identified and treated, predicate logic uses arbitrary names for predicates and relations which have no specific meaning until the logic is applied.

Though predicates are one of the features which distinguish first-order predicate logic from propositional logic, these are really the extra structure necessary to permit the study of quantifiers. The two important features of natural languages whose logic is captured in the predicate calculus are the terms "every" and "some" and their synonyms. Analogues in formal logic are referred to as the universal and existential quantifiers. These features of language refer to one or more individuals or things, which are not propositions and therefore force some kind of analysis of the structure of "atomic" propositions.

The simplest logic is *classical* or *Boolean*, first-order logic. The "classical" or "Boolean" signifies that propositions are either *true* or *false*.

First-order logic permits reasoning about the propositional and also about quantification ("all" or "some"). An elementary example of the inference is as follows:

1. All men are mortal.
2. John is a man.

The conclusion:

3. John is mortal.

Application of inference rules provides powerful logical deductions. With ontology pages on the Web, solutions to terminology problems begin to emerge. The definitions of terms and vocabularies or XML codes used on a Web page can be defined by pointers from a page to an ontology. Different ontologies need to provide equivalence relations (defining the same meaning for all vocabularies), otherwise there would be a conflict and confusion.

Software Agents

Many automated Web Services already exist without semantics, but other programs, such as agents have no way to locate one that will perform a specific function. This process, called service discovery, can happen only when there is a common language to describe a service in a way that lets other agents understand both the function offered and the way to take advantage of it. Services and agents can advertise their function by depositing descriptions in directories similar to the Yellow Pages.

There are some low-level, service-discovery schemes which are currently available. The Semantic Web is more flexible by comparison. The consumer and producer agents can reach a shared understanding by exchanging ontologies which provide the vocabulary needed for discussion. Agents can even bootstrap new reasoning capabilities when they discover new ontologies. Semantics also make it easier to take advantage of a service that only partially matches a request.

An intelligent agent is a computer system that is situated in some environment, that is capable of autonomous action and learning in its environment in order to meet its design objectives. Intelligent agents can have the following characteristics: reactivity—they perceive their environment, and respond, pro-active—they exhibit goal-directed behavior and social—they interact with other agents.

Real-time intelligent agent technology offers a powerful Web tool. Agents are able to act without the intervention of humans or other systems: they have control both over their own internal state and over their behavior. In complexity domains, agents must be prepared for the possibility of failure. This situation is called non-deterministic.

Normally, an agent will have a repertoire of actions available to it. This set of possible actions represents the agent's capability to modify its environments. Similarly, the action "purchase a house" will fail if insufficient funds are available to do so. Actions therefore have pre-conditions associated with them, which define the possible situations in which they can be applied.

The key problem facing an agent is that of deciding which of its actions it should perform to satisfy its design objectives. Agent architectures are really software architectures for decision-making systems that are embedded in an environment. The complexity of the decision-making process can be affected by a number of different environmental properties, such as:

- Accessible vs inaccessible.
- Deterministic vs non- deterministic.
- Episodic vs non-episodic.
- Static vs dynamic.
- Discrete vs continuous.

The most complex general class of environment is inaccessible, non-deterministic, non-episodic, dynamic, and continuous.

Trust and Proof

The next step in the architecture of the Semantic Web is trust and proof. If one person says that x is blue, and another says that x is not blue, will the Semantic Web face logical contradiction?

The answer is no, because applications on the Semantic Web generally depend upon context, and applications in the future will contain proof-checking mechanisms and digital signatures.

Figure 6-2 presents the W3C graphical view of the Semantic Web. It illustrates many of the aspects of the Web, Web Services, and developing semantics. Proof and trust are a significant element in the development of logic and semantics.

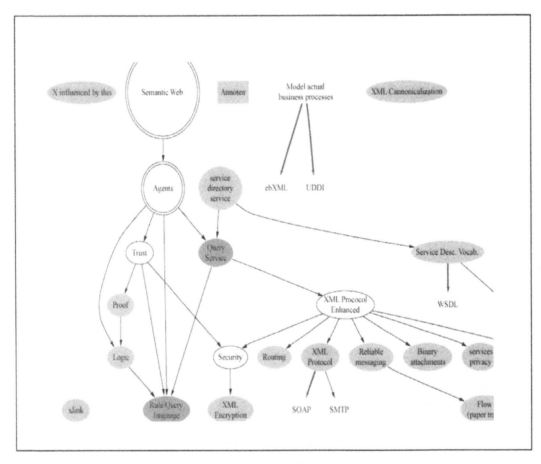

Figure 6-2. Graphical view of the Semantic Web.

Semantic Web Capabilities and Limitations

The Semantic Web promises to make Web content machine understandable, allowing agents and applications to access a variety of heterogeneous resources, processing and integrating the content, and producing added value for the user. The Semantic Web aims to provide an extra machine understandable layer, which will considerably simplify programming and maintenance effort for knowledge-based Web Services.

Current technology at research centers allow many of the functionalities the Semantic Web promises: software agents accessing and integrating content from distributed heterogeneous Web resources. However, these applications are really ad-hoc solutions using wrapper technology. A wrapper is a program that accesses an existing Website and extracts the needed information. Wrappers are screen scrapers in the sense that they parse the HTML source of a page, using heuristics to localize and extract the relevant information. Not surprisingly, wrappers have high construction and maintenance costs since much testing is needed to guarantee robust extraction and each time the Website changes, the wrapper has to be updated accordingly.

The main power of Semantic Web languages is that anyone can create one, simply by publishing RDF triplets with URIs. We have already seen that RDF Schema and OWL are very powerful languages.

One of the main challenges the Semantic Web community faces for the construction of innovative and knowledge-based Web Services is to reduce the programming effort while keeping the Web preparation task as small as possible.

The Semantic Web's success or failure will be determined by solving the following:

The availability of content.
Ontology availability, development, and evolution.
Scalability—Semantic Web content, storage, and search are scalable.
Multilinguality—information in several languages.
Visualization—Intuitive visualization of Semantic Web content.
Stability of Semantic Web languages.

Conclusion

In this chapter, we provided an introduction to the Semantic Web and discussed its background and potential. By laying out a roadmap for its likely development, we described the essential stepping stones including: knowledge representation, inference, ontology, and search. We

183

also discussed several supporting semantic layers of the Markup Language Pyramid Resource Description Framework (RDF) and Web Ontology Language (OWL).

In addition, we discussed using RDF and OWL for supporting software agents, Semantic Web Services, and semantic search.

Chapter Seven

Resource Description Framework (RDF)

Overview

It is often said that XML tags add meaning to documents. However, the meaning is only meaningful to humans. For example, given the following XML markup tags:

```
<book>
   < title>War and Peace<title>
</book>
```

a human might infer that "The book has the title *War and Peace*." This simple grammatical sentence is understood as a subject [book], a predicate [has title], and an object [*War and Peace*]. A machine, however, could not make this inference based upon the XML alone. We could, however, include an XSLT style sheet to transform the XML markup into the following string:

"The book has the title *War and Peace*."

Nevertheless, the computer would still see this as a simple string and take no action (such as checking to see related titles, prices, availability, etc.) based upon the information.

For machines to do more, we will have to go beyond the notion of a content data model to a "meaning" model. This is where Resource Description Framework (RDF) and metadata can provide new machine capabilities. RDF builds on XML terminology.

RDF constructs its own grammatical representation using the triple (subject, predicate, object) to represent information. RDF is built upon this very simple model, but the basic logic can support large-scale information management and processing. An RDF document delineates precise relationships between vocabulary items. The assertions in different RDF documents can be combined to provide far more information together than they contain separately. As a result, RDF provides a powerful and flexible query structure.

In this chapter, we provide a simple primer for RDF and RDF Schema. We include a discussion of RDF classes and properties, as well as RDF's capabilities and limitations. This will act as a supportive infrastructure for expanding our presentation of Web architecture with additional advanced markup, such as Web Ontology Language (OWL) (see Chapter 8).

Background

Though not as well-known as other W3C specifications, Resource Description Framework (RDF) is actually one of the older specifications. The earliest editors, Ora Lassila and Ralph Swick, established the foundation for RDF in 1997. They constructed RDF as a mechanism for working with metadata that promotes the interchange of data between automated processes. In 1999, they released the first recommendation. A candidate recommendation for RDF Schema was co-edited by Dan Brickley and R.V. Guha in 2000.

As efforts proceeded on RDF, discussions continued on the Semantic Web. Tim Berners-Lee's 2001 article in *Scientific America* outlined the Semantic Web as an ability to discover relevant information. The Semantic Web suggests that metadata can link information in a direct and useable way. To achieve this, the Semantic Web would use new Web languages based upon RDF which goes beyond XHTML's presentation capabilities or XML's data characterization.

Today, when we search for a Web site or a paper on a particular topic, we use search engines, such as Google, which do a good job of sorting through billions of possibilities. On specialized Websites, domain-specific search engines do even better; for example, a mathematician can find papers on "symplectic geometry" on a site devoted to theoretical mathematics. However, as science continues its exponential growth in complexity and scope, the need for more collaboration among scientists and disciplines requires information searching that is much more semantic capable. Imagine searching for papers across the Web on the topic of LaPlacean invariants (found under symplectic geometry). Clearly, this would be a difficult and time consuming task.

While there are many syntaxes you can use to store, transport, and search RDF/XML has emerged as the best. Because RDF requires modeling knowledge, it often requires more research and planning than XML alone. The structure of an XML document produces exactly one graphical tree model. In contrast, a RDF model is made up conceptually of a variable number of triplets. Each triplet contains a subject, predicate, and object and RDF triplets exist independently. As a result, RDF models using XML syntax are referred to as RDF/XML and they exist as RDF triplets within the XML tree structure.

The RDF/XML model is easier to query in comparison to the complex XML structure which makes parsing and searching difficult. Using XML without RDF, the order of the data is very important. In fact, if you change the order of the nodes, a parser will be unable to process the document. However, the order of "facts" in an RDF model does not affect the ability to process data.

For two applications to talk together and process XML data, they require that the two parties first agree on a common syntax for their documents. After re-engineering their documents with new syntax the exchange can happen. However, using the RDF/XML model, two parties may communicate with different syntax using the concept of equivalencies. For example, in RDF/XML we could say "car" and specify that it is equivalent to "automobile."

Artificial intelligence (AI) scientists have long pondered that, although computers overtake the human brain in processing speed and storage capacity, they can't compare to human intelligence. At least one reason for this is that the brain can make connections between partially-stored information and assemble this into knowledge. Achieving this level of understanding with RDF and RDFS (RDF Schema) would require countless resources on servers all over the world that would have to be methodically classified and described. However, the Semantic Web will manage this complexity (see Chapter 9) by using software agents that can figure out some things by themselves. Software agents can run unattended for however long they need to complete their tasks.

Fortunately, AI also gives us two tools to help cope with this complexity problem. First, knowledge-representation defines how we might represent what is stored in our brains and second, inference, provides a way of using formal logic to extrapolate new knowledge. All of this forms a system of representing and synthesizing knowledge that is called ontology.

Vocabulary can be defined using ontologies so that when describing data using an RDF model, it is possible to use an existing vocabulary or design our own. This combination of RDF models and associated ontologies gives the computer enough information to discover the meaning of the data. The resulting RDF/XML models allow intelligent applications to be built where new facts may be surmised from existing ones.

Until 2003, the leading ontology system for RDF/XML was the DARPA Agent Markup Language (DAML). DAML incorporated useful concepts from the Ontology Inference Layer (OIL), a European project to provide some AI primitives in RDF form. The combined language

189

DAML+OIL has been standardized by the W3C into Web Ontology Language (OWL). OWL let's us formally express ontologies so that while W3C RDFS provides primitive classification, OWL extends them.

Most of OWL's power comes from primitives for expressing classifications. OWL provides a toolbox of class expressions, which provides the power of mathematical logic and set theory to the important task of mapping ontologies through classifications (see Chapter 8).

RDF Primer

The RDF model/syntax specification and the RDF Schema specification build upon existing Web standards XML and XML Schema (see Chapter 4). The RDF Schema describes how to use RDF to build RDF vocabularies (collections of resources that can be used as predicates in RDF statements).

RDF data can be expressed using an XML syntax thereby allowing it to be passed over the Internet as a document and parsed using existing XML based software.

The RDF model is based on statements made about resources which can be anything with an associated URI. The basic RDF model produces a triple, where a resource (the subject) is linked through an arc labeled with a property (the predicate) to a value (the object).

We can say that:

```
A thing[subject] has a property[predicate] with a specific value[object].
```

Or, more succinctly:

```
[subject] has [predicate]  [object].
```

Or, as a triple:

```
(subject, predicate, object).
```

Alternatively, we could refashion the statement as:

```
A property[predicate] of a thing[subject] is a specific value[object]
```

Or, more succinctly:

```
[predicate] of [subject] is [object].
```

We will keep this form, nevertheless, as the triple (subject, predicate, object).

And we can define subject, predicate, and object as follows:

- Subject: The resource (a person, place, or thing) that the statement describes. A RDF Resource can be anything in the data model (document, user, product, etc). A RDF Resource is uniquely identified by a URI.

- Predicate: The property (name, city, title, color, shape, characteristic) of the subject (person, place, or thing). A RDF Property is uniquely identified by a URI.

- Object: The value (Peter, San Jose, "War and Peace," blue, circle, strong) for the property (name, city, title, color, shape, characteristic) of the subject (person, place, or thing). This value can be any valid RDF data type. RDF supports all of the XML data types.

There are four important facts about RDF triplets to be aware of:

1. Each RDF triple is made up of subject, predicate, and object.
2. Each RDF triple is a complete and unique fact.
3. Each RDF triple is a 3-tuple that the subject is either a uriref or a bnode,[1] the predicate is a uriref, and the object is a uriref, bnode, or literal.
4. Each RDf triple can be joined to other RDF triples, but still retains its own unique meaning, regardless of complexity.

The simple model of triple URIs used by RDF to describe information has many advantages. One of the most important is that any data model can be reduced to a common storage format based on a triple. This makes RDF ideal for aggregating disparate data models because all of the data from all models can be treated the same. Information can be combined from many sources and processed as if it came from a single source.

In addition, each RDF statement can be represented either as a document statement or as a graph. We can represent a set of RDF statements as a triple {s, p, o} illustrated as a directed labeled

---

[1] A blank node (bnode) represents a resource that isn't currently identified, similar to the null value from a relational database.

graph: each subject and object is shown as a vertex and the predicate is shown as an arc directed from subject (s), to object (o), labeled by predicate (p). This is illustrated in Figure 7-1.

Each arc in an RDF graph is called a statement. For example, the triple in Figure 7-1 shows the relational database equivalent as well as the graphical relationship of an RDF triple expressed as a statement.

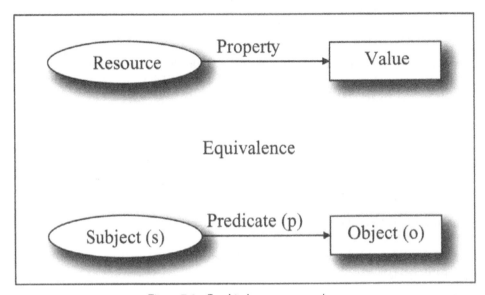

Figure 7-1. Graphical statement template.

The subject is shown as an oval, the predicate as an arc, and the object as a box. Graphs are easy to read and the directed arc removes any possibility of confusion over what are subject and objects. An RDF graph is considered grounded if there are no blank nodes.

Notice how the triple (resource, property, value) identified above relates to our triple (subject, predicate, object) relationship in Figure 7-1.

Let's try a very simple first step by creating an example (Example 7-1) of a statement and identifying the components that construct an RDF model.

192

Example 7-1. Listing 7-1. Interpreting a Sentence as an RDF Statement.

For Example 7-1, let's consider the statement, "The book has the title *War and Peace*." We can express this statement within RDF in several forms. The first form of this statement can be broadly identified as follows:

The book[resource] has the title[property of resource] *War and Peace*[specific value of property].

Or, more relevantly to RDF as:

The book[subject] has the title[predicate] *War and Peace*[object].

Or, more succinctly:

The book has title *War and Peace*.

With the triple:

(book, title, *War and Peace*).

Alternatively, we could retain the meaning, while rearrange the statement:

The title[property of the resource] of the book[resource] is *War and Peace*[specific value].

Or, more relevantly to RDF as:

The title[property] of the book[resource] is *War and Peace*[value].

Or, more succinctly:

The title[predicate] of the book[subject] is *War and Peace*[object].

We create a graphical representation of this example in Figure 7-2.

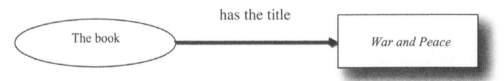

Figure 7-2. Graphical RDF statement of "The book has the title War and Peace."

It is worth mentioning that ill-formed statements should be exposed. For example, the statement, "The chair is brown" can not be represented as a triple, since the subject "chair" has not identified an explicit property, such as color with which to set the value "brown." While a human may understand and infer more about chairs and the color brown, a machine requires an explicit statement, such as "The color of the chair is brown."

The graphical nature of XML is a tree structure while the graphical nature of RDF is a much flatter, triple-based directed graph (see Chapter 12). While XML is hierarchical, which means that all related elements are nested within elements they relate to, RDF is not nested. In RDF you can associate two separate XML structures with each other through a URI. RDF/XML is well formed XML, but includes the URI of the relationship. URIs can use the same simply naming way to refer to resources under different protocols: HTTP, FTP, GOPHER, EMAIL, URLs (Uniform Resource Locator), a widely used type of URI. In addition, RDF adds a layer of complexity on XML that is more difficult to read.

On the other hand, RDF/XML can be easily processed and provides more responsive answers to queries. RDF/XML relates to a relational database (depends on the use of identifiers to relate data), while XML relates more directly to a hierarchical database (have a physical location dependency that requires data to be bi-located). RDF/XML can join data from two disparate vocabularies easily without negotiating structural differences that simple XML would require.

The W3C has developed an XML serialization of RDF that is considered to be the standard interchange format for RDF on the Semantic Web.

Serialization

Unfortunately, recording the RDF data in a graph is not the most efficient method of storing or retrieving data. Instead, transporting RDF data occurs with RDF/XML in a process know as serialization. RDF/XML is well-formed XML with an overlay of additional constraints that allow for interchange, collection, and merging of data from multiple models. RDF/XML can be parsed with simple XML technology.

Serialization converts an object into a persistent form. The RDF/XML syntax provides a means of documenting an RDF model in a text-based format that literally serializes the model as XML. As a result, the contents are required to meet both XML well-formedness and the additional constraints of RDF.

While RDF does require well-formedness, it does not require XML-style validation. The RDF/XML parsers do not use DTDs or XML Schema to ensure that the RDF/XML is valid.

We can use some prefixes to avoid writing URI references completely. There are some well-known QName prefixes:

```
rdf:    URI:   http//www.w3.org/1999/02/22-rdf-syntax-ns#
rdfs:   URI:   http//wwww3.org/2000/01/rdf-schema#
xsd:    URI:   http//wwww3.org/2001/XMLschema#
```

Now let's take the statement from Example 7-1, "The book has the title *War and Peace*," and serialize the statement by wrapping RDF in an XML document.

```
<?xml version="1.0"?>
<rdf:RDF
    xmlns:rdf=http://www.w3.org/1999/02/22-rdf-syntax-ns#
    xmlns:dc="http://purl.org/dc/elements/1.1/">
    <rdf:Description rdf:about="http://www.amazon.com/books" >
      <dc:title>War and Peace</dc:title>
    </rdf:Description>
</rdf:RDF>
```

We can try another serialization for the following statement:

```
http://www.w3.org/[subject] has the title[predicate] World Wide Web
Consortium[object].
```

The resulting serialization is:

```
<?xml version="1.0"?>
<rdf:RDF xmlns:rdf="http://www.w3.org/1999/02/22-rdf-syntax-ns#"
    xmlns:dc="http://purl.org/dc/elements/1.1/">
    <rdf:Description rdf:about="http://www.w3.org/">
     <dc:title>World Wide Web Consortium</dc:title>
   </rdf:Description>
</rdf:RDF>
```

where the subject, predicate, and object are indicated in capital letters below:

```
<?xml version="1.0"?>
 <rdf:RDF xmlns:rdf="http://www.w3.org/1999/02/22-rdf-syntax-ns#"
    xmlns:dc="http://purl.org/dc/elements/1.1/">
   <rdf:Description rdf:about="SUBJECT">
    <dc:PREDICATE>"OBJECT"</dc:PREDICATE>
   </rdf:Description>
 </rdf:RDF>
```

In Example 7-2, we discuss the interpretation of multiple statements in relationship to RDF statements.

Example 7-2. Listing 7-2. Interpreting Multiple Sentences as an RDF Statement.

Let's create an RDF example (Example 7-2) by starting with five simple facts that we wish to represent as RDF triplets.

1. The name of this URI (mailto: alesso@web-iq.com) is Peter Alesso.
2. The type of this URI (mailto: alesso@web-iq.com) is a person.
3. The author of this URI (mailto: alesso@web-iq.com) is isbn:0201730634.
4. The id of this URI (isbn:0201730634) is a book.
5. The title of this URI (isbn:0201730634) is "The Intelligent Wireless Web."

We can express these statements alternatively as:

1. This URI (mailto: alesso@web-iq.com) has the name Peter Alesso.
2. This URI (mailto: alesso@web-iq.com) has a type of person.
3. This URI (mailto: alesso@web-iq.com) has an author of isbn:0201730634.
4. This URI (isbn:0201730634) has the identity of a book.
5. This URI (isbn:0201730634) has the title of "The Intelligent Wireless Web."

We represent these five facts as RDF triplets in Table 7-1. Then in Figure 7-2 we illustrate this table.

Subject	Predicate	Object
mailto: alesso@web-iq.com	name	Peter Alesso
mailto: alesso@web-iq.com	type	Person
mailto: alesso@web-iq.com	author-of	isbn: 0201730634
isbn:0201730634	type	book
isbn: 0201730634	title	The Intelligent Wireless Web

Table 7-1. RDF Triplet Data Table.

Figure 7-2 illustrates the simple RDF statements as five simple directed graphs with subject, predicates, and objects.

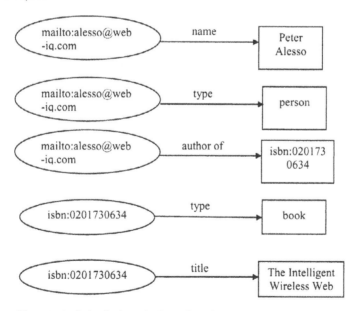

Figure 7-3. Individual graphs for each triplet statement of Example 7-2.

197

Then in Figure 7-4, we draw a composite graph that represents all the statements in an efficient form. Finally, we write the RDF serialization tags for this example.

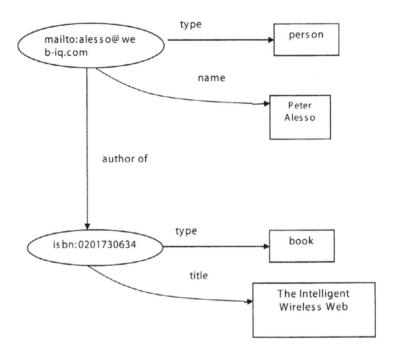

Figure 7-4. Merged RDF graph for Example 7-2.

We can write the serialized form of the RDF document for this example as:

Listing 7-3. Serialization of RDF Statement.

```xml
<?xml version="1.0"?>
<Class rdf:ID="book"
       xmlns:rdf="http://www.w3.org/1999/02/22-rdf-syntax-ns#"
       xmlns="uri">
    <title> The Intelligent Wireless Web </title>
    ...
</Class>
```

198

In any RDF graph, a subgraph would be a subset of the triples contained in the graph. Each triple is its own unique RDF graph (see Figure 7-2). N-Triples is a format that breaks an RDF graph into separate triples, one for each line (see Table 7-1). The union of two or more graphs is a new graph called a merged graph (see Figure 7-3). An RDF graph is called grounded if it has no blank nodes.

The RDF Model and Syntax specification defines an abstract data model. The model is abstract because it is defined in terms of abstract mathematical structures such as triples and sets. It is a data model only, because no formal semantics is given. It is suggested that RDF statements represent facts, but nothing formal is defined. RDF does not provide a complete first order predicate logic (FOPL). While the RDF Model and Syntax defines how to represent data conforming to the XML model. An RDF graph may also represent the data structure.

All the triples result in a direct graph whose nodes and arcs could all be labeled with qualified URIs. Instead of using the full URI, you could use a relative URI reference which resolves the base document concatenation with a relative URI reference. In the following, the relative URI reference "#value.htm":

```
<rdf:Description rdf:about = "#value">
```

then becomes http://address#value. With xml:base you can specify a base document that is used to generate the full URI when given a relative URI reference:

```
<rdf:RDF xml:base= http://address /> </rdf:RDF>
```

By default, all literals are plain literals and can be strings, integers, etc. Their format would be the string value plus optional xml:language. You can also embed XML within an RDF document by using rdf:parseType attribute set to a value of "literal".

Notations3, N3, and N-Triples

RDF/XML is the official serialization technique for RDF data, but Notation3 (N3) is an alternative notation sometimes used as a convenience.

Since RDF information is simply a collection of statements, each with a subject, predicate, and object, N3, let's us write an RDF triple just like that, with a period:

```
subject predicate object.

<#book> <#title> <#War and Peace>.
```

In this syntax, subject, predicate, and object are separated by spaces and the triple is terminated by a period.

Each subject, predicate, or object can be identified with a URI. This is something like <http://www.w3.org/> or but when everything is missed out before the "#" it identifies <#book> in the current document, whatever it is.

There is one exception: the object (only) can be a literal, such as a string or integer.

The predicate "title" is called a "property" and thought of as a noun expressing a relation between the two. In fact, we can write:

```
<#book> <#title> <#War and Peace>.
```

or, to make it more readable, as

```
<#book> has <#title> <#War and Peace >.
```

The property which tells us what type something is is rdf:type. This can be abbreviated in N3 to just "a." So we can define a class of book as:

```
:book a rdfs:Class.
```

The easiest way to help people find documentation is to make the URIs we create as vocabulary terms, also work in a Web browser. This happens automatically if we follow the naming convention we use here, where the vocabulary definition document has a URI like http://example.com/terms and it refers to its terms like <#book>. This gives the URI http://example.com/terms#book which in any browser displays the definition document.

Namespaces

An RDF goal is to record knowledge in machine-understandable format and provide mechanisms to allow the combination of the data. By combining combinations of models, additions can be incorporated without impacting an existing RDF Schema. To ensure that RDF/XML data from various documents can be successfully merged together, namespaces are added to the specification to prevent element collisions. To add namespace support, a namespace attribute is added to the document. As an example:

```
<rdf:RDF xmlns:rdf="http://www.w3.org/1999/02/22-rdf-syntax-ns#">
```

The namespace declaration for RDF vocabularies points to the URI of the RDF Schema document for the vocabulary. There is no formal checking of this document involved in RDF/XML the document is useful for the schema. RDF/XML uses the QName which is a namespace prefix followed by a colon (:) followed by an XML local name.

In particular, the prefix for the RDF Syntax is given as "rdf", the RDF Schema is given as "rdfs", and the Dublin Core schema is given as "dc".

To add a namespace to an RDF document, a namespace attribute can be added anywhere in the document, but is usually added to the RDF tag itself. The namespace declaration for RDF vocabularies usually points to a URI of the RDF Schema document for the vocabulary.

Vocabulary

The Resource Description Framework (RDF) specification is composed of two parts—a Syntax Speciation and a Schema Specification.

RDF W3C Specifications

RDF Model and Syntax Specification:

http://www.w3.org/TR/1999/REC-rdf-syntax-19990222/

RDF Schema Specification:

http://www.w3.org/TR/2003/WD-rdf-schema-20030123/

The RDF Syntax Specification shows how RDF constructs relate to one another and how they are diagrammed in XML. For example, elements such as rdf:type are used to describe a resource. The prefix sets the schema that a particular element is defined by.

A RDF/XML vocabulary or schema is a rule-based dictionary that defines the elements of importance to a domain and then describes how these relate to one another. It provides a type system that can be used by domain owners to create site-specific RDF/XML vocabularies. The rdf:type element is from the RDF Vocabulary.

RDF is about metadata—data about data. You may have already been working with metadata for a long time without realizing it. Relational databases, such as Oracle, MS SQL, Sybase, and MySQL, all use data schema for many different applications, and store many different types of data by using metadata structures. For instance, an application database could have three database tables for customer, order, and customer_order, with both the customer and order tables related to the third table by using a primary key relationship.

The relational database schema defines elements such as database tables, primary and foreign keys, and columns that describe information to facilitate multiple uses of the same storage mechanism. At runtime, the database management system hides the higher-level functions and allows applications to access objects directly. This process works so well that many companies throughout the world have relational database. Large multi-use applications such as PeopleSoft, SAP, and Oracle make use of the concept of real-time metadata which expedites recording metadata as records rather than columns within a table. With this, the application follows Customer Record Management (CRM) systems.

RDF acts in similar manner as a relational database to allow automatic access and processes (see Figure 7-5).

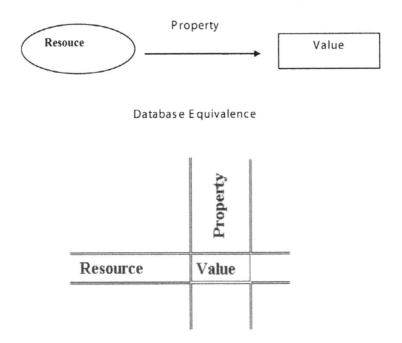

Figure 7- 5. RDF and relational databases.

This domain neutral approach allows us to store resources as rdf:Description element and uses RDF to define the properties for this resource. The RDF Schema provides some of the same functionality as a relational database schema. It provides the resources necessary to describe objects and property.

Vocabularies

What kind of vocabularies can be used to model business resources using syntax/schema of RDF? The answer is any kind of business resource. Because RDF creates domain-specific vocabularies that are then used to model resources, we can use RDF to model business-specific resources. The only limitation is the need for industry cooperation in developing an interoperable vocabulary.

We can consider RDF as a way of recording information about resources. RDF can be serialized using XML for specific business domains using a set of elements defined within the rule of the RDF data model and constrained through RDF syntax, vocabulary, and schema. We can recognize that RDF recorded in XML is a powerful tool. By using XML we have access to a great number of existing XML applications, such as parsers and APIs. However, RDF provides the same level of functionality to XML as the relational data model adds to commercial databases. RDF provides predefined data grammar that can be used for business information.

The way to start defining the vocabulary for a business is to first create domain elements and their properties within the given business scope. Defining the business elements for a new system is the same process as being defined for use within a more traditional relational database. Following the existing data-modeling techniques, first describe the major entities and their properties, then describe how these entities are related to one another. Once the elements for the vocabulary are defined, they can be compared to existing Web resource domain vocabulary for matches.

The benefit of RDF is that the information maps directly and unambiguously in to a decentralized model that differentiates the semantics of the application from any additional syntactic.

Before creating a formal RDF document for a new vocabulary, a prototype should be developed to test the model. During the process, the document is checked for validity with an RDF validator, which validates the result against the standard and also provides an edge graph and N-Triplet breakdown of the RDF.

RDF Validator

The RDF Validation Tool is available at:

http://www.w3.org/RDF/Validtor/

References with rdf:ID

The rdf:about attribute is used to provide the URI reference, but another way to reference a URI for a resource is to use the rdf:resource or rdf:ID attributes. Unlike rdf:about, which refers to an exisiting resource, rdf:ID generates a URI by concatenating the URI of the enclosing document (or the one provided by xml:base) to the identifier given, preceded by the relative URI # symbol.

Representing Structured Data with rdf:value

Not all data relations in RDF represent straight, binary connections between resources and object values. Some data values have both a value and additional information about the value. For example, the following RDF/XML is ambiguous:

```
<tag>17</tag >
```

because we do not know what 17 means. We could provide additional information as:

```
<tag>17 days</tag >
```

But this information requires us to splitter the data appropriately at some later time. Instead, we could define a second vocabulary element to detail the qualifications as:

```
<tag>17</tag>

<tagUnit>days</tagUnit>
```

While this works, there is a disconnect between the data and the unit because the two are only indirectly related. This rdf:value is appropriate to structure the data. The rdf:value predicate includes the actual value in this field as:

```
<tag rdf:parseType = "Resource">
    <rdf:value>17</rdf:value>
    <tagUnit>days</tagUnit>
</tag>
```

Now we know the data structure and the actual value.

One piece of information about the RDF resource that is consistent is the resource type or class. To explicitly define the resource we use rdf:type property. The value of rdf:type property is a URI identifying an rdfs:Class-typed resource (rdf:Class).

XML Schema restricts the syntax of XML applications and using it in conjunction with RDF may be useful for creating some datatypes.

Embedded RDF/XML can be achieved through scripts. For example, using, <script> tag around rdf tags could be included in an HTML file.

No provision is made in the RDF data model for a resource to have multiple URIs. Other URIs could be associated with a resource through some property, but the RDF specifications define no such property. The implication is clear, that as far as RDF is concerned, resources have a distinguished URI.

However, there is no way to stop many individuals from independently assigning URIs to represent, say, the trees in a particular park. Each such URI defines a new resource. Thus, there may be many resources which represent the same tree. The RDF specifications do not define a mechanism for stating the equivalence of resources; i.e., that multiple resources represent the same conceptual mapping. This is left to higher layers of the language stack such as OWL.

Notice that the RDF design pattern is an alternating sequence of resource-property. This pattern is known as "striping."

```
<?xml version="1.0"?>
<Resource-A>
      <property-A>
            <Resource-B>
                  <property-B>
                        <Resource-C>
                              <property-C>
                                    Value-C
                              </property-C>
                        </Resource-C>
                  </property-B>
            </Resource-B>
      </property-A>
</Resource-A>
```

Properties are resources which are identified by URIs. In RDF/XML, properties are often represented by XML in the form namespaceprefix:LocalPart, in which case the URI of the property is the concatenation of the URI associated with the namespaceprefix and the LocalPart.

RDF/XML parsers retain this information, representing properties not just by their URI, but by the pair consisting of their namespace URI and LocalPart. This will enable them to acquire and process the RDF Schema that describes each property and to write correctly an RDF graph as XML.

Collections

A collection is considered to be a finite grouping of items with a given terminator. Within RDF/XML, a collection is defined through the use of rdf:parseType="Collection" and through listing the collected resources within the other collection block.

Dublin Core MetaData Element Set

The Dublin Core metadata set consists of a core set of elements that comprise what is known as simple Dublin Core.

Dublin Core Specifications

Dublin Core metadata set is available at:

http://www.dblincore.org/documents/1999/07/02/dces/

These elements are given in Table 7-2 and we will use them in several of the following examples.

Name	Description
title	A name given to the resource.
creator	An entity responsible for making the content of the resource.
subject	The topic of the content of the resource.
description	An account of the content of the resource.
public	An entity responsible for making the content available.
contributor	An entity responsible for making contributions to the content of the resource.
date	A date associated with an event the life cycle of the resource.
type	The nature or genre of the content of the resource.
format	The physical or digital manifestation of the resource.

Table 7-2. Dublin Core Elements.

identifier	An unambiguous reference to the resource within a given context.
source	A reference to the resource from which the present resource is derived.
language	A language of the intellectual content of the resource.
relation	A reference to a related resource.
coverage	The extent or scope of the content of the resource.
rights	Information about reights held in and over the resource.

Table 7-2 (continued). Dublin Core Elements.

RDF Schema

RDF provides a very simple yet powerful model for describing information. The meaning of the information is described using an RDF Schema. Computers that process RDF can share disparate information by mapping from one schema to another. The purpose of RDF Schema is to provide an XML vocabulary to which we can express classes and their (subclass) relationships, as well as to define properties and associate them with classes.

As a result, RDF Schema facilitates inference and enhances searching. RDF Schemas are focused on defining taxonomies (class hierarchies) which in turn is what facilitates inference and search. RDF Schema uses the RDF/XML design pattern to define classes and properties. Recall RDF/XML design pattern:

```
<?xml version="1.0"?>
<Class rdf:ID="resource"
          xmlns:rdf="http://www.w3.org/1999/02/22-rdf-syntax-
ns#"
          xmlns="uri">
      <property rdf:resource="…"/>
      <property>value</property>
      ...
</Class>
```

The rdf:ID provides a name for the class.

The conjunction (AND) of two subClassOf statements is a subset of the intersection of the classes:

```
<rdfs:Class rdf:ID="Set1 AND Set 2">
        <rdfs:subClassOf rdf:resource="#Set1"/>
        <rdfs:subClassOf rdf:resource="#Set2"/>
</rdfs:Class>
```

The RDF Schema is simply a document that defines a data-typing model for an RDF document. By using RDF Schema, for example, we could define a "Desktop" as a type of "Computer," and "Computer" as a sub class of a "Machine." We can also create properties and classes, as well as ranges and domains for those properties.

When a relationship exists between two things, we can express it as a class. The subject of any property is a *domain* of the property. The object of the class is called the *range* of a property. A property can have many domains and ranges.

The first three most important RDF concepts are "Resource" (rdfs:Resource), "Class" (rdfs: Class), and "Property" (rdf:Property). These are all "classes," in that terms may belong to these classes. Class is in the rdfs namespace. Property is in the rdf namespace. For example, all terms in RDF are types of resources. We just use the rdf:type property, to declare that something is a "type" of something else. The following:

```
rdfs:Resource rdf:type rdfs:Class.
rdfs:Class  rdf:type  rdfs:Class.
rdf:Property rdf:type rdfs:Class.
rdf:type rdf:type rdf:Property.
```

means that "Resource is a type of Class, Class is a type of Class, Property is a type of Class, and type is a type of Property".

If we wish to create a class called "Computer", which contains all of the computers in the world, we would use the RDF triple:

```
rdfs:Computer rdf:type rdfs:Class .
```

Then, the following allows us to say that "Desktop is a type of Computer":

```
rdfs:Desktop rdf:type rdfs:Computer .
```

To create properties that a term is a type of rdf:Property, and use:

```
rdfs:name rdf:type rdf:Property .
```

```
rdfs:Dell rdfs:name "Desktop" .
```

RDF Schema includes rdfs:subClassOf and rdfs:subPropertyOf. These allow one class or property as a subclass or sub-property of another. For example, we could say that the class "Computer" is a subclass of the class "Machine" as follows:

```
rdfs:Computer rdfs:subClassOf rdfs:Machine .
```

As a result, when we say that Desktop is a Computer, we are also saying that Desktop is a Machine. We can also say that there are other sub classes of Machine:

```
rdfs:Calulator rdfs:subClassOf rdfs:Machine .

rdfs:Notepad rdfs:subClassOf rdfs:Machine .
```

While RDF Schema is very simple, it is powerful enough to allow us to build up knowledge bases of data in RDF. In most Object-Oriented languages, when a class is defined, the properties (attributes) are simultaneously defined.

However, for RDF Schema the approach is to define a class, and then separately define properties and state that they are to be used with the class. You can define a class (and indicate its relationships to other classes). Separately, you define properties and then associate them with a class. The advantage of this approach is that anyone, anywhere, anytime can create a property and state that it is usable with the class.

When we want to define a new vocabulary or ontology, we define new classes of things and new properties. When we say what type of thing something is, we say what *Class* it belongs to. The property which tells us what type something is, is rdf:type. So we can define a class of person as:

```
rdfs:Person rdf:type rdfs:Class.
```

In the same document, we could introduce an actual person:

```
rdfs:John rdf:type rdfs:Person.
```

Classes just tell us about the thing. An object can be in many classes without a hierarchical relationship. The properties of classes in RDF Schema form ontology vocabularies.

The Semantic Web provides the architecture for constructing a logical language for making inferences. There is debate about RDF's lacks th power to quantify; however, there are already a great range of tools with which to build the Semantic Web: assertions, and quoting in RDF, classes, properties, ranges and documentation in RDF Schema, disjoint classes, unambiguous and unique properties, datatypes, inverses, equivalencies, lists, as well as OWL.

Let's create an example for RDF/XML, Example 7-3, using our previous data and information from examples in Chapter 3 (Example 3-3) and Chapter 4 (Example 4-1). Listing 7-4 shows the RDF/XML from the Bookcatalog database. Listing 7-5 provides the RDF/XML Schema document. Finally, the Dublin Core Properties are given in Listing 7-6.

Example 7-3. Listing 7-4. RDF/XML Document.

```
<?xml version="1.0"?>
<rdf:RDF xmlns:rdf="http://www.w3.org/1999/02/22-rdf-syntax-ns#"
        xmlns:dc="http://purl.org/metadata/dublin-core#">
    <rdf:Description rdf:about="http://www.web-iq.com/
BookCatalogue.xml">
        <dc:Creator>H. Peter Alesso</dc:Creator>
        <dc:Subject>Book information</dc:Subject>
        <dc:Date>Sept 2003</dc:Date>
    </rdf:Description>
</rdf:RDF>
```

Now let's create an RDF Schema for the previous RDF/XML instance:

Example 7-3. Listing 7-5. RDF/XML Schema Document.

```
<?xml version="1.0"?>
<rdf:RDF xmlns:rdf="http://www.w3.org/1999/02/22-rdf-syntax-
ns#"
                xmlns:rdfs="http://www.w3.org/2000/01/rdf-
schema#"
                xml:base="http://www.publishing.org">
    <rdfs:Class rdf:ID="Catalogue">
        <rdfs:subClassOf rdf:resource="http://www.
w3.org/2000/01/rdf-schema#Resource"/>
    </rdfs:Class>

    <rdfs:Class rdf:ID="Book">
        <rdfs:subClassOf rdf:resource="http://www.
w3.org/2000/01/rdf-schema#Resource"/>
    </rdfs:Class>

    <rdf:Property rdf:ID="item">
        <rdfs:domain rdf:resource="#Catalogue"/>
        <rdfs:range rdf:resource="#Book "/>
    </rdf:Property>
    ...
</rdf:RDF>
```

Now let's create the Dublin Core properties - Title, Creator, Date, Publisher—defined in the Dublin Core RDF Schema:

Example 7-3. Listing 7-6. Dublin Core Properties.

```
<?xml version='1.0'?>
<rdf:RDF xmlns:rdf="http://www.w3.org/1999/02/22-rdf-
syntax-ns#"
        xmlns:rdfs="http://www.w3.org/TR/1999/PR-rdf-
schema-19990303#"
        xml:base="http://purl.org/metadata/dublin-core">

  <rdf:Description rdf:ID="Title">
     <rdf:type rdf:resource="http://www.w3.org/1999/02/22-
     rdf-syntax-ns#Property"/>
     <rdfs:label>Title</rdfs:label>
     <rdfs:comment>The name given to the resource, usually by
the Creator or Publisher.</rdfs:comment>
  </rdf:Description>

  <rdf:Description rdf:ID="Creator">
     <rdf:type rdf:resource="http://www.w3.org/1999/02/22-
rdf-syntax-ns#Property"/>
     <rdfs:label>Author/Creator</rdfs:label>
     <rdfs:comment>The person or organization primarily
responsible for creating the intellectual content of the
resource. For example, authors in the case of written
documents, artists, photographers, or illustrators in the
case of visual resources.</rdfs:comment>
  </rdf:Description>

  <rdf:Description ID="Date">
     <rdf:type rdf:resource="http://www.w3.org/1999/02/22-
rdf-syntax-ns#Property"/>
     <rdfs:label>Date</rdfs:label>
     <rdfs:comment>A date associated with the creation or
availability of the resource. Such a date is not to be
confused with one belonging in the Coverage element, which
would be associated with the resource only insofar as the
intellectual content is somehow about that date. Recommended
best practice is defined in a profile of ISO 8601 [Date and
Time Formats (based on ISO8601), W3C Technical Note,
```

```
http://www.w3.org/TR/NOTE-datetime] that includes (among
others) dates of the forms YYYY and YYYY-MM-DD. In this
scheme, for example, the date 1994-11-05 corresponds to
November 5, 1994.</rdfs:comment>
  </rdf:Description>

  <rdf:Description ID="Publisher">
    <rdf:type rdf:resource="http://www.w3.org/1999/02/22-
rdf-syntax-ns#Property"/>
    <rdfs:label>Publisher</rdfs:label>
    <rdfs:comment>The entity responsible for making the
resource available in its present form, such as a publishing
house, a university department, or a corporate entity.</
rdfs:comment>

  </rdf:Description>
    ...
  </rdf:RDF>
```

Classes and Properties

RDF and RDFS Classes are presented in Table 7-3 and their properties are presented in Table
7-4. Additional details are available in Appendix A and also at www.w3.org/rdf.

Class Name	Comment
rdfs:Resource	The class resource, everything.
rdfs:Literal	This represents the set of atomic values
rdfs:XMLLiteral	The class of XML literals.
rdfs:Class	The concept of class.
rdf:Property	The concept of a property.
rdfs:Datatype	The class of datatypes.
rdf:Statement	The class of RDF statements.

Table 7-3. RDF Classes.

rdf:Bag	An unordered collection.
rdf:Seq	An ordered collection.
rdf:Alt	A collection of alternatives.
rdfs:Container	This represents the set Containers.
rdfs:ContainerMembershipProperty	The container membership properties, rdf:1, rdf:2, ..., all of which are sub-properties of 'member'.
rdf:List	The class of RDF Lists.

Table 7-3 (continued). RDF Classes.

We have listed the RDF properties in Table 7-4.

Property Name	Comment
rdf:type	Indicates membership of a class.
rdfs:subClassOf	Indicates membership of a class.
rdfs:subPropertyOf	Indicates specialization of properties
rdfs:domain	A domain class for a property type
rdfs:range	A range class for a property type.
rdfs:label	Provides a human-readable version of a resource name.
rdfs:comment	Use this for descriptions.
rdfs:member	A member of a container.
rdf:first	The first item in an RDF list. Also often called the head.
rdf:rest	The rest of an RDF list after the first item, called the tail.
rdfs:seeAlso	A resource that provides information about the subject resource
rdfs:isDefinedBy	Indicates the namespace of a resource.
rdf:value	Identifies the principal value (usually a string) of a property when the property value is a structured resource.
rdf:subject	The subject of an RDF statement.
rdf:predicate	The predicate of an RDF statement.
rdf:object	The object of an RDF statement.

Table 7-4. RDF Properties.

Constraints on Properties

We can show the constraints on properties through rdfs:domain and rdfs:range. The property rdfs:domain restricts the set of resources that may have a given property (ie., its domain). The rdfs:range property restricts the set of values for a given Property (i.e., its range). The domain and range force subjects and objects of a Property to be a certain type.

Friend of a Friend (FOAF)

Friend of a Friend (FOAF) allows the expression of personal information and relationships, and is a useful building block for creating information systems that support online communities. Search engines can find people with similar interests through FOAF.

One of the latest episodes in the personal Web publishing trend is weblogs, which often have a very personal and informal tone. One of the technologies that underpins this form of publishing is Rich Site Summary, or RSS, an XML document that contains metadata about content items on a site. Part of its appeal is the way you can connect your content to the larger Web, enabling others to find you more easily.

Many communities have proliferated on the Internet, from companies to professional organizations to social groupings. The FOAF vocabulary, originated by Dan Brickley and Libby Miller, gives a basic expression for community membership. The FOAF project describes people and their basic properties such as name, e-mail address, and so on found at http://www.foaf-project.org/.

FOAF is simply an RDF vocabulary. Its typical use is akin to that of RSS: We create one or more FOAF files on your Web server and share the URLs so software can use the information inside the file. The creation of FOAF data is decentralized. An example application that uses these files might be a community directory where members maintain their own records. However, as with RSS, the interesting parts of FOAF come into play when the data is aggregated and can then be explored and cross-linked.

FOAF has the potential to become an important tool in managing communities. In addition to providing simple directory services, information from FOAF is accessible in many ways.

For the naming of people, mailto:, we have found that the "e-mail address" is a convenient URI scheme to use. A naive approach might lead a developer to write down, for example: mailto: alesso@web-iq.com lives in the USA.

Clearly, a person and that person's e-mail address are not the same thing so we can't use a person's e-mail address as the global name. Furthermore, a person may have multiple e-mail addresses, each used for a different purpose.

Yet the principle of using an e-mail address to identify a person is reasonable. While we can never create a global name for a person, we could reasonably assume that all descriptions of a person that included this person's e-mail address is "alesso@web-iq.com" might reasonably refer to the same person.

So, you might correctly write: The person with the e-mail address mailto: alesso@web-iq.com lives in the USA.

This is the way that FOAF works. In order to combine information about particular individuals, the assumption is made that an e-mail address is an unambiguous property and that only one person owns a particular mailbox. We illustrate this as an RDF document in Listing 7-7.

Listing 7-7. A sample FOAF description of the author.

```
<rdf:RDF
     xmlns:rdf="http://www.w3.org/1999/02/22-rdf-syntax-
ns#"
     xmlns:foaf="http://xmlns.com/foaf/0.1/">


<foaf:Person>
     <foaf:name>H. Peter Alesso</foaf:name>
     <foaf:mbox rdf:resource="mailto:alesso@web-iq.com" />
</foaf:Person>

</rdf:RDF>
```

Listing 7-8 is an expanded FOAF description for the author.

Listing 7-8. A complete FOAF description of the author.

```
<rdf:RDF
     xmlns:rdf="http://www.w3.org/1999/02/22-rdf-syntax-
ns#"
     xmlns:rdfs="http://www.w3.org/2000/01/rdf-schema#"
     xmlns:foaf="http://xmlns.com/foaf/0.1/">
<foaf:Person>
<foaf:name>Peter Alesso</foaf:name>
<foaf:firstName>Peter</foaf:firstName>
```

215

```
<foaf:surname>Alesso</foaf:surname>
<foaf:mbox_sha1sum>0dac4adeb17cff7cfe42e37fccf4f2fe2398fea9
</foaf:mbox_sha1sum>
<foaf:homepage rdf:resource="http://www.web-iq.com/"/>
<foaf:phone rdf:resource="tel:9254843415"/>
<foaf:workplaceHomepage rdf:resource="http://www.web-
iq.com/"/>
<foaf:schoolHomepage rdf:resource="http://web.mit.edu/"/>
<foaf:knows>
<foaf:Person>
<foaf:name>Craig Smith</foaf:name>
<foaf:mbox_sha1sum>b4071300c3be54d757893673727eba4a7d8b727e
</foaf:mbox_sha1sum>
<rdfs:seeAlso rdf:resource="http://www.video-software.
com/"/></foaf:Person></foaf:knows>
<foaf:knows>
<foaf:Person>
<foaf:name>Dominick Zingerelli</foaf:name>
<foaf:mbox_sha1sum>843c6e91e363606989c358724bf7e1d096e991b1
</foaf:mbox_sha1sum>
<rdfs:seeAlso rdf:resource="http://www.video-software.
com/"/></foaf:Person></foaf:knows>
<foaf:knows>
<foaf:Person>
<foaf:name>Chris</foaf:name>
<foaf:mbox_sha1sum>5354e2778494d56a99833af81988c11e0e86337c
</foaf:mbox_sha1sum>
<rdfs:seeAlso rdf:resource="http://www.semaview.com"/>
</foaf:Person>
</foaf:knows>
</foaf:Person>
</rdf:RDF>
```

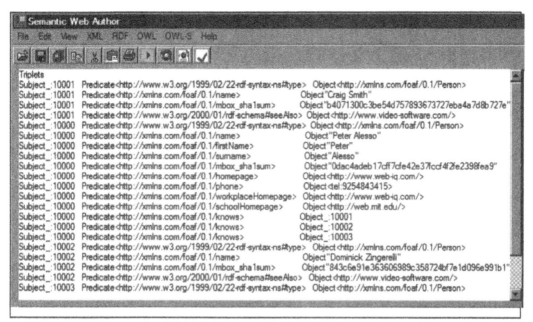

Figure 7-6. Friend of a Friend displayed in Semantic Web author Example 7-3.

FOAF is all about creating and using machine-readable home pages that describe people, the links between them, and the things they create and do. The *Semantic Web Author* (see Chapter 14) includes a FOAF template for generating RDF FOAF documents.

Figure 7-6 is a screen shot of the *Semantic Web Author* displaying the RDF FOAF Example 7-3.

Friend of a Friend displayed in a Semaview Java browser as a graphical representation is shown in Figure 7-7. FOAF is a way of describing yourself and your friends and relations. You can create a FOAF RDF file using the Semantic Web Author (see Chapter 14). After entering your input you must save the FOAF file, as an RDF file. Then load the RDF file to your Web site. You can view the FOAF RDF file using the Semaview Java Browser applet see Figure 7-7.

217

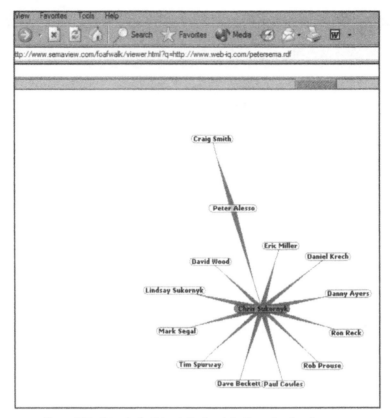

Figure 7-7. Friend of a Friend displayed in Semaview Java browser.

RDF Capabilities and Limitations

RDF provides a syntax convention for representing the semantics of data in a standardized interoperable manner. RDF provides a means of describing the relationships among resources (nameable by a URI) in terms of named properties and values.

The W3C also developed RDF Schema (RDFS), an object-oriented type system as a minimal ontology modeling language. Although RDF and RDFS are building blocks for defining a Semantic Web markup language, they lack expressive power. For example, they can't define: (1) the properties of properties, (2) necessary and sufficient conditions for class membership, or (3) equivalence and disjointness of classes. In addition, the only constraints expressible are domain and range constraints of properties. As a result, the semantics remains weakly specified.

We can compare several characteristics of RDF and XML Schemas in Table 7-5.

XML Schema	RDF Schema
XML Schemas is all about syntax.	RDF Schema is all about semantics.
An XML Schema tool is intended to validate that an XML instance conforms to the XML Schema.	An RDF Schema tool is intended to provide additional facts to supplement the facts in RDF/XML instances.
XML Schema prescribes what an element may contain, and the order the child elements may occur.	RDF Schema describes classes and properties.
	Tools can characterize the structure, "this element is a type (class), and here are its properties."
	RDF promotes the use of standardized vocabularies, standardized types (classes) and standardized properties.
	The RDF format gives us a structured approach to designing the XML documents. The RDF format is a regular, recurring pattern.
	It enables us to identify weaknesses and inconsistencies of non-RDF-compliant XML designs.
	We can use standard XML editors and validating to create, edit, and validate XML.
	RDF applies inference to the data.
	It positions data for the Semantic Web.

Table 7-5. Comparing XML and RDF.

Conclusion

Resource Description Framework (RDF) is built upon a very simple model, but the basic logic can support large-scale information management and processing. In this chapter, we provided a primer for RDF and RDFS as a basis for laying the infrastructure for Chapter 8, Web Ontology Language (OWL).

Chapter Eight

Web Ontology Language (OWL)

Overview

If a program wants to compare conceptual information across two knowledge bases on the Web, it has to know when any two given terms are being used to mean the same thing. Ideally, the program must have a way to discover common meanings for whatever knowledge bases it encounters. A solution to this problem is provided by the Semantic Web in the form of collections of information called ontologies. AI and Web researchers use the term ontology as a document that defines the relations among terms. A typical ontology for the Web uses a taxonomy and a set of inference rules.

A taxonomy defines classes of objects and relations among them. Classes, subclasses, and relations among entities are important tools for manipulating information. We can express a large number of relations among entities by assigning properties to classes and allowing subclasses to inherit such properties.

Inference rules in ontologies express rules for manipulating conceptual information.

In this chapter, we provide an introduction to the Web Ontology Language called OWL. We provide background on the development of ontology for the Web which has undergone significant change in the last few years. In addition, we introduce each of the three OWL versions currently available: Lite, DL, and Full. Some comparisons of OWL and RDFS are made and several illustrative examples are included. Finally, we discuss the basis of using this markup language for supporting the development of the Semantic Web.

Background

Building upon XML, the World Wide Web Consortium (W3C) developed a standard for metadata called the Resource Description Framework (RDF). The goal was to add semantics defined on top of XML. As a result, RDF provided a means of describing the relationships among resources in terms of named properties and values.

Since RDF and XML were developed about the same time, RDF was defined as an excellent complement to XML. As RDF expanded to include the requirements of the Semantic Web, however, the limitations of its lightweight schema language became evident.

In general, RDF provides a basic feature set for information modeling, including a basic directed graph. RDF is a sort of assembly language on top of which almost every other information-modeling method can be overlaid. However, users have desired more from RDF, such as data types and a consistent expression for enumerations. In addition, logicians have found that RDF offers a limited set of facilities for their particular needs.

As a result, W3C developed RDF Schema (RDFS), an object-oriented type system as a minimal ontology modeling language. Although RDF and RDFS are building blocks for defining a Semantic Web, together they still lack sufficient expressive power. For example, they can't define: (1) the properties of properties, (2) necessary and sufficient conditions for class membership, or (3) equivalence and disjointness of classes. In addition, the only constraints expressible are domain and range constraints on properties. As a result, the semantics have remained weakly specified.

Developing a Web Ontology Language

Since 1995, efforts have been made to build upon RDF and RDFS using AI-powered knowledge representation languages to overcome their limitations. As a result, Ontology grew rapidly as a research area. Simple HTML Ontology Extensions (SHOE), DARPA Agent Markup Language (DAML), DAML-ONT, Ontology Inference Layer (OIL), and DAML+OIL were all early efforts. The U.S. and EU governments began to invest in ontology research projects to stimulate rapid development.

In 1995, SHOE (Simple HTML Ontology Extensions) was initiated by James A. Hendler of the University of Maryland. In 1996, Meta-Content Format was provided as a note and then Ontobroker was developed by University of Karlsruhe. From 1997 to 1999, Ontology Inference Layer (OIL) was an ongoing work in Amsterdam, as a leading EU project.

DARPA Agent Markup Language (DAML)

Following on the heels of the eXtensible Markup Language revolution, and the ontology research projects, the Defense Advanced Research Projects Agency (DARPA) began working on DARPA Agent Markup Language (DAML). In Boston, in August 2000, the DAML Program formally began with a kick-off meeting. An integration contractor and 22 technology teams worked together to develop the DAML vision of an AI-powered knowledge representation language. Tools, data, and other results of their efforts were posted at the Web site: http://www.daml.org.

Michael Dean, principal investigator for the DAML integration and transition effort and a principal engineer for BBN Technologies of Cambridge, Mass, had been involved with DAML research almost since its inception. Dean envisioned DAML using XML as a transport vehicle for data, but with a greater capacity for describing objects and the relationships between them. It was designed to link disparate data from different sources and determine the relationships among the data.

DARPA developed DAML as a technology with intelligence built into the language through the behavior of agents. These agents would be programs that could dynamically identify and comprehend sources of information. As a consequence, DAML would allow agents to interact autonomously.

DAML continued to be extended with the addition of well-defined semantics. The technology is similar to defining fields and tables within a database, as well as defining the relationships among the fields and tables themselves.

Ontology Inference Layer (OIL)

At the same time that DAML was developing, Dr. Ian Horrocks at the University of Manchester found that standards were needed for the definition and interchange of ontologies. With the assistance of some of his European colleagues, Horrocks embarked on a project to further develop Ontology Inference Layer (OIL) in parallel with DAML.

As a result, OIL became a language built on the long history of research in Description Logics (DL). Description Logic is a subfield of Knowledge Representation and aims to provide a means for expressing structured information for reasoning. Description Logic provides a formal foundation for frame-based systems, object-oriented representations, semantic data models, and type systems (see Chapter 9). OIL was developed to produce a well-defined language for integrating ontologies with Web standards XML/XMLS and RDF/RDFS. It is a Web-based representation and inference layer for ontologies using the constructs found in many frame languages.

Unifying Ontology Efforts

By 2000, the U.S. National Science Foundation was funding activities in Japan and Australia to jumpstart additional work. At about this time, efforts were underway around the world to begin unifying the various ontology efforts. This rapidly led to the development of the DAML+OIL 1.0 specification. DAML+OIL was the second in the DAML family of markup languages, replacing DAML-ONT as an expressive ontology description language for markup. Building on top of RDF and RDFS, with AI-description logics, DAML+OIL overcame many of the expressiveness inadequacies of RDFS. It had well-defined semantics as well as an axiomatic specification. Since DAML+OIL produced unambiguously computer-interpretable results, it was amenable to agent interoperability and automated reasoning techniques.

In 2003, the W3C began final unification of the disparate ontology efforts into a standardized ontology called the Web Ontology Language (called OWL). OWL is a vocabulary extension of RDF and is derived from DAML+OIL. OWL is currently evolving into the semantic markup language for publishing and sharing ontologies on the World Wide Web.

OWL Primer

Comparing OWL with XML, RDF, and RDFS

A set of XML statements by itself does not allow us to reach a conclusion about any other XML statements. To employ XML to generate new data, we need knowledge embedded in some procedural code that exists as a server page on a remote server. A set of Web Ontology Language (OWL) statements by itself, however, can allow us to reach a conclusion about another OWL statement.

An ontology differs from an XML schema in that it is a knowledge representation rather than a message format. XML Schema and XML messages focus on the specific data and nothing from XML allows us to derive information outside of the context of its specific use. OWL differs from XML Schema in that it allows us to record data about an object outside of the specific transaction associated with the data.

OWL W3C Specifications

OWL Syntax Specification:

http://www.w3.org/TR/owl-features/

Other Web languages such as RDFS go a step further than XML, and could support some semantics, but OWL also offers a host of other standard properties such as equivalence (see Figure 8-1).

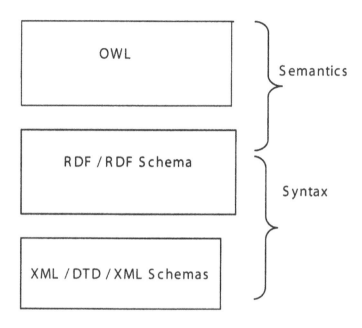

Figure 8-1. OWL enables machines to understand data.

OWL facilitates greater machine readability of Web content than that supported by XML, RDF, and RDFS by providing additional vocabulary along with a formal semantics.

An ontology defines the terms used to describe and represent concepts. Ontologies are used to describe concepts as well as their inter-relationships. Being able to standardize the definition of real-world concepts becomes very powerful as we begin to investigate knowledge that spans across multiple domains.

For example, an ontology may define knowledge such as the following:

A paperback is a type of book.
A book is a written document.
Documents have writers.
Writers are humans.
Humans read paperbacks.

OWL Versions

OWL comes in several flavors as three increasingly-expressive sublanguages: OWL Lite, OWL DL, and OWL Full. By offering three versions, W3C hopes to attract a broad following with multipicity of applications.

The OWL Guide provided by W3C provides an overview of three different versions of OWL as follows:

- *OWL Lite*—supports a classification hierarchy and simple constraints. It supports cardinality constraints, but only permits cardinality values of 0 or 1. It is simpler for tool support and provides a quick migration path for taxonomies.
- *OWL DL (Descriptive Logics)*—supports the maximum expressiveness while retaining computational completeness and decidability. OWL DL includes all of the OWL Full language constructs under certain restrictions.
- *OWL Full*—supports maximum expressiveness and the syntactic freedom of RDF, but with no computational guarantees. For example, in OWL Full, a class can be treated simultaneously as a collection of individuals and as an individual in its own right.

The major difference between OWL Full and OWL lite is the inclusion of OWL descriptions. For example:

```
<description> = <classID>
                    <restriction>
        unionOf( <description>)
        intersectionOf( <description>)
        complementOf( <description>)
        oneOf( <individualID>)
```

Primarily, an OWL description is one of a class identifier, a property restriction, or a complex class association. Any of which enriches the overall description of the class.

A key problem in achieving interoperability over the Web is recognizing when two pieces of data are talking about the same thing, even though different terminology are being used. OWL may be used to bridge this "terminology gap" (see Example 8-2).

Specifically, ontology includes four concepts that form the basis of an OWL document:

1. Classes.
2. Relationships between classes.

3. Properties of classes.
4. Constraints on relationships between the classes and properties of classes.

As a result, an OWL document identifies the following information:

- Class hierarchy—defines class/subclass relationships.
- Synonym—identifies equivalent classes and equivalent properties.
- Class association—maps one or more classes to one or more classes, through the use of a property (i.e., domain/range).
- Property metadata—contains metadata for properties.
- Class definition—specifies the composition of classes.

Since these OWL concepts can be used equally with RDF and RDFS, there is some confusion about the overlap between RDFS and OWL.

OWL defines the classes and properties, as well as their relationship to each other in the document, and as a result they are extremely similar to RDF Schema. For instance, an owl:Class element categories elements that are classes.

The purpose of OWL is similar to RDF Schemas—to provide an XML vocabulary to define classes, their properties and their relationships among classes. In comparison, RDF Schema enables us to express very rudimentary relationships and has limited inferencing capability while OWL enables us to express much richer relationships, thus yielding a much enhanced inferencing capability.

The OWL reference document at http://www.w3.org/TR/owl-ref/ provides a formal specification of the Web Ontology Language (OWL). Unlike RDF, the OWL vocabulary is quite large. Like RDF, OWL makes use of elements from RDF Schema.

However, OWL has several concepts unique to it, such as Boolean combination of class expressions and property restrictions, which add a layer of reasoning to applications.[1]

RDF Schema and OWL are compatible, which is why there are RDFS elements within the OWL element set.

OWL Lite Synopsis

The list of OWL Lite language constructs is given in Table 8-1 and includes RDF Schema Functions, (In)Equality, PropertyType Restrictions, Property Characteristics, and Class Intersection. OWL provides lots of metadata for properties: SymmetricProperty, FunctionalProperty,

---

[1] Note: owl:Thing is a legacy from DAML+OIL and is not formally defined in OWL.

TransitiveProperty, inverseOf, InverseFunctionalProperty, allValuesFrom, someValuesFrom, hasValue, cardinality, minCardinality, and maxCardinality.

RDF Schema Features:	(In)Equality:
Class	equivalentClass
rdf:Property	equivalentProperty
rdfs:subClassOf	sameIndividualAs
rdfs:subPropertyOf	differentFrom
rdfs:domain	allDifferent
rdfs:range	
Individual	
Property Type Restrictions:	**Property Characteristics:**
allValuesFrom	inverseOf
someValuesFrom	TransitiveProperty
	SymmetricProperty
	FunctionalProperty
	InverseFunctionalProperty
Class Intersection:	
intersectionOf	

Table 8-1. OWL Lite Language Features.

OWL DL and OWL Full Synopsis

The list of OWL DL and OWL Full language constructs that are in addition to those of OWL Lite is given in Table 8-2.

Class Axioms:	Boolean Combinations of Class Expressions:
oneOf	
disjiontWith	unionOf
equivalentClass	intersectionOf
(applied to class expressions)	complementOf
rdfs:subClassOf	
(applied to class expressions)	

Table 8-2. OWL Classes.

Samples of the OWL Vocabulary

The following three OWL elements are samples of the OWL vocabularies (see Table 8-1):

- subClassOf—this OWL element is used to assert that one class of items is a subset of another class of items. Example: Laptop is a subClassOf Computer.

- equivalentProperty—this OWL element is used to assert that one property is equivalent to another. Example: Memory is an equivalentProperty to RAM.

- sameIndividualAs—this OWL element is used to assert that one instance is the same as another instance. Example: George Washington is the sameIndividualAs "the Father of his Country."

Creating An OWL Document

An OWL Document looks very much like all XML and RDF documents in terms of elements, tags, and namespaces. In addition, an OWL document starts with a header and then defines properties and classes.

OWL Header

The first part of an OWL document is the outer OWL block, delimited by owl:Ontology, containing version information (owl:versionInfo), and an import section (owl:imports) (see Listing 8-1).

An example OWL header could look as shown in Listing 8-1. This is the OWL equivalent of the RDF Listing 6-1.

Listing 8-1. OWL Header.

```
<?xml version="1.0" encoding="UTF-8"?>
<rdf:RDF
        xmlns:iq = "http://www.web-iq.com">
        xmlns:owl = "http://www.w3.org/2002/07/owl#"
        xmlns:rdf = "http://www.w3.org/1999/02/22-rdf-
syntax-ns#"
        xmlns:rdfs = "http://www.w3.org/1999/02/22-rdf-
schema#"
```

```
            xmlns:dc = "http://purl.org/dc/elements/1.1/"
            xmlns:xsd = "http://www.w3.org/2000/1/XMLSchema#">
<owl:Ontology rdf:about = "http://www.web-iq.com">
<owl:versionInfo>
          $ID: Overview.html,v 1.2 2002/11/08 16:42:25 west
Exp
</owl:versionInfo>
<dc:creator>H. Peter Alesso</dc:creator>
<dc:title>e-Video:Producing Internet Video</dc:title>
</owl:Ontology>
</rdf:RDF>
```

These namespaces are familiar standards as well as the outer rdf:RDF opening and closing elements. However, we have not defined a schema for the existing RDF vocabulary. Rather, we are using RDF/XML and building a new ontology. Also introduced in the header is the outer Ontology block to contain the ontology definitions and version information elements. This section could also include import statements. An import section includes an rdf:resource attribute that identifies a separate RDF resource providing definitions used by the ontology. This may include the schema for the ontology.

Dublin Core (DC) elements are included in the header to provide title, creator, and other information since the ontology is a published resource. DC was designed to document metadata about published resources (see Chapter 7).

Defining Properties

After the OWL header, the document includes the definitions for classes and properties of the ontology. OWL classes define entities through properties.

A property in RDF provides information about the entity it is describing. Property characteristics increase our ability to understand the inferred information within the data.

The RDF Schema provides three ways to characterize a property:

- range—used to indicate the possible values for a property.
- domain—used to associate a property with a class.
- subPropertyOf—used to specialize a property.

The OWL documents can use rdfs:range, rdfs:domain, and rdfs:subPropertyOf as well.

230

An OWL property is very similar to an RDFS property. They both share the same use of rdfs:domain and rdfs:range, but OWL adds some constraints.

The relationship of the knowledge bank (OWL) to the Web application is shown in Figure 8-2. Generally, the inference engine is the component that takes the semantics and ontology definitions and deduces relationships to handle queries.

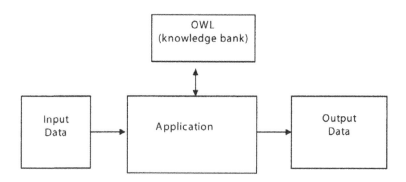

Figure 8-2. OWL and applications.

Defining Properties in OWL vs RDF Schema

All OWL definitions are nested within an RDF element rdf:RDF and the class can be defined as in Listing 8-2.

```
Listing 8-2. OWL Class.

<?xml version="1.0" encoding="UTF-8"?>
<rdf:RDF xmlns:rdf="http://www.w3.org/1999/02/22-rdf-syntax-
ns#"
               xmlns:rdfs="http://www.w3.org/2000/01/rdf-
schema#"
       xmlns:owl="http://www.w3.org/2002/07/owl#"    ...>
    <owl:Class rdf:ID="Book">
       ...
    </owl:Class>
</rdf:RDF>
```

231

Large resources can be managed using the RDF property called partOf which relates a piece of a document. However, this process does not capture which is the parent document and which is the child. OWL property characteristics are however able to capture this information.

On the other hand, RDFS and OWL are very different when it comes to data typing. Both use XML Schema data types; both allow the use of data type within the schema definition; and both allow annotation of instances with data type. The two differ in that RDF limits data types to those types that can be referenced by URI, while OWL extends the concept of data type to include creating classes of data types that are then used to constrain the range of properties. This ability of OWL to attach more nuance of meaning to the data being modeled is a clear advantage over RDFS.

Defining OWL Classes

OWL classes permit much greater expressiveness than RDF Schema classes. Consequently, OWL has created their own Class, owl:Class. For example:

```
<rdfs:Class rdf:ID="Computer">
        <rdfs:subClassOf rdf:resource="#Laptop"/>
</rdfs:Class>

becomes

<owl:Class rdf:ID="Computer">
        <rdfs:subClassOf rdf:resource="#Laptop"/>
</owl:Class>
```

which permits additional nuance of meaning.

OWL Constructs

In the next sections, we will present the definitions for several of the more important constructs including: transitive, symmetric, functional, and inverse.

Transitive

An important specialization of properties in OWL is transitivity. For instance, the ancestor of your ancestor is also your ancestor. There is at least one common transitive property built into RDFS: owl:subClassOf. If class A is a subclass of B, and class B is a subclass of C, then class

A must be a subclass of C. OWL allows one to give this behavior to any object property.

The OWL property characteristic for the TransitiveProperty has the following logic associated. If a property P is specified as transitive then for any x, y, and z:

$$P(x,y) \text{ and } P(y,z) \text{ implies } P(x,z)$$

We can illustrate this by using the property locatedIn, which is transitive (see Listing 8-3).

Listing 8-3. locatedIn.

```
<owl:ObjectProperty rdf:ID="locatedIn">
  <rdf:type rdf:resource="&owl;TransitiveProperty" />
  <rdfs:domain rdf:resource="&owl;Thing" />
  <rdfs:range rdf:resource="#Region" />
</owl:ObjectProperty>

<Region rdf:ID="SanJoseRegion">
  <locatedIn rdf:resource="#CaliforniaRegion" />
</Region>

<Region rdf:ID="CaliforniaRegion">
  <locatedIn rdf:resource="#USRegion" />
</Region>
```

Because the SanJoseRegion is locatedIn the CaliforniaRegion, then SanJoseRegion must also be locatedIn the USRegion, since locatedIn is transitive.

The TransitiveProperty characteristic is attached to the property partOf.

Symmetric

The second property characteristic is the SymmetricProperty which has a logic as follows:

$$P(x,y) \text{ iff } P(y,x)$$

Functional

And a third property characteristic is FunctionalProperty with a logic that:

$$P(x,y) \text{ and } P(x,z) \text{ implies } y = z$$

Inverse

Inverse properties are quite common. If A is the parent of B, then B is the child of A. The properties "parent" and "child" are the inverse of each other. OWL allows us to declare this systematically, so that if we assert one property, its inverse is inferred. Only one of the properties need carry the `owl:inverseOf` property, as it is reflexive. Also note that the range of one property is the domain of its inverse and vice versa.

The inverseOf characteristic is straight forward. If a property, P1, is tagged as the owl: inverseOf P2, then for all x, y, and z:

$$P1(x,y) \text{ iff } P2(y,x)$$

Note that A iff B means (A implies B) and (B implies A).

Computers have makers, which in the definition of a computer are restricted to manufacturers. Each manufacturer produces the computer that identifies it as a maker. This is shown as:

```
<owl:ObjectProperty rdf:ID="hasMaker">
  <rdf:type rdf:resource="&owl;FunctionalProperty" />
</owl:ObjectProperty>

<owl:ObjectProperty rdf:ID="producesComputers">
  <owl:inverseOf rdf:resource="#hasMaker" />
</owl:ObjectProperty>
```

If partOf shows a child section's relationship to a parent section, then the property hasChild defines a parent section's relationship to a child. For example:

```
<owl:ObjectProperty rdf:ID="hasChild">
    <owl:inverseOf rdf:resource="#partOf" />
</owl:ObjectProperty>
```

Finally, InverseFucntionalProperty gives:

$$P(x,y) \text{ and } P(z,x) \text{ implies } y = z$$

If property characteristics enhance reasoning by extending meaning behind element relationships, then property restrictions fine-tune the reasoning properties in specific context.

OWL provides property restrictions, which are a way to restrict classes to a set of resources based on particular properties. Restrictions differ from characteristics in that the former apply

234

to a sub-set of the data, instead of globally, as do the latter. One restriction is cardinality which indicates the exact number of individual instances of a property allowed within a class. OWL Lite specifies only values of 0 or 1 for the cardinality restriction. However, OWL Full allows owl: maxCardinality which can be used to set an upper cardinality and owl:minCardinality which sets a lower limit. A range is defined by using both.

More complex class relationships exist beyond simple hierarchy defined through the use of subClassOf. These relationships are managed through a set of properties that control how each class relates to another. All classes constructed using set operations, such as intersectionOf, are closed.

An intersection of a class and one or more properties is created using the intersectionOf property. All members of a class defined with intersectionOf are explicitly defined by the intersection of the class membership and the property specified.

The unionOf construct creates a class whose members combine the properties of both classes joined.

A class that consists of all members of a specific domain that do not belong to a specified class can be formed using the complementOf construct.

An enumeration is a class with a predetermined, closed set of members.

Finally, a disjoint construct lists all of the classes that a particular class is guaranteed not to be a member.

OWL offers considerable advantages over RDF and RDFS when modeling a specific domain that requires that the data respond to sophisticated queries.

OWL Example—Comp Inc.

In the following example, we illustrate many of the OWL features for a fictitious computer company called Comp Inc.

We build our OWL example as an online computer store called Comp Inc. First using RDF Schema, we define appropriate Product classes by direct declaration:

```
<rdfs:Class rdf:ID="Product">
  <rdfs:label>Product</rdfs:label>
  <rdfs:comment>An item sold by Comp Inc.</rdfs:comment>
</rdfs:Class>
```

We can make definitions for some simple, Product properties, such as Product Number:

```
<rdfs:Property rdf:ID="productNumber">
  <rdfs:label>Product Number</rdfs:label>
  <rdfs:domain rdf:resource="#Product"/>
  <rdfs:range rdf:resource="http://www.w3.org/2000/01/rdf-
schema#Literal"/>
</rdfs:Property>
```

We have defined the Product Number with the domain of the Product and the range indicated is a literal.

We define instances of Product classes by defining resources of the relevant RDF type, and then give them relevant properties. For example, we define a sound card as a product and identify its Product Number as 123:

```
<Product rdf:ID="Sound Card">
  <rdfs:label> Sound Card </rdfs:label>
  <productNumber>123</productNumber>
</Product>
```

One problem with this however, is that the values of the productNumber property are numbers. We specify them as literals, but literals can be any string, including those we can't interpret as numbers. OWL allows property values to be restricted to the data types defined in XSD or to user-defined data types. This is done by using a specialization of RDF properties DatatypeProperty:

```
<owl:DatatypeProperty rdf:ID="productNumber">
  <rdfs:label>Product Number</rdfs:label>
  <rdfs:domain rdf:resource="#Product"/>
  <rdfs:range rdf:resource="http://www.w3.org/2000/10/XMLSchema#no
nNegativeInteger"/>
</owl:DatatypeProperty>
```

The "owl" prefix represents the OWL namespace. OWL adds the primitives, like DatatypeProperty. There are some changes to the semantics of rdfs:domain and rdfs:range in OWL systems, such as a property can have multiple ranges. OWL effectively considers every literal used as the value of a property to have some data type.

OWL expresses property identity as with either the owl:sameAs or owl:equivalentProperty property. Suppose Comp Inc. has deployed its RDF-based system, and then an online competitor comes up with a standardized vocabulary for computer equipment information. If this new vocabulary uses a property called productID to indicate Product Number, Comp Inc. does not

have to alter all their code to use the new property. Since OWL simply extends the definition
of productNumber as:

```
<rdf:Description about="#productNumber">
  <owl:equivalentProperty rdf:resource="http://competitor.org/
vocab/productID"/>
</rdf:Description>
```

This relates the company's productNumber to its competitor's productID and enforces their
equivalence.

Unique Properties

We can specify that a property is unique by requiring that each Comp Inc. product have a
unique product number by modifying the property definition to:

```
<owl:DatatypeProperty rdf:ID="productNumber">
  <rdfs:label>Product Number</rdfs:label>
  <rdfs:domain rdf:resource="#Product"/>
  <rdfs:range rdf:resource="http://www.w3.org/2000/10/XMLSchema#no
nNegativeInteger"/>
  <rdf:type rdf:resource="http://www.w3.org/2001/10/
OWL#UniqueProperty"/>
</owl:DatatypeProperty>
```

We specify that the productNumber property has two properties: owl:DatatypeProperty
and owl:UniqueProperty. It permits a product to have more than one product number, as long
as each is unique. OWL allows an expression for the cardinality of a property.

Class

The class owl:Class is defined as a subclass of rdfs:Class, and adds new facilities. However, the
enumeration is not closed. OWL allows a class to be defined by being one of a given set of
instances (see Listing 8-4).

Listing 8-4. OWL Collection.

```
<owl:Class ID="Availability">
  <owl:oneOf parseType="owl:collection">
    <owl:Thing rdf:ID="InStock">
```

```
        <rdfs:label>In stock</rdfs:label>
    </owl:Thing>
    <owl:Thing rdf:ID="BackOrdered">
        <rdfs:label>Back ordered</rdfs:label>
    </owl:Thing>
    <owl:Thing rdf:ID="SpecialOrder">
        <rdfs:label>Special order</rdfs:label>
    </owl:Thing>
  </owl:oneOf>
</owl:Class>
```

The owl:oneOf element defines an enumeration, using a OWL construct the owl:collection parse type that allows us to define closed lists.

The owl:collection parse type allows an OWL agent to interpret the body of a property element as a special form of list. This list has a special representation in the RDF model—it is actually a set of statements that recursively breaks the list down into the first element and the sub-list consisting of the rest of the elements. Figure 8-3 illustrates this data structure.

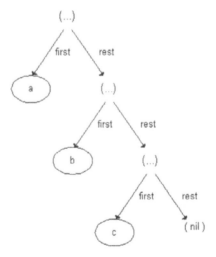

Figure 8-3. Data structure.

Now, we define a user-defined type to use in the product descriptions. The following listing is an XML schema definition for our data type for a hard drive product within Comp Inc. (see Listing 8-5).

Listing 8-5. Hard Drive XML Schema.

```
<?xml version="1.0" encoding="UTF-8"?>
<xsd:schema
  targetNamespace="http://rdfinference.org/eg/comp/dt"
  xmlns:dt="http://rdfinference.org/eg/comp/dt"
  xmlns:xsd="http://www.w3.org/2001/XMLSchema"
>
  <xsd:simpleType name="harddriveCapacity">
    <xsd:restriction base="xsd:positiveInteger">
      <xsd:maxExclusive value="50"/>
    </xsd:restriction>
  </xsd:simpleType>
```

We define a hard drive capacity as an integer range from 1 to 50 MB using a restriction on the core positive integer type from XSD.

We use this customized data type in the following OWL schema for the Comp Inc. product catalog (see Listing 8-6).

Example 8-1. **Listing 8-6.** Comp Inc. Catalog Document.

```
<?xml version="1.0" encoding="UTF-8"?>

<rdf:RDF
  xmlns:rdf="http://www.w3.org/1999/02/22-rdf-syntax-ns#"
  xmlns:rdfs="http://www.w3.org/2000/01/rdf-schema#"
  xmlns:owl="http://www.w3.org/2001/10/owl#"
  xmlns:dt="http://rdfinference.org/eg/comp/dt"
  xmlns:ss="http://rdfinference.org/eg/ comp /metadata"
  xmlns:xsd="http://www.w3.org/2000/10/XMLSchema#"
  xml:base="http://rdfinference.org/eg/ comp /metadata"
>

  <owl:Ontology rdf:about="">
    <owl:versionInfo>1.0</owl:versionInfo>
    <rdfs:comment>An ontology of Comp Inc. store products
    </rdfs:comment>
<owl:imports rdf:resource="http://www.w3.org/2001/10/owl"/>
```

```
</owl:Ontology>

<owl:Class rdf:ID="Product">
  <rdfs:label>Product</rdfs:label>
  <rdfs:comment>An item sold by Comp Inc.</rdfs:comment>
</owl:Class>

<owl:Class rdf:ID="Department">
  <rdfs:label>Department</rdfs:label>
  <rdfs:comment>A Comp Inc. department</rdfs:comment>
</owl:Class>

<!--enumeration-- >

<owl:Class rdf:ID="wordprocessing">
  <rdfs:label> Wordprocessing </rdfs:label>
  <rdfs:comment>A computer process wordprocessing </rdfs:
comment>
  <owl:oneOf rdf:parseType="owl:collection">
    <owl:Thing rdf:ID="Database">
      <rdfs:label>Database</rdfs:label>
    </owl:Thing>
    <owl:Thing rdf:ID="Spreadsheet">
      <rdfs:label> Spreadsheet </rdfs:label>
    </owl:Thing>
    <owl:Thing rdf:ID="Presentations">
      <rdfs:label> Presentations </rdfs:label>
    </owl:Thing>
   <owl:Thing rdf:ID="Multimedia">
      <rdfs:label> Multimedia </rdfs:label>
    </owl:Thing>
   </owl:oneOf>
  </owl:Class>

  <owl:Class rdf:ID="Availability">
    <rdfs:label>Availability</rdfs:label>
    <rdfs:comment>The availability of a product</rdfs:
comment>
    <owl:oneOf parseType="owl:collection">
      <owl:Thing rdf:ID="InStock">
        <rdfs:label>In stock</rdfs:label>
      </owl:Thing>
      <owl:Thing rdf:ID="BackOrdered">
        <rdfs:label>Back ordered</rdfs:label>
```

```
    </owl:Thing>
    <owl:Thing rdf:ID="SpecialOrder">
      <rdfs:label>Special order</rdfs:label>
    </owl:Thing>
   </owl:oneOf>
  </owl:Class>

  <!--datatype properties >

  <owl:DatatypeProperty rdf:ID="productNumber">
    <rdfs:label>Product Number</rdfs:label>
    <owl:equivalentProperty rdf:resource="<a
href="http://rosettanet.org/FundamentalBusiness">http://
rosettanet.org/FundamentalBusiness</a>
DataEntities#ProprietaryProductIdentifier"/>
    <rdfs:domain rdf:resource="#Product"/>
    <rdfs:range rdf:resource="http://www.w3.org/2000/10/XMLS
chema#nonNegativeInteger"/>
    <rdf:type rdf:resource="http://www.w3.org/2001/10/
owl#UniqueProperty"/>
  </owl:DatatypeProperty>

  <owl:DatatypeProperty rdf:ID="harddriveCapacity">
    <rdfs:label>capacity</rdfs:label>
    <rdfs:comment>The capacity of harddrive</rdfs:comment>
    <rdfs:domain rdf:resource="#harddrive"/>
    <rdfs:range rdf:resource="http://rdfinference.org/eg/
supersports/dt#packCapacity"/>
  </owl:DatatypeProperty>

  <!--object property >

  <owl:ObjectProperty rdf:ID="usedFor">
    <rdfs:label>usedFor</rdfs:label>
    <rdfs:comment>The wordprocessing for which a product is
used</rdfs:comment>
    <owl:domain rdf:resource="#Product"/>
    <owl:range rdf:resource="# wordproceesing"/>
  </owl:ObjectProperty>

</rdf:RDF>
```

At the top level of the document is the RDF envelope element, as in most RDF/XML files. Special namespaces are used to construct URIs in the descriptions. We use an xml:base attribute to set the base URI. This affects the actual URI to which RDF IDs are mapped. For instance, given our declared base URI, rdf:ID="Product" yields a resource with URI http://rdfinference. org/eg/supersports/metadata#Product. This allows an RDF/XML document to retrieve from different URIs.

Next, the OWL header is listed. This provides certain metadata for the ontology itself. By having an empty rdf:about, we are treating the very document as the resource, using the XML base. The owl:imports allows us to incorporate other RDF models.

Next we show the classes. Then we define an enumeration of activities associated with Comp Inc. products and an enumeration of product availability codes. We next define some properties, using standard XSD data types, as well as the custom type we defined. One of these properties, productNumber, is a unique property: each product can only have one product number.

OWL provides a rich expressiveness. It is not a schema language, but an ontology language, providing primitives that support the general representation of knowledge. It allows one to express classifications by inference.

OWL Disjoint Classes

Another important OWL feature is the ability for one class to be disjoint from another. This means that neither of the two classes have any instances in common. For example, if we wanted to state that something is either a current product or a discontinued product. We could write:

```
<owl:Class rdf:ID="CurrentProduct">
  <rdfs:label>Current Product</rdfs:label>
  <rdfs:comment>An item currently sold by Comp Inc.
    at the time of query</rdfs:comment>
</owl:Class>
<owl:Class rdf:ID="DiscontinuedProduct">
  <rdfs:label>Discontinued Product</rdfs:label>
  <rdfs:comment>An item no longer sold by Comp Inc.
    at the time of query</rdfs:comment>
  <owl:disjointWith rdf:resource="#CurrentProduct"/>
</owl:Class>
```

The key is the owl:disjointWith property on the second class. Its value asserts that the two classes can have no instances in common. This property applies

---

to OWL classes and is known as class expressions. In this case, the class expression is the URI of the target class. But OWL allows more complex algebra with class expressions.

We are clear that all products are either current products or discontinued products. The owl:disjointUnionOf property allows us to express this:

```
<owl:Class rdf:ID="Product">
  <rdfs:label>Product</rdfs:label>
  <rdfs:comment>An item sold by Comp Inc.</rdfs:comment>
  <owl:unionOf parseType="owl:collection">
    <owl:Class rdf:ID="CurrentProduct">
      <rdfs:label>Current Product</rdfs:label>
      <rdfs:comment>An item currently sold by Comp Inc.
        at the time of query</rdfs:comment>
    </owl:Class>
    <owl:Class rdf:ID="DiscontinuedProduct">
      <rdfs:label>Discontinued Product</rdfs:label>
      <rdfs:comment>An item no longer sold by Comp Inc.
        at the time of query</rdfs:comment>
    </owl:Class>
  </ owl:unionOf >
</owl:Class>
```

In Figure 8-4 there are properties of Class1. The name of the property is shown (e.g., property1), and its range is shown in italics (e.g., Type1).

An alternate notation to the above class hierarchy is to use a Venn Diagram, as shown in the bottom of Figure 8-4.

Each item in the enumeration is defined as an instance of owl:Thing, a special OWL type which universally includes all instances of all Classes.

Ontology Example—Birthplace

For this section, we illustrate various OWL capabilities and properties with Example 8-2. In this example we ask the question: "What is the birthplace of George Washington?"

Upon searching the Web, three documents provided information about George Washington's birthplace. The first document stated that George Washington was born in Virginia, the second document said he was born in the Mother State, while the third document stated that George

Taxonomy (Class Hierarchy)

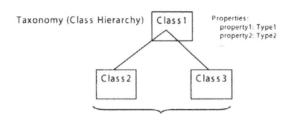

Class2 and Class3 are subclasses of Class1.

Venn Diagram

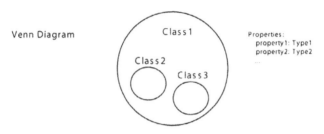

Figure 8-4. Taxonomy and Venn diagram.

Washington was born in the Old Dominion State. We can recognize that historically these are all the same location, but how could OWL help equate their meaning on the Web?

Consider the RDF/XML, Listing 8-7 which defines a person, ontology, and birthplace.

> **Example 8-2.** "What is the birthplace of George Washington?"
> **Listing 8-7.** RDF/XML Statements.
>
> ```
> <Person rdf:about="http://www.person.org# GeorgeWashington
> ">
>     <birthplace rdf:about="http://www.states.org#Virginia"/>
> </Person>
> <Person rdf:about="http://www.person.org# GeorgeWashington
> ">
> ```

244

```
     <birthplace rdf:resource="http://www.history.org# Mother
State "/>
</Person>
<Person rdf:about="http://www.person.org# GeorgeWashington
">
     <birthplace rdf:resource="http://www.tourism.org# Old
Dominion State"/>
</Person>
```

In Figure 8-5, we can represent the OWL Ontology which shows that the person OWL ontology indicates that a Person has only one birthplace location.

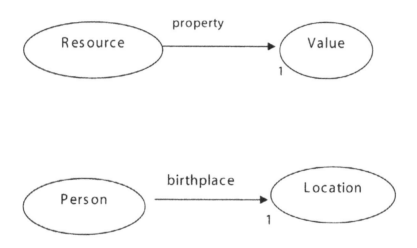

Figure 8-5. Birthplace ontology.

Figure 8-5, therefore, is a specific instance of a general capability in OWL to specify that a subject Resource has exactly one value. OWL properties that relate a resource to exactly one other resource are said to have a cardinality=1. Therefore this example is read as: "A person has exactly one birthplace location."

As a result, applying the person OWL ontology to Listing 8-7 results in the interpretation that makes the following inference:

Inference: Virginia, Mother State, and Old Dominion State are the same location.

This example demonstrates the that:

1. An OWL instance document can be enhanced with an OWL property to indicate that it is the same as another instance.
2. OWL provides the capability to construct taxonomies (class hierarchies). Such taxonomies can be used to dynamically understand how entities in an RDF/XML instance relate to other entities.
3. OWL provides the capability to specify that a subject can have only one value.
4. OWL facilitates a dynamic understanding of the semantics of data.

OWL Example—Book

In this section, we address several important issues with a book buying example of Web Bots utilizing OWL. An agent is a Web application (Bot) capable of a chosen autonomous action in its environment.

We start by asking a simple question: "Where on the Web can we purchase a book on abstract mathematics that includes Boolean Algebra and Functions?"

This query is expressed in XML in Listing 8-8.

Example 8-3. Book Buying Catalog.
Listing 8-8. Question: "Where on the Web can we purchase a book on abstract mathematics that includes Boolean Algebra and Functions?"

```
<?xml version="1.0" encoding="UTF-8"?>
<Book xmlns:rdf="http://www.w3.org/1999/02/22-rdf-syntax-ns#"
           xmlns="http://www.book.org#">
     <math>
          <Abstract>
               <BooleanAlgebra>Disjunctive Normal Form</
BooleanAlgebra>
               <Functions>binary</Functions>
          </Abstract>
     </math>
     <body>
          <Body>
               <available rdf:parseType="Resource">
                    <min>3</min>
```

```
                    <max>10</max>
                    <units>days</units>
                </ available >
            </Body>
        </body>
    </Book>
```

We can recast the query as: "Find all XML documents which overlap with the above XML document."

Is This Document Relevant?

After we launch our Web Bot to find this book information, we get responses to our query which we have to evaluate. The Bot finds a document (Listing 8-9) at a Web site:

Listing 8-9. Web Bot finds a document at a Web site.

```
<BookStore rdf:ID="Smiths"
                    xmlns:rdf="http://www.w3.org/1999/02/22-rdf-syntax-
ns#">
    <store-location>Malden, MA</store-location>
    <phone>617-555-1234</phone>
    <catalog rdf:parseType="Collection">
        <eBook rdf:ID="Abstract Algebra"
                xmlns="http://www.book.org#">
        <math>
            <Abstract>
                < PropositionalCalculus >Disjunctive Normal Form</Proposition-
alCalculus>
                < relationships >binary</ relationships >
            </Abstract>
        </math>
        <body>
            <Body>
            <available rdf:parseType="Resource">
```

```
            <min>3</min>
            <max>10</max>
            <units>days</units>
        </ available >
      </Body>
    </body>
    <cost rdf:parseType="Resource">
        <rdf:value>32.5</rdf:value>
        <currency>USD</currency>
    </cost>
  </eBook>
 </catalog>
</BookStore>
```

To determine if the document provides a book which is a match to our query, the following questions must be answered:

1. What's the relationship between "eBook" and "Book"?
2. What's the relationship between " PropositionalCalculus " and "BooleanAlgebra"?
3. What's the relationship between "Functions" and "Relationships"?

Relationship Between eBook and Book

This OWL statement (from the Book Ontology Listing 8-10 and Figure 8-6) tells the Web Bot that an eBook is a type of book. See Listing 8-10 and Figure 8-6:

Listing 8-10. eBook SubClass.

```
<owl:Class rdf:ID="eBook">
    <rdfs:subClassOf rdf:resource="#Book"/>
</owl:Class>
```

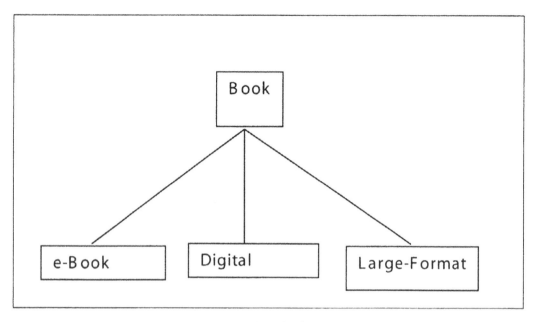

Figure 8-6. Book subClass

PropositionalCalculus Synonymous with BooleanAlgebra

The OWL statement in listing 8-11 says that PropositionalCalculus is equivalent to Boolean-Algebra.

```
Listing 8-11. Equivalence.

<owl:DatatypeProperty rdf:ID=" PropositionalCalculus ">
        <owl:equivalentProperty rdf:resource="#BooleanAlge
bra"/>
        <rdfs:domain rdf:resource="#Abstract"/>
        <rdfs:range rdf:resource="&xsd;#string"/>
</owl:DatatypeProperty>
```

Relationships Synonymous with Functions

Is Relationships synonymous with Functions? The OWL statement in listing 8-12 says the Web Bot that "relationships" is equivalent to "Functions."

> **Listing 8-12.** Equivalence.
>
> ```
> <owl:DatatypeProperty rdf:ID="Relationships">
>         <owl:equivalentProperty rdf:resource="#Functions"/>
>         <rdfs:domain rdf:resource="#Abstract"/>
>         <rdfs:range rdf:resource="&xsd;#string"/>
> </owl:DatatypeProperty>
> ```

The Web Bot now recognizes that the XML document it found at the Web site (Listing 8-9):

1. is talking about Books.
2. does show BooleanAlgebra.
3. does show functions for the book.

Thus, the Web Bot has determined that this Abstract Algebra eBook is an instance and an acceptable (though maybe not a perfect) match for the query we posed in Listing 8-8. We could therefore proceed to order the book from Smith's Bookstore at a cost of $32.50 and expect to receive it in 3 to 10 days.

We will see more examples of book purchasing on the Web with OWL and OWL-Services (OWL-S) in Chapter 11.

Markup Languages Comparisons

Table 8-3 provides comparisons that show the tradeoffs and differences among markup languages. It compares XML Schema (XSD), RDFS (Resource Description Framework Schema), and OWL (Web Ontology Language) by showing a description and examples of how each language addresses common knowledge- representation requirements.

	XML Schema	RDF Schema	OWL
Contexts	namespace:xmlns Declaring others : xmlns:<label> XMLSchema namespace (xsd) xmlns:xsd="www.w3.org/2001/XMLSchema"	RDF uses XML namespaces. RDF Syntax Namespace xmlns:rdf="http://www.w3.org/1999/02/22-rdf-syntax-ns#" RDF Schema namespace xmlns:rdfs = "http://www.w3.org/2000/01/rdf-schema#"	OWL also uses XML namespaces. It uses RDF and RDFS elements by referring to their respective namespaces. OWL namespace xmlns:owl="http://www.owl.org/2001/03/owl#."
Object Classes and Properties	No concept of classes and properties, only elements of certain types.	Resource is the top level class. (http://www.w3.org/2001/01/rdf-schema#Resource) Example of Classes, and Properties Cycles in class hierarchy were not allowed till a little while ago. Latest revisions to the RDF spec allow this.	OWL also has classes and properties. Classes can also be a subClassOf . Two kinds of Properties are defined: ObjectProperties (Relate an object to another object - the value of the property is also an object) and DatatypeProperties (Relate an object to a primitive data type - the value of the property is a primitive data type) Cycles in the class hierarchy are allowed.
Inheritance	no concept of inheritance.	A class can be a subClassOf other classes (multiple inheritance is allowed.) Properties can also be subPropertyOf other	Same as in RDF.

Table 8-3. Markup Languages Comparisons.

251

Property/ Element Range	Can be specified globally. For a locally specified (element specific) range, the element has to be declared locally.	Can only be specified globally <rdfs:range....> Multiple range statements imply conjunction	Can be specified globally (<rdfs:range...>) as well as locally <owl:Restriction> <owl:onProperty...><owl:allValuesFrom....> </owl:Restriction> Multiple range statements imply conjunction.
Property/ Element Domain	No explicit declaration of the domain of the element. The domain is implicitly the element in which the definition appears.	Can only be specified globally <rdfs:domain....> Multiple domain statements imply conjunction	Can be specified globally (<rdfs:domain...>). Multiple domain statements imply conjuction
Property/ Element Cardinality	Can be specified using minOccurs, maxOccurs.	Not defined in the core RDF Schema. By default there are no cardinality restrictions on properties.	Can be specified locally minCardinality, maxCardinality, cardinality. Can also be specified globally although only as a UniqueProperty (single valued i.e. having cardinality of 1).
Basic Data Types	Datatypes supported by XMLSchema are mainly variations of numerical, temporal, and string data types.	The core RDF Schema only includes 'Literals' which is the set of all strings.	Allows the use of XMLSchema Datatypes by just referring to the XMLSchema URI.

Table 8-3 (continued). Markup Languages Comparisons.

Basic Data Types	Datatypes supported by XMLSchema are mainly variations of numerical, temporal, and string data types.	The core RDF Schema only includes 'Literals' which is the set of all strings.	Allows the use of XMLSchema Datatypes by just referring to the XMLSchema URI.
Enumeration of Property Values	Possible with the <enumeration> tag.	Not possible.	Enumeration of property types is possible with the <oneOf rdf:ParseType="owl:collection"...> tag It is also possible to simply point to an enumerated data type declared using XMLSchema.
Ordered Data Set	Data Sets maintain order by default.	Data Set ordered with the <rdf:Seq...> tag.	Can use the <owl:list> tag.
Bounded Lists	No.	No.	Possible with the <owl:collection> tag
Transitive Properties	No.	No.	Possible with the <owl:TransitiveProperty> tag.
Negation	No.	No.	Possible with the <owl:complementOf..> tag.
Disjunctive / Disjoint Classes Conditions for Class Membership	A union of possible types for an element is possible with the <union> tag.	Can use a Bag to Indicate unordered collections (or unions of properties). However, we cannot	A class can be a union of 2 other classes. Possible with the <unionOf...> tag. We can represent disjoint unions with the

Table 8-3 (continued). Markup Languages Comparisons.

253

Necessary and Sufficient	No. (although \<unique\> could be interpreted as an UnambigousProperty.)	No.	Yes. sameClassAs, equivalent, using boolean combinations of Class Expressions. UnambigousProperty specifies a property which identifies the resource (i.e., a primary key).

Table 8-3 (continued). Markup Languages Comparisons.

OWL Capabilities and Limitations

Some OWL applications have encountered problems attaching semantics on a per-application basis or with burying semantic definitions within each application. This can lead to duplicate effort since each application must express the semantics and variability of its own interpretation.

Additional OWL problems include no ad-hoc discovery and exploitation, and applications that may have the semantics pre-wired; thus an application may not be able to effectively process new data when it is encountered. The result can be a brittle application. A better approach would be to provide extricate semantic definitions from applications and express semantic definitions in a standard vocabulary.

Why should we use OWL? OWL offers us:

- Less code to write.
- Less chance of misinterpretation.
- We can understand each other's data's semantics.
- OWL uses existing XML syntax to express semantics.
- OWL is a W3C recommendation.

There are many reasons for keeping the OWL semantic information separate from the application:

- Extensible—the OWL document can grow independent of the application.
- Reusable—the OWL document can be used by multiple applications.
- Avoid misinterpretation—the information in an OWL document is expressed using a well-defined, standardized vocabulary.

Conclusion

In this chapter, we provided an introduction to the Web Ontology Language called OWL. We provided background on the development of ontology which has undergone significant change in the last few years. In addition, we introduced each of the three OWL versions currently available; Lite, DL, and Full. A comparison to RDFS was made and several illustrative examples were included. Finally, we discussed the basis of using this markup language for developing the Semantic Web.

Chapter Nine

Machine Intelligence

Overview

New Web markup languages, such as Resource Description Framework (RDF) (see Chapter 7) and Web Ontology Language (OWL) (see Chapter 8) provide new powerful semantic and ontology capabilities for the next generation of Web architecture. However, for Semantic Web Services to succeed, the Web will have to become a much "smarter" place. How we define and implement new knowledge to make the Web "smarter" remains open to debate.

In this chapter, we describe key concepts essential for Semantic Web Services including: machine intelligence, computational complexity, Knowledge Representation, inference, Ontology, and software agents.

After a few brief comments on the concept of intelligence, we discuss the delineation of complexity and the issue of scaling semantic applications for the Web. Then, we outline several important research areas in Knowledge Representation theories, such as logic models, rule-based expert systems, frames and semantic networks, and description logics. This is followed by a presentation on inference rules and engines. Then we comment on the importance and application of Ontology and how to utilize languages such as Web Ontology Language (OWL). Finally, we discuss using software agents to carry out independent tasks on the Web to minimize complexity and take advantage of inference rules and ontologies.

Background

Before discussing "thinking machines" or artificial intelligence, it is appropriate to consider what we mean by real, as opposed to artificial, intelligence. The Greek philosopher Aristotle considered intelligence to be the main distinguishing feature of humans: he described man as a "rational animal." He also established many precedents in the study of logic and began the process of codifying syllogisms, a process later extended by the mathematician Leibnitz. In addition to his work in developing the mathematics of calculus, Leibnitz initiated an effort to represent human logic and reasoning as a series of mechanical and symbolic tasks. Later, George Boole developed Boolean logic paving the way for the use of mechanical rules to carry out logical deductions.

While it is still not possible to resolve controversial differences of opinion over the nature of human intelligence, it is possible to recognize certain attributes that most would agree reflect the concept. These include such elements as: the ability to learn; the ability to assimilate; the ability to organize and process information; and the ability to apply knowledge to solve complex problems. By extension then, many of these real intelligence attributes can be traced into the various areas of research in the field of artificial intelligence. Artificial intelligence addresses the basic questions of what it means for a machine to have intelligence.

In 1947, shortly after the end of World War II, English mathematician Alan Turing first started to seriously explore intelligent machines. By 1956, John McCarthy of MIT contributed the term "Artificial Intelligence (AI)." And by the late 1950s, there were many researchers in AI, most basing their work on programming computers. Eventually, AI became more than a branch of science—it expanded far beyond mathematics and computer science into fields such as philosophy, psychology, and biology.

In Turing's seminal work, more than 50 years ago, he determined that a computer can be called intelligent if it could deceive a human into believing that it was human. His test—called the Turing Test—consists of a person asking a series of questions to both a human subject and a machine. The questioning is done via a keyboard so that the questioner has no direct interaction between subjects, man, or machine. A machine with true intelligence will pass the Turing Test by providing responses that are sufficiently human-like that the questioner cannot determine which responder is human and which is not. A scaled down version of the Turing Test, known as the Loebner Prize, requires that machines "converse" with testers only on a limited topic in order to demonstrate their intelligence.

Human Intelligence

How far is AI from reaching human-level intelligence? Some have suggested that human-level intelligence can be achieved by writing large numbers of programs and assembling vast databases of facts in the languages used for expressing knowledge. However, most AI researchers believe that new fundamental ideas are required before true intelligence can be approached.

There are two main lines of AI research. One is biological, based on the idea that since humans are intelligent, AI should study humans and imitate the psychology or physiology of human intelligence. The other is phenomenological, based on studying and formalizing common sense facts about the world and the problems that the world presents to the achievement of goals thereby providing functionality that, in humans, would be considered intelligent behavior, even if the approach used is quite different from what would be found in a human.

Today, AI still means different things to different people. Some confusion arises because the word 'intelligence' is so ill-defined. AI is sometimes described in two ways: strong AI and weak AI. Strong AI asserts that computers can be made to think on a level (at least) equal to humans. Weak AI simply holds that some thinking-like features can be added to computers to make them more useful tools. Examples of weak AI abound: expert systems, drive-by-wire cars, smart browsers, and speech recognition software. These weak AI components may, when combined, begin to approach some aspects of strong AI.

Machine Intelligence

Central to the concept of the Semantic Web is Machine Intelligence. Machine Intelligence is often referred to in conjunction with Machine Learning, Computational Intelligence, Soft-Computing, and Artificial Intelligence. Although these terms are often used interchangeably, they are different branches of study.

For example, Artificial Intelligence involves symbolic computation while Soft-Computing involves intensive numeric computation. The following sub-branches of Machine Intelligence relate specifically to the Semantic Web:

- Computational Complexity.
- Knowledge Representation.
- Ontology.
- Inference.
- Search.
- Software Agents.

Although symbolic AI is currently built and developed into Semantic Web data representation, there is no doubt that software tool vendors and software developers will eventually incorporate the soft-computing paradigm as well. The benefit of such a step will be the creating of adaptive software. This would imply that Soft-Computing applications will have the ability to adapt to changing environments and input.

While the Semantic Web is under development, concepts surrounding machine intelligence will continue to evolve. The extent of the usefulness of the Semantic Web will be tested in various ways, but the controversy involving the meaning of Machine Intelligence will undoubtedly not end in the foreseeable future.

One point where Machine Intelligence is likely to be controversial is in the application of Semantic Web Services. Semantic Web Services will require automation of vital Web Service functions, such as service discovery, service execution, and service composition. In addition, intelligent agents will be required to interact and perform complex tasks (see Chapter 11). The results are bound to be interesting as methods evolve.

In the following sections, we will discuss each of the key machine-intelligence topics starting with computational complexity, then Knowledge Representation, inference, Ontology, (we will leave a detailed presentation on search to Chapter 15), and software agents are presented in the following sections.

Computational Complexity

Knowledge Representation, search, and software agents are all severely limited by the complexity of their particular applications. Various ways have been proposed to overcome complexity limitations of the Semantic Web.

Computational-complexity theory is the study of how much of a resource (such as time, space, parallelism, or randomness) is required to perform certain classes of computations. Problems have been classified according to how difficult they are to solve. Among the many different classifications are the following most commonly encountered:

- P—Problems that can be solved in polynomial time. An example problem in P, is the task of sorting a list of numbers. Since by systematically swapping any disordered pair the task can be accomplished within quadratic time, the problem is considered to be in P.
- NP—Problems are "nondeterministic in polynomial time." A problem is in NP if a selected (or guessed) trial solution can be quickly (in polynomial time) tested to determine if it is correct.

- PSPACE—Problems that can be solved using an amount of memory that is limited as a polynomial in the input size, regardless of how much time the solution takes.
- EXPTIME—Problems that can be solved in exponential time. This class contains problems most likely to be encountered, including everything in the previous three classes.
- Undecidable—For some problems, it can be proved that there is no algorithm that always solves them, no matter how much time or space is allowed.

In the 1930s, the mathematical logician, Kurt Gödel along with Alan Turing, established that, in certain important mathematical domains, there are problems that cannot be solved or propositions that cannot be proved or disproved and are therefore undecidable. Whether a certain statement of First Order Logic (FOL) is provable as a theorem is one example; and whether a polynomial equation in several variables has integer solutions is another. While humans solve problems in these domains all the time, it is not certain that arbitrary problems in these domains can always be solved. This is relevant for AI since it is important to establish the boundaries for problem solutions.

The theory of the difficulty of general classes of problems is called computational complexity. Algorithmic complexity theory was developed by Solomonoff, Kolmogorov and Chaitin. It defines the complexity of a symbolic object as the length of the shortest program that will generate it.

In the 1960s computer scientists Steve Cook and Richard Karp developed the theory of NP-complete problem domains. Problems in these domains are solvable, but take an exponential amount of time in proportion to its size. Humans often solve problems in NP-complete domains in times much shorter than is guaranteed by the general algorithms, but, in general, can't solve them quickly.

NP-complete problems are encountered frequently in AI. Alternatives to addressing them include:

- Using a heuristic—If the problem cannot be quickly solved deterministically in a reasonable time, a heuristic method may be used in certain cases.
- Accepting an approximate instead of an exact solution—In some cases, there is a provably fast algorithm that doesn't solve the problem exactly but comes up with an acceptable approximate solution.
- Using an exponential time solution anyway—If an exact solution is necessary, an exponential time algorithm may be the best approach.

- Redefining the problem—Normally, the NP-complete problem is based on an abstraction of the real world. Revising the abstraction to eliminate unnecessary details may make the difference between a P and NP problem.

Evaluating different knowledge-representation methodologies is highly dependent on the issue of scaling semantic applications for the Web. The complexity introduced with each methodology will have to be closely analyzed.

Knowledge Representation

An important element of AI is the principle that intelligent behavior can be achieved through processing of symbol structures representing increments of knowledge. This has given rise to the development of knowledge-representation languages that permit the representation of knowledge and allow for its manipulation to deduce new facts from the existing knowledge. Thus, knowledge-representation languages must have a well-defined syntax and semantics system, and, at the same time, support inference.

Three techniques have been popular to express knowledge representation and inference:

- logic based approaches.
- rule based systems.
- frames and semantic networks.

Logic-based approaches use logical formulas to represent complex relationships. They require a well-defined syntax, semantics, and proof theory. The formal power of a logical theorem proof can be applied to the knowledge, to derive new knowledge. Logic is used as the formalism for programming languages and databases. It can also be used as a formalism to implement knowledge methodology. Any formalism that admits a declarative semantics and can be interpreted both as a programming language and a database language is a knowledge language. However, the approach is inflexible and requires great precision in stating the logical relationships. In some cases, common sense inferences and conclusions cannot be derived, and the approach may be inefficient, especially when dealing with issues that result in large combinations of objects or concepts.

Rule-based approaches are more flexible. They allow the representation of knowledge using sets of IF-THEN or other condition action rules. This approach is more procedural and less formal in its logic. Reasoning can be controlled in a forward or backward chaining interpreter.

Frames and semantic networks capture declarative information about related objects and concepts where there is a clear class hierarchy and where the principle of inheritance can be used to infer the characteristics of members of a subclass from those of the higher-level class. The two forms of reasoning in this technique are matching (i.e., identification of objects having common properties), and property inheritance in which properties are inferred for a subclass. Frames and semantic networks are limited to representation and inference of relatively simple systems.

In each of these approaches, the knowledge-representation component (i.e., problem-specific rules and facts) is separate from the problem-solving and inference procedures.

Knowledge-based systems contain knowledge as well as information and data. The information and data can be modeled and implemented as a database. Let's define what we mean by the fundamental terms "data," "information," and "knowledge." An item of data is a fundamental element of an application. Data can be represented by population and labels. Information is an explicit association between data things. Associations represent a function relating one set of things to another set of things. A rule is an explicit functional association from a set of information things to a specific information thing. As a result, a rule is knowledge.

Higher Order Logic

Higher Order Logics have the greatest expressive power. However, higher order logics do not have nice computational properties. For example, there are true statements which are not provable (Godel's Incompleteness Theorem). There are two aspects of this issue: a higher-order syntax and a higher-order semantics. If a higher-order semantics is not needed (and this is often the case), a second-order logic can be translated into a first-order logic.

By higher-order syntax, logicians mean a language in which variables are allowed to appear in places where normally predicate and/or function symbols do. In contrast, a higher-order semantics is manifested by semantic structures in which variables may range over domains of relations and functions constructed out of the domains of individuals. In first-order semantics, variables can only range over domains of individuals or over the names of predicates and functions, not over sets as such.

Predicate calculus is the primary example of a logic where syntax and semantics are both first-order. There are logics that have a higher-order syntax but a first-order semantics. Under a higher-order semantics, an equation between predicate (or function) symbols is true if and only if, logics with a higher-order semantics and higher-order syntax are statements expressing trust about other statements.

First Order Logic (FOL)

Full First Order Logic (FOL) for specifying axioms requires a full-fledged automated theorem prover. FOL is semi-decidable and doing inferencing is computationally intractable for large amounts of data and axioms.

This means that the Web would not scale up to handle knowledge complexity. Proving full first theorems would mean maintaining consistency throughout the Web, which is improbable.

A different approach is taken by CYC; The Cyc Knowledge Server is a very large, multi-contextual knowledge base and inference engine developed by Cycorp, consisting of roughly 1MB of axioms and using the first-order framework: CYC organizes its axioms in contexts, maintaining consistency just for one context, and limiting deductions only to a few steps. Compared to a future Web architecture, CYC is still small—deduction must be further limited—thus neglecting the inference approach as a whole.

Rule-Based Systems

The term "expert system" can be considered a particular type of knowledge-based system where the knowledge is deliberately represented "as it is." Expert systems are applications that make decisions in real-life situations, which would otherwise be performed by a human expert.

Expert systems can take many different forms. In general, they are programs designed to mimic human performance at specialized, constrained problem-solving tasks. Frequently, they are constructed as a collection of IF-THEN production rules combined with a reasoning engine that applies those rules, either in a forward or backward direction, to a specific problem.

A key element of an expert system is the acquisition of the body of knowledge that is contained within the system. Such information is normally extracted from human experts, and is frequently in the form of rules of thumb or heuristic information, rather than statements of absolute fact. Simply put, an expert system contains knowledge derived from an expert in some narrow domain. This knowledge is used to help individuals using the expert system to solve some problem.

The traditional definition of a computer program is usually:

algorithm + data structures = program

In an expert system, the definition changes to:

inference engine + knowledge = expert system

Rule-based systems have the following attributes: symbolic representation, inference mechanism that allows conclusions to be drawn from facts and rules, and certainty factors and truth maintenance that allows rules to deal with uncertainty.

However, rules are cumbersome as a way of encoding relational knowledge and knowledge about objects.

Problem Solving Methods (PSM)

Problem Solving Methods (PSMs) are small algorithms discussed in the field of Knowledge Based Systems and Knowledge Acquisition. They are performing inferences within expert systems. A PSM specifies which inferences and actions have to be carried out to achieve the goal of a task and define the data flow and the control flow between subtasks. However, PSM are very specific, and every new task needs a new PSM.

Semantic Networks and Frames

Semantic nets facilitate processing of information and have been found to be useful as a modeling tool. The way that the information is processed is known as arc traversal. This is used to identify the complex relationships between nodes. One method of obtaining information from the network is though intersection search. This finds relationships between nodes by spreading a pattern of activation out from two nodes and then seeing where they meet.

A more complex type of semantic net is sometimes used in expert systems. These are known as frames and use a hierarchical structure. Semantic nets are important to cognitive science, but are rarely used on their own due to limitations in representing some concepts.

The problem is dealing with the concepts "some of" and "all of" which are known as quantifiers. They are impossible to represent in normal semantic nets and extensions have been proposed to deal with the problem. However, there are still limitations to semantic nets and the only way to get around this is to use a more complex calculus such as that offered by frames.

Frames offer a more highly structured hierarchy of nodes. Basically, each level in the hierarchy is of a given type, and there are certain options for filling the slot of this node type. In this way, specific knowledge can be represented and reasoned about. A lot of work has been done in the field of hypertext network organization. It is a long, recognized fact that hypertext structures mimic semantic networks. Similar to hypertext, semantic networks are composed of nodes and links. Nodes represent concepts, and links represent relationships between them. A hypertext system with arbitrary link types corresponds to a free semantic net. If the hypertext system allows just a limited number of link types, the underlying semantic net is restricted. Semantic nets are tightly coupled to the notion of associative networks.

We can say that in general, knowledge is stored in the human mind in information packets which are interrelated in a network structure. This view of the organization of the human memory may be used as a model to organize the information in hypertext. The evolution of associative network theory provides the foundation for the development of hypertext structures.

The semantic network formalism can be used as a general inferential representation mechanism of knowledge. In *spreading activation*, concepts surrounding a starting concept are viewed while problem solving. Starting from two different nodes is called an intersection search. Spreading activation fans out by following all links from the original two nodes. Then, all of these "second generation" nodes are activated. If one node is activated from both directions, a conclusion is drawn. It is the intersection between the two spheres of activation. The resulting path indicates a potential relationship between the original two concepts. Other inferential mechanisms in semantic networks are *inheritance hierarchies* and *analogical structures*. Both draw on the assumption that relevant facts about nodes can be inferred from neighboring nodes.

Frame-based representation adds *methods* to handle inference to the declarative knowledge representation in semantic networks. Each node in the semantic network (and in the corresponding hypertext structure) is represented as a single frame. Links are defined as slots of frames. Frame-based systems support inheritance, defaults of slot values, integration of truth maintenance, inference engines, and rule-based reasoning.

Reasoning with Semantic Networks

There is no formal semantics or agreed upon notion of what a given representational structure means. Meaning is assigned only by the nature of the programs that manipulate the network. Most common reasoning schemes use a network fragment as constructed for the query and matching the template is attempted against the network. Sets of things in a semantic network are termed types while individual objects in a semantic network are termed instances.

Semantic networks consist of nodes (objects, concepts, or situations) and arcs (relations). In Figure 9-1, we follow our way through the example net by obeying the following rules:

- If the property is not attached to that node, "climb" the *isa* link to the node's parent and search there.
  - o *isa* signifies set membership
  - o *ako* signifies the subset relation
- Repeat, using *isa/ako* links, until the property is found or the inheritance hierarchy is exhausted.

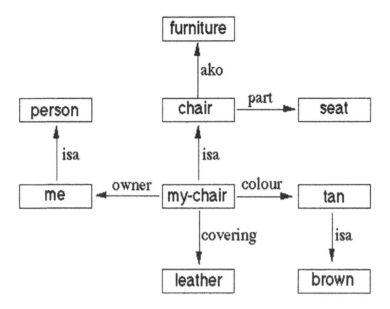

Figure 9-1. Semantic networks—state: I own a tan leather chair.

Description Logics (DLs)

The main research effort in knowledge representation is to provide theories and systems for expressing structured knowledge and for accessing and reasoning with it. Description Logics (DL) is an important powerful class of logic-based knowledge-representation languages.

The basic principles of Description Logics (DLs) are a family of knowledge representation formalisms designed for the representation of and reasoning about semantic networks and frame-based systems. DLs are also closely related to Modal and Dynamic Logics and it has turned out that DLs are also well-suited to the representation of and reasoning about database conceptual models, information integration, and ontologies. A variety of different DLs exist, with different expressive power and different computational complexity of the corresponding inference problems.

The Semantic Web provides a language that expresses both data and rules for reasoning about the data and allows rules from any existing knowledge-representation system to be imported. XML and the RDF are important technologies for developing the Semantic Web. The meaning is expressed by RDF, which encodes it in sets of triples, each triple acting as a sentence with a subject, predicate and object. These triples can be written using XML tags.

For the Semantic Web to function, computers must have access to structured collections of information (as RDF statements) and sets of inference rules that they can use to conduct automated reasoning. A Knowledge Representation language includes Language Syntax (describes configurations that can constitute sentences) and Semantics (determines the facts based upon the sentences). Traditional knowledge-representation systems typically have been centralized, requiring everyone to share exactly the same definition of common concepts. But central control is stifling, and increasing the size produces complexity which becomes rapidly unmanageable. These systems limit the questions that can be asked reliably. In avoiding the problems, traditional knowledge-representation systems narrow their focus and use a limited set of rules for making inferences.

A possible Inference Engine for the Semantic Web could be based upon Horn-logic, which is a fragment of First Order Predicate logic. Horn-logic was studied in the area of deductive databases and logic programming and a number of efficient evaluation strategies are available for this fragment of predicate logic. Integrating Horn-rules from different sources distributed on the Web introduces rules which can interfere with each other.

Inference Engines

Inference engines process the knowledge available in the Semantic Web. Inference engines deduce new knowledge from already specified knowledge. Two different approaches are applicable here: general logic based inference engines, and specialized algorithms (Problem Solving Methods).

An inference engine controls overall execution of a set of rules. It searches through a knowledge base, attempting to pattern match facts or knowledge present in memory to the antecedents of rules. If a rule's antecedent is satisfied, the rule is ready to fire and is placed in the agenda. When a rule is ready to fire it means that since the antecedent is satisfied, the consequent can be executed.

Salience is a mechanism used by some expert systems to add a procedural aspect to rule inferencing. Certain rules may be given a higher salience than others, which means that when the inference engine is searching for rules to fire, it places those with a higher salience at the top of the agenda.

There are two types of chaining: forward and backward. In forward chaining, the expert system is given data and chains forward to reach a conclusion. In backward chaining, the expert system is given a hypothesis and backtracks to check if it is valid.

We can make the analogy: inferencing is to computers, as reasoning is to humans. Figure 9-1 depicts a user relating to an Inference Engine and Knowledge Base.

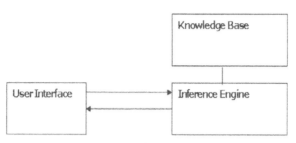

Figure 9-2. Inference engine.

Table 9-1 lists some available Inference Engines.

Inference Engines	Company	Site
Closed World Machine	W3C	http://www.w3.org/2000/10/swap/doc/cwm.html
RDFGateway	Intellidimension.com	http://www.intellidimension.com/
CYC	CYCORP	http://www.cyc.com/products.html

Table 9-1. Inference Engines.

Closed World Machine (CWM)

The Closed World Machine (CWM) inference engine written in Python by Tim Berners-Lee and Dan Connolly is a popular Semantic Web program that can perform the following tasks:

- Parse RDF formats: XML RDF, Notation3, and NTriples.
- Store triples in a query able triples database.
- Perform inferences as a forward chaining FOPL inference engine.
- Perform built in functions, such as comparing strings, or retrieving resources.

CWM is a general-purpose data processor for the Semantic Web. It is a forward-chaining reasoner which can be used for querying, checking, transforming, and filtering information. Its core language is RDF, extended to include rules, and it uses RDF/XML or N3 serializations as required.

RDFGateway

RDF Gateway is a fully functional logical inference engine that allows inference rules to dynamically generate additional RDF statements and execute complex recursive and non-recursive algorithms while executing a query. Inference rules can be extremely useful for aggregating, transforming, and validating information. Inference rules are essential for semantic processing of RDF data.

The inference rules are capable of dynamically generating RDF statements based on existing statements. The rule infers the type of a resource based on RDF schema information. It infers that a resource is a type of all of its base classes. When executing a query with this rule a resource will be treated like any of its base classes.

Ontology

If a program wants to compare conceptual information across two knowledge bases on the Web, it has to know when any two given terms are being used to mean the same thing. Ideally, the program must have a way to discover common meanings for whatever knowledge bases it encounters. A solution to this problem is provided by the Semantic Web in the form of collections of information called ontologies. Artificial Intelligence and Web researchers use the term ontology as a document that defines the relations among terms. A typical ontology for the Web uses a taxonomy and a set of inference rules.

The taxonomy defines classes of objects and relations among them. Classes, subclasses and relations among entities are important tools. We can express a large number of relations among entities by assigning properties to classes and allowing subclasses to inherit such properties.

Inference rules in ontologies may express rules for manipulating information. Inference rules may express the rule "If a city code is associated with a state code, and an address uses that city code, then that address has the associated state code." A program could then readily deduce, for instance, that a Cornell University address, being in Ithaca, must be in New York State, which is in the U.S., and therefore should be formatted to U.S. standards.

The real power of the Semantic Web will be realized when people create many programs that collect Web content from diverse sources, process the information and exchange the results. The effectiveness of software agents will increase exponentially as more machine-readable Web content and automated services become available. The Semantic Web promotes this synergy: even agents that were not expressly designed to work together can transfer semantic data.

Software Agents

An intelligent agent is a computer system that is situated in some environment, and that is capable of autonomous action and learning in order to meet its design objectives. Agents have the following characteristics: reactivity—they perceive their environment, and respond, pro-active—they exhibit goal-directed behavior, and social—they interact with other agents.

Real-time intelligent agent technology offers a powerful Web tool. Agents are able to act without the intervention of humans or other systems: they have control both over their own internal state and their behavior. In complexity domains, agents must be prepared for the possibility of failure. This situation is called non-deterministic. Normally, an agent will have a repertoire of actions available to it. This set of possible actions represents the agent's capability to modify its environments. Similarly, the action "purchase a house" will fail if insufficient funds area available to do so. Actions therefore have pre-conditions associated with them, which define the possible situations in which they can be applied.

The key problem facing an agent is that of deciding which of its actions it should perform to satisfy its design objectives. Agent architectures are really software architectures for decision-making systems that are embedded in an environment. The complexity of the decision-making process can be affected by a number of different environmental properties:

- Accessible vs inaccessible.
- Deterministic vs non- deterministic.
- Episodic vs non-episodic.
- Static vs dynamic.
- Discrete vs continuous.

The most complex general class of environments are those that are inaccessible, non-deterministic, non-episodic, dynamic, and continuous.

Limitations and Capabilities

In Table 9-2, we compare the key aspects of the Semantic Web, Web Services, and Intelligent Agents. The table identifies the promising aspects of the combining Semantic Web with Web Services and intelligent agents.

The promise of combining these three important innovations will mean that the Semantic Web will move information from keywords to concepts and allow information retrieval to answer questions in way that makes sense. Web Services will allow business applications to communicate over an existing, low cost infrastructure and if we add intelligent software agents to this mix, we allow task delegation as well as aggregation and coherent presentation of distributed content. The challenge will be in the automation of many of theses tasks.

	Semantic Web	**Web Services**	**Intelligent Agents**
Promising aspects	From keywords to concepts. From information retrieval to question answering to sense-making. An open semantic Layer understandable by third-party agents.	Business applications communicate over an existing, low-cost infrastructure. Configure 'new' systems from distributed existing. Applications.	Task delegation. Aggregation and Coherent presentation of distributed content.
Current limitations	Manual annotation of content with metadata is not scalable.	Systems exchange data, but do not understand it. Communication at low, syntactic level. People have to do the configuration.	Need clearly defined representation. User profiles are still poor from business point of view.
Challenges	Automatic annotation of metadata using ontologies. Security and trust.	Automatic discovery and orchestration of Web services into business services.	Exploit the content of the Semantic Web.

Table 9-2. Aspects of the Semantic Web, Web Services and Intelligent Agents.

Conclusion

In this chapter, we described key related concepts essential for Semantic Web Services including: machine intelligence, computational complexity, Knowledge Representation, Ontology, inference, and software agents.

From this chapter, we may conclude that Artificial Intelligence may play a role in bringing intelligence into future Web applications and that as AI agents, services, and applications are introduced into individual Web applications. We can expect that these applications will become increasingly user friendly and productive.

Chapter Ten

Web Ontology Language
for Services (OWL-S)

Overview

The World Wide Web Consortium (W3C) is currently developing architecture and markup languages to support both Web Services and the Semantic Web. Tim Berners-Lee has suggested that both of these technologies would benefit from integration. Integration would combine Web Services' business logic with the Semantic Web's meaningful content. There are several areas where the two could work well together. For example, the current discovery (UDDI), binding (WSDL), and messaging (SOAP) technologies could use Web Ontology Language (OWL) to interact with Web business rules engines, thereby laying the foundation for an ontology for Web Services.

In this chapter, we present Web Ontology Language for Services (OWL-S) currently under development by the W3C as the technology for building Semantic Web Services. We include discussions on related Web architectures and grounding OWL-S services with WSDL and SOAP.

Background

In 1994, the original concept of distributed objects through CORBA was intended to develop a Web architecture that would let applications plug into an "application bus" and call a service. Based on object-oriented units, it would call on specialized software components. However,

275

component software developers were unable to achieve the desired interoperability due to the lack of universal acceptance of CORBA. In 2002, it took unprecedented vendor cooperation and commitment to accept the XML-based Web standards SOAP, WSDL, and UDDI to make Web Services happen.

XML-based Web Services

Currently, a Web Service is a software system identified by a URI, whose public interfaces and bindings are defined and described using XML. Its definition and function can be discovered by other software systems. These systems may then interact with the Web Service using XML-based messages over Internet protocols.

A Web Service interaction involves two or more software agents exchanging information in the form of messages, using a variety of Message Exchange Patterns (MEP). A very common Message Exchange Pattern for Web Services is the Request Response MEP. A sender sends a request and the receiver responds. The data that is exchanged in the request, or the response, is usually XML carried over the transfer protocol, HTTP.

In a Web Service, the agent sends and receives messages based upon their architectural roles as shown in Figure 10-1. A requester is an entity that wishes to make use of a provider's Web Service. It will use a requester agent to exchange messages with the provider agent. In order for this message exchange to be successful, the requester and the provider must first agree on both the semantics and the mechanics of the message exchange.

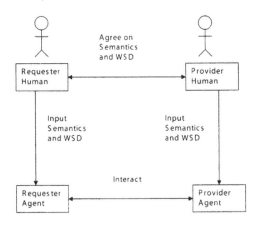

Figure 10-1. Basic architectural roles.

The mechanics of the message exchange are documented in a Web Service Description (WSD). The service description is a machine process-able specification of the message formats, data types, and protocols that are used between the requester and provider. It also specifies the network location of the provider, and may include some information about the MEP that is expected.

Web services technologies aim to enable a Service Oriented Architecture (SOA) on the Internet. In this system discrete software agents must work together to implement some intended functionality. Furthermore, the agents do not all operate in the same processing environment so they must communicate by hardware/software protocol stacks that are less reliable than direct code invocation. This has important implications because distributed systems require developers to consider the unpredictable latency of remote access, and taking into account issues of partial failure and concurrency.

Web Service Architecture (WSA)

Web Services provide a standard means of interoperating between different software applications, running on a variety of platforms. The Web Service Architecture (WSA), as defined by the W3C, is intended to provide a common definition of a Web Service.

WSA involves many layered and interrelated technologies (see Chapter 5). Figure 10-2 illustrates some of these technology families supporting Web Services including the XML technologies SOAP, WDSL, and UDDI.

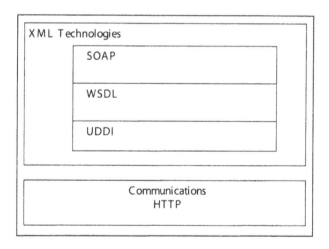

Figure 10-2. Web Service standards.

XML provides the extensibility and language neutrality that is key for standards-based interoperability of Web Services. Furthermore, XML helps combine the payload and protocol data. Thus, the base technology of WSA consists of key XML specifications.

Services are invoked and provide results through messages that must be exchanged over some communications medium. WSA encompasses a wide variety of communications mechanisms including HTTP, SMTP, FTP, JMS, and IIOP.

Today, WSDL is an obvious choice as the means for the precise description of Web Service messages, while SOAP is the key messaging technology in WSA. SOAP's envelope structure has proven to be a very robust and powerful framework.

SOAP, WSDL, and UDDI Limitations

Since a critical mass of knowledge and technology has formed around SOAP and WSDL, they will likely continue at the center of the Web Service Architecture. However, these technologies have limitations including:

- Integration with the Web—While SOAP Web Services use the HTTP infrastructure, they are not able to hyperlink SOAP Web Service through HTML links or XSLT functions.

- Extension mechanism—SOAP provides an extension mechanism only through headers.

- Overall understanding of modules and layering—SOAP provides a framework within which additional features can be added via headers, but there is little agreement on the specific categories of functionality.

- Automation—the future of Web Services greatly depends on their ability to automate as much of the Web Service process as possible under interoperable standards. Matchmaking, or service discovery, is one important aspect of Web Services' e-commerce interactions, and advanced matchmaking services require rich and flexible metadata that are not currently supported by UDDI.

Next Generation Web Services

To make use of a Web Service, a software agent needs a computer-interpretable description of the service and the means for access. An important goal for Semantic Web markup languages is to establish a framework for making and sharing these descriptions. Web sites should be able to employ a set of basic classes and properties for declaring and describing services, and the ontology structuring mechanisms of OWL provides the appropriate framework to do this.

Ontology and Taxonomy

We can express an Ontology as:

Ontology = < taxonomy, inference rules>

And we can express a Taxonomy as:

Taxonomy = < {classes}, {relations}>

As a result, an ontology for Web Services would make Web Services machine understandable and support automated Web Service composition and interoperability. Central to an ontology for Web Services is providing three automated functions:

- service discovery.
- service execution.
- service composition.

None of these three tasks is entirely realizable with today's Web technology, primarily because of a lack of a suitable markup language. However, over the last several years, a number of Semantic markup languages have been developed that could improve this situation, including RDF, RDFS, and most recently OWL. The DAML project, which was developed between 1999 and 2003 in conjunction with OIL, has now evolved into the Web Ontology Language (OWL). OWL is the W3C markup language for publishing and sharing ontologies on the World Wide Web (see Chapter 8). Now, OWL-S offers to extend the capability to form the required ontology for Web Services.

The next generation of Web Services could be built on Semantic Web Architecture (SWA) and related technologies including RDFS and OWL-S. We will present a basic outline of the OWL-S specification in the following sections.

OWL-S Primer

The Semantic Web is rapidly becoming a reality through the development of Semantic Web markup languages such as OWL. These markup languages enable the creation of arbitrary domain ontologies that support the unambiguous description of Web content.

Web-accessible programs and devices are among the most important resources on the Web. These Web Services have garnered significant interest from industry, and standards are being developed for low-level descriptions of Web Services including WSDL which provides a communication level description of the messages and protocols.

To make use of a Web service, a software agent needs a computer-interpretable description of the service and the means to access it. The OWL ontology for Web Services, called OWL-S, could make Web Services computer-interpretable in order to perform the tasks listed in Table 10-1.

Task	Description
Discovery	Locating Web Services.
Invocation	Execution of service by an agent or other service.
Interoperation	Breaking down interoperability barriers and automatic insertion of message parameter translations.
Composition	New services through automatic selection, composition and interoperation of existing services.
Verification	Verify service properties.
Execution Monitoring	Tracking the execution of composite tasks and identifying failure cases of different execution traces.

Table 10-1. Computer-Interpretable Tasks.

An Upper Ontology for Services

In OWL, abstract categories of entities are defined in terms of classes and properties. OWL-S uses OWL to define a set of classes and properties specific to the description of services. The class Service is at the top of the OWL-S ontology.

The ontology of services provides three essential types of knowledge about a service:

1. The class Service *presents* a ServiceProfile: "What does the service provide for and require of agents?"

2. The class Service is *describedBy* a ServiceModel: "How does it work?"

3. The class Service *supports* a ServiceGrounding: "How to access the service?"

The ServiceProfile provides information about a service that can be used by an agent to determine if the service meets its rough needs, and if it satisfies constraints such as security, locality, and quality requirements.

The ServiceModel enables an agent to: (1) perform an in-depth analysis of whether the service meets its needs, (2) compose service description from multiple services to perform a specific task, (3) coordinate the activities of different agents, and (4) monitor the execution of the service.

The ServiceGrounding specifies the details of how to access the service such as protocol and message formats, serialization, transport, and addressing. A grounding is a mapping from an abstract to a concrete specification of those service description elements that are required for interacting with the service; basically, the inputs and outputs of atomic processes.

Building upon SOAP and WSDL technologies, the OWL-S ontology-based Web services can be dynamically invoked by other services on the Web.

OWL-S Specifications

The OWL-S 1.0 specification are available at:

http://daml.semanticweb.org/services/owl-s/1.0/

Upper Ontology for Services is available at:

http://daml.semanticweb.org/services/owl-s/1.0/Service.owl

http://daml.semanticweb.org/services/owl-s/1.0/Profile.owl

http://daml.semanticweb.org/services/owl-s/1.0/Process.owl

http://daml.semanticweb.org/services/owl-s/1.0/Grounding.owl

The upper ontology for services requires all three of the following properties to be fully characterized: *presents, describedBy* and *supports*.

In general, the ServiceProfile provides the information needed for an agent to discover the service while the ServiceModel and ServiceGrounding objects provide information for an agent to use the service (see Figure 10-3).

We will describe each of these three classes (ServiceProfile, ServiceModel, ServiceGrounding) in the following sections.

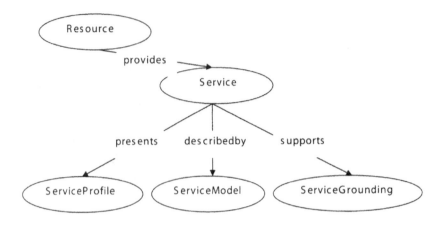

Figure 10-3. Upper ontology of services.

ServiceProfile

A service profile provides a high-level description of a service and its provider and is used by discovery registries to request and advertise services. It includes: a human readable description (see Table 10-2), a specification of functionalities (see Table 10-3), and functional attributes (see Table 10-4).

A transaction in the Web service marketplace involves three parties: the service requester, the service provider, and the infrastructure components. The service requester (buyer) seeks a service to complete its work and the service provider (seller) offers a service. The infrastructure components facilitate the process, such as registries to match the request with the offers available.

Within the OWL-S ontology, the ServiceProfile describes the services. A ServiceProfile describes a service as a function of three basic types of information: what organization provides the service, what functions the service computes, and what features characterize the service.

There is a two-way relationship between a service and a profile which is expressed by the properties *presents* (relates an instance of service and an instance of profile) and *presentedBy* (specifies the inverse of presents).

ServiceProfile can be viewed as an expression of two functions: first, the information transformation and second, the state change produced by the execution of the service. The information transformation includes the input and output properties of the profile. For example, a bookselling service could require the buyer's credit-card number and information on the book. The state change produced by the execution of the service results from the precondition and effect properties of the profile. Precondition presents logical conditions that should be satisfied prior to the service being requested. Effects are the result of the successful execution of a service.

For example, to complete the sale, a book-selling service requires a credit card number and expiration date, but also the precondition that the credit card actually exists and is not overdrawn. The result of the sale is the transfer of the book from the warehouse to the address of the buyer.

In addition, the ServiceProfile provides a description of the service to a registry. Although the ServiceProfile and the ProcessModel play different roles during the transaction, they reflect the same service, and so the iopes (inputs, outputs, parameters and effects) are related.

Table 10-2 lists the Profile properties used to provide a description of the service.

Property	Description
serviceName	The name of the service.
intendedPurpose	Constitutes successful execution.
textDescription	Human readable description.
role	Link to Actors.
providedBy	Sub-property of role referring to the requester.
requestedBy	Sub-property of role referring to the provider.

Table 10-2. ServiceProfile Property Description.

The class Actor: (name, phone, fax, email, physicalAddress, WebURL) describes entities that provide or request Web Services. Two specific classes are derived from the Actor class; the Service-Requester and Service-Provider. Properties of Actor include: name, phone, email, fax, email, physicalAddress, and WebURL. Figure 10-4 presents the relationship of the Actor property to the Service-Profile.

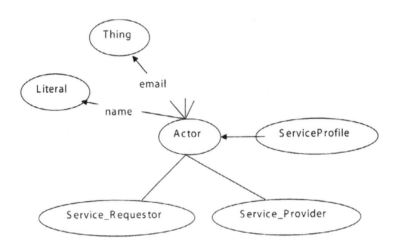

Figure 10-4. Actor relationships.

Table 10-3 lists the functional description parameters.

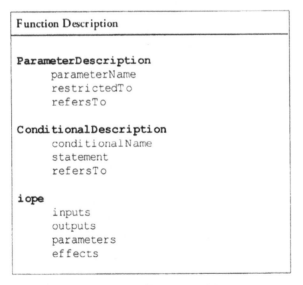

Table 10-3. Service Profile Functional Description.

Additional information is provided by functional attributes, such as guarantees of response time or accuracy, the cost of the service, or the classification of the service in a registry. In Table 10-4, we list the functional attributes available for the service.

Functional Attribute	Description *Note this set of functional attributes can easily be extended.
geographicRadius	Geographic scope of the service.
degreeofQuality	Qualifications, such as the cheapest or fastest.
serviceParameter	Properties that characterize the execution.
communicationThru	How a service may communicate (e.g., SOAP).
serviceType	Ontology of service types, such as B2B, B2C etc.
serviceCategory	May include Products, Information Services etc.
qualityGuarantees	Service promises to deliver.
qualityRating	Industry-based ratings.

Table 10-4. ServiceProfile Functional Attribute*.

In Figure 10-5, we illustrate the overall relationships of ServiceProfile.

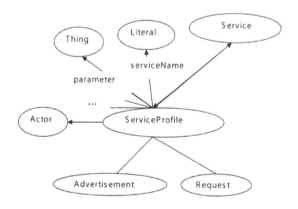

Figure 10-5. ServiceProfile relationships.

285

ServiceModel

A detailed perspective of a service can be viewed as a process. A subclass of the ServiceModel is defined as the ProcessModel which draws upon Artificial Intelligence, planning and workflow automation to support a wide array of services on the Web. Figure 10-6 presents the relationships of ServiceModel and includes the Process and ProcessControl, iopes, and constructs.

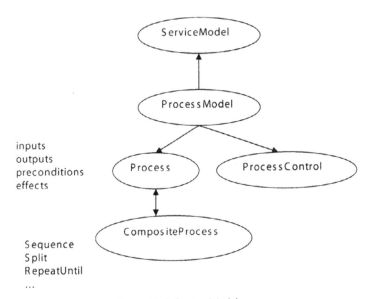

Figure 10-6. Service Model.

ProcessModel

The process model comprises subclasses and properties of the ProcessModel class.
The chief components of the process model are the:

- Process Ontology which describes a service in terms of its inputs, outputs, preconditions, effects, and component subprocesses.

- Process Control Ontology which describes each process in terms of its state, including initial activation, execution, and completion.

The process control model allows agents to monitor the progression of a service request as part of the Process Control Ontology.

Process Ontology

Process Ontology can have any number of inputs and outputs representing the information required for execution. Besides inputs and outputs, parameter for physical devices, such things as rates, forces, and control settings can be included.

The Process Ontology serves as the basis for specifying a wide array of services on standardizations.

OWL-S defines three types of processes (see Figure 10-7):

1. Atomic: directly invokable.
2. Simple: single-step, but not directly invokable.
3. Composite: decomposable into other processes.

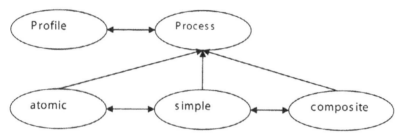

Figure 10-7. Process ontology.

In Figure 10-7, the three types of processes are related: atomic, simple, and composite. They are represented in the following serializations. Listing 10-1 illustrates Process as encompassing the three disjoint sub-processes: atomic, simple, and composite, where a simple process can include atomic processes and a composite process can include more than one simple process.

Listing 10-1. Process.

```
<owl:Class rdf:ID="Process">
  <rdfs:comment> The most general class of processes </rdfs:comment>
  < owl:disjointUnionOf rdf:parseType=" owl:collection">
    < owl:Class rdf:about="#AtomicProcess"/>
    < owl:Class rdf:about="#SimpleProcess"/>
    < owl:Class rdf:about="#CompositeProcess"/>
  </ owl:disjointUnionOf>
</ owl:Class>
```

287

AtomicProcess

The atomic processes can be invoked directly and are executed in a single step. For each atomic process, there is a grounding that enables a service requester to construct messages. Listing 10-2 identifies an AtomicProcess as a subclass of a Process.

Listing 10-2. AtomicProcess.

```
<owl:Class rdf:ID="AtomicProcess">
 < owl:subClassOf rdf:resource="#Process"/>
</ owl:Class>
```

SimpleProcess

Simple processes are not associated with a grounding. They are single-step executions. Simple processes are used as elements of abstraction; a simple process may be used either to provide a view of some atomic process, or a simplified representation of some composite process. Listing 10-3 shows a SimpleProcess.

Listing 10-3. SimpleProcess.

```
<owl:Class rdf:ID="SimpleProcess">
 < owl:subClassOf rdf:resource="#Process"/>
</ owl:Class>

<rdf:Property rdf:ID="realizedBy">
 <rdfs:domain rdf:resource="#SimpleProcess"/>
 <rdfs:range rdf:resource="#AtomicProcess"/>
 < owl:inverseOf rdf:resource="#realizes"/>
</rdf:Property>

<rdf:Property rdf:ID="expandsTo">
 <rdfs:domain rdf:resource="#SimpleProcess"/>
 <rdfs:range rdf:resource="#CompositeProcess"/>
 < owl:inverseOf rdf:resource="#collapsesTo"/>
</rdf:Property>
```

This listing identified a SimpleProcess as a subclass of the Process and says that a simple process can realize an atomic process, and may be the result of collapsing a composite process.

CompositeProcess

Composite processes are decomposable into other processes. The decomposition shows how the various inputs and outputs are accepted. For example, see Listing 10-4.

Listing 10-4. CompositeProcess.

```
<owl:Class rdf:ID="CompositeProcess">
  < owl:intersectionOf rdf:parseType=" owl:collection">
  < owl:Class rdf:about="#Process"/>
  < owl:Restriction owl:cardinality="1">
    < owl:onProperty rdf:resource="#composedOf"/>
  </ owl:Restriction>
  </ owl:intersectionOf>
</ owl:Class>
```

A CompositeProcess must have a composedOf property by which is indicated the control structure of the composite, using a ControlConstruct.

```
<rdf:Property rdf:ID="composedOf">
  <rdfs:domain rdf:resource="#CompositeProcess"/>
  <rdfs:range rdf:resource="#ControlConstruct"/>
</rdf:Property>

<owl:Class rdf:ID="ControlConstruct">
</owl:Class>
```

Constructs

A CompositeProcess must have a composedOf property to indicate the control structure using a ControlConstruct. Each control construct is associated with an additional property called components to indicate the ordering and conditional execution of the subprocesses. For instance, the control construct Sequence, has a components property that ranges over a ProcessComponentList (see Table 10-5).

Process Control Ontology

To monitor the execution of a process, an agent uses a model with three characteristics that provide:

1. Mapping rules for the input state properties and preconditions to the corresponding output state properties.

2. A model of the temporal or state dependencies described by constructs such as sequence, split, and split+join.

3. Representation for messages about the execution state of atomic and composite processes sufficient to do execution monitoring. This allows an agent to keep track of the status of executions, including successful, failed and interrupted processes.

Process Ontology Control is still an area under significant development.

Construct	Description
Sequence	A list of Processes to be done in order.
Split	A bag of process components to be executed concurrently. Similar to other ontologies' use of Fork, Concurrent, or Parallel.
Split+Join	Invoke elements of a bag of processes and synchronize.
Concurrent	Execute elements of a bag of processes concurrently.
Unordered	Allows the process components (specified as a bag) to be executed in some unspecified order, or concurrently.
Choice	Choose between alternatives and execute one.
If-Then-Else	If specified condition holds, execute "Then," else execute "Else".
Repeat-Until	Iterate execution of a bag of processes until a condition holds.
Repeat-While	Iterate execution of a bag of processes while a condition holds.

Table 10-5. Process Constructs.

ServiceGrounding

In OWL-S, both the ServiceProfile and the ServiceModel are thought of as abstract representations; only the ServiceGrounding deals with the concrete level of specification. The grounding of a service specifies the details of how to access the service, including protocol and message formats, serialization, transport, and addressing.

Relationship between OWL-S and WSDL and SOAP

An OWL-S/WSDL grounding involves complementary use of the two languages. Both languages are required for the full specification of grounding even though there is some overlap (see Figure

10-8). WSDL specifies abstract types using XML Schema (XSD) (see Chapter 5), but OWL-S allows for the definition of logic-based OWL classes.

WSDL/XSD is unable to express the semantics of an OWL class. Similarly, OWL-S has no means to express the binding information that WSDL captures. Therefore, an OWL-S/WSDL grounding uses OWL classes as the abstract types of message parts declared in WSDL. The job of an OWL-S/WSDL grounding is to define the messages and operations for the atomic processes that are accessed and then specify correspondences.

Because OWL-S is an XML-based language, and its atomic process declarations and input/output types already fit with WSDL, it is useful to extend existing WSDL bindings for OWL-S, such as the SOAP binding.

Grounding OWL-S with WSDL and SOAP involves the construction of a WSDL service description with the message, operation, port type, binding, and service constructs.

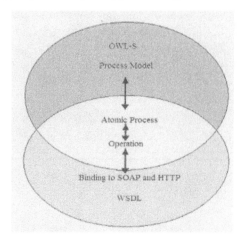

Figure 10-8. OWL-S relationship to WSDL.

OWL-S atomic processes specify the basic actions for larger processes and can also communicate the primitives of a process specification.

The central function of the OWL-S grounding is to show how the inputs and outputs of an atomic process are realized as messages in transmittable format. WSDL has been used in developing the initial grounding mechanism for OWL-S.

The OWL-S concept of grounding is generally consistent with WSDL's concept of binding. WSDL is used as the ground of an OWL-S atomic process.

OWL-S WSDL Correspondences

OWL-S / WSDL groundings are based upon the following correspondences:

I. An OWL-S atomic process corresponds to a WSDL operation.

Different types of operations relate as follows:

An atomic process with both inputs and outputs corresponds to a WSDL request-response operation.

An atomic process with inputs, but no outputs, corresponds to a WSDL one-way operation.

An atomic process with outputs, but no inputs, corresponds to a WSDL notification operation.

A composite process with both outputs and inputs, and with the sending of outputs specified as coming before the reception of inputs, corresponds to WSDL's solicit-response operation.

II. The set of inputs and set of outputs of an OWL-S atomic process correspond to WSDL's concept of message.

III. The types (OWL-S classes) of inputs and outputs of an OWL-S atomic process corresponds to a WSDL's extensible notion of abstract types.

We illustrate several of these correspondences in Figure 10-9.

Grounding OWL-S Services with WSDL and SOAP

Because OWL-S is an XML-based language and its atomic process declarations and input/output types already fit with WSDL, we can extend existing WSDL bindings for use with OWL-S, such as the SOAP binding.

Grounding OWL-S with WSDL and SOAP involves the construction of a WSDL service description with all the usual parts (message, operation, port type, binding, and service constructs, see Chapter 5), except that the type element can be omitted.

The OWL-S extensions are:

1. The owl-property attribute is used in each part of the WSDL message definition to indicate the fully-qualified name of the OWL-S input or output property. The property name yields the appropriate OWL range class.

2. The owl-s-process attribute is used in each WSDL operation element, to indicate the corresponding name of the OWL-S atomic process.

3. The encodingStyle attribute is given a value within the WSDL binding element to indicate that the message parts will be serialized for class instances of the given types.

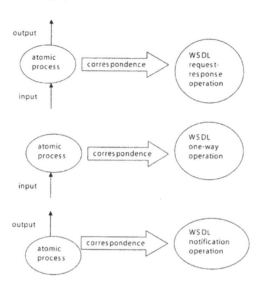

Figure 10-9. OWL-S correspondence to WSDL.

Once the WSDL service description is completed, a WsdlGrounding object is constructed. The WsdlGrounding object refers to specific WSDL specification elements using the properties listed in Table 10-6.

Creating an Ontology for a Web Service

Creating an OWL-S based Ontology for a Web Service requires five steps:

1. Describe individual programs—describe the individual programs that comprise the service. The process model provides a declarative description of a program's properties.

2. Describe the grounding for each atomic process—relate each atomic process to its grounding.

3. Describe compositions of the atomic processes—describe the composite process which is a composition of its atomic processes.

4. Describe a simple process—describe a simple process for the service (optional).

5. Profile description—provide a declarative advertisement for the service. It is partially populated by the process model.

In Chapter 11, we will follow these five steps and develop an ontology for the Congo.owl Web Service which is an example on-line, book buying store.

WsdlGrounding Object	Properties
wsdlReference	URI indicating the version of WSDL.
otherReferences	A list of URIs for standards used by WSDL (e.g., SOAP, HTTP).
wsdlDocuments	A list of the URIs of the WSDL documents that give the grounding.
wsdlOperation	The URI of the WSDL operation corresponding to the given atomic process.
wsdlInputMessage	An object containing the URI of the WSDL message definition that carries the inputs of the given atomic process, and a list of mapping pairs, for the correspondence between OWL-S input properties and WSDL message parts.
wsdlOutputMessage	Similar to wsdlInputMessage, but for outputs.

Table 10-6. Properties for WsdlGrounding Objects.

Conclusion

In this chapter, we introduced an OWL-S-based Ontology for a Web Service. We showed that OWL-S will enable users and software agents to automatically discover, invoke, compose, and monitor Web resources offering services, under specified constraints. Three aspects of OWL-S were presented: the ServiceProfile, the ProcessModel, and the ServiceGrounding. The Service-Grounding was identified as critical to the successful deployment of OWL-S, since it provides the connection between the Semantic Web approach and the current industry standards for Web Service Description Language (WSDL).

Part Three

Developing Semantic Web Services

Chapter Eleven

OWL-S Example: Congo.owl

Overview

In order to design an automatic, self-regulating OWL-S-based Web Service Ontology, it is necessary to understand how the automatic service will operate within a complex dynamic environment and how it will respond to a wide variety of outside stimuli. Unlike traditional computer projects, designing a OWL-S-based Web Service requires detailed analysis that exposes and eliminates semantic logic conflicts and indeterminacies. Because OWL-S-based Web Services seeks to remove humans from the interactions and leave automated processes in place, logic conflicts would result in unacceptable transaction failure rates.

In this chapter, we present the phases and steps necessary to design and implement a OWL-S-based Web Service. We illustrate the design process through an example for an on-line book service that includes the ability to select a book, collect buyer information, collect payment and deliver the book. We walk through an OWL-S on-line book buying example "Congo.owl" provided by www.daml.org and available for download at http://daml.semanticweb.org/services/owl-s/1.0/. This example provides details of the transactions, processes, and flow paths of the service performance. Afterward, we discuss general service-design features.

As part of the preliminary design process, we review the XML-based Web Service book store: Amazon.com and its Software Developer's Kit. In addition, we will use a semantic tool called WSDL2DAML-S Converter (see Chapter 13) to convert the Amazon.wsdl document into DAML-S/OWL-S document.

Then, in Chapter 12, we apply graphical analysis methodologies to the "Congo.owl" example. Through this analysis, we show that it is possible to improve the logic flow and transaction reliability of OWL-S-based Web Service.

Background

Since 1996, Web Services have connected computers and devices using the Internet to exchange and combine data in new ways. The key to Web Services has been software composition through the use of reusable software components. This has fundamental implications in both technical and business terms.

Web Services can be completely decentralized and distributed over the Web and accessed by a wide variety of communications devices. An example application would be a supply-chain relationship where an enterprise manufactures short-lived goods and must frequently seek suppliers as well as buyers. Instead of employees constantly searching for both suppliers and buyers, the Web Service infrastructure could perform these requirements automatically.

OWL-S-based Web Services can significantly improve the capabilities and performance of traditional Web Services by using the Web architectural potential provided by automated program communications and services. It could also achieve automatic interoperability between systems to accomplish organizational tasks.

Current XML-based Web Service technology provides limited support in mechanizing service recognition, service configuration and combination, service comparison, and automated negotiation. In a business environment, the vision of flexible and autonomous Web Services translates into automatic cooperation between enterprise services. Any enterprise requiring a business interaction with another enterprise needs to automatically discover and select the optimal Web Services. Any necessary mediation would be applied based on data and process ontologies using automatic translation for semantic interoperations.

Planning OWL-S-based Web Services

Intuitively, planning is a simple matter. Mentally we lay out a sequence of actions, and through a process of forward and reverse planning, eventually, we find our way from the starting point to our goal.

For us to develop a Web Service we must complete the following three phases:
1. Design and Initiation.
2. Execution.
3. Deployment.

Having a well-defined goal is the first step in dealing with complex problems. Gathering information and formulating models enables us to analyze and choose between alternative options. Since we are working toward automation of many features of our service, self-regulating feedback and self-optimizing mechanisms must be incorporated into the service design.

For our example, we plan to illustrate an on-line book shopping, payment, and delivery store.

Design and Initiation Phase

In the design and initiation phase, a comprehensive list of tasks to be performed is prepared and information flows including: inputs, outputs, preconditions, and effects (iope) assigned to established transactions.

The general project design and implementation steps include:

1. Define the service objectives.
2. Identify its transactions.
3. Create definitions for successful outcomes.
4. Make assumptions about relevant factors that can affect performance.
5. Evaluate inputs, outputs, preconditions, and effects.
6. Discuss alternative scenarios when failures occur.
7. Design contingency flow paths.

After identifying the service objectives, we identify the component elements, transactions and events that constitute the service. The remaining tasks include how transactions are performed, and what constitutes a transaction completion.

An OWL-S-based Web Service development project has additional burdens which are due to semantic logic conflicts and indeterminacies. Because OWL-S-based Web Services seeks to remove humans from the interactions logic conflicts can arise from simple contradictions in designing transaction instructions or from deeper logic misconstructions that are a result of convoluted relationships within a complex interaction of processes. During the design phase, analysis using several methodologies, such as Petri nets, reliability analysis, and Digraph Matrix Analysis may be performed that searches for logical inconsistencies (see Chapter 12).

Execution Phase

In the project execution phase, we:

- Analyze requirements.
- Create low-level detailed design.
- Conduct performance analysis and testing.

In analyzing the customer's needs and constraints, we can develop the project requirements. This establishes the transactions involved as well as their iopes.

Next, construction of logic models of the Web Service not only analyzes the service for logic conflicts, but provides a methodology for analyzing and testing efficiencies of individual transactions using reliability tools and collected execution data. Such modeling allows for trial testing and evaluation of alternatives.

Substantial user testing provides an accurate way of identifying remaining conflicts, deadlocks, or inefficiencies in performance. In addition, performance data can be collected from the server concerning detailed transaction performance. This data can be used within the logic models to complete reliability analysis for the service (see Chapter 12).

Deployment Phase

The final phase makes the service available to clients by registering and advertising the service. In addition, operations and maintenance schedules are developed to insure that the Web Service continues to perform as promised even after it is deployed and implemented by the client. Once deployed the following processes are available:

- Automatic Web Service discovery.
- Automatic Web Service invocation.
- Automatic Web Service composition and interoperation.

OWL-S-based Web Service Example: Congo.owl

In the following sections, we will present the OWL-S-based Web Service example, "Congo.owl" created by the www.daml.org.

OWL-S Specification and Congo.owl Example

The OWL-S specification for encoding of the profile ontology, the process ontology and the grounding ontology was developed by the DAML-S Coalition (also know as the OWL-S Coalition) and can be found at:

http://daml.semanticweb.org/services/owl-s/1.0/

The "Congo.owl" example source code is available at:

http://daml.semanticweb.org/services/owl-s/1.0/

Design of an On-line Book Store

In order to design an on-line book service, we require the following transactions: the ability to make a selection of books, collect information about the buyer, collect payment, and deliver the book. These transactions are delineated as follows:

1. Book search capability to locate the desired book.
2. Place book in individual's shopping cart.
3. Individual signs-in.
4. Load profile, or
5. Create new account, and
6. Create new profile.
7. Specify delivery details.
8. Finalize purchase.
9. Book distribution.
10. Book delivery.

But before we jump into a design for an OWL-S-based on-line book buying service, let's first examine today's existing book-buying XML-based Web Service: Amazon.com.

Amazon SDK Specifications, WSDL and DAML-S

 Amazon.SDK—The Amazon software development kit can be downloaded at:

http://www.amazon.com/gp/browse.html/002-4601444-0048069?node=3435361

Amazon.WSDL—The Amazon wsdl document is at:

http://soap.amazon.com/schemas2/AmazonWebServices.wsdl

Amazon.DAML-S—Place the Amazon.wsdl URL (above) into the URL conversion input at the WSDL2DAML-S conversion tool at:

http://www.daml.ri.cmu.edu/wsdl2damls/

and the DAML-S profile, service, process and grounding documents will be produced.

Amazon.com XML-based Web Service

Today, Amazon.com is one of the most successful Web enterprises. Amazon has provided an open-source code XML-based Web Service for developers to create advanced environments for on-line book selling using Amazon.com Web Services Software Development Kit 3.0 (see Figure 11-1).

Amazon.com Web Services offers developers the choice of XML over HTTP or SOAP to access information in catalogs and databases. There is significant industry debate over which Web Services method is the "best." Amazon.com decided to take a neutral approach and offer access via both methods.

The Amazon.com developer's kit contains everything needed to start using Amazon Web Services including technical documentation and sample code.

Figure 11-1 Amazon.com XML-based Web Services SDK 3.0.

Within Amazon's SDK, we observe many of the basic features that we would like to use as a foundation for an OWL-S-based Web Service Ontology for an on-line book-buying service.

Listing 11-1 is an abbreviated pseudo code of the Amazon.WSDL document. By using the Semantic Web Service tool WSDL2DAML-S Convertor (see Chapter 13) we create the OWL-S/DAML-S documents for the Amazon.daml-s., including the OWL-S/DAML-S profile, service, process and grounding documents.

Listing 11-1. Abbreviated Pseudo Code for Amazon.Wsdl Document.

```
<wsdl:definitions xmlns:typens="http://soap.amazon.com"
xmlns:xsd="http://www.w3.org/2001/XMLSchema"
xmlns:soap="http://schemas.xmlsoap.org/wsdl/soap/" xmlns:
soapenc="http://schemas.xmlsoap.org/soap/encoding/"
xmlns:wsdl="http://schemas.xmlsoap.org/wsdl/" xmlns="http://
schemas.xmlsoap.org/wsdl/" targetNamespace="http://soap.
amazon.com"
name="AmazonSearch">
<wsdl:types>
<xsd:schema xmlns="" xmlns:xsd="http://www.w3.org/2001/
XMLSchema" targetNamespace="http://soap.amazon.com">
<xsd:complexType name="ProductLineArray">
<xsd:complexContent>
<xsd:restriction base="soapenc:Array">
<xsd:attribute ref="soapenc:arrayType" wsdl:
arrayType="typens:ProductLine[]"/>
</xsd:restriction>
</xsd:complexContent>
</xsd:complexType>
...
<xsd:all>
<xsd:element name="Url" type="xsd:string" minOccurs="0"/>
<xsd:element name="Asin" type="xsd:string" minOccurs="0"/>

<xsd:element name="ProductName" type="xsd:string"
minOccurs="0"/>
...
</xsd:all>
</xsd:complexType>
<xsd:complexType name="KeyPhraseArray">
<xsd:complexContent>
<xsd:restriction base="soapenc:Array">
<xsd:attribute ref="soapenc:arrayType" wsdl:
```

```
arrayType="typens:KeyPhrase[]"/>
</xsd:restriction>
</xsd:complexContent>
</xsd:complexType>
...
</xsd:schema>
</wsdl:types>
<message name="KeywordSearchRequest"> <!-- Messages for
Amazon Web APIs -->
<part name="KeywordSearchRequest" type="typens:
KeywordRequest"/>
</message>
<message name="KeywordSearchResponse">
</message>
...
<portType name="AmazonSearchPort"><!-- Port for Amazon Web
APIs -->
<operation name="KeywordSearchRequest">
<input message="typens:KeywordSearchRequest"/>
<output message="typens:KeywordSearchResponse"/>
</operation>
...
</portType>
<binding name="AmazonSearchBinding" type="typens:
AmazonSearchPort">
<soap:binding style="rpc" transport="http://schemas.xmlsoap.
org/soap/http"/>
<!-- Binding for Amazon Web APIs - RPC, SOAP over HTTP -->
<operation name="KeywordSearchRequest">
<soap:operation soapAction="http://soap.amazon.com"/>
<input>
<soap:body use="encoded" encodingStyle="http://schemas.
xmlsoap.org/soap/encoding/" namespace="http://soap.amazon.
com"/>
</input>
<soap:body use="encoded" encodingStyle="http://schemas.
xmlsoap.org/soap/encoding/" namespace="http://soap.amazon.
com"/>
</input>
<output>
<soap:body use="encoded" encodingStyle="http://schemas.
xmlsoap.org/soap/encoding/" namespace="http://soap.amazon.
com"/>
```

```
</output>
</operation>
...
</operation>
</binding>
<service name="AmazonSearchService">
<!-- Endpoint for Amazon Web APIs -->
<port name="AmazonSearchPort" binding="typens:
AmazonSearchBinding">
<soap:address location="http://soap.amazon.com/onca/soap2"/>
</port>
</service>
<!--Shopping Cart-->
</wsdl:definitions>
```

Conversion from WSDL to OWL-S/DAML-S was successful. If the WSDL file has a schema tag, an additional file called concept.daml will be generated. This is a list of files generated by the WSDL2DAML-S tool.

WSDL URL :	http://soap.amazon.com/schemas2/AmazonWebServices.wsdl
OWL-S/DAML-S Service :	Service.daml
OWL-S/DAML-S Service Profile file :	Profile.daml
OWL-S/DAML-S Process Model file :	Process.daml
OWL-S/DAML-S Process Grounding file :	Grounding.daml
DAML Conceptfile :	Concept.daml

These files form the basis for an OWL-S online book Web Service.

Congo.owl Example: The Congo, Inc. On-line Book Store

The Congo.owl example is a fictitious book-buying service offered by the fictitious Web Service provider, Congo, Inc. This book-buying service uses a suite of Web-accessible programs called LocateBook, PutInCart, SignIn, CreateAcct, CreateProfile, LoadProfile, SpecifyDeliveryDetails, and FinalizeBuy. The composite service CongoBuy is composed of this suite of smaller programs required for a user to buy books.

Congo Specifications

OWL-S descriptions for the Congo example are:

service instance:
   http://daml.semanticweb.org/services/owl-s/1.0/CongoService.owl

service profile:
   http://daml.semanticweb.org/services/owl-s/1.0/CongoProfile.owl

process model:
   http://daml.semanticweb.org/services/owl-s/1.0/CongoProcess.owl

process data flow model:
   http://daml.semanticweb.org/services/owl/s/1.0/CongoProcessDataFlow.owl

grounding models:
   http://daml.semanticweb.org/services/owl-s/1.0/CongoGrounding.owl

Task-Driven Markup of Web Services

In the Congo.owl example, Web Service provider Congo Inc. is considering using three automation tasks enabled with OWL-S markup:

- Automatic Web Service discovery.
- Automatic Web Service invocation.
- Automatic Web Service composition and interoperation.

In the following sections, we first provide a description of the Web-accessible programs through a process model and grounding description in order to provide automatic invocation and composition. Then, we provide a means of advertising the properties and capabilities through a profile description for automatic discovery (see Figure 11-2).

Describing the Congo.owl Transaction Programs

The development of an Ontology for the Congo.owl Web Service requires five steps:

1. Describe individual programs—describe the individual programs that comprise the service. The process model provides a declarative description of a program's properties.

2. Describe the grounding for Each Atomic Process—(for example; relate LocateBook to its grounding, LocateBookGrounding).

3. Describe compositions of the atomic processes—(for example; describe the composite process CongoBuyBook which is a composition of LocateBook, PutInCart, etc).

4. Describe simple process—describe a simple process for the service (optional).

5. Profile description—provide a declarative advertisement for the service. It is partially populated by the process model.

The Congo.owl Web Service begins by describing the program that utilize the service. OWL-S provides for a declarative description of the programs in terms of a process model. This provides the descriptors to automate Web Service invocation and Web Service composition and interoperation.

To enable automated Web Service invocation, a Web Service must be able to tell an external agent how to actually interact with the Web Service, such as, how to automatically construct an HTTP call to execute or invoke a Web Service, and what outputs are returned from the service. To compose services, the process model must describe the preconditions necessary for its execution and the effects. OWL-S provides the process ontology to accomplish this. The markup then enables the Web Service provider to include sufficient information for automating Web Service invocation as well as automating Web Service composition. The Congo Service Ontology is shown in Figure 11-2.

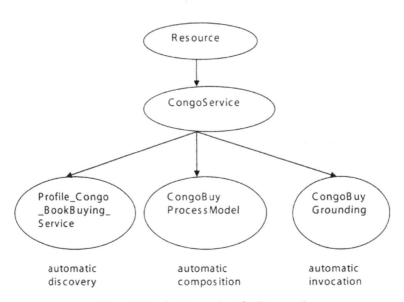

Figure 11-2. Service ontology for Congo.owl.

Step 1: Describe Individual Programs

The first step in developing Congo.owl is to describe the individual programs that are to comprise the service. The process model provides a declarative description of a program's properties.

Congo, Inc. provides the book-buying OWL-S-based Web Service for its customers called CongoBuy. This service is actually a collection of smaller Congo programs. We must first describe each of these individual programs, and then describe their composition, which becomes the ExpandedCongBuy interactive service.

Throughout this example, we will refer to the profile ontology and the process ontology. These ontologies define classes and properties that form a service description. For a particular service, we specialize the classes and properties by creating subclasses and sub-properties.

The Congo.owl book-buying service uses a suite of eight Web-accessible, transaction programs called LocateBook, PutInCart, SignIn, CreateAcct, CreateProfile, LoadProfile, SpecifyDeliveryDetails, and FinalizeBuy. The information flow through the Congo.owl example is illustrated in Figure 11-3. The names of the programs reflect their functions, starting with LocateBook where the user selects a book, through FinalizeBuy where the user completes his purchase. It is the process model that provides a declarative description of the properties of the Web-accessible programs.

We can follow the user's purchase process through the programs laid out in Figure 11-3. First the book selection is made and the book placed into a shopping cart. When the user is ready to check-out he can initiate a new account, use an existing account, or skip ahead if he had previously established a one-click option. If he proceeds through a normal check-out he will establish his method of payment and his preferred delivery method. The last step is finalizing the purchase. A more detailed analysis looking for logic conflict, deadlocks, and indeterminacies is presented in Chapter 12.

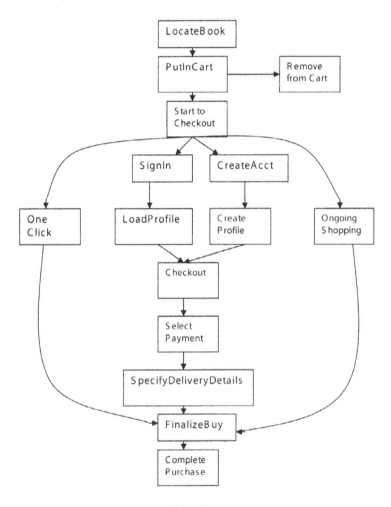

Figure 11-3. Client decision process.

The process model (see Listing 11-2) sees each program as either an atomic process or a composite process (see Chapter 10). Additional, it allows for the concept of a simple process, which will provide a simplied view of the composite CongoBuy program. A simple process is used to describe a view of an atomic or composite service to which it expands.

Listing 11-2. Process Model.

```
< owl:Class rdf:ID="Process">
  <rdfs:comment> The most general class of processes </rdfs:
comment>
  <owl:unionOf rdf:parseType=" owl:collection">
    < owl:Class rdf:about="#AtomicProcess"/>
    < owl:Class rdf:about="#SimpleProcess"/>
    < owl:Class rdf:about="#CompositeProcess"/>
  </ owl:unionOf>
</ owl:Class>
```

A non-decomposable, Web-accessible program is described as an atomic process. An atomic process is characterized by its ability to be executed by a single HTTP call that returns a response:

```
< owl:Class rdf:ID="AtomicProcess">
  < owl:subClassOf rdf:resource="#Process"/>
</ owl:Class>
```

The LocateBook program is an atomic process that takes as input the name of a book and returns a description of the book and its price (see Figure 11-4). For brevity, we refer to the inputs, outputs, preconditions and effects as iopes:

```
< owl:Class rdf:ID="LocateBook">
  <rdfs:subClassOf rdf:resource="&process;#AtomicProcess"/>
</ owl:Class>
```

If we want to put restrictions on the iopes, (such as cardinality restrictions), we need to define LocateBook as follows in Listing 11-3 with some or all of its iopes listed in the class definition.

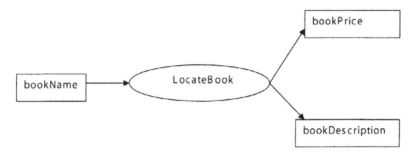

Figure 11-4. LocateBook atomic process with input and outputs.

Listing 11-3. LocateBook Input.

```
< owl:Class rdf:ID="LocateBook">
  <rdfs:subClassOf rdf:resource="&process;#AtomicProcess"/>
  <rdfs:subClassOf>
    < owl:Restriction owl:cardinality="1">
      <owl:onProperty rdf:resource="#bookName"/>
    </owl:Restriction>
  </rdfs:subClassOf>
</owl:Class>
```

Two types of parameters are the OWL-S properties input (see Listing 11-4) and output (see Listing 11-5).

Listing 11-4. Properties General Input.

```
<rdf:Property rdf:ID="parameter">
  <rdfs:domain rdf:resource="#Process"/>
  <rdfs:range  rdf:resource="http://www.daml.org/2001/03/
owl#Thing"/>
</rdf:Property>

<rdf:Property rdf:ID="input">
 <rdfs:subPropertyOf rdf:resource="#parameter"/>
</rdf:Property>
```

311

Associated with each process is a set of properties that have parameters associated with it. Two types of parameters are the OWL-S properties input and (conditional) output. An example of an input for LocateBook might be the name of the book. We proclaim this using the subPropertyOf construct.

An example of an input for LocateBook would be the name of the book, "bookName" as shown below:

```
<rdf:Property rdf:ID="bookName">
  <rdfs:subPropertyOf rdf:resource="&process;#input"/>
  <rdfs:domain rdf:resource="#LocateBook"/>
  <rdfs:range rdf:resource="&xsd;#string"/>
</rdf:Property>
```

Inputs can be mandatory or optional. In contrast, outputs are generally conditional. For example, when searching for a book in the Congo catalog, the output may be a detail description of the book if Congo carries it, or else it may be a "Sorry, unavailable" message. A conditional output class is ConditionalOutput which describes both a condition and the output based on this condition. An unconditional output has a zero cardinality restriction on its condition.

Listing 11-5. General Conditional Output Class.

```
<rdf:Property rdf:ID="output">
  <rdfs:domain rdf:resource="#parameter"/>
  <rdfs:range rdf:resource="#ConditionalOutput"/>
</rdf:Property>

<owl:Class rdf:ID="ConditionalOutput">
  <owl:subClassOf rdf:resource="http://www.daml.org/2001/03/
owl#Thing"/>
</owl:Class>

<rdf:Property rdf:ID="coCondition">
  <rdfs:domain rdf:resource="#ConditionalOutput"/>
  <rdfs:range rdf:resource="#Condition"/>
</rdf:Property>

<rdf:Property rdf:ID="coOutput">
  <rdfs:domain rdf:resource="#ConditionalOutput"/>
  <rdfs:range rdf:resource="http://www.daml.org/2001/03/
owl#Thing"/>
</rdf:Property>
```

The process bookDescription is output conditional and is dependent upon the book being in the Congo catalog (see Listing 11-6).

Listing 11-6. LocateBook Output bookDescription.

```
<rdf:Property rdf:ID="bookDescription">
  <rdfs:subPropertyOf rdf:resource="&process;#conditionalOutput"/>
  <rdfs:domain rdf:resource="#LocateBook"/>
  <rdfs:range rdf:resource="InCatalogueBookDescription"/>
</rdf:Property>

<owl:Class rdf:ID="InCatalogueBookDescription">
  <rdfs:subClassOf rdf:resource="&process;#ConditionalOutput"/>
  </owl:Class>

<rdf:Property rdf:ID="condInCatalogueBookDescription">
  <rdfs:subPropertyOf rdf:resource="&process;#coCondition"/>
  <rdfs:domain rdf:resource="#InCatalogueBookDescription"/>
  <rdfs:range rdf:resource="#InCatalogueBook"/>
</rdf:Property>

<rdf:Property rdf:ID="outInCatalogueBookDescription">
  <rdfs:subPropertyOf rdf:resource="&process;#coOutput"/>
  <rdfs:domain rdf:resource="#InCatalogueBookDescription"/>
  <rdfs:range rdf:resource="#TextBookDescription"/>
</rdf:Property>

<owl:Class rdf:ID="TextBookDescription">
  <rdfs:subClassOf rdf:resource="&owl;#Thing"/>
  </owl:Class>
```

The designation of inputs and outputs enables automation of the Web Service invocation. For automated composition and interoperation program, side-effects must be described. An action metaphor is used to conceive services having the properties, preconditions and (conditional) effects analogous to inputs and conditional outputs.

Preconditions specify what must be true in order for an agent to execute a service. Many Web Services have no preconditions except that the input parameters are known. However, Web-accessible devices may have many physical preconditions including bandwidth resources or battery power. Preconditions are described in the process ontology as a property and are described in the same manner as inputs.

```
<rdf:Property rdf:ID="precondition">
<rdfs:domain rdf:resource="#Process"/>
<rdfs:range  rdf:resource="http://www.daml.org/2001/03/
owl#Thing"/>
</rdf:Property>
```

Step 2: Describe the Grounding for Each Atomic Process

The grounding for LocateBook is LocateBookGrounding. For the class LocateBook, every instance of the class has an instance of the hasGrounding property, with value LocateBook-Grounding.

The hasGrounding property is defined in Process.owl.

```
<owl:Class rdf:about="LocateBook">
<owl:sameClassAs>
<owl:Restriction owl:cardinality="1">
<owl:onProperty rdf:resource="#hasGrounding"/>
<owl:hasValue rdf:resource="#LocateBookGrounding"/>
</owl:Restriction>
</owl:sameClassAs>
</owl:Class>
```

Listing 11-7 is an example of a OWL-S Grounding Instance.

Listing 11-7. LocateBookGrounding.

```
<grounding:WsdlGrounding rdf:ID="LocateBookGrounding">
<grounding:wsdlReference rdf:resource="http://www.w3.org/
TR/2001/NOTE-wsdl-20010315">
<grounding:otherReferences rdf:parseType="owl:collection">
"http://www.w3.org/TR/2001/NOTE-wsdl-20010315"
"http://schemas.xmlsoap.org/wsdl/soap/"
"http://schemas.xmlsoap.org/soap/http/"
</grounding:otherReferences>
<grounding:wsdlDocuments rdf:parseType="owl:collection">
"http://example.com/congo/congobuy.wsdl"
</grounding:wsdlDocuments>
<grounding:wsdlOperation
rdf:resource="http://example.com//locatebook.
wsdl#FindBook"/>
<grounding:wsdlInputMessage
rdf:resource="http://example.com/locatebook.
```

```
wsdl#LocateBookInput"/>
<grounding:wsdlInputMessageParts rdf:parseType="owl:
collection">
<grounding:wsdlMessageMap>
<grounding:damlsParameter rdf:resource=#bookName>
<grounding:wsdlMessagePart
rdf:resource="http://example.com//locatebook.wsdl#BookName">
</grounding:wsdlMessageMap>
... other message map elements ...
</grounding:wsdlInputMessageParts>
<grounding:wsdlOutputMessage
rdf:resource="http://example.com/locatebook.
wsdl#LocateBookOutput"/>
<grounding:wsdlOutputMessageParts rdf:parseType="owl:
collection">
... similar to wsdlInputMessageParts ...
</grounding:wsdlOutputMessageParts>
<grounding:WsdlGrounding>
```

Step 3: Describe Compositions of the Atomic Processes

So far, we have described each of the atomic processes and their iopes. Now we describe compositions of those programs that provide specific services. The CongoBuy composite service enables a user to buy a book.

Listing 11-8. General ConditionalEffect.

```
<rdf:Property rdf:ID="effect">
<rdfs:domain rdf:resource="#Process"/>
<rdfs:range  rdf:resource="#ConditionalEffect"/>
</rdf:Property>

<owl:Class rdf:ID="ConditionalEffect">
  <owl:subClassOf rdf:resource="http://www.daml.org/2001/03/
owl#Thing"/>
</owl:Class>

<rdf:Property rdf:ID="ceCondition">
    <rdfs:domain rdf:resource="#ConditionalEffect"/>
  <rdfs:range rdf:resource="#Condition"/>
</rdf:Property>
```

315

```
<rdf:Property rdf:ID="ceEffect">
  <rdfs:domain rdf:resource="#ConditionalEffect"/>
  <rdfs:range rdf:resource="http://www.daml.org/2001/03/
owl#Thing"/>
</rdf:Property>
```

In contrast to atomic processes, composite processes are composed of other composite or atomic processes (see Listing 11-8). They are composed through the use of control constructs and typical programming language constructs such as sequence, if-then-else, while a fork dictates the ordering and the conditional execution of processes in the composition.

In Listing 11-9, we provide the definition of a composite process in the process model. Notice that the composite process is composed of other processes.

In the Congo.owl example, CongoBuy is described in terms of two main steps: locating the book and then buying the book (see Figure 11-5).

ExpandedCongoBuy is the name of the composition for the sequence of the atomic process LocateBook followed by CongoBuyBook.

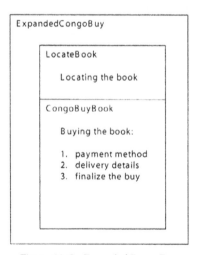

Figure 11-5. ExpandedCongoBuy.

While the locate book is an atomic process, the buying of a book involves a sequence of sub-processes corresponding to a payment method, the details of delivery, and finalizing the buy process. Figure 11-6 shows the Congo Service Model.

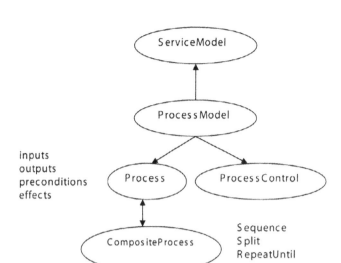

Figure 11-6. Service model.

Listing 11-9. CompositeProcess.

```
<owl:Class rdf:ID="CompositeProcess">
<owl:intersectionOf rdf:parseType="owl:collection">
    <owl:Class rdf:about="#Process"/>
    <owl:Restriction daml:minCardinality="1">
       <owl:onProperty rdf:resource="#composedOf"/>
    </owl:Restriction>
  </owl:intersectionOf>
</owl:Class>

<rdf:Property rdf:ID="composedOf">
<rdfs:domain rdf:resource="#CompositeProcess"/>
<rdfs:range rdf:resource="#ControlConstruct"/>
</rdf:Property>
```

The OWL-S composite process is recursively constructed from a top-down manner. Each CompositeProcess is composedOf a ControlConstruct, which may be a Sequence, Alternative, If-then-else, and so on. Each ControlConstruct has a property which specifies the classes of its subcomponents. These classes may also be processes or control constructs. Finally, the end is reached when the components of a composite process are atomic processes.

317

ExpandedCongoBuy is the name for the sequence of the atomic process LocateBook, followed by composite process CongoBuyBook. As was the case with atomic processes, composite processes have iopess (inputs, outputs, preconditions, and effects) and restrictions. Figure 11-5 represents CongoBuy, which corresponds to Listing 11-10.

Listing 11-10. ExpandedCongoBuy.

```
<owl:Class rdf:ID="ExpandedCongoBuy">
  <rdfs:subClassOf rdf:resource="&process;#CompositeProcess
"/>
  <rdfs:subClassOf>
    <owl:Restriction>
      <owl:onProperty rdf:resource="&process;#composedOf"/>
      <owl:toClass>
       <owl:Class>
        <owl:intersectionOf rdf:parseType="owl:collection">
         <owl:Class rdf:about="process:Sequence"/>
         <owl:Restriction>
           <owl:onProperty rdf:resource="process:
components"/>
           <owl:toClass>
            <owl:Class>
             <owl:listOfInstancesOf rdf:parseType="owl:
collection">
               <owl:Class rdf:about="#LocateBook"/>
               <owl:Class rdf:about="#CongoBuyBook"/>
             </owl:listOfInstancesOf>
            </owl:Class>
           </owl:toClass>
         </owl:Restriction>
        </owl:intersectionOf>
       </owl:Class>
      </owl:toClass>
    </owl:Restriction>
  </rdfs:subClassOf>
  <rdfs:subClassOf>
    <owl:Restriction owl:cardinality="1">
      <owl:onProperty rdf:resource="#expCongoBuyBookName"/>
    </owl:Restriction>
  </rdfs:subClassOf>
  <rdfs:subClassOf>
    <owl:Restriction owl:cardinality="1">
```

```
            <owl:onProperty rdf:resource="#expCongoBuyCreditCardN
umber"/>
        </owl:Restriction>
    </rdfs:subClassOf>
    <rdfs:subClassOf>
      <owl:Restriction owl:cardinality="1">
        <owl:onProperty rdf:resource="#expCongoBuyCreditCardT
ype"/>
        </owl:Restriction>
    </rdfs:subClassOf>
    <rdfs:subClassOf>
      <owl:Restriction owl:cardinality="1">
        <owl:onProperty        rdf:resource="#expCongoBuyCredi
tCardExpirationDate"/>
        </owl:Restriction>
    </rdfs:subClassOf>
    <rdfs:subClassOf>
      <owl:Restriction owl:cardinality="1">
        <owl:onProperty rdf:resource="#expCongoBuyDeliveryAdd
ress"/>
        </owl:Restriction>
    </rdfs:subClassOf>
    <rdfs:subClassOf>
      <owl:Restriction owl:cardinality="1">
        <owl:onProperty rdf:resource="#expCongoBuyPackagingSe
lection"/>
        </owl:Restriction>
    </rdfs:subClassOf>
    <rdfs:subClassOf>
      <owl:Restriction owl:cardinality="1">
        <owl:onProperty rdf:resource="#expCongoBuyDeliveryTyp
eSelection"/>
        </owl:Restriction>
    </rdfs:subClassOf>
</owl:Class>
```

Creating a Service

Although the CongoBuy service is a composition of several of Congo's transaction programs, it is useful to view it as a black-box process that expands the composite process. The black-box process enables the details of the operation of the composite process to be hidden. In the Congo example, a simple process called CongoBuy is (see Listing 11-11):

319

```
<owl:Class rdf:ID="CongoBuy">
  <rdfs:subClassOf rdf:resource="&process;#SimpleProcess"/>
</owl:Class>
```

The simple process is related to the composite process, ExpandedCongoBuy through the expand property. CongoBuy expands to ExpandedCongoBuy.

Listing 11-11. CongoBuy.

```
<owl:Class rdf:about="#CongoBuy">
  <rdfs:subClassOf>
    <owl:Restriction>
      <owl:onProperty rdf:resource="&process;#expand"/>
      <owl:toClass rdf:resource="#ExpandedCongoBuy"/>
    </owl:Restriction>
  </rdfs:subClassOf>
</owl:Class>
```

As was the case with ExpandedCongoBuy, the black-box process CongoBuy, has a variety of properties that characterize its black-box view. The iopes for the black-box process are designed for the computed iopes of the associated composite process. For now, OWL-S leaves this decision up to the Web Service provider.

Step 4: Simple Process (intentionally omitted)

This step was intentionally omitted for this example.

Step 5: Profile Description—Advertising the Services

OWL-S has been designed to enable automated Web Service discovery by providing descriptions of the properties and capabilities. These descriptors exist in a registry of services, to provide better indexing and retrieval features by search engines. Markup for Web-service discovery requires a process model constructed and the profile made available.

For Congo.owl, the following XML namespaces shown in Table 11-1.

concepts	http://www.daml.ri.cmu.edu/ont/DAML-S/concepts.daml
congo	http://www.daml.org/services/daml-s/0.9/Congo.daml
country	http://www.daml.ri.cmu.edu/ont/Country.daml
daml	http://www.daml.org/2001/03/daml+oil
profile	http://www.daml.org/services/daml-s/0.9/Profile
rdf	http://www.w3.org/1999/02/22-rdf-syntax-ns
rdfs	http://www.w3.org/2000/01/rdf-schema
service	http://www.daml.org/services/daml-s/0.9/Service
xsd	http://www.w3.org/2000/10/XMLSchema

Table 11-1. XML Namespaces.

Unlike the process model which describes services as classes, a service profile is an instance of the class Profile defined in the profile ontology. rdf:ID provides an ID to the instance so it can be referred to by other ontologies.

The descriptive information about the service and information about the provider of the services is:

```
<profile:profile rdf:ID="Profile_Congo_BookBuying_Service">
```

The term isPresentedBy (see Table 10-1) relates the profile to the service it describes, in this case Congo_BookBuying_Service:

```
<service:isPresentedBy>
<service:Service df:resource = "&congo;#Congo_BookBuying_
    Service"/>
</service:isPresentedBy>
```

The term serviceName is an identifier of the service that can be used to refer to the profile:

```
<profile:serviceName>Congo_BookBuying_Agent</profile:serviceName>
```

The term textDescription is a human readable description of the service

```
<profile:textDescription>
      This service provides a
```

```
       book selling site
</profile:textDescription>
```

The term providedBy (see Table 10-1) describes the provider of the service and is shown in Listing 11-12.

Listing 11-12. Profile providedBy.

```
<profile:providedBy>
<profile:ServiceProvider rdf:ID="CongoBuy">

      <profile:name>CongoBuy</profile:name>

      <profile:phone>455 484 1256 </profile:phone>

      <profile:fax>455 484 1234 </profile:fax>

      <profile:email>congo@congo.com</profile:email>

      <profile:physicalAddress>


location, USA

      </profile:physicalAddress>
      <profile:webURL>
              http://www.daml.org/services/daml-s/0.9/
CongoBuy.html
      </profile:webURL>
</profile:ServiceProvider>
</profile:providedBy>
```

The profile specifies additional attributes of the service. These are attributes included in service constraints such as geographic radius.

The term geographicRadius specifies whether there is a limitation on the distribution of the service. By restricting the geographicRadius to United States, the service will not be offered outside the area. This field is used either by the register during matching or by the requester to decide whether to use this service:

```
<profile:geographicRadius rdf:resource="&country;#UnitedStates"/>
```

The term qualityRating specify the quality of the service provided. This field is used either by the register during matching to make sure that the quality requested is matched, or by the requester to decide whether to use this service.

```
<profile:qualityRating rdf:resource="&concepts;#qualityRatingGood"/>
```

The profile is a set of attributes for describing key elements of the process. The four key elements of the process model are the input parameters the output parameters and the preconditions and conditional effects of the service.

The property profile:input is used to describe each key input to the corresponding process, by using as values the descriptions of the class profile:ParameterDescription. ParameterDescriptions name the corresponding parameter properties of the process, and their value restrictions.

Due to limitations of the OWL language, there is no logical relationship between ParameterDescriptions in the profile and the actual input output parameters of the corresponding process model. Each input requires a name and a restriction to what information is requested and a reference to the process model input used.

An input parameter is described by a name, a restriction on its values, and a reference to the input parameter in the profile it represents. The value restriction is used during matching to check whether the inputs that the requester is willing to provide match what the provider needs. The requester uses the inputs to know what additional information it needs to provide to the service:

```
<input>
<profile:ParameterDescription>
        <profile:parameterName rdf:resource="bookTitle"/>
        <profile:restrictedTo rdf:resource="&xsd;#string"/>
        <profile:refersTo rdf:resource="&congo;#congoBuyBookName"/>
</profile:ParameterDescription>
</input>
```

Outputs are represented similar to inputs. The restriction is used by the Web register to specify whether the service provides the outputs that are expected by the requester. The requester uses the outputs to know what additional knowledge it will acquire from the service:

```
<output>
<profile:ParameterDescription>
        <profile:parameterName rdf:resource="EReceipt"/>
        <profile:restrictedTo rdf:resource="&congoProcess;#EReceipt"/>
        <profile:refersTo rdf:resource="&congo;#congoBuyReceipt"/>
        </profile:ParameterDescription>
</output>
```

Preconditions and effects have a structure similar to the structure of inputs and outputs. The main difference is that instead of a restriction to some class they have a statement which are defined as owl:Thing. Preconditions and effects are used by the registry in a way that is similar to the inputs and outputs:

```
<precondition>
        <profile:ConditionDescription>
        <profile:ConditionName rdf:resource="AcctExists"/>
        <profile:statement rdf:resource="&congoProcess;#AcctExists"/>
        <profile:refersTo
                    rdf:resource="&congo;#congoBuyAcctExistsPrecon
dition"/>
        </profile:ParameterDescription>
</precondition>
```

Finally, close the description of the service:

```
</profile:OfferedService>
```

The Congo.owl service code is given in Listing 11-13.

Listing 11-13. CongoService.owl.

```
<?xml version="1.0" encoding="ISO-8859-1" ?>
 <!DOCTYPE uridef (View Source for full doctype...)>

<rdf:RDF xmlns:rdf="http://www.w3.org/1999/02/22-rdf-
syntax-ns#" xmlns:rdfs="http://www.w3.org/2000/01/rdf-
schema#" xmlns:owl="http://www.w3.org/2002/07/owl#" xmlns:
service="http://www.daml.org/services/owl-s/0.9/Service.
owl#" xmlns="http://www.daml.org/services/owl-s/0.9/
CongoService.owl#">

<owl:Ontology rdf:about="">
  <owl:versionInfo>$Id: CongoService.owl,v 1.12 2003/09/19
05:06:47 martin Exp $</owl:versionInfo>

  <rdfs:comment>This ontology represents the DAML-S service
description for the Congo Web Service example.</rdfs:
comment>
```

```
   <owl:imports rdf:resource="http://www.w3.org/2002/07/owl"
/>
   <owl:imports rdf:resource="http://www.daml.org/services/
owl-s/0.9/Service.owl" />
   <owl:imports rdf:resource="http://www.daml.org/services/
owl-s/0.9/CongoProfile.owl" />
   <owl:imports rdf:resource="http://www.daml.org/services/
owl-s/0.9/CongoProcess.owl" />
   <owl:imports rdf:resource="http://www.daml.org/services/
owl-s/0.9/CongoGrounding.owl" />
   </owl:Ontology>

<service:Service rdf:ID="ExpressCongoBuyService">

<!-- Reference to the Profile -->

   <service:presents rdf:resource="http://www.daml.org/
services/owl-s/0.9/CongoProfile.owl#Profile_Congo_BookBuying_
Service" />

<!-- Reference to the Process Model -->

   <service:describedBy rdf:resource="http://www.daml.org/
services/owl-s/0.9/CongoProcess.owl#ExpressCongoBuyProcessM
odel" />

<!-- Reference to the Grounding -->

   <service:supports rdf:resource="http://www.daml.org/
services/owl-s/0.9/CongoGrounding.owl#CongoBuyGrounding" />
   </service:Service>
<service:Service rdf:ID="FullCongoBuyService">
   <service:presents rdf:resource="http://www.daml.org/
services/owl-s/0.9/CongoProfile.owl#Profile_Congo_BookBuying_
Service" />

<!-- Reference to the Process Model -->

   <service:describedBy rdf:resource="http://www.daml.org/
services/owl-s/0.9/CongoProcess.owl#FullCongoBuyProcessMode
l" />

<!-- Reference to the Grounding -->
```

```
    <service:supports rdf:resource="http://www.daml.org/
services/owl-s/0.9/CongoGrounding.owl#FullCongoBuyGrounding"
/>
    </service:Service>
    </rdf:RDF>
```

Conclusion

In this chapter, we presented the phases and steps necessary to design and implement a OWL-S-based Web Service. We illustrated the design process by developing an example design for a semantic online book service that includes the ability to select a book, collect buyer information, collect payment,and deliver the book. As part of the preliminary, design process, we reviewed the explicit information available about online book services from Amazon.com's Software Developer's Kit which is available as open source.

We walked through an OWL-S on-line book-buying example "Congo.owl" provided by the daml.org organization and available for download at http://daml.semanticweb.org/services/owl-s/1.0/. This example provides details of the transactions, processes and flow paths of the service performance. Afterward, we discussed general service-design features.

In Chapter 12, we will expand our discussion of "Congo.owl" to include graphical analysis methodologies applied to the OWL-S example. This analysis improves the logic flow and transaction reliability of the OWL-S-based Web Service Ontology.

Chapter Twelve

Design and Analysis

Overview

Designing and analyzing Semantic Web Services will become increasingly more difficult as the number of components increases and there are more calls to interfacing services. Not only will this increase complexity, but more logic conflicts and indeterminacy problems will occur. While the logic structures of OWL and RDFS will assist in controlling conflicts and uncertainties, such problems can not be completely excluded. To minimize and resolve these issues the design of Semantic Web Services should be subjected to logic methods and analysis that expose loops, conflicts and deadlocks. Graph theory offers important methods for addressing these issues since XML trees and RDF graphs will flow naturally toward graphical evaluation and resolution. In addition, First Order Logics have been successfully represented and evaluated as logic-oriented directed graphs for many years.

In 2002, S. Narayanan and Sheila McIlraith first explored Petri net models as a way of analyzing Semantic Web Services. In their work, the book-buying on-line store example, Congo.owl Web Service (presented in Chapter 11), was modeled as a Petri net and simulations were run. Several problems were identified including a deadlock. This was despite the fact that the model design was relatively straightforward and less than 20 nodes. We can expect that a complete on-line Web Service similar to the actual Amazon.com site which includes electronics, apparel, CDs, DVDs, toys, and many other store fronts, and features besides books, would result in a

Petri net model of many hundreds of nodes. This might be simplified by segregating services that acted independently into modules. Nevertheless, the interfaces between multiple modules could be highly complicated.

As a result, designing and analyzing Semantic Web Services can be expected to become increasingly complex as the number of component processes increases and more services begin to interact.

In this chapter, we present methods, analysis and tools for reducing the complexity and conflicts, even as the number of Web Service process nodes increases from a few dozen to several thousand. We introduce the use of unmarked Petri nets for an initial analysis of very large models (before attempting to run Petri net simulations). This will expose higher-order loops and conflicts, and in addition, identify separable modules. We describe how unmarked Petri nets can use traditional reliability tools, such as reachability, minimum path sets, and modularization, in order to reduce higher-order loops, and logic conflicts. In addition, breaking higher-order conflicts will expose additional reaches that were previously hidden due to the inability to resolve the "knotted" logical conflict.

Background

Leonhard Euler (1707-1783) was one of the first mathematicians to experiment with graph theory. He attempted to solve the problem of traversing seven bridges on to an island without crossing any bridge more than once. From that point on, the study of graphs has been applied to a large number of real-world problems. Today, graphs are all around us. They are used in many diverse industries, from urban planning to computer networks such as the Web.

In Chapter 4, we saw that XML uses graphs (trees) to partition, organize, and manipulate data. In Chapter 7, we found that RDF used directed graphs to represent simple statements of fact. In both cases, the graphs consisted of vertices and arcs. Now the Semantic Web with OWL's introduction of logic will require a more complex graphic representation.

For the Semantic Web to provide computer-interpretable markup of the Web's content, it is necessary to provide automation features that will wind graph-like over convoluted networks. Semantic markup will enable automation of a variety of reasoning tasks, currently performed manually by human beings, such as automated Web Service discovery, automated invocation, automated interoperation, automated selection and composition, and automated execution monitoring. But for Semantic Web Service to be an effective automated function, it must be reliable.

Web Services will continue to proliferate to include more services like the book-buying service at www.amazon.com or the travel service at www.travelocity.com. Compositions of Web Services can be created manually by the service provider who takes a simple Web-accessible program, such as a form-validation program or database-lookup program, and composes them using typical procedural programming running on the server. The book-buying service at www. amazon.com is an example of a composite service.

Regardless of how the compositions originated, it is necessary to test the system under different input conditions and to logically verify conditions associated with the service. The Web Services will readily provide statistical information on service performance that can be feed into reliability and fail rate models that will support important design information.

The OWL-S ontology describes a set of classes and properties, specific to the description of Web Services. The upper ontology of OWL-S comprises the Service Profile for describing service advertisements, the Process Model for describing the actual program that realizes the service, and the Service Grounding for describing the transport-level messaging information associated with the execution of the program. The Service Grounding builds upon WSDL.

In this chapter, starting from OWL-S ontology for Web Services, compositions of Web Services are described. We consider using semantics graph methodologies, such as Petri nets to describe decision procedures for Web Services to be a helpful methodology. We also provide an analysis of the complexity of these tasks.

In addition, we present reliability and fault analysis in order to establish a relationship between a simplified (unmarked) Petri net and these powerful analytical toolkits which will provide valuable feedback on the performance and reliability of Semantic Web Services designs.

Graph Theory

A graph consists of a non-empty set of points or vertices, and a set of edges that link the vertices together. A simple real-world example of a graph could be your house and your workplace. Where the house and the workplace are the vertices and the road between them is the edge connecting the two vertices.

A graph can be either directed or undirected. A directed graph is one in which the direction of any given edge is defined. Conversely, an undirected graph indicates motion in both directions between vertices (see Figure 12-1). In addition, the edges can also be weighted or unweighted. Using the previous example, weights can be thought of as the number of blocks between your house and the school (see Figure 12-2).

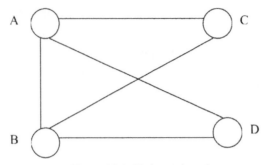

Figure 12-1. Undirected graph.

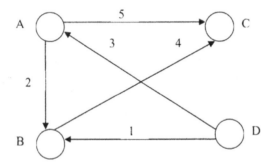

Figure 12-2. Directed graph with weighted edges.

The type of graph depends upon the attributes of the vertices and edges. A vertex within a graph may or may not have a label. Similarly, an edge may have a label, weight, and/or direction associated with it. As an example, a mixed graph is one that contains both directed and undirected edges, while a null graph is one that contains only isolated vertices (i.e., no edges).

An edge in a graph that joins two vertices is said to be incident to both vertices. Furthermore, the degree of a vertex is determined by the number of distinct edges that are incident to it. Specifically, the indegree and outdegree of a vertex represent the number of edges that terminate in and originate from a vertex, respectively.

Two edges in a graph are termed adjacent if they connect to the same vertex. Similarly, two vertices are termed adjacent if they are connected by the same edge. A loop is an edge that links a vertex to itself. A simple graph is one that contains no loops or parallel edges (i.e., where more than one edge connects two given vertices). A multi-graph is a graph that contains multiple edges and finally, a complete graph is a simple graph in which every pair of vertices is adjacent.

There are several different ways to represent a graph. Although graphs are usually shown diagrammatically, this is only possible when the number of vertices and edges is reasonably small. Graphs can also be represented in the form of matrices. The major advantage of matrix representation is that the calculation of paths and cycles can easily be performed using well known operations of matrices. However, the disadvantage is that this form of representation takes away from the visual aspect of graphs. Properties that are easily illustrated graphically, are often difficult to illustrate in a matrix.

Representing Graphs as Matrices

Consider the following directed graph, G (with vertices as v_1, v_2, v_3, v_4, and v_5), and its equivalent adjacency matrix, A, representation (see Figure 12-3).

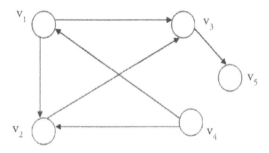

	v_1	v_2	v_3	v_4	v_5
v_1	0	1	1	0	0
v_2	0	0	1	0	0
v_3	0	0	0	0	1
v_4	1	1	0	0	0
v_5	0	0	0	0	0

Figure 12-3. Adjacency matrix for simple graph.

333

In Figure 12-3, we examine the graph and if a path of length 1 exists from one vertex to another (e.g., the two vertices are adjacent) there must be an entry of 1 in the corresponding position in the matrix. For example, from the vertex v_1, we can reach vertices v_2 and v_3. Therefore, we have a corresponding entry of 1 in the matrix in the first row and the second and third columns. In general, the number of 1s in the the ith row, correspond to the number of edges leaving the vertex v_i, and the number of 1s in the jth column, correspond to the number of edges entering the vertex v_j.

An adjacency matrix, A, is defined as follows: Let G be a graph with "n" vertices that are assumed to be ordered from v_1 to v_n.

The n x n matrix A, in which

$a_{ij} = 1$ if there exists a path from v_i to v_j,

$a_{ij} = 0$ otherwise,

is called an adjacency matrix.

Paths

As shown in the previous example, the existence of an edge between two vertices v_i and v_j is shown by an entry of 1 in the ith row and j^{th} column of the adjacency matrix. This entry represents a path of length 1 from v_i to v_j. To compute a path of length 2, the matrix of length 1 must be multiplied by itself, and the product matrix is the matrix representation of path of length 2. To compute a path of length n, the matrix of length 1 must be multiplied by itself to the nth power.

Trees

A tree is defined as an undirected, acyclic and connected graph (or more simply, a graph in which there is only one path connecting each pair of vertices).

Assume there is an undirected, connected graph G. A spanning tree is a subgraph of G, is a tree containing all the vertices of G. A Minimum Spanning Tree (MST) is a spanning tree, but has weights or lengths associated with the edges, and the total weight of the tree (the sum of the weights of its edges) is at a minimum. The MST applies to a couple of real-world examples:

1.   One practical application of a MST would be in the design of a network. For instance, a group of individuals who are separated by varying distances wish to be

connected together in a telephone network. MST can be used to determine the least costly paths in this network with no cycles, thereby connecting everyone at a minimum cost.

2. Another useful application of MST would be finding airline routes. The vertices of the graph would represent cities, and the edges would represent routes between the cities. Normally, the further one has to travel, the more it will cost, so MST can be applied to optimize airline routes by finding the least costly paths with no cycles.

Networks

One important use of graphs and graph theory can be illustrated with the following scenario.

An exporter who needs to ship several boxes to a major city has various routes that the shipment could take. The possible routes are laid out in the directed graph below.

The weighted, labeled, and directed graph in Figure 12-4 is called a network. The vertex s, referred to as the source of the network, represents the city in which the company is located. Notice that the indegree of the source must always be 0. The vertex t, referred to as the sink of the network, represents the city to which we are shipping the product. Notice that the outdegree of the sink must always be 0. The other vertices (a, b, c, d) represent several middlemen. The number assigned to each edge, called the capacity of the edge, represents the

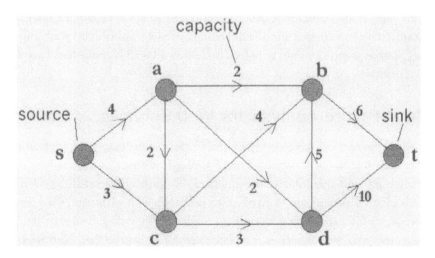

Figure 12-4. Network example.

maximum rate at which your product can be shipped over that particular edge. We seek to send the boxes of the product at the highest possible rate through the graph, but without exceeding the capacity of each edge.

Now, in order to show the rate at which the product is sent, each edge must also be labeled with a non-negative number called the flow. A flow must also hold certain properties. The flow on an edge must not exceed the capacity of the edge. This is referred to as the capacity constraint. The total flow into any vertex must equal the total flow out of the vertex. This is referred to as flow conservation. And due to flow conservation, it follows that the total flow out of the source must equal the total flow into the sink.

In order to find the maximum flow through the graph we would set the flow on each edge to 0 and recursively attempt to improve on each flow until we could no longer send the product at a greater rate.

Traveling Salesman Problem

The traveling salesman problem in graph theory involves finding the most efficient tour (i.e., minimum distance) through a graph, visiting each vertex in the graph exactly once. There is no general method to solve this problem. The solution is determined by trying all possible elementary paths. Once this is done, it is possible to conclude which is the optimum path (i.e., the one with the lowest distance/cost). However one must try all possibilities before you can determine this.

For a trip with many nodes, exhaustive experiment to find an optimal path is a complexity problem. In fact, the traveling salesman problem is categorized as an NP-hard problem. This means that this type of problem can only be solved by testing all possible solutions in order to find the optimum one.

Reliability and Failure Analysis for Web Services

Reliability and failure analysis can provide critical information for design and application of Semantic Web Services in terms of scalability, as well as proof and trust models.

Fault tree analysis provides quantitative assessment of reliability characteristics of Web Services. A fault tree is a logic diagram composed of a directed graph with a superimposed Boolean algebra. The objective of fault tree construction is to model a system or service that results in a failure event (e.g., the Web Service fails to complete the desired transaction). Normally, fault trees used to analyze physical service where improved performance of individual components does not degrade the performance of the service as a whole. Such systems are called coherent structures.

The following sections present structural relationships, path-sets, cut-sets, reliability, modularization, and other analysis methods that may be applied to evaluate Web Service performance and design.

Service Representation

A binary variable x may assume values of 0 or 1 and can be used to indicate the functioning of a service component.

The state of the ith component is given as

x_i = 1 if the ith service component is functioning,
 0 otherwise.

The vector x, denoted as $\mathbf{x}$, represents the state of n components as

$x = (x_1,\ldots x_i,\ldots x_n).$

The state of the service is indicated by the binary variable φ

φ_i = 1 if the service is functioning,
 0 otherwise.

If the components determine the state of the service, then

$\varphi = \varphi(\mathbf{x}),$

which is called the structure function and assumes the values of 0 and 1.

The dual of a reliability coherent structure function is defined as

$\varphi_d(\mathbf{x}) = 1 - \varphi(1 - \mathbf{x}).$

Path-sets and Cut-sets

Coherent structures may be represented in either path-sets or cut-sets. A path-set is defined as a set of components whose functioning ensures the functioning of the system. Thus, a path vector $\mathbf{x}$ yields $\varphi(\mathbf{x}) = 1$. A minimum path-set is a path-set which cannot be reduced. We can define minimum path sets as:

$$P_j(\mathbf{x}) = \prod x_i$$

This takes the value 1 if all the service components are in the jth minimal path-set function. The service ϕ will function only if at least one minimum path-set is functioning:

$$\varphi(\mathbf{x}) = \coprod P_j(\mathbf{x}) = \coprod {}^* \prod x_i.$$

A minimum path-set of a service is defined as the minimum combination of service components, transactions, or processes that must be successfully executed within the service in order for the service to successfully perform its function.

A cut-set is a set of components whose failure results in the failure of the service. A cut vector $\mathbf{x}$ produces the function $\phi(\mathbf{x})$. A minimum cut-set is a cut-set without irrelevant components. The binary function $k_j(\mathbf{x})$ is associated with the jth minimal cut-set k_j,

$$k_j(\mathbf{x}) = \coprod x_i.$$

which has the value 0 if all the service components of that cut-set fail, and 1 otherwise. When at least one complete cut-set fails then $\phi(\mathbf{x})$ equals zero. This is represented as

$$\varphi(\mathbf{x}) = \prod k_j(\mathbf{x}) = \prod {}^* \coprod x_i.$$

Fault Tree, Reliability Spaces, and their Duals

While reliability analysis is concerned with the functioning of services, fault tree analysis is concerned with service failure. Their correspondence is given by

$$1 - x_i = 1 \text{ if the } i^{th} \text{ component fails,}$$
$$0 \text{ otherwise.}$$

The fault tree top event is given as

$$\Phi(1-\mathbf{x}) = 1 - \varphi(\mathbf{x}) = 1 \text{ if the service fails,}$$
$$0 \text{ otherwise.}$$

The fault tree dual space representation is defined as

$$\Phi_d(1-\mathbf{x}) = 1 - \Phi(1-(1-\mathbf{x})) = 1 \text{ if the service fails,}$$
$$0 \text{ otherwise.}$$

338

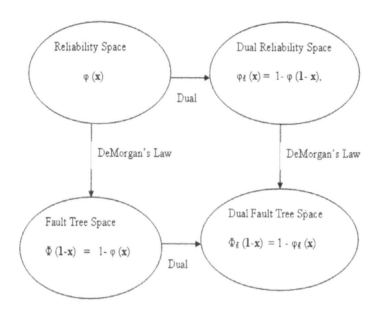

Figure 12-5. The relationship between fault trees and reliability spaces and their duals.

Dual spaces are often useful for mathematical manipulation. Note that path-sets of reliability space are the cut-sets of its dual space. Also, note that DeMorgan's Law operating on path-sets of reliability space yields the cut-sets of fault tree space.

Reliability Example

In this section, we present Example 12-1 a detailed analysis of success and failure modes for a simple directed graph. Figure 12-6 is a simple directed graph with four vertices v_i and four edges x_i.

We will find the path-sets, cut-sets and fault trees for Figure 12-6. The set of minimal path-sets:

$$P_j(\mathbf{x}) = \prod x_i$$

is equal to $P_j(x_1, x_2, x_3, x_4)$ where the edge x_i takes the value 0 or 1. There are two path-sets from vertex one to vertex four:

$$P_1 = (1, 1, 0, 0),$$
$$P_2 = (0, 0, 1, 1).$$

339

The minimal path-sets of Figure 12-6 can be represented as:

$$\varphi\,(\mathbf{x}) = \amalg\; P_j\,(\mathbf{x}) = (\;x_1 \cdot x_2 \;+\; x_3 \cdot x_4\;),$$

which means that if either path $x_1 \cdot x_2$ or path $x_3 \cdot x_4$ are functioning, then the service is functioning. The Success Tree in Figure 12-6 shows that either one of two paths is successful the service succeeds.

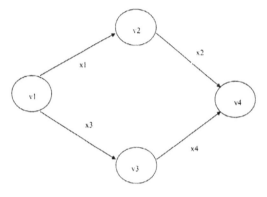

Figure 12-5. Relationships between reliability and fault tree spaces and their duals.

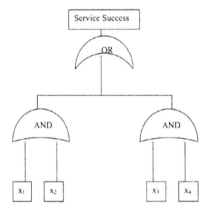

Figure 12-6. Finding path-sets of directed graph for Example 12-1.

340

DeMorgan's Law

DeMorgan's Law represents the complement function so that for any x, the complement is 1-x.

Applying DeMorgan's law to the set of minimal path-sets transforms them into the set of minimal cut-sets as

$$\overline{\varphi(\mathbf{x})} = \overline{\sum P_i} = \overline{(x_1 \cdot x_2 + x_3 \cdot x_4)} = \Phi(1-\mathbf{x})$$

$$\Phi(1-\mathbf{x}) = \bar{x}_1 \cdot \bar{x}_3 + \bar{x}_1 \cdot \bar{x}_4 + \bar{x}_2 \cdot \bar{x}_3 + \bar{x}_2 \cdot \bar{x}_4 = 1 - \varphi(\mathbf{x}).$$

The fault tree value of the service $\Phi(1-\mathbf{x})$ has the value 1 meaning that the service fails when the components of any minimal cut-set fails, and 0 otherwise.

Which means for example, that if components x_1 and x_3 both fail $(x_1 = 0)$ and $(x_3 = 0)$ then

$$\bar{x}_1 \cdot \bar{x}_3 = (1-0) * (1-0) = 1*1 = 1.$$

When at least one complete cut-set fails then $\phi(\mathbf{x})$ equals 0 and $\Phi(1-\mathbf{x}) = 1$.

The minimal cut-sets for Figure 12-6 yields the component failures as

$K_1 = (1, 0, 1, 0),$

$K_2 = (1, 0, 0, 1),$

$K_3 = (0, 1, 1, 0),$

$K_4 = (0, 1, 0, 1),$

and the service will fail. Figure 12-8 shows the resultant fault tree for service failure. It consists of one OR gate with four minimal cut-sets each showing that if the two designated components fail the service fails.

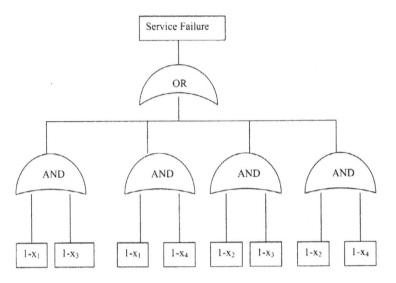

Figure 12-8. Fault tree for Example 12-1.

Probability Analysis

In establishing a probability analysis of a coherent service, we first assume that the components are statistically independent. Then, the probability of state x_i of the ith component is

$$P(x_i = 1) = Ex_i = p_i \quad \text{for } (i-1,\ldots,n)$$

where Ex_i is the expected value of the random variable x_i, and p_i is the reliability of the ith component.

The reliability h of the service is given by:

$$h = p(\varphi(\mathbf{x}) = 1) = E \varphi(\mathbf{x}).$$

By assuming that the components are statistically independent, the service reliability is given as a function of component reliability.

$$h = h(\mathbf{p})$$

where

$$\mathbf{p} = (p_i,\ldots,p_n).$$

Then for path sets

$$h(\mathbf{p}) = E \varphi(\mathbf{X}) = E * \amalg p_j(\mathbf{x}) = E * \amalg * \prod x_i,$$

For Figure 12-6 then, the reliability of the path sets yield

$$h(\mathbf{p}) = E(x_1 \cdot x_2 \ \amalg \ x_3 \cdot x_4) = E\,x_1 \cdot E\,x_2 + E\,x_3 \cdot E\,x_4 - E\,x_1 * E\,x_2 * E\,x_3 * E\,x_4$$

or

$$h(\mathbf{p}) = p_1 * p_2 + p_3 {}^* p_4 - p_1 {}^* p_2 * p_3 {}^* p_4.$$

(Note: $p_1 {}^* p_2 * p_3 {}^* p_4$ is set to 0 if there is statistical independence.)

In general, however, a basic event may appear in more than one minimal path set and if so the probability is not statistically independent.

Modularization

One way to simplify analysis of coherent services is to first decompose it into disjoint sub-systems or modules. A module is a coherent sub-system that acts as if it were a single component. The modular decomposition of a coherent system is a set of disjoint modules along with an organizing structure.

Reachability

Reachability is an important characteristic of a directed logic graph which finds all paths from every node n_j, to any node n_j within the graph.

Reachability R can be found using the Adjacency Matrix A with V vertices where the ij location will be 0 if there is no path from vertex i to vertex j and one otherwise

$$R = \sum_{i=1}^{V-1} A\!\char94\!i$$

The reachability of a directed graph with a superimposed logic is the linear sum of the graphical reachability solution plus the logic structure reachability which was developed by I.J. Sachs:

$$R = R_N + R_L.$$

We will return to the contributions of reliability analysis after we introduce Petri nets.

Petri Nets for Web Services

Petri nets are a well-established modeling technique used to analyze many processes including complex nuclear reactor systems and business processes. A Petri net is a directed, connected, and bipartite graph in which each node is either a place or a transition. Tokens occupy places. When there is at least one token in every place connected to a transition, the transition is enabled.

A Web Service behavior is basically a partially ordered set of operations. Therefore, it maps into a Petri net. Operations are modeled by transitions and the state of the service is modeled by places. The arrows between places and transitions are used to specify causal relations.

A Petri net structure, C, is a four-tuple, C = <P, T, I, O>

> where

>> P = $\{p_1, \ldots, p_n\}$ is a finite set of places, $n \geq 0$ and

>> T = $\{t_1, \ldots, t_m\}$ is a finite set of transitions, $m \geq 0$.

The set of places and the set of transitions are disjoint, $P \cap T = 0$, and

>> I : T → P is the transition input function, a mapping from transitions to a multi-set of places.

>> O : T → P is the set of transition output functions, a mapping from transitions to multi-set of places.

Corresponding to these, a Petri net graph has two types of nodes. A circle represents a place; a bar represents a transition.

A Petri net graph G is a bipartite multi-graph, G = (V, A), where A = $\{a_1, \ldots, a_n\}$ is a bag of directed arcs, $a_1 = (v_j, v_k)$, with v_j, v_k elements of V. The set V can be partitioned into two disjoint sets P and T such that V = P $\cup$ T, P $\cap$ T = 0, and for each directed arc, $a_1 \in$ A, is a_1 = (v_j, v_k) then either $v_j \in$ P and $v_k \in$ T, or $v_j \in$ T and $v_k \in$ P.

A marking μ is an assignment of tokens to the places of a Petri net. A token is a primitive concept for Petri nets. Tokens are assigned to places. The number and position of tokens may change during the execution of a Petri net. The tokens are used to define dynamic execution of a Petri net.

Therefore, a marked Petri net is M(C, μ).

Petri Net Reachability

Reachability is an important characteristic of a directed logic graph which find all paths from every node n_i to any node n_j within the graph.

For a Petri net, a marking M is reachable if it is the marking reached by some occurrence sequence. The reachability problem for a net N is the problem of deciding for a given marking M of N if it is reachable.

344

Semantic Web Services

The Semantic Web requires precise interpretation of automatic Web search, discovery and use. Services are an important component of the Semantic Web. Petri net analysis offers an important contribution to this precision.

Minimizing Higher-Order Conflicts

In OWL-S, both iterate and choice introduce conflict constructs, iterate introduces a conflict between the repeat and finish transitions, while choice is by definition a structural conflict. No other control construct introduces structural conflicts.

Also, a marking of a net is a deadlock if it enables no transitions. The deadlock problem for a net is the problem of deciding if any of its reachable markings is a deadlock.

For large Semantic Web Services there are advantages to analyzing the unmarked representation of a Petri net in search of logical conflicts, loops, and deadlocks.

An unmarked Petri net, C, is isomorphic to a directed graph with a logic structure superimposed. The places are simple nodes and the transitions are logic gates. If we consider the graph as a failure mode graph then the transition gates are treated as AND gates and the cut-sets of the graph yield all the combination of events that will result in the failure of the Web Service to perform correctly. The process of finding cut-sets however, will require breaking any conflict loops in the graph first. Reachability analysis plays a major role in achieving this.

Once the failure modes are evaluated, the success modes can be processed through conversion to path-sets by traditional means.

In the following sections, we analyze the Congo.owl example, provided in Chapter 11, as a digraph and find its cut-sets, modules, path-sets, and reachability, and expand the model to include additional stores that produce conflicts.

The Relationship Between Digraph Matrix Analysis and Petri Nets

Digraph Matrix Analysis (DMA) is a tool for mathematically representing large complex systems and services in order to evaluate their design structure and reliability. DMA is based upon a matrix representation of logical connective superimposed on a directed graph structure. Computer reachability processing and evaluation of matrix representations of large, complex digraphs (thousands of nodes) has been demonstrated for nuclear power plant systems and services.

In 1985, H. P. Alesso provided a proof demonstrating that there exists an isomorphism between an unmarked Petri net model and DMA which is useful for our analysis.

Software Testing and Reliability

The purpose of software testing is to assess and evaluate the quality of work performed at each step of the software-development process. The goal of testing is to ensure that the software performs as intended and improve software quality, reliability and maintainability.

Testing involves the operation of a system or application under controlled conditions and evaluating the results. The controlled conditions should include both normal and abnormal conditions. Testing should intentionally attempt to make things go wrong to determine if things happen when they shouldn't or if things don't happen when they should.

Software reliability engineering is a practice that helps develop software that is more reliable. Software reliability engineering works by quantitatively characterizing and applying two things about the product the expected relative use of its functions and its required major quality characteristics. The major quality characteristics are reliability, availability, and life-cycle cost.

Software reliability is the application of statistical techniques to data collected during system development and operation to specify, predict, estimate, and assess the reliability of software-based systems. Software reliability engineering estimates failure intensity from failure data. By tracking software reliability growth, you can uncover possible problems and take timely corrective action.

Analyzing the Congo Example

For the Congo.owl example, the on-line book seller service, presented in Chapter 11, the step-by-step process for a client to purchase a book on our on-line service is given as:

1. Book search capability to locate the desired book.
2. Place book in individual's purchase cart.
3. Individual signs-in.
4. Load profile, or
5. Create new account, and
6. Create profile.
7. Specify delivery details.
8. Finalize purchase.
9. Book distribution.
10. Book delivery.

The Congo.owl book-buying service uses a suite of Web-accessible programs called Locate-Book, PutInCart, SignIn, CreateAcct, CreateProfile, LoadProfile, SpecifyDeliveryDetails, and FinalizeBuy.

Figure 12-9 provides a definition for AND and OR gate representations which appear in the logic graph in Figure 12-11.

Figure 12-10 represents the Congo.owl book-buying data flow model with the suite of Web-accessible programs. It shows four routes from "Start to Checkout" to finalizeBuy. The four paths follow from the one-click option, on-going shopping, sign-in, and create account programs.

Figure 12-11 reduces the named programs to corresponding numbered nodes with two logic gates added (L_1 and L_2) and illustrates a success-oriented graph.

We reduce this figure to symbolic form in Figure 12-11 and find its Adjacency Matrix A.

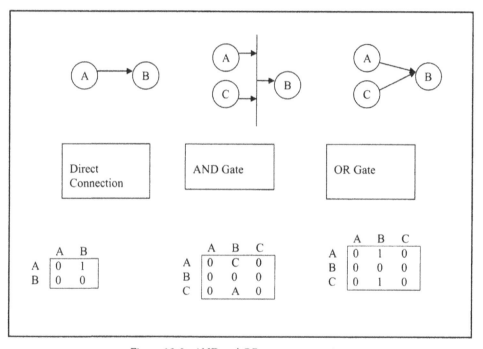

Figure 12-9. AND and OR gate representation.

Figure 12-11 has indicated that transition gates L_1 and L_2 represent logical connectives. L_1 and L_2 are OR gate connectives when evaluating Figure 12-11 as a success-oriented graph. In fact, Figure 12-11 is a success graph in the same fashion as Figure 12-7.

347

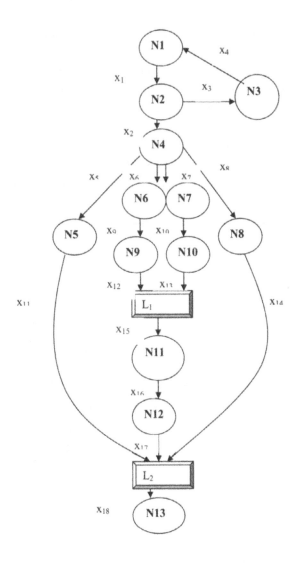

Figure 12-10. Digraph of client decision process.

The cut-sets require failure modes and AND gates at transition, while path sets require OR gates at transitions and AND gates at output nodes.

Matrix Representation of Congo Example

Adjacency Matrix = A = [n x n] =

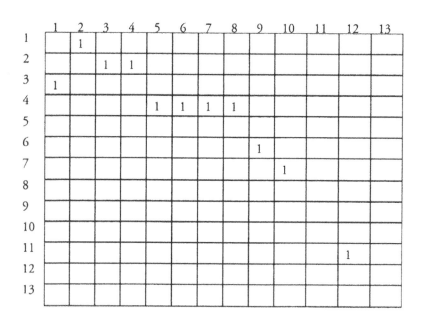

	1	2	3	4	5	6	7	8	9	10	11	12	13
1		1											
2			1	1									
3	1												
4					1	1	1	1					
5													
6									1				
7										1			
8													
9													
10													
11												1	
12													
13													

Reachability for Congo Example

Recall that, R = A^n and that

$$R = R_N + R_L.$$

The overall relationships are illustrated as:

N = {n_1, n_2, n_3, n_4, n_5, n_6, n_7, n_8, n_9, n_{10}, n_{11}, n_{12}, n_{13}}
L = {l_1, l_2}

$$I\{ l_1 \} = \{n_9, n_{10}\} \qquad\qquad O\{ l_1 \} = \{n_{11}\}$$
$$I\{ l_2 \} = \{n_5, n_8, n_{13}\} \qquad\qquad O\{ l_2 \} = \{n_{13}\}$$

$$I\{ n_1 \} = 0 \qquad\qquad O\{ n_1 \} = \{n_2\}$$
$$I\{ n_2 \} = \{n_1\} \qquad\qquad O\{ n_2 \} = \{n_4\}$$
$$I\{ n_3 \} = \{n_2\} \qquad\qquad O\{ n_3 \} = \{n_1\}$$
$$I\{ n_4 \} = \{n_2\} \qquad\qquad O\{ n_4 \} = \{n_5, n_6, n_7, n_8\}$$
$$I\{ n_5 \} = \{n_4\} \qquad\qquad O\{ n_5 \} = 0$$
$$I\{ n_6 \} = \{n_4\} \qquad\qquad O\{ n_6 \} = \{n_9\}$$
$$I\{ n_7 \} = \{n_4\} \qquad\qquad O\{ n_7 \} = \{n_{10}\}$$
$$I\{ n_8 \} = \{n_4\} \qquad\qquad O\{ n_8 \} = 0$$
$$I\{ n_9 \} = \{n_6\} \qquad\qquad O\{ n_9 \} = 0$$
$$I\{ n_{10} \} = \{n_7\} \qquad\qquad O\{ n_{10} \} = 0$$
$$I\{ n_{11} \} = 0 \qquad\qquad O\{ n_{11} \} = \{n_{12}\}$$
$$I\{ n_{12} \} = \{n_{11}\} \qquad\qquad O\{ n_{12} \} = 0$$
$$I\{ n_{13} \} = 0 \qquad\qquad O\{ n_{13} \} = 0$$

Path-Set for Congo Example

$$P_j (\mathbf{x}) = \prod x_i$$

Successful book-buying transactions can happen through four minimal path-sets. The loop responsible for searching for a book returns a superfluous path $x_1 * x_3 * x_4$ that is not minimal. The complete set of successful minimal path-sets is

$$P_1 = x_1 * x_2 * x_5 * x_{11} * x_{18}$$

$$P_2 = x_1 * x_2 * x_6 * x_9 * x_{12} * x_{15} * x_{16} * x_{17} * x_{18}$$

$$P_3 = x_1 * x_2 * x_7 * x_{10} * x_{13} * x_{15} * x_{16} * x_{17} * x_{18}$$

$$P_4 = x_1 * x_2 * x_8 * x_{10} * x_{14} * x_{18}$$

Reliability for Congo Example

Recall that the reliability is

$$h(\mathbf{p}) = E\, \varphi (\mathbf{X}) = E * \amalg P_j (\mathbf{x}) = E * \amalg * \prod x_i$$

or

$$h(\mathbf{p}) = E\left(P_1 + P_2 + P_3 + P_4\right)$$

after substituting the paths for P_i we could find the overall reliability of the service to perform once we have collected statistically significant data while running the Web site.

Cut-Sets for Congo Example

$$k_j(\mathbf{x}) = \coprod x_i$$

Failure to complete a book-buying transaction can happen through minimal cut-sets. The loop responsible for searching for a book returns a superfluous path $x_1 * x_3 * x_4$ that is not minimal.

The complete set of 42 minimal cut-sets is (note for simplicity we have omitted the negation sign for each of the elements x_i in Table 12-1 below:

Singleton cut-set:	$K_{19} = x_5 * x_9 * x_7 * x_{14}$
	$K_{20} = x_5 * x_9 * x_{10} * x_{14}$
$K_1 = x_1$	$K_{21} = x_5 * x_9 * x_{13} * x_{14}$
$K_2 = x_2$	
$K_3 = x_{18}$	$K_{22} = x_{11} * x_{12} * x_7 * x_{14}$
	$K_{23} = x_{11} * x_{12} * x_{10} * x_{14}$
Doubleton cut-sets	$K_{24} = x_{11} * x_{12} * x_{13} * x_{14}$
none	$K_{25} = x_{11} * x_6 * x_7 * x_8$
	$K_{26} = x_{11} * x_6 * x_{10} * x_8$
Triplet cut-sets:	$K_{27} = x_{11} * x_6 * x_{13} * x_8$
$K_4 = x_{11} * x_{15} * x_{14}$	$K_{28} = x_{11} * x_9 * x_7 * x_8$
$K_5 = x_{11} * x_{16} * x_{14}$	$K_{29} = x_{11} * x_9 * x_{10} * x_8$
$K_6 = x_{11} * x_{17} * x_{14}$	$K_{30} = x_{11} * x_9 * x_{13} * x_8$
Quadruplet cut-sets:	
$K_7 = x_5 * x_6 * x_7 * x_8$	$K_{31} = x_{11} * x_{12} * x_7 * x_8$
$K_8 = x_5 * x_6 * x_{10} * x_8$	$K_{32} = x_{11} * x_{12} * x_{10} * x_8$
$K_9 = x_5 * x_6 * x_{13} * x_8$	$K_{33} = x_{11} * x_{12} * x_{13} * x_8$
$K_{10} = x_5 * x_9 * x_7 * x_8$	$K_{34} = x_{11} * x_6 * x_7 * x_{14}$
$K_{11} = x_5 * x_9 * x_{10} * x_8$	$K_{35} = x_{11} * x_6 * x_{10} * x_{14}$
$K_{12} = x_5 * x_9 * x_{13} * x_8$	$K_{36} = x_{11} * x_6 * x_{13} * x_{14}$

Table 12-1. Complete Set of Minimal Cut-sets.

$$K_{13} = x_5 * x_{12} * x_7 * x_8$$
$$K_{14} = x_5 * x_{12} * x_{10} * x_8$$
$$K_{15} = x_5 * x_{12} * x_{13} * x_8$$

$$K_{16} = x_5 * x_6 * x_7 * x_{14}$$
$$K_{17} = x_5 * x_6 * x_{10} * x_{14}$$
$$K_{18} = x_5 * x_6 * x_{13} * x_{14}$$

$$K_{37} = x_{11} * x_9 * x_7 * x_{14}$$
$$K_{38} = x_{11} * x_9 * x_{10} * x_{14}$$
$$K_{39} = x_{11} * x_9 * x_{13} * x_{14}$$

$$K_{40} = x_{11} * x_{12} * x_7 * x_{14}$$
$$K_{41} = x_{11} * x_{12} * x_{10} * x_{14}$$
$$K_{42} = x_{11} * x_{12} * x_{13} * x_{14}$$

Table 12-1 (continued). Complete Set of Minimal Cut-sets.

Analyzing the Analysis

Once the analysis is completed and raw data collected and turned into statically meaningful information about each transaction and the process as a whole, then re-engineering can take place. The goal would be to improve performance of each and every transaction as well as offering a guarantee that shoppers aren't prevented from completing a book buying process through some difficulty with the process itself.

Conclusion

In this chapter, we introduced Petri nets to analyze Semantic Web Service designs. The Semantic requires precise interpretation of automatic Web search, discovery and use. Services are an important component of the Semantic Web. Petri net analysis offers an important contribution to this precision. The benefits include:

- A service description is represented using Petri nets.
- Analysis of Petri nets allows a rich repository of analysis techniques and tools.
- Complexity and reasoning supports ordinary Petri nets.

Chapter Thirteen

Semantic Tools

Overview

In this chapter, we introduce some of the many rapidly developing semantic tools and their toolmakers. The current available Semantic Web tools include RDF/XML and OWL editors, parsers, servers, databases and inference engines. Some of the more widely used include RDF Gateway, Jena, SMORE, and Drive.

In addition, we present a review of the semantic search tool TAP. TAP is a distributed project involving researchers from Stanford, IBM, and W3C. TAP leverages automated and semi-automated techniques to extract knowledge bases from unstructured and semi-structured bodies of text. The system is able to use previously learned information to learn new information, and can be used for information retrieval and word processing.

We also examine some of the new Semantic Web Services tools. The early development tools in this area include WSDL2DAML-S, DAML-S Converter, Web Service Composer, DL Mapping, and DAML-S Matchmaker.

Background

Artificial Intelligence (AI) software helps engineers create better jet engines. In factories, it boosts productivity by monitoring equipment and signaling when preventive maintenance is needed.

The Department of Defense uses AI software to coordinate logistic operations. And in the pharmaceutical sector, it is used to gain new insights into the data on the human genome.

As AI technologies contribute to both the Semantic Web and Web Services, it is important that open standards develop. A layered approach to ontology creation and annotations has been adopted to support open standards. Tool support is also essential to take a significant step forward in the construction of the Semantic Web. The tools themselves are partly dependent on the Ontology language they are supposed to work with. As a result, XML-based integration and interoperability become central issues.

Semantic Web Services are harder to build than XML-based Web Services since Microsoft .NET Visual Studio generates all the SOAP code for us. SOAP may be generated easier, but it has its problems. There is risk of breakage if functions change. Semantic Web Services, while requiring some more work at the outset, make it more likely that the program will last and automatically play well with others.

If Semantic Web Services development tools become powerful and reduce the problems of constructing Semantic Web Services, then we can expect important progress on the Semantic Web. This chapter looks at the Semantic Web Service development tools currently available and under construction.

Semantic Tools

Semantic Web tools and classic Web tools (browsers) use different interpretations of a URI. Browsers fetch a Web page while the Semantic Web tools treat the URI as an opaque object that can only be compared to another one. Certain tools are under development that may help us understand the vocabulary for relating the two.

The languages for the future of the Semantic Web will depend upon distributed computing principles. Software agents that can move as mobile code from host to host carry their state with them and they will be built for moving data (mobile data) around between different applications. The ability to act autonomously occurs through true mobility of the code, because the code does the execution of computational task not the data. There is a variety of Java-based Semantic tools available that strongly support mobile solutions.

Table 13-1 displays a list of some of the leading Semantic Web software tool developers.

Developer	Product	Category
AIdministrator http://www.aidministrator.nl/	Sesame Spectacle	RDF(S) storage and retrieval Ontology-based information presentation
Applied Semantics (formerly Oingo) http://www.appliedsemantics.com/	Circa	Ontology-based automatic categorization
Cycorp http://www.cyc.com/	Cyc Knowledge Server	Multi-contextual knowledge base / inference engine
DigitalOwl http://www.digitalowl.com/	KineticEdge	Content management / publishing
Empolis http://www.empolis.co.uk/	K42	Topic map server
Eprise http://www.eprise.com/	Participant Server	Content management
Epigraph http://www.epigraph.com/	Xcellerant	Content management / ontology management
Forward look inc http://www.forwardlook.com/	ContextStreams	Data asset management
GlobalWisdom http://www.globalwisdom.org/	Bravo engine	Facilitated ontology construction / dynamic knowledge engine
Intellidimension http://www.intellidimension.com/	RDF Gateway	RDF data management system
Inxight http://www.inxight.com/	ThingFinder Server Star Tree Viewer	Content extraction Web content navigation
Mohomine	Several	Information

Table 13-1. Semantic Software Tools.

Network Inference http://www.networkinference.com/	Cerebra	Inference engine and tools
Ontoprise http://www.ontoprise.de/	Ontobroker	Inference middleware
Persist http://www.persistag.com/	Semantic Base	Knowledge management system
Profium http://www.profium.com/	Smart Information Router (SIR)	Semantic content management based on RDF
R-Objects http://www.r-objects.com/	Pepper website: pepper.r-objects.com	Personal knowledge management
SC4 Solution Clustering http://www.sc4.org/	SemTalk website: http://www.semtalk.com/	RDFS editor based on Visio
Semio http://www.semio.com/	SemioMap	Content categorization and indexing
SMORE – Semantic Markup, Ontology and RDF Editor http://www.mindswap.org	MindSwap	SMORE is a application that incorporates four applications in one.
Tarragon Consulting Corporation http://www.tgncorp.com/	High-performance knowledge and content management systems	Custom systems design and development
TheBrain.com http://www.thebrain.com/	TheBrain	Information organizer
Unicorn Solutions http://www.unicorn.com/	Unicorn Coherence	Ontology modeling and data integration
Verity http://www.verity.com/	K2	Business portal infrastructure
Voquette (formerly Taalee)	Semantic Engine	Knowledge-based

Table 13-1 (contineud). Semantic Software Tools.

In the following sections, we present and evaluate several of the more prominent tools.

RDF Gateway

One of the leading tool and server developers for RDF and OWL is a young company named Intellidimension, Inc. The president of Intellidimension, Inc. (http:\\www.intellidimension.com) is Geoff Chappell, a veteran software developer with extensive technology start-up experience and co-founder, Derrish Repchick. Derrish gained his expertise as a technology consultant for the financial services industry, as a software architect for Tally Systems Corp., and as an information technology professional for United Technologies.

Intellidimension, Inc.'s RDF Gateway is one of the first Web Server applications built completely upon the RDF standard. It makes interoperate metadata possible across Web sites and enables everything from powerful search agents to extensive inference database engines.

While RDF is the core technology behind the W3C's Semantic Web effort, adoption of RDF has been slow, especially when compared with XML, upon which RDF is based.

RDF Gateway, however, runs as both a Web application server and database, with the database especially designed to handle RDF content. This makes the product easy to deploy.

To develop applications to run on RDF Gateway, RSP (RDF Server Pages), a format developed for RDF Gateway by Intellidimension, is provided. Anyone who has worked with JSP (Java Server Pages) or ASP (Active Server Pages), will find learning and coding in RSP to be a simple task.

Administration of RDF Gateway is done through a simple browser-based interface that manages content on the server, assigns users to the server and creates usage roles.

A Windows-based query tool allows access to the database and creates and tests server-side scripts. Server-side scripts are written in RDF Query Language, which, being based on ECMAScript, is easy to use.

RDF builds upon XML to provide a mechanism for exchanging semantics as well as data in real time. RDF enables a dynamic network of distributed information sources to share information over the Internet. RDF is open and does not require a common schema for systems to exchange information (see Figure 13-1).

The simple model of triple URIs used by RDF to describe information has many advantages. One of the most important is that any data model can be reduced to a common storage format based on a triple. This makes RDF ideal for aggregating disparate data models because all of the data from all models can be treated the same. Information can be combined from many sources and processed as if it can from a single source.

The information in Figure 13-1 shows an individual, H. Peter Alesso, with some related facts represented in the RDF triplet graphical form that translates into a triplet table with (subject, predicate, object) shown in Table 13-1.

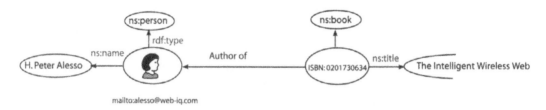

Figure 13-1. RDF graph example.

Subject	Predicate	Object
mailto:alesso@web-iq.com	rdf:type	ns:Person
mailto:alesso@web-iq.com	ns:name	H. Peter Alesso
isbn:0201730634	ns:type	ns:book
isbn: 0201730634	ns:title	The Intelligent Wireless Web
isbn: 0201730634	ns:author-of	mailto:alesso@web-iq.com

Table 13-2. RDF Triplet Data Table.

RDF Gateway is designed from the ground up to work with RDF data. Its native database engine fully supports the RDF model and syntax. RDF Gateway allows developers to create applications for the Semantic Web. As a result, Semantic Web applications can integrate and share disparate information over the Internet.

RDF Gateway has a native RDF Database Engine with its own SQL-like query language called RDFQL. Since with RDF Gateway all tables have four columns there is no need to use column names in a query. RDFQL uses the statement syntax to identify columns based on position.

RDF Gateway offers such an attractive server-based system for creating, deploying, and managing RDF applications. In tests, the authors used RDF Gateway to build a wide variety of Web applications that incorporated and understood RDF.

Jena—Java API for RDF

Researchers at HP Labs have been developing a Java-based open source Semantic Web toolkit called Jena. Jena is compliant with the current decisions made by the RDF-core and WebOnt Working Groups. Jena can be downloaded from SourceForge and includes:

- Readers and writers for RDF/XML N-Triples RDF/N3.
- The ARP RDF parser used by the W3C Validator site.
- An RDF API including RDF datatyping.
- An ontology API (OWL DAML+OIL, RDFS).
- Ontology readers (OWL, DAML+OIL, RDFS).
- Storage mechanisms (in-memory, database).
- Plug-in reasoner API (so you can connect to your favorite DL engine).
- Reasoners for RDFS and for the rules-based subset of OWL (i.e., the OWL-Lite subset of OWL-Full).
- Query language and implementation: RDQL.

Jena is in widespread use within the semantic community. Such toolkits enable the development of myriad example applications, helping to embody the Semantic Web vision.

Included with the Jena toolkit are examples. The only requirement is JRE 1.2. The Jena developers are refactoring many of the classes, changing class structure as well as making modifications to the API itself. Included within the Jena toolset is an RDF parser.

Jena's API architecture focuses on the RDF model, the set of statements that comprises an RDF document, graph, or instantiation of a vocabulary. A basic RDF/XML document is created by instantiating one of the model classes and adding at least one statement (triple) to it. To view the RDF/XML, read it into a model and then access the individual elements, either through the API or through the query engine. The ModelMem class creates an RDF model in memory. It extends ModelCom—the class incorporating common model methods used by all models—and implements the key interface, Model.

In addition, the DAML class, DAMLModelImpl, and subclasses ModelMem are included. The ModelRDB class is an implementation of the model used to manipulate RDF stored within a relational database such as MySQL or Oracle. Unlike the memory model, ModelRDB persists the RDF data for later access, and the basic functionality between it and ModelMem is opening and maintaining a connection to a relational database in addition to managing the data.

We can access data in a stored RDF model directly using specific API function calls, or via RDQL—an RDF query language. Querying data using an SQL-like syntax is a very effective way of pulling data from an RDF model, whether that model is stored in memory or in a relational database. Jena's RDQL is implemented as an object called Query. Once instantiated, it can then be passed to a query engine (QueryEngine) and the results stored in a query result.

Once we query data using the Query object, or if we access all RDF/XML elements of a specific class, we can assign the results to an iterator object and iterate through the set, displaying the results or looking for a specific value.

Starting with later versions of Jena, support for DAML+OIL was added to the tool suite. DAML+OIL is a language for describing ontologies, a way of describing constraints and refinements for a given vocabulary that are beyond the sophistication of RDFS. Much of the effort on behalf of the Semantic Web is based on the Web Ontology Language (OWL) at the W3C, which owes much of its effort to DAML+OIL. The principle DAML+OIL class within Jena, outside of the DAMLModel, is the DAMLOntology class.

Automating the process of creating an RDF/XML document is actually a fairly simple process, but you have to first understand how your RDF triples relate to one another. One approach to using Jena to generate RDF/XML for a particular vocabulary is to create a prototype document of the vocabulary and run it/them through the RDF Validator.

SMORE: Semantic Markup, Ontology and RDF Editor

SMORE is a tool that allows users to markup their documents in RDF using Web ontologies in association with user-specific terms and elements.
The aim of this software is:

- To provide the user with a flexible environment to create a Web page.
- To allow the user to markup a document with minimal knowledge of RDF terms and syntax. However, the user should be able to semantically classify his data set for annotation, i.e., breakup sentences into the basic subject-predicate-object model.
- To provide a reference to existing ontologies on the Internet in order to use more precise references in Web pages/text. The user can also create his own ontology from scratch and borrow terms from existing ontologies.
- To ensure accurate and complete RDF markup with scope to make modifications easily.

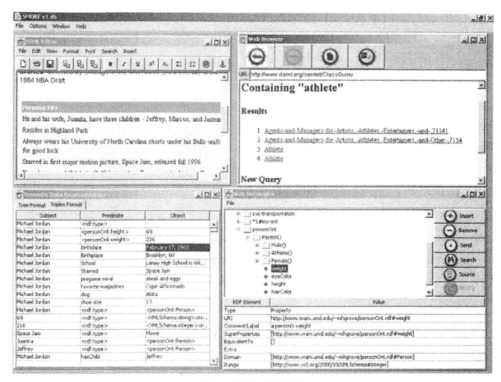

Figure 13-2. SMORE.

Drive

A C# parser named "Drive" is a relatively uncomplicated API providing three classes; Softagents. Drive.RDFEdge, Softagents.Drive.RDFEGraph, and Softagents.Drive.RDFENode, available at http://www.daml.ri.cmu.edu/drive/news.

The Drive RDF browser is a tool for parsing and validating RDF documents using the Drive RDF Parser. It works like a standard Web browser. The browser displays any document just like a regular Web browser with one exception—if you type in a URL and hit enter or click the Parse RDF button, the browser will attempt to parse and validate the RDF document at that URL. If it doesn't find any RDF, it switches back to standard browser mode.

Drive parses RDF/XML documents and builds an abstract graph that can be recursively traversed. Drive is fully compliant with the RDF Syntax Specification. The full list of features:

- C# based RDF parser for the .NET platform.
- Builds a directed linked graph.

363

- Can be used with any .NET language.
- RDF to N-Triples output.
- Extensible API built using the Factory design pattern.
- Supports xml:base.
- Supports xml:lang.

Drive builds an in-memory model of an RDF graph from the RDF/XML serialization. The graph is encapsulated in the RdfGraph class which implements the IRdfGraph interface. The graph consists of a collection of nodes maintained and managed by the RdfNodeCollection class.

TAP

TAP is a distributed project involving researchers from Stanford, IBM, and W3C. TAP leverages automated and semi-automated techniques to extract knowledge bases from unstructured and semi-structured bodies of text. The system is able to use previously learned information to learn new information, and can be used for information retrieval and word processing.

Existing documents are analyzed using semantic techniques and converted into Semantic Web documents using automated techniques or manually by the author using standard word-processing packages. Traditional information retrieval techniques are enhanced with more deeply structured knowledge to provide more accurate results. Both automated and guided analysis use intelligent reasoning systems and agents.

The difficulty of creating the knowledge itself is that it requires a "knowledge engineer" who translates documents into the symbolic and logical languages required. Ontologies forming the core vocabulary of the knowledge are required in order to define concepts and relations that hold instances of the concepts.

Activity Based Search (ABS) is an application of TAP which complements traditional search results. Given the search query, Activity Based Search retrieves real-time data relevant to that query from TAP. Internet search engines are primarily targeted at text and not data. Further, the crawl, grab, and index model of search does not work well for searching across dynamically changing sites. ABS uses TAP to overcome these two search shortcomings.

Users search in the context of an activity. Even a very shallow understanding of the potential activities that make sense in the context of a given search can make a dramatic difference in the search experience. We generalize what Google does when the user types in an address into the search box. It identifies that the search term is an address and provides a link to Mapquest for that address, because getting a map is one of the common activities associated with street addresses.

Given the search term, we look up the term in the TAP Knowledge Base. If the term is found in the Knowledge Base (KB), based on the type of the concept it denotes, we determine the kinds of activities that are typically associated with that concept. Based on that, we determine the kinds of data from the global graph that should be used to augment the search results. This data is fetched from the global graph using GetData and used to augment traditional search results. In the case that the search term has multiple denotations the system selects one and offers the user the ability to choose the other denotation.

TAP is inspired by DNS, and early Web architecture which used simple contracts with everything decentralized. TAP development would be to proceed through bootstrapping of comprehensive chunks of the Semantic Web in a few areas (for more on TAP and semantic search see Chapter 15).

Semantic Web Services Tools

There are a number of new development tools and toolmakers for the Semantic Web Services already available and more are coming. The currently available Semantic Web Services tools under development include: profile, process and profile tools for services, as well as composition, conversion and parsing tools.

Table 13-1 displays a list of some of the leading Semantic Web Services software tool developers.

Author and Affiliation	Product	For More Information Visit
Massimo Paolucci, Carnegie-Mellon University	WSDL2DAML-S Converter	http://www.daml.ri.cmu.edu/wsdl2damls
Ervin Sirin, Mindswap.org	Web Service Composer	http://www.daml.ri.cmu.edu/wsdl2damls
Joachin Peer, University of St. Gallen	DL Mapping Tool	http://sws.mcm.unisg.ch/xmldl/mapper-win32.zip for win32 systems.
Katia Sycara, Carnegie-Mellon University	DAML-S Matchmaker	http://www.damlsmm.ri.cmu.edu/

Table 13-3. Semantic Web Services Software Tools.

Each of these software tools is discussed in further detail in the following sections.

WSDL2DAML-S Converter

Massimo Paolucci of Carnegie-Mellon University has developed a tool for converting WSDL into DAML-S called "WSDL2DAML-S Converter."

The WSDL2DAML-S Converter is a Web-based tool that provides a partial conversion from WSDL Web-services descriptions to DAML-S descriptions. The tool provides a complete specification of the Grounding and the atomic processes of the DAML-S Process Model. In addition, it provides a partial specification of the DAML-S Profile. After the transformation, the specification of the complex processes in the Process Model requires providing the XSLT transformation from the data types used by WSDL and the DAML ontologies used by the DAML-S description. Finally, it is necessary to complete the description of the DAML-S Profile.

Web Service Composer

Ervin Sirin of Mindswap.org has developed a tool called the "Web Service Composer." (See http://www.mindswap.org/~evren/composer/).

This is a prototype that guides a user in the dynamic composition of Web Services. The semi-automatic process includes presenting matching services to the user of a composition, and filtering the possibilities by using semantic descriptions of the services. The generated composition is then directly executable through the WSDL grounding of the services.

The basic functionality of the composer is to let the users invoke Web Services annotated with DAML-S. The user is presented a list of services registered to the system and can execute an individual Web service by entering input parameters. The DAML-S services are executed using the WSDL grounding information.

Using the composer it is possible to create a workflow of Web Services. The composition is done in a semi-automatic fashion where composer presents the available choices.

Composer provides a filtering mechanism to limit the services shown and let the user locate the most relevant service for the current task. The ontology of DAML-S ServiceProfiles are used to dynamically build up a filtering panel where constraints on various properties of the service may be entered.

DL Mapping Tool

Joachin Peer University of St. Gallen has created a Semantic Web Services description (using DAML-S) for XML Web Services, that tell agents how to transform an XML element into a Description Logic (DAML/OWL) construct and vice versa. In DAML-S, there exists an attribute

366

"xsltTransformation" which carries this kind of "mapping information" using XSL, the XSL document specifies how the mapping between XML grammars and Description Logic concept descriptions is carried out. Since the construction of such mapping documents is an error prone this tool is aimed to support developers during this process; the tool allows mapping documents via mouse clicks and the tool allows verification of the mappings created "on the fly."

The mapping tool was developed using Java2 and the Eclipse SWT library.

DAML-S Matchmaker

Katia Sycara of Carnegie-Mellon University(CMU) has developed the DAML-S Matchmaker.

The Matchmaker is a Web Services tool that helps make connections between service request-ers and service providers. The Matchmaker serves as a "yellow pages" of service capabilities. The Matchmaker allows users and/or software agents to find each other by providing a mechanism for registering service capabilities. Registration information is stored as advertisements. When the Matchmaker agent receives a query from a user or another software agent, it searches its dynamic database of advertisements for agents that can fulfill the incoming request. The Match-maker serves as a liaison between a service requester and a service provider.

The DAML-S Matchmaker employs techniques from information retrieval, AI, and soft-ware engineering to compute the syntactical and semantic similarity among service capability descriptions. The matching engine of the matchmaking system contains five different filters for namespace comparison, word frequency comparison, ontology similarity matching, ontol-ogy matching, and constraint matching. The user configures these filters to achieve a tradeoff between performance and matching quality.

Conclusion

In this chapter, we introduced some of the rapidly developing tools and toolmakers for the Se-mantic Web Services. The currently available Semantic Web tools under development include editors, parsers, servers, databases, and inference engines.

The early Semantic Web Services development tools included: WSDL2DAML-S, DAML-S Converter, Web Service Composer, DL Mapping, and DAML-S Matchmaker.

Chapter Fourteen

Semantic Web Author

Overview

The Semantic Web Author for XML, RDF, and OWL is a new tool which combines a text editor, parser, validator, and Integrated Development Environment (IDE) into a single program. Many of the basic components necessary for developing Semantic Web Services are available from this single IDE running on Windows.

The Semantic Web Author is available with this book on disc and updates are available at http://www.web-iq.com. It provides a traditional Windows user interface and combines a traditional editor, parser, and validator for XML, RDF/XML, and OWL. It is written in C# and well annotated. Some of the key features for each of these integrated components include:

- Multiple view architecture.
- Standard editor features (cut, paste, delete).
- Well-formedness and validation checks.
- Design form templates.

In this chapter, we explain the key features of the C# source code for the Semantic Web Author including methods for editing, parsing, and validating of XML, RDF, and OWL documents.

369

Background

Programming a computer means that we must create a sequence of instructions that the computer will use to perform a series of tasks. While it is possible to create programs directly in machine language, it is uncommon for programmers to work at this level because of the abstract nature of the instructions. It is better to write programs in a simple text file using a high-level programming language which can later be compiled into executable code.

Integrated Development Environments (IDE)

Of course, there are easier ways to create fully compiled programs. Integrated Development Environments (IDE) have proven to be tremendously useful. Microsoft's IDE Visual Studio and its suite of languages offer an important developer's tool to meet today's demands.

However, even with all of today's technical support, detailed instructions, and sample code, the process of achieving program performance for a feature-rich application is demanding. Add to this, the ability to interface with Web applications and services and it is easy to understand the challenge to meeting the demand for more powerful, yet user-friendly development environments.

We chose to write Semantic Web Author for Windows in C# in order to build a powerful and user-friendly Semantic Web development tool.

C# Programming Language

C# is the Visual Studio language built specifically to program the complete set of capabilities within the Microsoft .NET Framework. The .NET framework consists of a runtime environment called the Common Language Runtime (CLR), and a set of class libraries, which provide a rich development platform that can be exploited by a variety of languages and tools.

The C# language specification was written by Anders Hejlsberg and Scott Wiltamuth. Anders Hejlsberg also created the Turbo Pascal compiler and led the team that designed Delphi. Programming languages are evaluated based upon performance, reliability, and simplicity. C# is designed to provide an optimum blend of simplicity, expressiveness, and performance for Windows Desktop and Windows-based Web servers. Many features of C# were designed in response to the strengths and weaknesses of other languages, particularly Java and C++.

An excellent way to manage complexity in a program is to sub-divide it into several interacting components. C# was designed to make component building easy and provides component-oriented language constructs such as properties, events, and declarative constructs called attributes.

Everything pertaining to a declaration in C# is localized to the declaration itself, rather than being spread across several source files. C# provides features such as explicit interface implementations, hiding inherited members, and read-only modifiers, which help new versions of a component work with older components that depend on it. In addition, C# is type-safe, which ensures that a variable can be accessed only through the type associated with that variable.

All C# types derive from a single-base type. This means all types—structs, interfaces, delegates, enums, and arrays—share the same basic functionality, such as the ability to be converted to a string, serialized, or stored in a collection.

C# relies on a runtime that performs automatic memory management which eliminates problems such as dangling pointers, memory leaks, and coping with circular references.

However, C# does not eliminate pointers; it merely makes them unnecessary for most programming tasks. An advantage of C# over other languages is its close fit with the .NET.

Common Language Runtime (CLR)

Of fundamental importance to the .NET Framework is the fact that programs are executed within a managed execution environment provided by the Common Language Runtime (CLR). The CLR improves runtime interactivity between programs, portability, security, development simplicity, and cross-language integration. In addition, Visual Studio includes features such as XML, SOAP, and Web service support that makes it useful as our development tool for the Semantic Web Author.

Each language targeting .NET compiles source code into metadata and Microsoft Intermediate Language (MSIL) code. Metadata includes a complete specification for a program including all its types, apart from the actual implementation of each function. These implementations are stored as MSIL, which is machine-independent code that describes the instructions of a program. The CLR uses this "blueprint" to bring a .NET program to life at runtime, compiling code directly to assembly language.

Key features of the CLR include:

- Runtime interactivity—Programs can interact with each other at runtime through their metadata. A program can search for new types at runtime, then instantiate and invoke methods on those types.

- Portability—Programs can be run without recompiling on any operating system and processor combination that supports the CLR. A key element of this platform independence is the runtime's JIT (Just-In-Time) Compiler, which compiles the MSIL code it is fed to native code that runs on the underlying platform.

- Security—Security considerations permeate the design of the .NET Framework.

- Simplified deployment—An assembly is a completely self-describing package that contains all the metadata and MSIL of a program.

- Versioning—An assembly can function properly with new versions of assemblies it depends on without recompilation.

- Simplified development—The CLR provides many features that greatly simplify development, including services such as garbage collection, exception handling, debugging, and profiling.

- Cross-language integration—The Common Type System (CTS) of the CLR defines the types that can be expressed in metadata and MSIL and the possible operations that can be performed on those types. The CTS is broad enough to support many different languages including Microsoft languages, such as C#, VB.NET, and Visual C++ .NET, and such third-party languages as COBOL, Eiffel, Haskell, Mercury, ML, Oberon, Python, Smalltalk, and Scheme.

The Common Language Specification (CLS) defines a subset of the CTS, which provides a common standard that enables .NET languages to share and extend each other's libraries. For instance, an Eiffel programmer can create a class that derives from a C# class and override its virtual methods. The CLR is interoperated with COM and C.

The .NET Framework provides the .NET Framework Class Library (FCL), which can be used by all languages. The FCL offers features ranging from core functionality of the runtime, such as threading and runtime manipulation of types (reflection), to types that provide high-level functionality, such as data access, rich client support, and Web Services (whereby code can even be embedded in a Web page). C# has almost no built-in libraries; it uses the FCL instead.

'Hello, World' C# program

Listing 14-1. A Simple C# Program.

```
namespace FirstProgram {
  using System;
  class Test {
    static void Main ( ) {
      Console.WriteLine ("Hello, World");
    }
  }
}
```

A C# program is composed of types (classes) that we organize into namespaces. Each type contains function members methods, as well as data fields. The Console class encapsulates standard input/output functionality, providing methods such as WriteLine. To use types from another namespace, we use the "using" directive.

To compile this program into an executable, paste it into a text file, save it as Test.cs, then type csc Text.cs in the command prompt. This compiles the program into an executable called Test.exe. Add the /debug option to the csc command line to include debugging symbols in the output. This will let you run your program under a debugger and get meaningful stack traces that include line numbers.

In C#, functions are always associated with a type, or instances of that type. Also C# recognizes a method named Main as the default entry point of execution.

The Purpose of Semantic Web Author

The Semantic Web Author's purpose is to aid the developer in creating, parsing, validating and testing Semantic Web pages using XML, RDF, OWL, and OWL-S.

The Semantic Web Author combines a text editor, parser and code generator into a single program. All components needed to Semantic Web Service programs are available from this single Semantic Web Author IDE running on Windows 95/98/Me/2000 and XP.

Semantic Web Author System Requirements:

Processor: 90-megahertz (MHz) Intel Pentium-class processor
Memory: 32 megabytes (MB) of RAM, 96 MB recommended
Hard-disk: 1MB
Display: 800 x 600 or higher-resolution display with 256 colors
Browser: Internet Explorer 5.01 or higher is required
Supported OS: Microsoft Windows

Semantic Web Author IDE adopts the Microsoft Windows XP look and feel and features a completely customizable user interface (see Figure 14-1).

The principal elements of the Semantic Web Author include: three document areas, menus and toolbar.

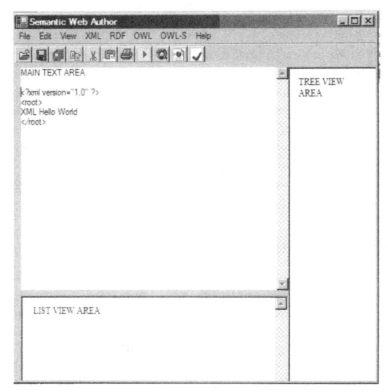

Figure 14-1. Semantic Web Author with XML, RDF, OWL development tools.

Document Areas

Semantic Web Author IDE provides several views that show various aspects of the working markup document. Figure 14-1 illustrates the three areas of Semantic Web Author: Main Text Area, List View Area, and Tree View Area.

The left area consists of the Main Document Text Area where you edit and view all types of XML, RDF and OWL documents. The bottom area contains the List-View Area which displays the parsed results of the file. The right area contains the Tree-View Area which displays the graphics results of the file.

Main Menu

The Main Menu is shown in Figure 14-2.

Figure 14-2. Semantic Web Author main menu.

The Main Menu includes Files, Edit, Language Features (XML, RDF, OWL, OWL-S), and Help.

Toolbar

With keyboard shortcuts you can perform tasks a lot faster. In addition, icons on the Toolbar offer quick operations for the main features (see Figure 14-3).

Figure 14-3. Semantic Web Author icon bar.

Main Application Screen

The most important commands such as Save, Open, New, Print, and Edit, are right at your fingertips. Just click on the icon without going through the menus.

You can even copy, cut/paste with a single click. WordPad has lots of icons, this makes your job much easier (see Figure 14-2). To get even faster use CTRL C, CTRL X, CTRL V and copy, cut, and paste.

Creating and Saving an XML Document

The word-processor-style interface is clear and straightforward.

As you create pages using the editor, be sure to save and save often. Use the File: SaveAs to make sure you know where the file will be saved. You may wish to create a folder on your hard drive for all the pages you create, or you may simply wish to save pages in a Temp folder.

Select the menu option File | New, and select the .xml XML Document entry from the dialog then confirm with OK. Edit the document as needed within the edit window and save using the Save option from the File menu selection.

Editing

Semantic Web Author IDE features a structured editing text view with traditional editing features including copy, cut, and paste.

You can also create or edit your documents with the text editor just like using NotePad or WordPad. As you type your text, you must enclose it in the appropriate tags that tell the browser how to display your text.

To copy a section of text:

1. Select the item you want to copy.

2. To copy the item, click Copy.

3. Click Paste on the toolbar.

The Paste button appears in the Edit menu. When you click the button, you paste to the location of the arrow.

Print

A useful feature for Printing is Print Preview You can preview your files before printing go to File then Print Preview.

Schema

Check the for well-formednesses and validity of any XML document against the official W3C XML Schema.

Understanding or developing complicated data schemas becomes easy with Semantic Web Author IDE advanced, visualization capabilities, which includes full support for graphical design of XML Schema.

Validating

Validation of a document is checked against a Document Type Definition (DTD) or XML Schema document.

In XML, there are two types of validation: well-formedness and grammatical validity. A well-formed document must follow the XML rules for the physical document structure and syntax. For example, all XML documents must have a single-root element; the first element in the document that contains all the other elements. A well-formed document is not checked against an external XML Schema.

To check for well-formedness: Select the menu option XML | Well-Formed.

A valid XML document is a well-formed document that also conforms to the stricter rules specified in the XML Schema. The XML Schema describes a document's structure, specifies which element types are allowed, and defines the properties for each element. If a XML Schema is not present, an XML document is not valid.

To check for validity: Select the menu option XML | Validate

Semantic Web Author performs both types of validation. If a document is not well-formed, errors are displayed in an Errors folder in the structure pane. If a document isn't grammatically valid, errors are displayed in the message pane.

The document you created in the previous step is well-formed because the Errors folder does not appear in the structure pane. If you remove the root element, which is required for a well-formed XML document, the Errors folder appears in the structure pane.

Displaying Errors

Now, we'll introduce an error into this well-formed document to see how Semantic Web Author displays errors.

1. Select the root element in the editor and cut it from the document. In a well-formed document, all elements must have start and end tags, so this should display as an error. Note that an Errors folder displays in the structure pane.

2. Open the Errors folder and select the error to highlight it in the code. Double-click the error to change the focus to the line of code in the editor. The line of code indicated by the error message may not be the origin of the error. In this example, the error occurs because the start tag for the root element is missing.

3. Re-enter the root element in the XML document. Notice that the Errors folder disappears. The document is now well-formed again.

A message appears at the bottom of the main window declaring that the document is well-formed. Click OK to confirm and close the message. Being well-formed, means that the XML document syntax is correct (i.e., there is a root element, each start tag has a corresponding end tag, all elements are nested correctly etc.).

This check does not check against a schema file (or any other external file). Element sequence or element content are not checked either.

Partial Listing of C# Source Code for Semantic Web Author

In this section, we will explore some of the more illustrative parts of the C# source code of the Semantic Web Author. The complete source code is available in Appendix C and on the companion disc. Updates are also available from http://www.web-iq.com.

Listing 14-2 shows the parsing code for the XML documents.

Listing 14-2. Partial Listing of C# Source for Semantic Web Author.

```
// //////////////////////////////////////////////////////////
//////
//
// -----XML Read - Write - Validate-------------------
//
// //////////////////////////////////////////////////////////
//////
private void MyXMLReader04()
{
//Reads an XML document and populates the listbox with node
names
listBox1.Items.Clear();
// Create the root node
TreeNode rootNode = new TreeNode("Tree Structure of Element
");
rootNode.Tag = "element1";
treeView1.Nodes.Clear();
treeView1.Nodes.Add(rootNode);
TreeNodeCollection nodeCollection = rootNode.Nodes;
string errmsg = "";
// //////////////////////////////////////////////////////////
//////
// Create new text reader from xml file
// //////////////////////////////////////////////////////////
//////
XmlTextReader objTxtRd = new XmlTextReader(textBox1.Text,
XmlNodeType.Document, null);
try
{
// //////////////////////////////////////////////////////////
//////
//iterate through document nodes
// //////////////////////////////////////////////////////////
//////
```

```
while(objTxtRd.Read())
{
// add the VALUE property of each node
      if (strMyXMLReader04Variable == "NodeValue")
      {
      listBox1.Items.Add(objTxtRd.Value);
      }

// add the  NodeTYPE property of each node
      if (strMyXMLReader04Variable == "NodeType")
      {
      while (objTxtRd.Read())
      {
// ////////////////////////////////////////////////////////
//////
      //Check node type and write out message
      // ////////////////////////////////////////////////////////
////////////
if ((objTxtRd.NodeType == XmlNodeType.Element) ||
      (objTxtRd.NodeType == XmlNodeType.EndElement) ||
      (objTxtRd.NodeType == XmlNodeType.XmlDeclaration))
      {
listBox1.Items.Add(objTxtRd.Name + " is type " + objTxtRd.
NodeType.ToString());
      //
      if (objTxtRd.NodeType == XmlNodeType.Element)
      {
      rootNode.Nodes.Add(objTxtRd.Name.ToString());
      //
      }
      }
      }
      }
      // ////////////////////////////////////////////////////////
////////////
// add the TEXT Node Values of each node
      // ////////////////////////////////////////////////////////
////////////
if (strMyXMLReader04Variable == "NodeText")
      {
      if (objTxtRd.NodeType == XmlNodeType.Text)
      {
      listBox1.Items.Add(objTxtRd.Value);
      }
```

```
        }
        // ////////////////////////////////////////////////
////////////
// add the ATTRIBUTE Node Values
        // ////////////////////////////////////////////////
////////////
if (strMyXMLReader04Variable == "NodeAttribute")
        {
        if (objTxtRd.NodeType == XmlNodeType.Element)
        {
        //Does this element have any attributes?
        if (objTxtRd.HasAttributes)
        {
        //It does, how many?
        listBox1.Items.Add("The element " +
        objTxtRd.Name.ToString() + " has " +
        objTxtRd.AttributeCount.ToString() + " attributes.");
        listBox1.Items.Add("The attributes are : ");
        //Iterate through each attribute & write value
        while (objTxtRd.MoveToNextAttribute())
        {
        listBox1.Items.Add(objTxtRd.Name + " = " + objTxtRd.
Value);
        }
        }
        else
        {
        //No attributes on this element
        listBox1.Items.Add("The Element " + objTxtRd.Name +
        " has no attributes.");
        }
        listBox1.Items.Add("");
        }
        }
        }
        }
        catch (Exception err)
        {
        errmsg = errmsg + "Error Occurred While Reading" +
MyDATAFILE + " " + err.ToString();
        listBox1.Items.Add(errmsg);
        }
        finally
        {
```

```
      if (objTxtRd != null)
      {
      objTxtRd.Close();
      }
      }
      }
      // ///////////////////////////////////////////////////////
///////////////
      // ///////////////////////////////////////////////////////
//////
      // ///////////////////////////////////////////////////////
//////
private void MyXMLValidator()
      {
      XmlTextReader objXTRead = new XmlTextReader(textBox1.
Text, XmlNodeType.Document, null);

//Layer validation on top of this
XmlValidatingReader objXValRead = new XmlValidatingReader(o
bjXTRead);

//Set the validation type to a DTD
      objXValRead.ValidationType = ValidationType.DTD;
      try
      {
      //Perform validation
      while (objXValRead.Read()){ }
      MessageBox.Show("Validation Completed");
      }
      catch (Exception exception)
      {
      MessageBox.Show(exception.Message);
      }
      finally
      {
      if (objXValRead != null)
      {
      objXValRead.Close();
      }
      }
}
```

381

The source code for Semantic Web Author provides a basic framework for developers to expand and improve. Using Visual Studio with C# developers can add and customize various features and options within Semantic Web Author.

To start, first copy the SemanticWebAuthorFolder from the source disc onto your hard drive. Using Microsoft Visual Studio open the solution file for Semantic Web Author, "SemanticWebAuthor.sln" (see Figure 14-2).

XML Menu Selection

Figure 14-4 shows the XML Menu Selections.

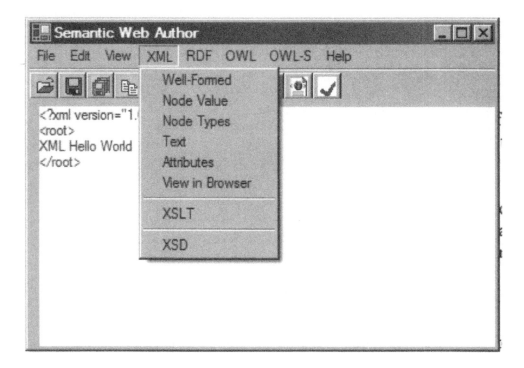

Figure 14-4. Visual Studio IDE for Semantic Web Author.

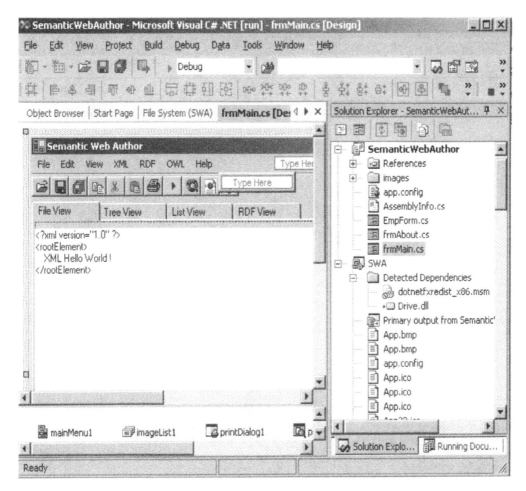

Figure 14-5. Visual Studio IDE for Semantic Web Author.

383

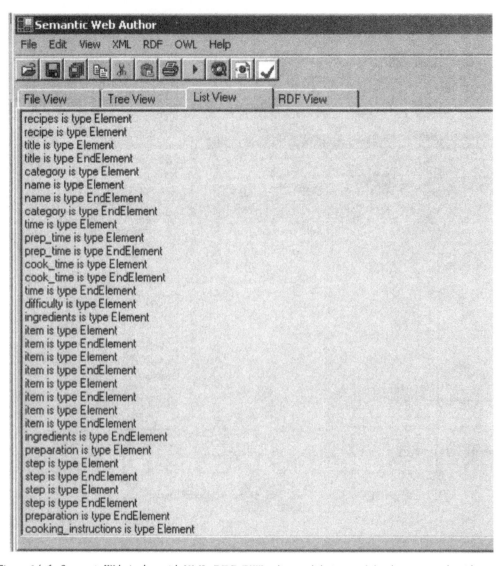

Figure 14-6. Semantic Web Author with XML, RDF, OWL editor, validation, and development tools with source file recipes.xml.

Conclusion

In this chapter, we explained the key features of the C# source code for the Semantic Web Author, which is on the disc included with this book (updates will be available from site http://www. web-iq.com/swa/).

The Semantic Web Author combines a text editor, parser and software generator into a single program. All components needed to Semantic Web Service programs are available from this single Semantic Web Author IDE running on Windows 95/98/Me/2000 and XP.

The integrated editor includes:

- Multiple document and multiple view architecture.

- Standard editor features (cut, paste, delete).

- Built in file text search.

It provides a user interface similar to that of Microsoft's Visual Studio. It combines an editor, parser, and code generator for XML, RDF/XML, and OWL. Some of the key features for each of these integrated components were presented in this chapter.

Chapter Fifteen

Semantic Search

Overview

As the use of the World Wide Web has become increasingly widespread, the business of commercial search has become a vital and lucrative part of the Web. Search engines have become commonplace tools for virtually every user of the Internet, and company names such as Google and Yahoo have become commonly recognized. Commercial search is based upon two forms of Web search technologies: human-directed search and automated search.

The human directed search engine technology utilizes a database of keyword concepts and references. A great deal of existing search-engine technology uses keyword searches to rank pages, but this often leads to irrelevant and spurious results. In its simplest form, a content-based search engine will count the number of query words (keywords) that occur in each of the pages that are contained in its index. The search engine will then rank the pages. More sophisticated approaches take into account the location of the keywords. For example, keywords occurring in the title tags of the Web page are more important than those in the body.

Other types of human-directed search engines, like Yahoo, use topic hierarchies to help narrow the search and make search results more relevant. These topic hierarchies are human created. Because of this, they are costly to produce and maintain in terms of time, and are subsequently not updated as often as the fully automated systems.

The automated form of Web search technology is based on the Web crawler, spider, robot (bot), or agent which follows HTTP links from site-to-site and accumulates information about

Web pages. This agent-based search technology accumulates data automatically and continuously updates information.

AI technologies become more powerful, it is reasonable to ask for better search capabilities which can truly respond to detailed requests. This is the intent of semantic-based search engines and semantic-based search agents. A semantic search engine seeks to find documents that have similar '*concepts*' not just similar '*words.*' However, most semantic-based search engines suffer performance problems from the scale of a very large semantic network. In order for the semantic search to be effective in finding responsive results, the network must contain a great deal of relevant information. At the same time, a large network creates difficulties in processing the many possible paths to a solution.

In this chapter, we explore semantic search engines and semantic search agents, including their current development and progress. We present efforts being made to implement semantic search by Google, MSN, and other innovators.

Background

In early 1994, Jerry Yang and David Filo of Stanford University started the heirarchical search engine, Yahoo!, in order to bring some order to the otherwise chaotic collection of documents on the Web. Some months later, Brian Pinkerton of the University of Washington, developed the search crawler WebCrawler. Also in 1994, Dr. Michael Maldin of Carnegie Melon University created Lycos.

In late 1995, Metacrawler, Excite, AltaVista, and later Inktomi/HotBot (mid-1996), AskJeeves, and GoTo appeared. At that time, Yahoo, though actually a directory, was the leading search engine. But as soon as it was launched, AltaVista began to gain popularity.

By late 1998, Stanford's Larry Page and Sergey Brin reinvented search-ranking technology with their paper *"The Anatomy of a Large-Scale Hypertextual Web Search Engine"* and started what became the most successful search engine in the world, Google. The uncluttered interface, speed and relevancy of the search results were cornerstones in winning the tech-literate public.

As experts tried to boost the rankings of their commercial Websites in order to attract more customers, search engine optimization became more important. In 2000, Yahoo and Google become partners, with Google handling over 100 million daily search requests. In 2001, AskJeeves aquired Teoma, and GoTo was renamed Overture.

Google is undeniably the most capable search engine of today with its 300 million hits per day, and over 5 billion indexed WWW pages,. The prevaling attitude is: When you have a question—fire up Google, the answer's out there somewhere.

Web Search Engines

Current search engines are based upon huge databases of Web-page references. There are two implementations of search engines:

- Individual—Individual search engines compile their own searchable databases on the Web (e.g., Google).
- Meta—Metasearchers do not compile databases. Instead, they search the databases of multiple sets of individual engines simultaneously (e.g., Yahoo!).

Agent-based search engines compile their databases by employing "spiders" or "robots" ("bots") to crawl through Web space from link-to-link, identifying and perusing pages. Sites with no links to other pages may be missed by spiders altogether. Once the spiders get to a Web site, they typically index most of the words on the publicly available pages at the site. Web-page owners may submit their URLs to search engines for "crawling" and eventual inclusion in their databases.

When ranking Web pages, search engines follow a certain set of rules. Their goal, of course, is to return the most relevant pages at the top of their lists. To do this, they look for the location and frequency of keywords and phrases in the Web page document and, sometimes, in the HTML Meta tags (see Chapter 3). They check out the title field and scan the headers and text near the top of the document. Some of them assess popularity by the number of links that are pointing to sites; the more links, the greater the popularity of the page.

Search Engine Categories

Search can be categorized by several fundamental types including lexical, linguistic, semantic, mathematical, meta, SQL structured query, and XML query:

- Lexical—searches for a word or a set of words, with Boolean operators (AND, OR, EXCEPT).
- Linguistic—allows words to be found in whatever form they take, and enables the search to be extended to synonyms.
- Semantic—the search can be carried out on the basis of the meaning of the query.
- Mathematical—semantic search operates in parallel with a statistical model adapted to it.
- Metasearch—searches the databases of multiple sets of individual search engines simultaneously. Metasearchers provide a quick way of finding out which engines are retrieving the best results for you in your search.

- SQL structure query—a search through a sub-set of the documents of the database defined by SQL.

- XML structured query—the initial structuring of a document is preserved and the request is formulated in XPath.

Linguistic Phenomena

There are two basic forms of Web search engine technology: (1) Small-scale human-based search engines that use a category hierarchy for each category described by a set of keywords, and (2) Large-scale agent/robot-based search engines which rely on bots to retrieve Web pages and store them in a centralized database.

Both forms of Web search engines are based on keywords and are subject to the two well-known linguistic phenomena that strongly degrade a query's precision and recall:

- Polysemy (one word might have several meanings).

- Synonymy (several words or phrases, might designate the same concept).

Several systems have been built to overcome these problems based on the idea of annotating Web pages with RDF and OWL tags to represent semantics. However, the limitation of these systems is that they can only process Web pages that are already annotated with semantic tags.

To be truly useful search engines must:

- Maximize relevant information.

- Minimize irrelevant information.

- Provide meaningful ranking, with the most relevant results first.

The first of these criteria—getting all of the relevant information available—is called recall. Without good recall, we have no guarantee that valid, interesting results won't be left out of our result set. We want the rate of false negatives—relevant results that we never see—to be as low as possible.

The second criterion—minimizing irrelevant information so that the proportion of relevant documents in our result set is very high—is called precision. With too little precision, our useful results get diluted by irrelevancies, and we are left with the task of sifting through a large set of documents to find what we want. High precision means the lowest possible rate of false positives.

There is an inevitable trade-off between precision and recall. Search results generally lie on a continuum of relevancy, so there is no distinct place where relevant results stop and extraneous ones begin. The wider we cast our net, the less precise our result set becomes.

This is why the third criterion, ranking, is so important. Ranking has to do with whether the result set is ordered in a way that matches our intuitive understanding of what is more and what is less relevant. Of course the concept of 'relevance' depends heavily on our own immediate needs, our interests, and the context of our search. In an ideal world, search engines would learn our individual preferences so well that they could fine-tune any search we made based on our past expressed interests and peccadilloes. In the real world, a useful ranking is anything that does a reasonable job of distinguishing between strong and weak results.

Current Semantic Search Efforts

As AI Web technologies become more advanced, using RDF and OWL tags will offer semantic opportunities for search. However, the size of the network being searched will establish the complexity of solution space and therefore drastically affect the likelihood of our success.

As a result, one problem with implementing a semantic search engine is the ability to solve the resultant complexity. However, there are ways to implement semantic search engines cost-effectively and efficiently.

Several major companies are seriously addressing the issue of semantic search. Microsoft's growth on the Web may depend on its ability to compete with search leader Google. As a result, Microsoft has launched a new search program called MSNBot, which scours the Web to build an index of HTML links and documents. The homegrown system, which performs agent/robot functions previously done by Inktomi, may pose a significant threat to Google.

At first glance, Figure 15-1 seems to indicate that Yahoo and AOL lead Google in the percentage of searches; however, Google actually powers both Yahoo and AOL searches. In addition, the numbers seem to add up to over 100%, but this is because many users use more than one search engine when seeking a solution.

MSNBot is believed to be the first step toward building a new search technology that bridges Microsoft's home and business customers. It is planned as a technology that binds applications to the Windows operating system.

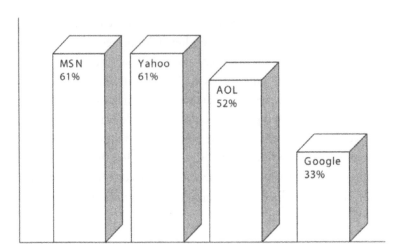

Figure 15-1. Use comparison of search engines for 2003.

Microsoft could then connect its MSN portal into its next version of Windows (code-named Longhorn) which will make it easier to search e-mail, spreadsheets, documents on PCs, corporate networks, and the Web.

Google has increased their commitment to content-targeted advertising with products that are based on semantic technology, which understands, organizes, and extracts knowledge from Websites and information repositories in a way that mimics human thought and enables more effective information retrieval. A key application of the technology is the representation of the key themes on Web pages to deliver highly relevant and targeted advertisements.

The business of commercial search has become very profitable, not only for Google and rival Overture Services, but also for their partners MSN, America Online and Yahoo. Google and Overture share revenues with their distribution partners every time someone clicks on a sponsored link. With an estimated 500 million on-line searches taking place daily, the targeted ad business is predicted to generate more than $7 billion annually within four years, according to analysts.

Google Search

At the heart of Google Search software is PageRank, a system for ranking Web pages developed by the founders Larry Page and Sergey Brin at Stanford University.

PageRank relies on the uniquely democratic nature of the Web by using its vast link structure as an indicator of an individual page's value. Essentially, Google interprets a link from page A to page B as a vote, by page A, for page B. But, Google analyzes the page that casts the vote. Votes cast by pages that are themselves "important" weigh more heavily and help to make other pages "important."

Important sites receive a higher PageRank, which Google remembers. Google combines PageRank with sophisticated text-matching techniques to find pages that are both important and relevant to the search. Google goes far beyond the number of times a term appears on a page and examines all aspects of the page's content (and the content of the pages linking to it) to determine if it's a good match for the query.

Example 15-1 presents the PageRank calculation.

Example 15-1. Google PageRank algorithm.

```
PR(A) = (1-d) + d (PR(T₁)/C(T₁) + ... + PR(Tₙ)/C(Tₙ))
where:

PR(A) is the PageRank of a page A
PR(T1) is the PageRank of a page T1
C(T1) is the number of outgoing links from the page T1
d is a damping factor in the range 0 < d < 1, usually set to
0.85

The PageRank of a Web page is therefore calculated as a sum
of the PageRanks of all pages linking to it (its incoming
links), divided by the number of links on each of those
pages (its outgoing links).
```

A Stanford University start-up, Kaltix, was recently purchased by Google after it had taken Google's model one step further, so that different search results are produced for every user based on their preferences and history. Without discussing Kaltix's plans publicly, the company's founders have published research that claims to offer a way to compute search results nearly 1,000 times faster than what's currently possible. Kaltix's method is similar to looking for a tree in a forest by examining only a clump of trees rather than the whole forest.

Link Structure Analysis

Link-structure analysis has emerged in recent years as an alternative to content-based search engines. One of the major aims of these link-based approaches is to combat some of the problems of Polysemy and Synonymy. For link-based Web searching, there is a link from Website A to Website B that it analyzes.

We can identify two types of Web sites: hubs and authorities. Some Web sites provide the most prominent sources of primary content, and are called the authorities on the topic; other sites assemble high-quality guides and resource lists that act as focused hubs, directing users to recommended authorities (see Appendix C: Graphical Structure of the Web).

Originally, the algorithm developed by Kleinberg addressed this dichotomy of Web sites. The algorithm developed by Kleinberg can be broken down into two stages:

1. Create a subgraph of the Web to use as the search space.
2. Compute the hub and authorities in the subgraph.

Example 15-2. Kleinberg's Subgraph Algorithm.

Subgraph(σ,ε,t,d)

    σ : a query string.
    ε: a text-based search engine.
    t, d: natural numbers.

Let $R\sigma$ denote the top t results of σ on ε.
Set $S\sigma := R\sigma$

For each page p . $R\sigma$
    Let $\Gamma+ (p)$ denote the set of all pages p points to.
    Let $\Gamma- (p)$ denote the set of all pages pointing to p.
    Add all pages in $\Gamma+(p)$ to $S\sigma$.

If $|\Gamma- (p)| <= d$ then
    Add all pages in $\Gamma- (p)$ to $S\sigma$.
Else
    Add an arbitrary set of d pages from $\Gamma- (p)$ to $S\sigma$.
End
Return $S\sigma$

The aim of the algorithm is to find authoritative pages on a given query. It is obviously not feasible to try and apply this algorithm to the Web as a whole. One possibility is to apply the algorithm to a sub-graph of the Web where pages in the graph contain the query string. However, this could result in a sub-graph of a million or more nodes. The first part of the algorithm takes the query string and inputs it to some text-based search engine. The first results are then considered for expansion. The reason why this set alone cannot be used is that it will not contain enough authority sites to be useful. Kleinberg observed that although an authority is unlikely to be in this set, it is likely to be pointed to by at least one member of the set.

We need to find a small enough sub-graph to work on, such that the hubs and authorities can be located. One simple way of doing this would be to consider the best authorities to be those pages. However, this is not sufficient. Some pages that remain will have a large number of incoming links but they will not be related to the query topic. For example, popular sites (such as Yahoo) will always have a very high number of incoming links not all of which are relevant to immediate interests.

The idea is that good hub pages will point to many good authorities and good authority pages will be pointed to by many good hubs. The algorithm makes use of this relationship by assigning to each page, p, an authority score $x(p)$ and a hub score $y(p)$. The sum of the square of all authority scores is normalized to 1. The sum of the square of the hub scores is normalized to 1. Larger scores mean better authorities or better hubs (for $x(p)$ and $y(p)$ respectively).

Web Search Engine Problems

If we examine the practical problems of semantic search, we will find that the search tree faces an incompleteness of logic resulting in the "Halting Problem" or "The Incompleteness Problem."

In Chapter 9, we describe how inference can be viewed as a sequence of logical deductions chained together. At each point along the way, there might be different ways to reach a new deduction. So, in effect, there is a branching set of possibilities for how to reach a correct solution. And that branching set can spread out in novel ways.

For example, you might want to try to determine "Who does Kevin Bacon know?" based on information about his family relationships, his movies, or his business contacts. So, there's more than one path to some conclusions. This results in a branching set of possibilities. Therefore, the inference in our system is a kind of search problem, just like a search tree.

It is possible to start at the top of the tree, the root, or with the branches. The top of the tree can be the query asked. Down to child nodes each step in this tree can be viewed as one potential logical deduction that moves toward trying to prove the original query into trying to prove a different query below using this logical deductive step. The fan out of possibilities can be viewed as this branching tree, getting bushier and deeper.

So, for the purposes of explaining this process, each of the approaches ends up being one of the child steps to a child node.

Imagine that each node in this tree represents something to prove. Each link from a parent node higher up to a child node below represents one logical statement. For a proof to end, or be successful, it must find a child node where there nothing left to prove. This would be the leaf node is 'true.' We refer to this kind of node in the tree as a 'Goal Node.' The path all the way up represents one unique, justified reason for one set of answers for the variables in the query.

Now the problem is that we have a big tree of possibilities and often have cases where this proof could just go on forever.

In any sufficiently interesting or complex logical system, there is going to be an arbitrarily large number of potential proofs that can be derived. Some of them are arbitrarily long and it is uncertain if there is an end to this proof. In the 1930's, Gödel proved that any sufficiently complicated logical system is inherently incomplete (undecideable). In other words, there are statements that can not be logically proven. His argument for that is related to the other problem, the halting problem.

The halting problem infers that certain algorithms will never end in an answer. When we talk about the Web, we're talking about millions of facts and tens of thousands of rules that can chain together in arbitrarily complicated and interesting ways; so the space of potential proofs is infinite and the tree becomes logically infinite. Due to this, we will run into some inherent incompleteness issues: for example, we cannot simply say "let's just look at every possible proof and gather up all the answers."

We run into incompleteness because the search tree that we're describing here is too large. So our approach is to only search portions of the tree. There are well-known strategies for how one addresses search problems like this. One strategy is to search the tree in a "depth-first" fashion.

Depth-first Search

A depth-first search would start at the top of the tree and go as deeply as possible down some path, expanding nodes as we go, until we find a dead end. A dead end is either a goal (success) or a node where we are unable to produce new children (we don't have enough information to go deeper). So the system can't prove anything beyond that point.

Let's walk through a depth-first search and traverse the tree. We start at the top node and go as deeply as possible:

1. Start at the highest node.
2. Go as deeply as possible down one path.
3. When we run into a dead-end, back-up to the last node that we turned away from. If there is a path there that we haven't tried, go down it. Follow this option until we reach a dead-end or a goal.

4. This path leads to another dead-end, so go back up a node and try the other branch.
5. This path leads to a goal. In other words, this final node is a positive result to the query. So we have one answer. Keep searching for other answers by going up a couple more nodes and then down a path we haven't tried.
6. Continue until we reach more dead-ends and have exhausted search possibilities.

The advantage of a depth-first search is that it is a very algorithmically efficient way to search trees in one format. It limits the amount of space that we have to keep for remembering the things we haven't looked at yet. All we have to remember is the path back up.

The disadvantage with depth-first search is that once we get started down some path we must trace it all the way to its end, before going on to another branch.

Breadth-first Search

Another strategy for searching is a breadth-first search. Here we search layer-by-layer. First, we try to do all of the zero-step proofs, then we try to do all of the one-step proofs, etc. The advantage of breadth-first search is that we're guaranteed to get the simplest proofs before we get anything that's strictly more complicated. This is referred to as the Ockham's Razor benefit. If there is an n-step proof, we'll find it before we look at any $n+1$-step proofs. The disadvantage of breadth-first search is that we've got huge, deep trees and we also have huge, bushy trees where we could have thousands or tens of thousands of child nodes. Another disadvantage of breadth-first searching is the amount of space you have to use to store what we haven't examined as yet. So, if the third layer is explosively large, we would have to store all of the third-level results before we could even look at them. With a breadth-first search, the deeper we go into the tree, the more space is required.

So we find that two of the traditional algorithms for search—depth-first and breadth-first—are going to run into problems with large systems.

Heuristic Search

Another search strategy is to attempt to identify the most promising path before expanding each node in order of which ones look most promising at the time. This is called a heuristic search. We search the tree in order of heuristic quality, thereby pushing off the parts that might go on infinitely.

The problems solved by means of heuristic methods are considered invention.
Solving such problems is accomplished through Expert Systems (ES). Expert Systems state the problem and find its solution. The knowledge in ES is represented deterministically. The Knowledge Base (KB) of any ES contains the facts and rules of their processing.

Practically, the expert system is a Knowledge Base that depends on choosing the correct knowledge representation model. Knowledge Representation (KR) supports computer solutions of intellectual problems. The choice of the KR model helps to avoid the complications.

Web Search Agents

While Web search engines are powerful and important to the future of the Web, there is another form of search that is also critical: Web search agents. A Web search agent will not perform like a commercial search engine. Search engines use database lookups from a knowledge base. In the case of a Web search agent, the Web itself is searched and the computer provides interface with the user. The agent's percepts are documents connected through the Internet utilizing HTTP. The agent's actions determine if its goal of seeking a Website containing a specified target (e.g., keyword or phrase), has been met and if not, find other locations to visit in which to further the search to attain the goal. It acts on the environment using output methods to update the user on the status of the search or the end result(s).

What makes the agent intelligent is its ability to make a rational decision when given a choice. In other words, given a goal, it will follow the course of actions that would lead it to that goal in a timely manner.

Search Algorithms

An agent can usually generate all of the possible outcomes of an event, but then it will need to search through those outcomes to find the desired goal and execute the path (sequence of steps) starting at the initial or current state, to get to the desired goal state. In the case of the intelligent Web search agent, it will need to utilize a search to navigate through the Web to reach its goal.

There are two basic classes of search algorithms: uninformed and informed. Uninformed, or blind, searches are those that have no information about the number of steps or the path cost from the current state to the goal. These searches include: depth-first, breadth-first, uniform-cost, depth-limiting, and iterative deepening search. Informed, or heuristic, searches are those that have information about the goal; this information is usually either an estimated path cost to it or an estimated number of steps away from it. This information is known as the search agent heuristic. It allows informed searches to perform better than the blind searches and makes them behave in an almost "rational" manner. These searches include: best-first, hill-climbing, beam, A*, and IDA* (iterative deepening A*) searches (see Chapter 9).

Designing a Search Agent

Building an intelligent Web search agent requires mechanisms for multiple and combinational keyword searches, exclusion handling, and the ability to self-seed when it exhausts a search space. Given a target, the Web search agent should look for it through as many paths as are necessary. This agent will be keyword based. The advocated method is to start from a "seed" location (user provided) and find all other locations linked in a tree fashion to the root (seed location) that contain the target. The search agent needs to know the target (i.e., keyword or phrase), where to start, how many iterations of the target to find, how long to look (time constraint), and what methods should determine criteria for choosing paths (search methods). These issues are addressed in the software.

Implementation requires some knowledge of general programming, working with sockets, the Hypertext Transfer Protocol (HTTP), Hypertext Markup Language (HTML), sorting, and searches. There are many languages with Web-based utilities, advanced application programming interfaces (APIs), and superior text parsing capabilities that can be used to write a Web search agent. Using a more advanced, efficient sorting algorithm will help improve the performance of the Web search agent.

The Web search agent design consists of four main phases: initialization, perception, action, and effect. In the initialization phase, the Web search agent should set up all variables, structures, and arrays. It should also get the base information it will need to conduct the hunt—the target, the goal, a place to start and the method of searching. The perception phase is centered on using the knowledge provided to contact a site and retrieve the information from that location. It should identify if the target is present and identify paths to other URL locations. The action phase takes all of the information that the system knows and determines if the goal has been met (the target has been found and the hunt is over). If the hunt is still active, it must make the decision on where to go next. This is the intelligence of the agent, and the method of search dictates how "smart" the Web agent will be (see Figure 15-2). If a match is found, the hunt is complete, and it provides output to the user.

The Web search agent moves from the initialize phase to a loop consisting of the perception, action, and effect phases until the goal is achieved or can not be achieved.

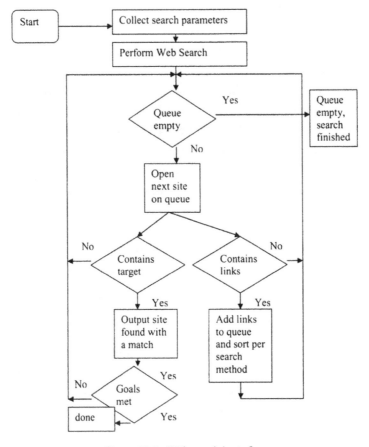

Figure 15-2. Web search basic flow.

Performance Metrics

An implemented Web search agent will not perform like a commercial search engine. Search engines use database lookups from a stored database created by similar Web search agents (i.e., industrial spiders). Despite being a low-level utility, good performance will make the Web search agent a more useful tool. Testing the speed of searches on a given target is a good way to measure performance. Goal achievement is also important. Some seed values are better than others. Utilizing more seed Web sites to execute sequentially after the previous has been exhausted may improve goal attainment. The program could even be modified to do seed look

400

ups itself, utilizing search engines or random/sequential IP number generation. The time and goal achievement are simple metrics for performance.

Web Search Agent Applications

The Web search agent could be used to create an entire search engine system defining its own dictionary word generator and a sequential IP number generator to perform an exhaustive search on a target. The results could be stored in a database for later retrieval. Provided with an HTML interface and its own Website, such an agent could be another Web search engine. The Web search agent could also be used to hunt through any data.

Using RDF and OWL for Search Engines

RDF is very straightforward to implement, which is both its advantage and disadvantage. It is inadequate when we want more strict data typing and a consistent expression for enumerations. For example, if we want to describe a book sold by Amazon, the RDF and RDFS form is given in Listing 15-1.

Listing 15-1. RDF/RDFS - Book Sold by Amazon.

```
<rdfs:Class rdf:ID="Book">
<rdfs:label>Book</rdfs:label>
<rdfs:comment>A book sold by Amazon</rdfs:comment>
</rdfs:Class>

<rdfs:Property rdf:ID="pages">
<rdfs:label>Pages</rdfs:label>
<rdfs:domain rdf:resource="#Book"/>
<rdfs:range rdf:resource="http://www.
w3.org/2000/01/rdf-schema#Literal"/>
</rdfs:Property>

<Book rdf:ID="MachineLearning">
<rdfs:label>Machine Learning</rdfs:label>
<pages>432</pages>
</Book>
```

Listing 15-2. OWL - Book Sold by Amazon.

```
<owl:DatatypeProperty rdf:ID="pages">
<rdfs:label>Pages</rdfs:label>
<rdfs:domain rdf:resource="#Book"/>
<rdfs:range rdf:resource="http://www.w3.org/2000/10/XMLSche
ma#positiveInteger"/>
</owl:DatatypeProperty>
<rdfs:Class rdf:ID="Book">
<rdfs:label>Book</rdfs:label>
<rdfs:comment>A book sold by Amazon</rdfs:comment>
</rdfs:Class>
<rdfs:Property rdf:ID="pages">
<rdfs:label>Pages</rdfs:label>
<rdfs:domain rdf:resource="#Book"/>
<rdfs:range rdf:resource="http://www.w3.org/2000/01/rdf-
schema#Literal"/>
</rdfs:Property>
<Book rdf:ID="MachineLearning">
<rdfs:label>Machine Learning</rdfs:label>
<pages>432</pages>
</Book>
```

The disadvantage of Listing 15-1 is that literals can be any string, but we want the pages to be a positive integer. Compared with RDF and RDFS, OWL allows us to use a more accurate data type (defined in XSD) to describe data as in Listing 15-2. Apart from these advantages, there are many OWL data-sets open to public on the Web.

Ontology

Ontology describes concepts and relationships with a set of representational vocabulary. The aim of building ontologies is to share and reuse knowledge. Since the Semantic Web is a distributed network, there are different ontologies that describe semantically equivalent things. As a result, it is necessary to map elements of these ontologies if we want to process information on the scale of the Web.

An ontology can be represented in a taxonomy tree where each node represents a concept with its attributes. Figure 15-3 shows two different publication ontologies in tree form. The

402

concept publication on the left of Figure 15-3 should be recognizable as an equivalent match
to the tree on the right.

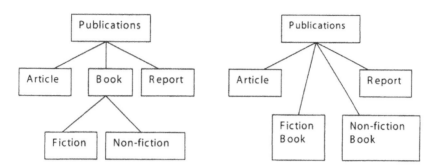

Figure 15-3. Meta-model.

The aim of ontology matching is to map the semantically equivalent elements. This is a
one-to-one mapping of the simplest type. We can also map the different types of elements: e.g.,
a particular relation maps to a particular attribute. Mapping can be more complex if we want to
map the combination of some elements to a specific element. For example, "FullName" could
map into the combination of "FirstName" and "LastName."

An approach for semantic search can be based on text categorization for ontology mapping
than compares each element of an ontology with each element of the other ontology, and then
determines a similarity metric on a per pair basis. Matched items are those whose similarity
values are greater than a certain threshold.

The meta-model maps assertions between two ontology elements and supports further description of that relationship. It has a mapping type, a mapping degree, and an assertion source.

Suppose there are two ontologies: O1 and O2. We could compute a similarity measure. The
node with the highest similarity would be ranked on top as a retrieval technique. In this approach,
we could apply the notion of the joint probability distribution between any two concepts.

There are four probabilities in the distribution: P(A,B), P(A,¬B), P(¬A,B), and P(¬A,¬B).
Suppose an instance is randomly chosen from the universe, P(A,B) is the probability that the
instance belongs to A and B, and P(A,¬B) is the probability that the instance belongs to A but
not to B, P(¬A,B) is the probability that the instance belongs to B but not to A, and P(¬A,¬B)
is the probability that the instance belongs to neither A nor B. There are two similarity functions depending on different cases. In most cases, we can use the relationship below, called the
Jaccard co-efficient, as the similarity measure (see Figure 15-4).

$$Jaccardsim(A, B) = \frac{P(A \cap B)}{P(A \cup B)} = \frac{P(A, B)}{P(A, B) + P(A, \neg B) + P(\neg A, B)}$$

Figure 15-4. Jaccardism metric.

Similarity measures play a very significant role in ontology matching. A set of similarity measures evaluate similarity between ontologies at two semiotic levels—the lexical level and the conceptual level.

There are many approaches that compare the similarity of two concepts between taxonomies, but few of these approaches compare two taxonomies themselves.

Semantic Search Agent

A dynamic machine-learning algorithm can be used in a search agent to crawl across the Semantic Web, so that the agent can capture and learn from user's interest, analyze the RDF metadata collected from Semantic Web and return Web pages that may be most relevant to the user interest through an optimized path.

So far, different kinds of learning algorithms have been adopted into the search process. One of the popular selections is the implementation of reinforcement learning—a dynamic machine-learning algorithm that usually involves agents to maximize the reward. Some examples of applying reinforcement learning in the Web searching include AltaVista and HotBot.

We can define the learning process as follow: A computer program is said to learn from experience E with respect to some class of tasks T and performance measure P, if its performance at tasks in T, as measured by P, improves with experience E.

Being a kind of machin- learning algorithm, reinforcement learning differs from other kinds of supervised learning in that the learner is never told the correct action to perform in order to reach a particular goal; instead, an optimal policy is learned by providing rewards or punishment to every step. Such a life-long, learn-by-experience approach adopted in reinforcement learning is very efficient in situations when the environment is subject to changes due to user preferences.

Given the possibility that machine agents can crawl across the Web and retrieve information with a certain degree of understanding the data, we can then consider the entire Web to be a gigantic relational database that the agent no longer needs a text parser to parse the page word-by-word, but an XML parser to parse the tags to retrieve the data and the metadata, so that the agent can further look up the description of the metadata if necessary. As a result, the

Semantic Web data model is very directly connected with the relational database model. A relational database consists of tables, which consist of rows or records. Each record consists of a set of fields. The record is nothing but the content of its fields, just as an RDF node is nothing but the connections the property values. The mapping is direct:

- A record is an RDF node.
- The field (column) name is an RDF property type.
- The record field (table cell) is a value.

The data retrieving process means mapping an RDF statement$\{s, p, o\}$ into a relational database table R$\{a_1, a_2, a_3\}$.

Consider that each record in the table has its own URI then the database table D has a schema. Where a_1 as the isbn of a book, has the title and a_3 = "The Intelligent Wireless Web," we can 'flatten' each single record in the database table as shown in Table 15-1.

Subject	Predicate	Object
a_1 s isbn: 0201730634	a_2 p has the title	a_3 o The Intelligent Wireless Web

Table 15-1. Relating RDF to a Relational Database Table.

This table has the same data model as RDF, and this implies that if the Web can evolve and all Web sites can present their data model in RDF, we will have the potential power to build a world-wide-gigantic relational database.

How can the search process improve by using the RDF framework in the Semantic Web? Consider the following example. We know the name of a song and we want to know the author and all other songs by the same author. In the current search process based on the existing Web, we will put in the name of the song we know as the search phrase in the engine, and locate manually the name of the creator from all the Web pages returned by the engine, and then manually perform another search by using the creator as the search phrase. Finally, we should be able to track all the songs from the author.

With the Semantic Web, the task can be solved. The agents crawl across the Web and find the metadata of the song in RDF format. As the structure of RDF is declarative triple, if we consider the search process as resolution in predicate logic, it will be something similar to: Author (A), resolve the value of A, and then apply, A to other predicates will expand the search space (see Figure 15-2).

The learning task should then be able to automatically identify all the relevant pages and return to the user according to the user's interest. The open question so far is to determine the predicates the agent should include in refining the search criteria—one obvious example is the user may not be interested in any other songs having the same duration. In order to achieve this, the agent should be able to capture the user's preference—reinforcement learning is a good choice to perform the task.

Conclusion

The use of software agents and search is becoming important tools in the information age and especially in information environments such as the Web. Creating a Web search agent may seem like a daunting task, but standards and other resources are available for programmers.

In this chapter, we explored semantic search engines and semantic search agents, including their current development and progress. In addition, we presented efforts being made to implement semantic search by Google, MSN, and other innovators.

Chapter Sixteen

Challenges and Opportunities

Overview

In this book, we have surveyed the on-going development of the World Wide Web focusing on its progression towards Semantic Web architecture. We presented the new generation of Web markup languages, including Resource Description Framework (RDF), Web Ontology Language (OWL), and OWL-Services (OWL-S) along with examples and software demonstrations. In addition, we have described the semantic software development tools and included design and analysis methodologies that support Semantic Web Services. The source code for the "Semantic Web Author," an Integrated Development Environment (IDE) for Semantic Markup Languages was presented and is available for download.

In this chapter, we summarize some fundamental conclusions about the development of the Semantic Web and Semantic Web Services. We find that both are well-launched, but that there are both challenges and opportunities ahead.

Background

Throughout this book, we've surveyed the Web—past, present and future. We began by recalling that the inventor of the World Wide Web, Tim Berners-Lee, is also the originator of the next generation Web architecture, the Semantic Web. Berners-Lee's World Wide Web consortium

(W3C) team also works to develop, extend, and standardize the Web's markup languages and tools. The objective of the Semantic Web Architecture is to provide a knowledge representation of linked data in order to allow machine processing on a global scale. Just as the W3C has developed a new generation of open markup languages providing logic, they have also opened the door to the next generation of Web Services: Semantic Web Services.

Since 2000, Web technology has been moving from Electronic Data Interchange (EDI) to XML and from CORBA to SOAP. These technological changes impact the industries providing services and products. But as high-tech companies focus on today's technology, they run the risk of becoming obsolete when technological discontinuities suddenly occur.

Web Service standards SOAP, WSDL, and UDDI are ideally suited to be merged with Semantic Web technology to produce a technological discontinuity.

Just as the World Wide Web presented a paradigm shift in communications, Semantic Web technology will accelerate the change from simply displaying information to actually understanding content. As a result, innovative companies currently providing Web Services are exploring the potential of adding semantics. There is, however, still a very long way to go before the Semantic Web vision becomes a reality. But ultimately, implementation of the Semantic Web will take us from syntax to semantics and from information retrieval to task delegation. The surprise, however, is that Semantic Web Services can be offered in the near term without waiting for complete implementation of the Semantic Web.

Challenges for the Semantic Web

Ultimately, Semantic Web opportunities will come and they will bring with new challenges including:

- Availability of semantic content.
- Ontology availability, development and evolution.
- Scalability of Semantic Web content.
- Semantic Web languages standardization.
- Proof and Trust models.

We will explore each of these challenges in the following sections.

The Availability of Semantic Content

The infrastructure of the Semantic Web is still being built upon RDFS and OWL and there is little actual Semantic Web content currently available. Semantic Web content is annotated according to particular ontologies, which define the meaning of the words or concepts. Apart from the infrastructure, researchers are currently building tools to support semantic annotation of Web content. Such tools are critical to the success of the Semantic Web. However, they have two limiting characteristics:

1. Most of them annotate only static pages.
2. Many of them focus on creating new content.

This leads to a non-optimal situation where dynamically generated content is not considered and existing content is runs the risk of being excluded from the Semantic Web.

A set of annotation services (middleware), addressing static and dynamic Web documents, may be necessary to address multimedia and Web Services. The output of these annotation services will be generated according to the language pyramid of the Semantic Web, so that different agents understanding different languages of the Semantic Web might always understand each other. Basically, automatic annotation of static content uses existing wrapping technology. Annotation of dynamic content is more complex. There are several alternatives, which can be explored, for example:

- Extract the dynamic content from its source, annotate it and store it. The problem with this is the almost infinite amount of static pages that can be generated from a dynamic site, including continuous updates, creations, and removals of pages when data changes in the databases.

- Leave the content in the database and annotate the query that retrieves the concerned content. This option is less space-consuming and provides consistency in the annotations with respect to the underlying sources of information, since the content is dynamically annotated when retrieved.

Ontology Availability, Development, and Evolution

Ontologies are central to the Semantic Web because they carry the meaning. They provide the vocabulary and semantics of the annotations. There are three associated ontology issues:

- The construction of kernel ontologies to be used by all the domains.

- The need to provide methodological and technological support for most of the activities of the ontology development process including: knowledge acquisition, conceptual modeling and ontology coding in Semantic Web languages; ontology alignment and mapping; ontology integration; ontology translation tools; and ontology reengineering tools.

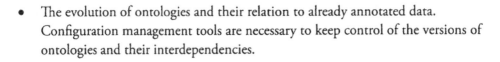

- The evolution of ontologies and their relation to already annotated data. Configuration management tools are necessary to keep control of the versions of ontologies and their interdependencies.

Scalability of Semantic Web Content

Once the Semantic Web content becomes available the resultant complexity of related facts will require management in a scalable manner including organizing, storing, and searching content. The storage and organization of Semantic Web pages includes the use of semantic indices to group content based on topics. Semantic indices may be generated dynamically using ontological information and annotated documents.

Semantic Web Language Standardization

In order to advance the Semantic Web, it is important that open standards dominate the Web. Currently, a layered approach to ontology creation and annotations has been adopted. Tool support is also essential to making a significant step forward in the construction of the Semantic Web, but the tools are partly dependent on the Semantic Web language themselves. Therefore, integration and interoperability will always be a concern.

XML might serve as the meta-language to facilitate future interoperation and integration. The functional architecture of the Semantic Web has three layers: the metadata layer, the schema layer, and the logical layer. Currently, RDF is believed to be the most popular data model for the metadata layer. RDFS extends RDF and is currently a popular schema layer language. OWL is the latest language to be developed.

Proof and Trust

As a logical, open, and distributed system, the Semantic Web asserts some statements which can be in conflict. Therefore the original source of a particular statement must establish itself as trustworthy. Digital signatures will play an important role in proof where the source signs the statement so that agents can check if information really comes from the source. In addition, other security technologies like encryption and access control can be used to ensure confidentiality of information.

Since it is unrealistic to define the extent of trust for each source, a mechanism is necessary to derive the degree of trust for each new source. When one trusts source A, he also trusts all other sources that are trusted by source A, but to a lower extent. In this way, a huge and hierarchical network is created which helps agents infer information based on their trusted knowledge.

412

Currently, Proof and Trust has yet to be formalized and a theory that integrates them into inference engines of the Semantic Web is yet to be developed. However, these technologies are very important and are the foundation of building real commercial applications.

Challenges for Semantic Web Services

OWL-S partitions a Semantic Web Service description into three components (1) service profile, (2) process model, and (3) service grounding. The service profile describes what the service does by specifying the input and output types, preconditions, and effects (iopes). The process model describes how the service works. Each service is either an AtomicProcess that is executed directly or a CompositeProcess that is a combination of other sub-processes. The service grounding contains the details of how an agent can access a service by specifying the communications protocol, parameters to be used in the protocol, and the serialization techniques to be employed for communications.

Using SOAP and WSDL technologies, Semantic Web Services can be dynamically invoked by other services in the network. In addition, Semantic Web Services can be marked up with the OWL-S ontology using WSDL as the service grounding.

Today, Web service developers must decide how to group their logical objects into services. They must create some technique to correlate messages sent to the service with particular objects.

Since a critical mass of knowledge and technology has formed around SOAP and WSDL, they will likely remain at the center of the Web Services architecture. However, questions remain in moving them toward a semantic capability including:

- Integration with the Web—SOAP Web services use the HTTP infrastructure. It is not possible to hyperlink SOAP Web Sservice via HTML links or XSLT functions.

- Extension mechanism—SOAP provides an extension mechanism via headers.

- Overall understanding of modules and layering—SOAP provides a framework within which additional features can be added via headers, but there is little agreement on the specific categories of functionality.

Semantic Opportunities

There are several areas were semantics will offer significant financial opportunities including: Semantic Search, Semantic Web Groupware, and Semantic Web Services.

Semantic Search

As AI technologies become more advanced, it is reasonable to ask for a better search engine which can truly understand our requests. This is the origin of semantic-based search engines. However, most semantic-based search engines suffer from building a very large semantic network in order to have a better performance.

Google has increased their commitment to content-targeted advertising with semantic products that are based on semantic technology, which understands, organizes, and extracts knowledge from Websites and information repositories in a way that mimics human thought and enables more effective information retrieval. A key application of the technology is understanding the key themes on Web pages to deliver highly relevant and targeted advertisements.

Microsoft's growth on the Web depends on its ability to compete with search leader Google. Microsoft launched a new search program called MSNBot, which scours the Web to build an index of HTML links and documents. The homegrown system—which performs robot functions previously left to Inktomi—may pose a significant threat to Google.

MSNBot is believed to be the first step to building new search technology that bridges Microsoft's home and business customers. It is planned as the technology that binds applications to the Windows operating system.

The business of commercial search has become a cash windfall not only for Google and rival Overture Services, but also for partners such as MSN, America Online, and Yahoo. Google and Overture share revenues with their distribution partners every time someone clicks on a sponsored link.

Reaching Conclusions

Table 16-1 shows projected Web characteristics as the Web acquires a new Semantic architecture. It moves from information to semantics and its resultant complexities.

Web Characteristics	Semantic Web Services
Distribution	Open standards
Reliability	Highly reliable
Fault Tolerance	Highly fault tolerant
Bandwidth	High bandwidth
search	Inference search

Table 16-1. Semantic Web Services Projected Characteristics.

414

Ultimately, there will be a competition between proprietary developers working toward focusing data flow through their portals and over their specialized framework servers and open standards which allows business logic to be implemented directly on the Web.

Balancing Proprietary and Open Standards

As the Web adds layered open markup languages upon its current language pyramid, proprietary forces will continue to compete.

In Table 16-2, we show that under complete open Web standards, the Web should grow in a basic distributed manner. However, proprietary standards could produce a decentralized network with critical portals. And finally, a monopoly on standards by one vendor could ultimately produce a centralized network around the owner of the standards. The later two cases will face security, trust, and reliability difficulties.

Standards	Network Type
Open Standards	Distributed
Proprietary Specialized Server Logic	Decentralized
Standard	Centralized

Table 16-2. How Standards Produce Network Types.

How will the standards of new Web languages be resolved? We can conclude that future search and Web Services will need metadata and logic constructs available globally. Therefore, we must address how global standards for search and logic will evolve.

Global Web standards (open vs proprietary) are truly a key element for the future of the Web. But how can we assure that the Web remains primarily based upon compatible standards despite fierce vendor competition for various standards' control?

Traditionally, standards have evolved through three methods:

1. A vendor dominates a market and sets a de facto standard (e.g., telephony by AT&T, or PC operating systems by Microsoft). This would lead to a Web monopoly and a centralized network.

2. Vendors and markets collaborate in ways that may not be clearly attributed to any one organization, but over time emerges as the leader (e.g., TCP/IP). This would lead to the Web as a decentralized network.

3. Standards organizations establish standards that are so useful that they are rapidly universally adopted (e.g., HTML by W3C). This would lead to a Web as a distributed network.

Currently, vendors support different frameworks on their specialized Web servers. The J2EE framework works to optimize UNIX flavor servers for Web service applications provided by one group of vendors and .NET framework works to optimize Windows servers for Web service applications provided by Microsoft and its supporters. So long as the business logic is controlled by vendor-specific frameworks, interoperability, overall efficiency, inference, and smooth growth will remain problematic. Moving toward an open markup language standard will level the playing field worldwide and allow business logic, inference, and other intelligent applications to be more fully utilized.

Ultimately, there will be a competition between proprietary developers working toward focusing data flow through their portals and over their specialized framework servers and open standards which allow business logic to be implemented directly on the Web.

Questions and Answers

The technology issues of the "Next Generation Web" create many problematic questions that must be answered before the full power and capability of the Semantic Web Services are available. However, we have endeavored to respond to the Semantic Web Services technological issues addressed in this book in Table 15-4.

Conclusion

The Semantic Web is still a vision. While the Web will grow toward this vision, the Semantic Web communities will appear and grow first, and then the interaction and interoperation among different communities will finally interweave them into the Semantic Web. But the surprise is that Semantic Web Services may be implemented even without waiting for the Semantic Web itself to be completed.

While Web Services meet many immediate technological needs of businesses, they have been limited by the Web's existing architecture. The Semantic Web which has the potential for significant Web architecture improvement has been limited by slow adoption.

Questions	Answers
Why is XML so critical to the future of Web architecture?	XML will generate and define future Web architecture languages.
How will Web Services using .NET and J2EE evolve toward automated discovery and delivery?	Proprietary automation efforts will fail to provide the interoperability necessary for financial success driving innovators toward Semantic Web Services.
How will Meta-languages, Ontologies, and Inference Engines produce powerful Web search capabilities?	B2B and B2C search engines represent a hugely profitable opportunity that piggy-back on automated Semantic Web Services.
Can Semantic Web Services be implemented immediately without waiting for the full development of the Semantic Web?	Semantic Web Services can be implemented immediately through business innovators specializing in today's Web Services.
Why would Semantic Web Services lead to open Web standards and a distributed Web?	Semantic Web Services are based on open standards and reduce the need for business logic on specialized proprietary servers which move the Web toward a decentralized network with major portals or hubs.

Table 16-3. Questions and Answers.

Berners-Lee has suggested that both the Semantic Web and Web Services would benefit from integration. Integration would combine the Semantic Web's data integration and Web Services' program integration. Berners-Lee has identified areas where the two could best work together. For example, discovery mechanisms, such as UDDI and WSDL are ideally suited to be implemented using Semantic Web technology. In addition, SOAP could use RDF payloads, remote RDF query and updates, and interact with Semantic Web business rules engines, thereby laying the foundation for Semantic Web Services.

An important opportunity exists, however, for Semantic Web Services. Web service providers and Web service standards (SOAP, WSDL, and UDDI) can adopt open standardized semantics and produce Semantic Web Services for Web B2B.

In this book, we have surveyed the Web's past, present, and future. In particular, we presented the opportunities that semantics will bring to the Web, and the challenges that we are facing to develop Semantic Web Services.

417

Bibliography

[1] Alesso, H.P., and Smith, C. F., *The Intelligent Wireless Web*, Addison-Wesley, 2001.

[2] Alesso, H.P., *e-Video: Producing Internet Video as Broadband Technologies Converge*, Addison-Wesley, 2000.

[3] Alesso, H.P., "On the Relationship of Digraph Matrix Analysis to Petri Net Theory and Fault Trees," *Reliability Engineering*, Vol.10, pp. 93-103, 1985.

[4] Alesso, H.P., "Some Algebraic Aspects of Decomposed Non-Coherent Structure Functions," *Reliability Engineering Journal*, Vol. 5, pp. 129-138, 1983.

[5] Alesso, H.P., and Benson, H.J., "Fault Tree and Reliability Relationships for Analyzing NonCoherent Two-State Systems," *Nuclear Engineering and Design*, Vol. 56, pp. 309-320, 1980.

[6] Ankolekar, A., Huch, F., and Sycara, K., "Concurrent Semantics for the Web Services Specification Language Daml-S," In *Proc. of the Coordination 2002 Conf.*, 2002.

[7] Berners-Lee, T., Primer, http://www.w3.org/2000/10/swap/Primer.html, 2002.

[8] Berners-L., T., Hendler, J., and Ora, L., "The Semantic Web", *Scientfic Amercian*, pp35-43, May 2001.

[9] Brin, S., and Page, L., *The Anatomy of a Large-Scale Hypertextual Web Search Engine*, Computer Science Department, Stanford University, Stanford, 1996.

[10] Bogdanowicz, K.D., Scapolo, F., Leijten, J., and Burgelman, J.C., "Scenarios for Ambient Intelligence in 2010," *ISTAG Report, European Commission*, Feb. 2001.

[11] Bollen, J. and Heylighen F., "Algorithms for the self-organization of distributed, multi-user networks." Trappl, R. (ed.), *Proceedings of the 13th European Meeting on Cybernetics and Systems Research*, Austrian Society for Cybernetic Studies, Vienna, p.911-917, 1996.

[12] Broder, A., Kumar, R., Maghoul, F., Raghavar, P., Rajagopalan, S., State, R., Tomkins, A., Wiener, J., *Graph Sstructure in the Web*, IBM Report, Oct. 1999.

[13] Brusilovsky, P., "Methods and Techniques of Adaptive Hypermedia," *User Modeling and User-Adapted Interaction*, Vol.6, pp 87-129, Kluwer Academic, 1996.

[14] Cawsey, A., *The Essence of Artificial Intelligence*, Prentice Hall, 1998.

[15] Chappell, G., and Repchick, D., http://www.intellidimension.com Intellidimension, Inc., 2003.

[16] Christensen, E. Curbera, F., Meredith, G., and Weerawarana, S., *Web Services Description Language (WSDL) 1.1.* http://www.w3.org/TR/2001/NOTE-wsdl-20010315, 2001.

[17] Costello, R.L., and Jacobs, D.B., "Inferring and Discovering Relationships using RDF Schemas," The MITRE Corporation, 2003.

[18] Costello, R.L., and Jacobs, D.B., "Examples Using the OWL Camera Ontology," The MITRE Corporation, 2003.

[19] The DAML Services Coalition (also known as the OWL-S Coalition), Anupriya Ankolenkar, Jerry Hobbs, Ora Lassila, David Martin, Drew McDermott, Sheila McIlraith, Srini Narayanan, Massimo Paolucci, Terry Payne, and Katia Sycara, "DAML-S: Web Service Description for the Semantic Web," *Proceedings of The First International Semantic Web Conference (ISWC), Sardina, Italia*, http://www.daml.org/services , June 2002.

[20] Dean, M., Connolly, D., van Harmelen, F., Hendler, J., Horrocks, I., McGuinness, L., Patel-Schneider, P., and Stein, L., "OWL Web Ontology Language 1.0," http://www.w3.org/TR/owl-ref/, July 2002.

[21] Fensel, D., "The Semantic Web and Its Languages," *IEEE Intelligent Systems*, Vol. 15, no. 6, p. 67–73, Nov./Dec. 2000,.

[22] Ferrara, A., and MacDonald, M., *Programming .NET Web Services,* O'Reilly & Associates, October 15, 2002.

[23] French, M., "DOD developers build on XML success DARPA researchers seek smart data sharing," White paper, March 31, 2003.

[24] Gil, Y., Ratnakar, V., "Markup Languages: Comparisons and Examples," Trellis Project, http://trellis.semanticweb.org/, 2002.

[25] Harold, E. R., Means, W. S., *XML in a Nutshell*, 2nd Edition, O'Reilly & Associates, 2nd edition, June 2002.

[26] Harmelen, F., and Horrocks, I., "FAQs on OIL: The Ontology Inference Layer," *IEEE Intelligent Systems*, Vol. 15, no. 6, pp. 69–72, Nov./Dec. 2000.

[27] Hendler, J., and McGuinness, D., "DARPA Agent Markup Language." *IEEE Intelligent Systems*, Vol. 15, No. 6, pp. 72-73, 2001.

[28] Highsmith, J.A. III, *Adaptive Software Development: A Collaborative Approach to Managing Complex Systems*, Dorset House, 2000.

[29] Hau, J., Lee, W., and Newhouse, S., "The ICENI Semantic Service Adaptation Framework," London e-Science Centre, Imperial College London, Science, Technology and Medicine, August 14, 2003.

[30] Jain, L.C., *Knowledge-Based Intelligent Techniques in Industry*, CRC Press, 1998.

[31] Jiang, G., Chung, W., and Cybenko, G., "Dynamic Integration of Distributed Semantic Services", Dartmouth College, Hanover, NH, 2003.

[32] Joint US/EU ad hoc Agent Markup Language Committee. "Reference Description of the DAML+OIL (March 2001) Ontology Markup Language." http://www.daml.org/2001/03/reference, March 2001.

[33] Kayam, A., and Bailey, S., "Intelligent Architectures for Service-Oriented Solutions," *Web Services Journal*, June 2003.

[34] Kleinberg, J., Authoritative sources in a hyperlinked environment. J. ACM, Vol. 46, http://www.cs.cornell.edu/home/kleinber/auth.pdf, 1999.

[35] Lassila, O., and Swick, R., Resource Description Framework (RDF) Model and Syntax Specification, W3C Recommendation, World Wide Web Consortium, Feb. 1999; www.w3.org/TR/REC-rdf-syntax, 11 Apr. 2001

[36] Lassila, O., "Serendipitous Interoperability," In E. Hyvönen, editor, The Semantic Web – *Proc. the Kick-O, Seminar in Finland*, 2002.

[37] Lesser, V., Horling, B., Klassner, F., Raja, A., Wagner, T., and XQ. Zhang, S., "BIG: A Resource-Bounded Information Gathering Agent," *Proceedings of the Fifteenth National Conference on Artificial Intelligence* (AAAI-98). 1998.

[38] Levesque, H., Reiter, R., Lesperance, Y., Lin, F., and Scherl, R., "GOLOG: A Logic programming language for dynamic domains." *Journal of Logic Programming*, Vol. 31, No. 1-3, pp. 59-84, April-June 1997.

[39] Lu, S., Dong, M., and Fotouhi, F., "The Semantic Web: opportunities and challenges for next-generation Web applications," *Information Research*, Vol. 7 No. 4, July 2002,

[40] Luke, S., and Heflin, J., "SHOE 1.01. Proposed Specification," www.cs.umd.edu/projects/plus/SHOE/spec1.01.html, 20 Mar. 2001.

[41] Martin, D., editor, "DAML-S: Semantic Markup For Web Services," http://www.daml.org/services/owl-s/1.0/owl-s.html, 2001.

[42] Martin, D., Burstein, M., Lassila, O., Paolucci, M., Payne, T., and McIlraith, S., "Describing Web Services using DAML-S and WSDL." http://www.daml.org/services/daml-s/0.7/daml-s-wsdl.html, August 2002.

[43] McBride, B., "Jena, An RDF API in Java." http://wwwuk.hpl.hp.com/people/bwm/rdf/jena

[44] McCool, R., Fikes, F., McGuinness, D., "Semantic Web Tools for Enhanced Authoring," Knowledge Systems Laboratory, Computer Science Department, Stanford University, 2003.

[45] McIlraith, S., Son, T. C., and Zeng, H., "Semantic Web Service," *IEEE Intelligent Systems*, Vol. 16, No. 2, pp. 46-53, 2001.

[46] McIlraith, S., Son, T. C., and Zeng, H., "Mobilizing the Web with DAML-Enabled Web Service." In *Proc. Second Int'l Workshop Semantic Web* (SemWeb'2001), 2001.

[47] MIT, "AI Labs," http://oxygen.lcs.mit.edu/, 2001.

[48] Narayanan, S., and McIraith, S., "Simulation, Verification and Automated Composition of Web Services," WWW2002, May 77-11, 2002, Honolulu, Hawaii, USA.

[49] Ogbuji, U., "An introduction to RDF: Exploring the standard for Web-based metadata," http://www.ibm.com, Dec. 2000.

[50] Ouellet, R., and Ogbuji, U. "Introduction to DAML," http://www.ibm.com, 2002.

[51] http://infomesh.net/2001/swintro/

[52] M. Paolucci, M., Kawmura, T., Payne, T., and Sycara, K., "Semantic Matching of Web Services Capabilities," In *First Int. Semantic Web Conf.*, 2002.

[53] Payne, T., Singh, R., and Sycara, K., "Browsing Schedules - An Agent-based approach to navigating the SemanticWeb," In *First Int. Semantic Web Conf.*, 2002.

[54] Powers, S., *Practical RDF*, O'Reilly & Associates, July 2003.

[55] Ray, E. T., *Learning XML: (Guide to) Creating Self-Describing Data,* Second edition, O'Reilly & Associates; September 22, 2003.

[56] Riva, A., Ramoni, M., "LispWeb: a Specialized HTTP Server for Distributed AI Applications," *Computer Networks and ISDN Systems*, Volume 28, issues 7–11, p. 953. 1999.

[57] Schmelzer, R., Vandersypen, T., Bloomberg, J., Siddalingaiah, M., Hunting, S., Qualls, M., Houlding, D., Darby, C., and Kennedy, D., *XML and Web Services*, SAMS, 2002.

[58] Tamura, T., Oguchi, M., and Kitsuregawa, M., "Parallel Database Processing on a 100 Node PC Cluster: Cases for Decision Support Query Processing and Data Mining," 2001.

[59] Weng, P., "A Search Engine Based on the Semantic Web," MSc in Machine Learning and Data Mining Project, University of Bristol, May 2003.

[60] Zue, V., "Talking with Your Computer," http://www.mit.com, 1999.

Part Four

Supplemental Information

Appendix **A**

RDF Specification

The syntax elements in the RDF XML syntax have been designed to allow the grouping of multiple statements about a resource into an rdf:Description element. These elements are not part of the model and are therefore not deserialized into triples.

Table A-1 presents the core RDF Classes with their properties below.

RDF Class	Properties
rdfs:Resource	All things described by RDF are called resources, and are members of the class rdfs:Resource.
rdfs:Literal	The class rdfs:Literal respresents the class of literal values such as strings and integers. Property values such as textual strings are examples of RDF literals.
rdfs:XMLLiteral	The class rdfs:XMLLiteral respresents the class of XML literal values.
rdfs:Class	This corresponds to the generic concept of a type or category of resource. RDF class membership is used to represent types or categories of a resource. Two classes may happen to have the same members, while remaining distinct resources.
rdf:Property	rdf:Property represents those resources that are RDF properties.

Table A-1. Core RDF Classes and Properties.

rdfs:Datatype	rdfs:Datatype represents those resources that are RDF data types.
rdf:type	The rdf:type property indicates that a resource is a member of a class. When a resource has an rdf:type property whose value is some specific class, we say that the resource is an instance of the specified class. The value of an rdf:type property will always be a resource that is an instance of rdfs:Class. The resource known as rdfs:Class is itself a resource of rdf:type rdfs:Class.
rdfs:subClassOf	The rdfs:subClassOf property represents a specialization relationship between classes of resource. The rdfs:subClassOf property is transitive.
rdfs: subPropertyOf	The property rdfs:subPropertyOf is an instance of rdf:Property that is used to specify that one property is a specialization of another. Sub-property hierarchies can be used to express hierarchies of range and domain constraints.
rdfs:range	An instance of rdf:Property that is used to indicate the class(es) that the values of a property will be members of. The value of an rdfs:range property is always a Class. The rdfs:range property can itself be used to express this: the rdfs:range of rdfs:range is the class rdfs:Class. This indicates that any resource that is the value of a range property will be a class. The rdfs:range property is only applied to properties. This can also be represented in RDF using the rdfs:domain property. The rdfs:domain of rdfs:range is the class rdf:Property. This indicates that the range property applies to resources that are themselves properties.
rdfs:domain	An instance of rdf:Property that is used to indicate the class(es) that will have as members any resource that has the indicated property. The rdfs:domain of rdfs:domain is the class rdf:Property. This indicates that the domain property is used on resources that are properties. The rdfs:range of rdfs:domain is the class rdfs:Class. This indicates that any resource that is the value of a domain property will be a class.
rdfs:label	The rdfs:label property is used to provide a human-readable version of a resource's name.
rdfs:comment	The rdfs:comment property is used to provide a human-readable description of a resource.

Table A-1 (continued). Core RDF Classes and Properties.

Appendix B

Web Ontology Language— OWL Specification Language Elements

Overview

This appendix presents the W3C Candidate Recommendation as of 18 August 2003 and provides index of all OWL language elements

OWL W3C Specifications

OWL W3C Specification is available at: http://www.w3.org/TR/owl-ref/

OWL Language Elements

The following table contains all the OWL language elements.

OWL Reference
owl:AllDifferent
owl:allValuesFrom
owl:AnnotationProperty
owl:backwardCompatibleWith
owl:cardinality

Table B-1. OWL Language Elements.

owl:Class
owl:complementOf
owl:DataRange
owl:DatatypeProperty
owl:DeprecatedClass
owl:DeprecatedProperty
owl:differentFrom
owl:disjointWith
owl:distinctMembers
owl:equivalentClass
owl:equivalentProperty
owl:FunctionalProperty
owl:hasValue
owl:imports
owl:incompatibleWith
owl:intersectionOf
owl:InverseFunctionalProperty
owl:inverseOf
owl:maxCardinality
owl:minCardinality
owl:Nothing
owl:ObjectProperty
owl:oneOf
owl:onProperty
owl:Ontology
owl:OntologyProperty
owl:priorVersion
owl:Restriction
owl:sameAs
owl:someValuesFrom
owl:SymmetricProperty
owl:Thing
owl:TransitiveProperty
owl:unionOf
owl:versionInfo

Table B-1 (contineud). OWL Language Elements.

NOTE: This appendix only contains the OWL-specific constructs. For the RDF/RDFS constructs see the relevant RDF documentation.

Appendix C

Graphical Models of the Web

Overview

In this appendix, we explore a graphical representation of the data flow of the Web.

Graphical Model of the Web

The study of the Web as a graph yields valuable insight into Web algorithms for crawling, searching, and the characteristics of its own evolution. Consider a directed graph whose nodes correspond to static pages on the Web, and whose arcs correspond to links between these pages. The key properties of the graphical form of the Web include its diameter, degree distributions, connected components, and macroscopic structure.

Much recent work has addressed the web as a graph and applied algorithmic methods from graph theory in addressing search, retrieval, and mining problems on the web. The graph theoretic analysis includes document content, as well as usage statistics, resulting in an understanding of domain structure and the role played by Web pages.

The power law in current Web crawls is a basic Web property. It has been found that most ordered pairs of pages cannot be bridged at all and there are significant numbers of pairs that can be bridged, but only using paths going through hundreds of intermediate pages.

The power law for in-degree states that the probability that a node has in-degree i is proportional to $1/i^x$, for some $x > 1$.

Thus, the Web is not the ball of highly connected spaghetti that it has been thought to be; instead the connectivity is strongly limited by a high-level global structure.

Characteristics of the Web

The pages and hyperlinks of the World-Wide Web may be viewed as nodes and edges in a directed graph. Today this graph has about a billion nodes, several billion links, and appears to grow exponentially with time. The study of the web as a graph is not only fascinating in its own right, but also yields valuable insight into web algorithms for crawling and searching which characterize its evolution. Experiments on local and global properties of the Web graph on over 200 million pages and 1.5 billion links indicated that the macroscopic structure of the Web was intricate and specific.

Analysis done by IBM Research revealed an interesting picture (see Figure C-1) of the Web's macroscopic structure. Over 90% of the approximately 203 million nodes in the study formed a single connected component. This connected Web breaks naturally into four pieces. The first piece is a central core, all of whose pages can reach one another along directed links — this is the "core" of the Web. The second and third pieces are called IN and OUT. IN consists of pages that can reach the core, but can not be reached from it. OUT consists of pages that are accessible from the core, but do not link back to it, such as corporate websites that contain only internal links. Finally, the TENDRILS contain pages that cannot reach the core and can not be reached from the core.

The core was comprised of about 56 million pages (out of the explored 203 million). Each of the other three sets contained about 44 million. For randomly chosen source and destination pages, the probability that any path exists from the source to the destination is only 24%.

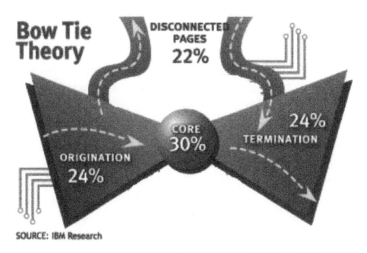

Figure C-1. Bow tie graphical characteristics of Web traffic flow.

Glossary

adjacent—Two vertices are adjacent if they are connected by an edge.

Amaya—An open source Web browser editor from W3C and friends, used to push leading-edge ideas in Web client design.

arc—A synonym for edge.

Apache—An open source Web server originally formed by taking all the "patches" (fixes) to the NCSA Web server and making a new server out of it.

bipartite—A graph is **bipartite** if its vertices can be partitioned into two disjoint sub-sets U and V such that each edge connects a vertex from U to one from V. A bipartite graph is a **complete bipartite** graph if every vertex in U is connected to every vertex in V. If U has n elements and V has m, then we denote the resulting complete bipartite graph by $K_{n,m}$.

browser—A Web client that allows a human to read information on the Web. Microsoft Internet Explorer and Netscape Navigator are two leading browsers.

chromatic number—The chromatic number of a graph is the least number of colors it takes to color its vertices so that adjacent vertices have different colors. For example, this graph has chromatic number three. When applied to a map this is the least number of colors necessary so that countries that share non-trivial borders (borders consisting of more than single points) have different colors.

CERN—Conseil Européen pour la Recherche Nucléaire, European Particle Physics Laboratory of the European Orgaization for Nuclear Research. The European Particle Physics Laboratory, located on the French-Swiss border near Geneva, Switzerland.

circuit—A circuit is a path which ends at the vertex it begins (so a loop is an circuit of length one).

class—A set of things; a one-parameter predicate; a unary relation.

client—Any program that uses the service of another program. On the Web, a Web client is a program, such as a browser, editor, or search robot that reads or writes information on the Web.

433

complete graph—A complete graph with n vertices (denoted K_n) is a graph with n vertices in which each vertex is connected to each of the others (with one edge between each pair of vertices). Here are the first five completed graphs:

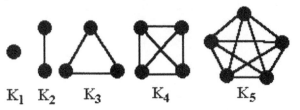

$$K_1 \quad K_2 \quad K_3 \quad K_4 \quad K_5$$

composition—of new services through automatic selection, composition and interoperation of existing Web services.

connected—A graph is connected if there is a path connecting every pair of vertices. A graph that is not connected can be divided into **connected components** (disjoint connected, subgraphs).

CSS (Cascading Style Sheets)—A W3C Standard that uses a rule-based declarative syntax that assigns formatting properties to the element either HTML or XML element content.

cut-set – A set of components whose failure results in the failure of the service. A cut vector **x** produces the function ϕ (**x**). A minimum cut-set is a cut set without irrelevant components. The binary function k_j (**x**) is associated with the jth minimal cut-set k_j.

cut vertex—A vertex that if removed (along with all edges incident with it) produces a graph with more connected components than the original graph.

CWM (Closed world machine)—A bit of code for playing with this stuff, as grep is for regular expressions.

Cyc—A knowledge-representation project in which a tree of definitions attempts to express real-world facts in a machine-readable fashion.

DAML (DARPA Agent Markup Language)—The DAML language is being developed as an extension to XML and the Resource Description Framework (RDF). The latest release of the language (DAML+OIL) provides a rich set of constructs with which to create ontologies and to markup information so that it is machine readable and understandable. http://www.daml.org/

DAML+OIL Web Ontology Language- A semantic markup language for Web resources. It builds on earlier W3C standards such as RDF and RDF Schema, and extends these languages with richer modelling primitives. DAML+OIL provides modelling primitives commonly found in frame-based languages. DAML+OIL (March 2001) extends DAML+OIL (December 2000) with values from XML Schema datatypes.

data model—A data model is what is formally-defined in a DTD (Document Type Definition) or XML Schema. A document's "data model" consists of the allowable element and attribute names and optional structural and occurrence constraints for a "type" or "class" of documents.

data typing—Data is said to be "typed" when it takes on additional abstract meaning than what its characters usually represent. Integers, dates, booleans, and strings are all examples of typed data (data types). A data value that is typed takes on additional meaning, due to the semantic properties known to be associated with specific named data types.

digraph—A digraph (or a directed graph) is a graph in which the edges are directed. (Formally, a digraph is a (usually finite) set of vertices V and set of *ordered* pairs (*a,b*) (where *a*, *b* are in V) called edges. The vertex *a* is the initial vertex of the edge and *b* the terminal vertex.)

discovery—computer-interpretable capability for locating Web Services

decentralized network—A computer network distributed across many peers rather than centralized around a server.

DMA (Digraph Matrix Analysis)—is a tool for mathematically representing large complex systems and services in order to evaluate their design structure and reliability

DOCTYPE declaration (Document type declaration)—The syntactical "glue" used by an XML document to locate an external DTD (Document Type Definition) so that it can be validated against it.

DTD (Document Type Definition)—A formal definition of the data model (the elements and attributes allowed and their allowable content and nesting structure) for a class of documents. XML DTDs are written using SGML DTD syntax.

DOM (Document Object Model)—Within a computer, information is often organized as a set of "objects." When transmitted, it is sent as a "document." The DOM is a W3C specification that gives a common way for programs to access a document as a set of objects.

domain—For a Property, a class of things which any subject of the Property must be in.

Dublin Core—A set of basic metadata properties (such as title, etc.) for classifying Web resources.

execution monitoring—tracking the execution of complex or composite tasks performed by a service or a set of services, thus identifying failure cases or providing explanations of different execution traces.

Four Color Theorem—Every planar graph can be colored using no more than four colors.

graph—Informally, a graph is a finite set of dots called **vertices** (or **nodes**) connected by links called **edges** (or **arcs**). More formally a **simple graph** is a (usually finite) set of vertices V and set of unordered pairs of distinct elements of V called edges.

HTML (Hypertext Markup Language)—A computer language for representing the contents of a page of hypertext; the language that most Web pages are written in.

HyperLink—A medium that includes links and includes media as well as text and is sometimes called hypermedia.

HTTP (HyperText Transfer Protocol)—This is the protocol by which web clients (browsers) and web servers communicate. It is stateless, meaning that it does not maintain a conversation between a given client and server, but it can be manipulated using scripting to appear as if state is being maintained. Do not confuse HTML (Markup language for our browser-based front ends), with HTTP (protocol used by clients and servers to send and receive messages over the Web).

Internet—A global network of networks through which computers communicate by sending information in packets. Each network consists of computers connected by cables or wireless links.

interoperation—Breaking down interoperability barriers through semantics, and the automatic insertion of message parameter translations between clients and Web services

Intranet—A part of the Internet or part of the Web used internally within a company or organization.

invocation—Execution of an identified Web Service by an agent or other service;

IP (Internet Protocol)—The protocol that governs how computers send packets across the Internet. Designed by Vint Cerf and Bob Khan.

Java—A programming language developed (originally as "Oak") by James Gosling of Sun Microsystems. Designed for portability and usability embedded in small devices, Java took off as a language for small applications ("applets") that ran within a Web browser.

GUI (Graphical User Interface)—An end-user sees and interacts with when operating (interacting with) a software application. Sometimes referred to as the "front-end" of an application. HTML is the GUI standard for Web-based applications.

link—A link (or hyperlink) is a relationship between two resources. HTML links usually connect HTML documents together in this fashion (called a "hyperlink"), but links can link to any type of resource (documents, pictures, sound and video files) capable of residing at a Web address.

loop—An edge that connects a vertex to itself.

markup—Comprised of several "special characters" that are used to structure a document's character data into logical components that can then be labeled (named) so that they can be manipulated more easily by a software application.

Markup Language—A language used to structure a document's character data into logical components, and "name" them in a manner that is useful. These labels (element names) provide either formatting information about how the character data should be visually presented (for a word processor or a Web browser, for instance) or they can provide "semantic" (meaningful) information about what kind of data the component represents. Markup languages provide a simple format for exchanging text-based character data that can be understood by both humans and machines.

meta—A prefix to indicate something applied to itself; for example, a metameeting is a meeting about meetings.

metadata—Data about data on the Web, including but not limited to authorship, classification, endorsement, policy, distribution terms, IPR, and so on. A significant use for the Semantic Web.

Meta-markup language—A language used to define markup languages. SGML and XML are both meta-markup languages. HTML is a markup language that was defined using the SGML meta-markup language.

multi-graph—Informally, a multigraph is a graph with multiple edges between the same vertices. Formally: a multigraph is a set V of vertices along, a set E of edges, and a function f from E to $\{\{u,v\}|u,v$ in V; u,v distinct$\}$. (The function f shows which vertices are connected by which edge.) The edges r and s are called parallel or multiple edges if $f(r)=f(s)$.

N3—Notation3, a quick notation for jotting down or reading RDF Semantic Web information, and experimenting with more advanced sematic Web features.

object—Of the three parts of a statement, the object is one of the two things related by the predicate. Often, it is the value of some property, such as the color of a car. See also: subject, predicate.

OIL (Ontology Inference Layer)—a proposal for a web-based representation and inference layer for ontologies, which combines the widely used modeling primitives from frame-based languages with the formal semantics and reasoning services provided by description logics. It is compatible with RDF Schema (RDFS), and includes a precise semantics for describing term meanings (and thus also for describing implied information). http://www.ontoknowledge.org/oil/index.shtml

Ontology—From an IT industry perspective, the word ontology was first used by artificial intelligence researchers and then the Web community to describe the linguistic specifications needed to help computers effectively share information and knowledge. In both cases, ontologies are used to define "the things and rules that exist" within a respective domain. In this sense, an ontology is like a rigorous taxonomy that also understands the relationships between the various classified items.

OWL – Web Ontology Language for markup ontology for the Internet (see Chapter 8).

OWL-S—Web Ontology Language for Services (see Chapter 10).

path—A path is a sequence of consecutive edges in a graph and the length of the path is the number of edges traversed.

path-set—A set of components whose functioning ensures the functioning of the system. Thus a path vector **x** yields ϕ (**x**) = 1. A minimum path-set is a path-set which cannot be reduced. We can define minimum path sets as:

peer—A conversation participant. An "equal" to whatever person or application it is communicating with across a network (bi-directional communication).

P2P or Peer-to-peer—A blanket term used to describe: (1) a peer-centric distributed software architecture, (2) a flavor of software that encourages collaboration and file sharing between peers, and (3) a cultural progression in the way humans and applications interact with each other that emphasizes two way interactive "conversations" in place of the Web's initial television-like communication model (where information only flows in one direction).

Petri net graph— A bipartite multigraph, G = (V, A), where A = $\{a_1, \ldots, a_n\}$ is a bag of directed arcs, $a_1 = (v_j, v_k)$, with v_j, v_k elements of V. The set V can be partitioned into two disjoint sets P and T such that V = P $\cup$ T, P $\cap$ T = 0. and for each directed arc, $a_1 \in$ A, is $a_1 = (v_j, v_k)$ then either $v_j \in$ P and $v_k \in$ T, or $v_j \in$ T and $v_k \in$ P.

predicate—Of the three parts of a statement, the predicate or verb, is the resource, specifically the Property, which defines what the statement means. See also: subject, object.

property—A sort of relationship between two things; a binary relation. A Property can be used as the predicate in a statement.

protocol—A language and a set of rules that allow computers to interact in a well-defined way. Examples are FTP, HTTP, and NNTP.

range—For a Property, its range is a class which any object of that Property must be in.

RDF (Resource Description Framework)—A framework for constructing logical languages that can work together in the Semantic Web. A way of using XML for data rather than just documents.

RDF Schema—or RDF Vocabulary Description Language 1.0: The Resource Description Framework (RDF) is a general purpose language for representing information in the Web. This describes how to use RDF to describe RDF vocabularies. This is a basic vocabulary for this purpose, as well as conventions that can be used by Semantic Web applications to support more sophisticated RDF vocabulary description. See http://www.w3.org/TR/rdf-schema/

reachability—An important characteristic of a directed logic graph which find all paths from every node n_i, to any node n_j within the graph.

resource—That identified by a Universal Resource Identifier (without a "#"). If the URI starts "http:", then the resource is some form of generic document.

rule—A loose term for a Statement that an engine has been programmed to process. Different engines have different sets of rules.

Semantic Web—The Web of data with meaning in the sense that a computer program can learn enough about what the data means to process it. The principle that one should separately represent the essence of a document and the style presented.

Semantic Web Services – Web Services developed using semantic markup language ontologies.

server—A program that provides a service (typically information) to another program, called the client. A Web server holds Web pages and allows client programs to read and write them.

SGML (Standard Generalized Markup Language)—An international standard in markup languages a basis for HTML and a precursor to XML.

SHOE Simple HTML Ontology Extension—A small extension to HTML which allows web page authors to annotate their web documents with machine readable knowledge. SHOE claims to make real intelligent agent software on the web possible. See http://www.cs.umd.edu/projects/plus/SHOE/

SQL (Structured Query Language)—An ISO and ANSI standard language for database access. SQL is sometimes implemented as an interactive, command line application and is sometimes used within database applications. Typical commands include select, insert, and update.

SGML (Standard Generalized Markup Language) -Since 1986, SGML has been the international ISO standard used to define standards-based markup languages. HTML is a markup language that is defined using SGML. The HTML DTD the specifies HTML is written in SGML syntax. XML is not a markup language written in SGML. There is no pre-defined DTD for "XML Markup." XML is a sub-set of the SGML standard itself.

statement—A subject, predicate and object which assert meaning defined by the particular predicate used.

stylesheets- A term extended from print publishing to online media. A stylesheet can contain either formatting information (as is the case with CSS—Cascading Style Sheets, or XSL FOs—XSL Formatting Objects), or it can contain information about how to manipulate the structure of a document, so it can be "transformed" into another type of structure (as is the case with XSLT Transformation "style sheets").

subject—Of the three parts of a statement, the subject is one of the two things related by the predicate. Often, it indicates the thing being described, such as a car whos color and length are being given. See also: object, predicate.

Taxonomy—This term traditionally refers to the study of the general principles of classification. It is widely used to describe computer-based systems that use hierarchies of topics to help users sift through information. Many companies have developed their own taxonomies, although there is also an increasing number of industry standard offerings. Additionally, a number of suppliers, including Applied Semantics, Autonomy, Verity and Semio, provide taxonomy-building software.

TCP (Transmission Control Protocol)—A computer protocol that allows one computer to send the other a continuous stream of information by breaking it into packets and reassembling it at the other end, resending any packets that get lost in the Internet. TCP uses IP to send the packets, and the two together are referred to as TCP/IP.

thing—In DAML, a generic name for anything—abstract, animate, inanimate, whatever. The class which anything is in. (In RDF parlance, confusingly, rdf:Resource.) Identified by a URI with or without a "#" in it.

transformation—In XSLT, a transformation is the process of a software application applying a style sheet containing template "rules" to a source document containing structured XML markup to create a new document containing a completely altered data structure.

UML (Unified Modeling Language)—Derived from three separate modeling languages.

URI (Universal Resource Identifier)—The string (often starting with http:) that is used to identify anything on the Web.

URL (Uniform Resource Locator)—The address of a file or resource on the Internet.

valid—An XML document is "valid" if it is both well-formed and it conforms to an explicitly-defined data model that has been expressed using SGML's DTD (Document Type Definition) syntax.

W3C (World Wide Web Consortium)—A neutral meeting of those to whom the Web is important, with the mission of leading the Web to its full potential.

WSDL (Web Service Description Language)—provides a communication level description of the messages and protocols used by a Web Service.

Weblogs—Weblogs (Blogs) are personal publishing Web sites that syndicate their content for inclusion in other sites using XML-based file formats known as RSS. Weblogs frequently include links to content syndicated from other Weblogs and organizations use RSS to circulate news about themselves and their business. RSS version 1.0 supports richly expressive metadata in the form of RDF.

Web Services—Web-accessible programs and devices.

Web server—A Web server is a program that, using the client/server model and the World Wide Web's Hypertext Transfer Protocol (HTTP), serves the files that form Web pages to Web users (whose computers contain HTTP clients that forward their requests).

well-formed—A document is "well-formed" if all of its start tags have end tags and are nested properly, with any empty tags properly terminated, and any attribute values properly quoted. An XML document must be well-formed by definition.

XML Schema—A formal definition of a "class" or "type" of documents that is expressed using XML syntax instead of SGML DTD syntax.

XSL (Extensible Stylesheet Language)—XSL has two parts to it: a transformation vocabulary (XSL Transformations—XSLT) and a formatting vocabulary (XSL Formatting Objects (XSL FOs).

XSL FOs (XSL Formatting Objects)—The formatting vocabulary part of XSL that applies style properties to the result of an XSLT transformation.

XSLT (XSL Transformations)—The transformation vocabulary part of XSL. An XSLT "stylesheet" contains template rules that are applied to selected portions of a source document's "source tree" to produce a "result tree" that can then be rendered for viewing, processed by another application, or further transformed into another data structure.

Index

Printed and bound by CPI Group (UK) Ltd, Croydon, CR0 4YY

22/10/2024

01777637-0008